DATE DUE

DEMCO 38-297

Modernity and Housing

The MIT Press
Cambridge, Massachusetts
London, England

Modernity and Housing

Peter G. Rowe

This book was set in Rockwell and Melior by DEKR Corporation and was printed and bound in the United States of America.

Library of Congress Cataloging-in-Publication Data

Rowe, Peter G.
    Modernity and housing / Peter G. Rowe.
      p.   cm.
    Includes bibliographical references and index.
    ISBN 0-262-18151-7
      1. Housing—History—20th century—Case studies. 2. Housing development—History—20th century—Case studies. 3. Architecture, Domestic—History—20th century—Case studies. I. Title.
    HD7287.R68 1993
    363.5'09'04—dc20
                                      92-45140
                                        CIP

To Far, homo nostrae aetatis

Contents

Acknowledgments

This book initially came about through ideas shared with Ada Louise Huxtable and José Rafael Moneo, two fellow travelers in Europe at the time, to whom I owe a special debt of gratitude. With Rafael I also enthusiastically shared a common responsibility for several studio classes in the fourth-semester architecture program at Harvard, to which this book is especially addressed.

I also owe a particular debt to my friend Joan Busquets for his constant enthusiasm about the project, his generous support, and his knowledgeable guidance toward unfamiliar examples. In a similar vein I must thank another friend, Gwendolyn Wright, for her constructive criticism, timely advice, and encouragement. Additionally, I remain grateful to two fine colleagues, Michael Hays and Alexander von Hoffman, who, each in his own way, acted as responsible sounding boards for many partially formed ideas and work in progress. Similarly, my dean, Jerry McCue, deserves gratitude for his unfailing support and special interest.

In working through the book, I received willing assistance from several remarkable graduate students from the urban design program at Harvard. To Deborah Torres, Christopher Procter, and Jacqueline Tatom, in particular, I owe a special debt of gratitude. My thanks also goes to Carmen Hurwitz-Morales for far more patience and splendid assistance than I deserved, and to Richard Aguilar who tirelessly converted my scrawl into a polished manuscript.

Finally, I wish to thank Marianne Rowe for her selfless support, aid in proofing the manuscript, and technical assistance in making several important translations. My son, Anthony, must also be acknowledged for his interest and forbearance, in addition to Lauretta Vinciarelli for her sweetness, light, and wise counsel.

Modernity and Housing

1 Conditions of Modernity

This book is about the architecture of housing in the modern age and, in particular, broaches the question: how can modern housing be made in an appropriate manner? In so doing, it also explores topics of broader theoretical interest in architecture, especially those concerning the cultural enterprise of modernity.

During the past two decades, severe criticism has been leveled at modern housing projects that dot the landscape of many American inner cities, and at the rows of monolithic flats that mark much of Europe's postwar development (figure 1). In spite of many good intentions and, indeed, a certain widespread enthusiasm for early designs, the building of modern housing seems to have floundered among plain unimaginative projects with no character, accommodations ill suited for their occupants, and building complexes with a significant lack of public amenity (figure 2). Curiously, however, there have been relatively few alternative proposals, and most of those have been primarily intent on reconstructing urban housing the way it was once. In an attempt to provide continuity with the past and to recover a lost sense of tradition, past practices and period styles have been closely emulated under the rubric of architectural post-modernity. Unfortunately, this has often proved to be a dubious undertaking on at least two counts. First, it has given little or no recognition to the wholesale character of social change that has taken place between the past period of emulation and present circumstances. Second, the backward-looking orientation has effectively stifled any attempt to remain open to contemporaneous influences, let alone visions of the future. Consequently, if we are modern, as we otherwise seem to be, the question of the architectural accompaniment to this modern condition still seems conspicuously unresolved.

1
Monolithic flats on the
European urban periphery:
the Polygonos of Barcelona.

2
Postwar American public
housing: Stateway Gardens,
Chicago, 1950s.

The book embraces three more or less parallel themes concerning modernity. The first is the rise and rearrangement of the modern technical orientation, which simultaneously compresses the experience of time and expands the experience of space until temporal experience is largely confined to the present and spatial experience becomes universal. The second theme concerns representational issues that arise out of an emphasis on subject-centered reason and relativism in place of a belief in metaphysical foundations, and the third concerns social practices that give rise to the production of mass housing on an unprecedented scale. Broadly speaking, an appreciation of space-time relationships in architecture will philosophically ground discussion of local and traditional building practices as these contrast universal and novel ways of making housing; the perspective of subject-centered reason will focus discussion of the use of abstract forms and the problem of providing authentic architectural expression; while the unprecedented production of housing, especially under conditions of considerable social diversity, raises the thorny issue of widely defining a normative building program for appropriate accommodations—of designing for everyone but for no one in particular. Mass production also simultaneously raises the equally difficult issue of standardization in design.

The time frame for most of the narrative is roughly from the end of World War I until the present day. While many architectural scholars mark the advent of the truly modern era with the rise of the avant-garde around 1910, it is the post–World War I period in housing that coincides with the actual effects of major sociocultural realignments in which widely accepted concepts of space and time were shattered, traditional architectural practices were abandoned, and new social relations were formed. Of particular importance in these regards are two historical moments. They are the postwar building boom from about 1920 to 1930, which witnessed the first widespread application of modern housing in both Europe and the United States; and the period from about 1970 to 1980, when many broadly based underlying conditions of western socioeconomic stability and prosperity were severely threatened. This latter period is also roughly congruent with the ascendancy of so-called postmodern culture, at least in architectural circles. As we shall see, both were self-conscious moments for architecture, when attention was directed inward toward the discipline itself and, as such, when the issue of architecture's presumed modernity was undergoing critical consideration. Moreover, again as we shall see, each period coincides with the predominance of a particular form of modern sense making—one concerned with technological order and universal truth, the other with a much less confident, fragmented, and circumscribed view. Throughout, for fairly obvious reasons of commonality and influence, the account, with one or two exceptions, will be confined to western Europe and North America.

Finally, among key examples of modern housing in each of the two periods other interesting symmetries can be seen to emerge. During the period between the World Wars, for instance, most notable modern housing estates were built in suburban and peripheral locations (figure 3). This is not surprising, given the unprecedented horizontal mobility that became available and the rather obvious cure for urban blight and squalor to be found in the countryside. By contrast, during the second period of the 1970s, emphasis primarily shifted to redevelopment of older urban areas largely abandoned by years of outward urban expansion. Also of interest is the parallel rise and subsequent collapse of modern housing programs in numerous technologically advanced nations. Beginning after World War I, with obvious interruptions during the Depression years and World War II, housing production followed a strong upward trend, both in absolute terms and as a proportion of population growth, until a period between the late 1960s and the mid-1970s when it either plummeted or sagged conspicuously. The general trend was much the same for each nation, as if the sheer limitations of a way of technologically engaging the world had been reached. Modern housing production largely coincided with the "second industrial revolution" and an emphasis on the management of throughput. When that was replaced during the dramatic technological rearrangements of the seventies, earlier housing programs were either abandoned or fell into disrepute.

3
Housing estates on the
suburban fringe: Römerstadt
in Frankfurt by Ernst May,
1925–1930.

The Rise and Rearrangement of the Modern Technical Orientation

Although the root causes of an epoch are seldom clear, there can be little doubt that technology has shaped the course of modern history and the affairs of modern civilization (Giedion 1948, Habakkuk 1962, Borgmann 1984, Colton and Bruchey 1987). The modern technical orientation, or more pervasively society's modern technical temperament, was shaped and is sustained by three complementary processes: a technological way of making things, a technocratic way of managing things, and a technical way of interpreting people and their world. Not all these, however, came into being at the same time. Rather there was, and continues to be, a persistent transformation in the technological fabric of our lives, in which there appear to have been three rather distinct episodes. The singular and rather monolithic pattern of development that is quite often depicted, especially from a postmodern architectural viewpoint (Rowe and Koetter 1978), is thus in need of revision.

The first episode was the early industrial revolution that brought with it the harnessing of steam power, mechanization, urbanization, and product economies of price. The second was the so-called second industrial revolution with its emphasis on mass production, mass consumption, and throughput, as well as a constant search for economies of scale. Finally, there were the more recent and perhaps still emerging business and technological arrangements based on flexible production, individualized consumption, and what have sometimes been referred to as economies of scope (Chandler 1990). While the first episode bore witness to the arrival of the factory system, the second saw the creation of the corporation, and the third the full-blown arrival of the service sector. Generally speaking, the technological centerpieces of each episode were steam power, electric power, and the computer, respectively.

The Early Industrial Revolution

It is well known that from the late eighteenth century through much of the nineteenth century, the industrial revolution dramatically changed the way in which we made things and the manner in which we moved about in the world. The steam engine was invented in or about 1776, bringing in its wake an unprecedented capacity for convenient mass transportation, at a rapidly declining cost, in the form of railroads and steamships. Simultaneously, mechanized power drove manufacturing processes that produced goods and finished products, formerly made by craftsmen and manual laborers. To a large degree the French historian Fernand Braudel was correct in defining technology as the way in which we transform and use energy, and equally correct when he conferred upon technology the status of the "queen that changes the economy and hence the world" (Colton and Bruchey 1987, p. 1).

By as early as 1850, American industry had developed a generic type of industrial production that was significantly different, at least in the breadth of its applications, from European counterparts, making far more use of mechanization and, in the process, of mass production (figure 4). Instead of relying on individual workers to produce unique products, mechanical production processes were geared to produce identical component parts that were then assembled into specific products. Once a commitment was made to a particular product line, this approach had the twin advantages of speed of manufacture and ease of later maintenance. A defective part was simply replaced. The key was standardization of product components and a high degree of interchangeability of those components to produce other, different products (Habakkuk 1962, Sparke 1987).

4
The American system of manufacture: crankshaft factory in Worcester, Massachusetts, 1911.

Nevertheless, until almost the end of the century, business enterprises in most parts of the world remained comparatively small and were usually personally managed. They certainly increased in number but remained fragmented in an economic sense, as single units specializing in a particular enterprise. Distributors, for instance, all the way through the nineteenth century, were either wholesalers or retailers but never assumed both roles. Throughout, competition was based on price and, until about 1865 in a place like the United States, the business environment was basically stable (Beddington 1981, Chandler 1987, DiBacco 1987).

The Second Industrial Revolution

Toward the end of the nineteenth century these industrial situations and business environments were to change radically, although in hindsight perhaps not unexpectedly. By 1890 larger enterprises replaced and even combined the former single units of production and distribution, in search of greater control over the marketplace and higher profits. Thus large integrated firms, or corporations, appeared for the first time, and throughput, the rate of production, became the index of performance, as input and industrial capacity alone were no longer decisive (Chandler 1987, 1990). Under conditions where high volumes of throughput could be anticipated, the first step was usually forward or vertical integration into transshipment, processing, and distribution. This was often followed, certainly later during the twentieth century, by multinational and multiproduct diversification. In the case of Standard Oil, for example, railroads were acquired to guarantee transport of both raw materials and products. Other production units were similarly acquired in order to rationalize, streamline, and control the overall process, so much so that in 1882 the Standard Oil Trust was formed from 40 companies. Shortly thereafter, kerosene dropped almost one third in price, such were the scale economies involved (Blum et al. 1963, Chandler 1987).

The corporate pools, trusts, and mergers that ensued during this period created very large and complex business arrangements, not to mention monopolistic and other "unfair" trade practices that, in the United States, prompted passage of special legislation in the form of the Sherman Antitrust Act of 1890. Interestingly, large integrated firms also appeared at the same moment in Europe, probably due to comparable improvements in the transportation and communications so necessary for transshipment and coordination (Chandler 1987). The employment effects of these relatively sudden agglomerations were also considerable. For example, by 1925, in Germany, about 2 percent of the industries employed some 55 percent of the workers (Friedrich 1972).

No doubt many of these changes, at least in the United States, were reactions to, and ways of coping with, the enormous business difficulties encountered after the Civil War. Numerous industrial inventions, representing an 18-fold increase in the number of patents issued over the previous 70 years, encouraged and simplified entry into business. For someone with enterprise, the costs seemed low and the prospects high. The resulting overcompetition and overproduction led to severe price deflation. For example, the overall price index in 1873 stood at 100, falling to 71 by 1896. In some ventures, like textiles, it fell still further, from 245 to 76 over the same period. Apart from creating a necessity of selling more goods in order to sustain a profitable throughput, these business cycles often proved to be ruinous. During the 30-year period roughly from the end of the Civil War until the turn of the century, only half the calendar years saw economic upturn or prosperity. Furthermore, there were no fewer than seven cycles from prosperity through depression, as shown in

Table 1
**United States Business Cycles
between 1865 and 1900**

Depression	Revival	Prosperity	Recession
1866–67	1868	1869	1870
1870	1871	1871–73	1873
1874–78	1878–79	1879–82	1882–83
1884–85	1885–86	1887	1888
		1889–90	1890
1891	1891	1892	1893
1893–95	1895		1896
1896–97			

Source: after DiBacco 1987, p. 143

table 1, and other related enterprises involved in capitalizing industries, such as banks, frequently failed (DiBacco 1987). Indeed, the latter part of the nineteenth century was a time of great risk, very much suited to the Spencerian description of the "survival of the fittest" (Blum et al. 1963).

In other parts of the world similar conditions were encountered, although in some places with added political upheavals. Germany, for instance, underwent unification in addition to rapid industrial change. Nevertheless, around the turn of the century the free-for-all Victorian era in Britain, the *Gründerzeit* in Germany, and the era of the so-called Gospel of Wealth in the United States were to come rather abruptly to a close. A new progressive spirit was abroad and with it a new emphasis on technology and technological expansion.

At the heart of the second industrial revolution that began around 1890 lay the "visible hand" of corporate management (Chandler 1977). Especially for capital-intensive industries, "production was increased not by adding more machinery and more workers but by improving and rearranging input, reorganizing production processes, and augmenting the importance of applied energy" (Colton and Bruchey 1987, p. 3). In short, it was a restructuring of industries in search of economies of scale, rather than a resizing, that was accomplished in order to maximize throughput, boost the market share of sales, and increase profits. Undoubtedly Henry Ford's production line (figure 5) is the most celebrated example of this overall procedure. Commenced in 1909 and perfected by about 1913, it reduced by half the time of production for one of Ford's Model T automobiles and roughly halved the cost, simultaneously allowing significant wage increases for production line workers (Nevins and Hill 1957, Hounshell 1985). Perhaps most important, Ford fixed in our minds the reciprocal concepts of mass production and mass consumption.

If Ford was the prime practical example, then Frederick W. Taylor, together with others like Frank B. Gilbreth, supplied the new managerial techniques and theoretical insights. Before Taylor in 1882 and Gilbreth around 1890 undertook their studies, management was primitive and based almost solely on prior experience or trial and error practices. By devising empirically verifiable principles for ordering and controlling even the simplest task, the new researchers helped create a new breed of managers in an emerging corporate hierarchy and gave them the tools they needed. Time and motion studies also helped create a rich conceptual framework for efficiency, replete with numerous yardsticks of performance (Taylor 1911). The terminology of maxima, minima, and optima gradually grew into a full-fledged "science of decision making," receiving widespread and immediate application shortly before and after World War I in business, government, and industry (Galbraith 1972, Borgmann 1984).

The effect in the workplace was both immediate and pervasive. There had been a long-standing division between employers and workers, toward which much of the social criticism of the nineteenth century was directed, but now a dramatic shift in numbers also occurred from blue-collar to white-collar workers, particularly as management and the service sector expanded to meet new corporate needs. In the United States, for instance, the occupational profile in 1930 was vastly different from that in 1870. The professional ranks increased tenfold and a watershed was reached as early as 1921, amid the new corporate alignments, when salaried workers accounted for 50 percent of the total work force (Vaile and Canoyer 1938).

Occupational specialization also occurred to meet the new employment needs, especially in the professional, service, and trade sectors. In fact, between 1870 and 1930 there was fully a 71 percent increase in the number of occupational designations in the United States. Public service alone accounted for a significant amount of this increase, reflecting a new role for government in business matters and an increasing complexity in related institutional arrangements. Between 1910 and 1930, for instance, the number of people entering public service almost doubled (Vaile and Canoyer 1938). Varying degrees of automation within specific industries also changed the complexion of the work force. Although relative employment declined within several manufacturing industries, such as petrochemicals, overall production or throughput actually rose. Similarly

5
Assembly plant for Model T
Fords.

6
An element in the technostructure: the Mercantile Exchange in Chicago.

there was a considerable reduction in agricultural employment in the United States, although farm productivity remained high (Colton and Bruchey, 1987).

At about this time another, less well known division took place within the modern technological setting, with widespread ramifications for patterns of employment. An occupational distinction developed between work at the "leading edge" of technology and work in its "wake" (Borgmann 1984). At the leading edge were to be found inventors, entrepreneurs, and those directly involved with the substance of the technology in question. In the wake mushroomed various developmental experts, financiers, as well as marketing and advertising specialists (figure 6). Soon a "technostructure" emerged, as Galbraith called it, usually extending far beyond the center of the technology itself (Galbraith 1972).

Finally, the overall shift from agrarian to urban occupations and lifestyles also became intensified at this time. In the United States, for example, the urban population was still slightly less than the rural population in 1914, quickly surpassing it by the end of the decade in 1920, in spite of the fact that the rural population actually peaked in 1916. By 1929, farm workers were only 21 percent of the total labor force, and America had truly made the transition from an agrarian to an urban society (U.S. Bureau of the Census 1975, Vatter 1987).

During the period between the wars, the division of labor, the specialization of labor, and the dispersion of the work force out from central production activities was to continue under corporate auspices. Moreover, by now many of Taylor's and others' management ideas had found their way into the home. A new simplicity in furnishing and new levels of efficiency in the functional layout of activities were stressed. Many of the same measures used in business and industry were adapted for application in the home (Frederick 1920, Forty 1986). Urbanization also continued, one effect of which was a decline in the natural rate of population growth.

By the 1920s the modern city in both Europe and North America began to emerge. Transportation improvements significantly relieved the need for overcrowding and congestion, and soon led to decentralized patterns of settlement and suburbanization. Use of the private automobile in the United States rose from a paltry 2 million vehicles in 1914 to over 26 million before 1930. By the beginning of the post–World War II era some 100 million had been produced (Rae 1971). With an extensive road-building program first aimed at simply improving existing roadways and then focusing on extensive interregional travel (figure 7), suburban decentralization of urban areas continued to intensify. Shortly before 1955 the suburban proportion of metropolitan populations in the United States passed 50 percent, continuing to climb since then (Muller 1981, Rowe 1991). Suburbanization was not nearly so extensive in Europe, especially not in the form of single-family houses on individual lots. Nevertheless, a higher-density sprawl of bedroom communities can be found on the outskirts of most cities and, in the larger metropolitan areas of Germany and the United Kingdom, suburbanization more closely approximated the American model (Clawson and Hall 1973).

Other technological changes that had started during the second industrial revolution also found large-scale application between the wars, and further consolidated the structure and makeup of the modern city. Domestic electrification, for instance, rose quickly from 24 percent of all United States homes in 1917 to 48 percent in 1920, finally reaching nearly 100 percent by 1930 (Cowan 1982). With electrical power also came appliances, changes in transshipping, and, perhaps above all, the arrival of new kinds of mass media. From the first broadcast in 1920, radios became commonplace in the United States by 1930, with sales rising during the early years of production between 1922 and 1926 by over 1,400 percent (Allen 1959).

Other facets of everyday life also changed from the turn of the century, including domestic habits of consumption. For instance, the use of commercial laundries in the United States, between 1914 and 1924, increased by 57 percent, and the output of bakeries over the same period rose by 60 percent. The sale of canned foods, a relatively new invention, also grew appreciably. Like the workplace, the resources and activities of daily life became more specialized, commodified, and, in a sense, compartmentalized. An astute commentator of the time observed: "With a job came a feeling of comparative economic independence. . . . For city dwellers the home was steadily becoming less of a shrine, and more of a dormitory—a place of casual shelter where one stopped overnight on the way from the restaurant and the movies to the office" (Allen 1959, p. 81).

In spite of progress, however, including rises in real income and the material quality of life, social concerns began to emerge, precisely at the points of technological application. First, fragmentation of production processes, together with the relative remoteness of many employees from objectives and products central to a corporation's livelihood, led to labor alienation. Similarly, expanding hierarchical levels of management and bureaucracy in many areas of daily life, including government services

7
An early American urban
freeway.

and the workplace, began to have a distancing effect. Third, there was an inevitable curtailment of craftsmanlike satisfaction in the workplace, and job obsolescence became a nagging fear in people's minds. Finally, with widespread increases in the sheer number and complexity of business and other relations, people began to feel less autonomous and, therefore, less in control.

After the Second World War, business arrangements and related technological developments at first essentially followed the prewar paradigm. There were, however, spectacular breakthroughs and technological transformations in agriculture, accelerating still further the exodus from farms in many countries and quickly completing the dispersed process of urbanization. New chemical and biological products, in particular, together with more controlled farming practices, resulted in very large increases in productivity at greatly reduced labor costs. The number of farm workers shrank from 21 percent of the labor force in the United States in 1929 to only about 3 percent in 1980, while the per capita food production index was maintained relatively constant (Vatter 1987). Similar experiences occurred in other places like West Germany, where the farm labor force declined to less than 6 percent of the total in the same period (Chandler 1990).

New Technological Arrangements

During the early seventies, the United States and several European countries relinquished full control of oil exploration and petrochemical facilities in many overseas producing countries. In 1973 OPEC was formed, followed by a sharp increase in oil prices and a general economic recession. In the United States the downturn was the sharpest and most ominous since the Great Depression years of the 1930s. The stock market, for example, lost almost half its value in under a year, and inflation doubled from 1970 levels, to about 10 percent in the United States by 1975 and as high as 13 percent in Europe (Watterson 1990, OECD 1987). The ensuing seven or eight years saw a numbing combination of recession and inflation. The social cost of this economic shock was considerable. Unemployment almost doubled from that of the 1960s, reaching 9 percent, for instance, in the United States by 1975. For the first time in decades, there was a decline in real wages and a leveling off, or slight decline, in American median family incomes; and trends in many parts of Europe were much the same (OMB 1980, OECD 1987). Consumer confidence was severely shaken; inventories remained unsold as discretionary incomes shrank and many customers changed their buying habits.

It is probably an oversimplification to point to one set of events, like the energy crises of 1973 and 1980, as the motivation for wholesale technocratic rearrangement. Indeed, some experts believe that economic fortunes had begun to change as early as 1968 (Watterson 1990). Nevertheless, these crises were undoubtedly instrumental in raising very serious questions about prevailing doctrines of mass production and economies of scale. Certainly the 1960s had seen substantial economic growth and expansion in the service sector, especially among the more industrially advanced countries of the world. In the United States, for instance, service sector employment went to well over 50 percent of the total labor force during this decade (U.S. Bureau of the Census 1975). Nevertheless the sudden specter of severe economic instability provided a definite call for action. In any event, new technological arrangements have emerged since the early seventies that appear to be as radical and potentially far-reaching as those of the waning years of the nineteenth century (Beniger 1986, Harvey 1989, Chandler 1990).

Probably the most profound technological transformation of the late 1960s and 1970s took the form of electronic breakthroughs that have revolutionized all manner of control and transmission devices (Hawkes 1971). The microprocessor was invented in California as early as 1968, allowing electronic devices to become much smaller and diversified in their applications (Behar 1990). Precise automation and robotics have become a reality and have quickly found their way onto the factory floor (figure 8). Today, we are still in the midst of the computer and information age and have probably only just begun to appreciate its full effects, not the least of which are the rapidity, directness, and malleability of communication and data processing. The continuing growth of the service sector—to around 66 percent of the United States work force by 1980, with parallel growth patterns in other industrialized countries—has been shaped for the most part by the newfound information-processing power.

Another real change seems to have come about in technological attitudes toward production and consumption. Here flexibility and diversity have partly displaced mass and scale as guiding notions. Thus production has become oriented toward more numerous and diversified markets, some of which never existed before. Consumption is now more individualized, specializing in particular options as well as other marks of distinction. Technically speaking, the use of small production batches across a greater product range and offering a more timely response to consumer demands have become primary industrial objectives (Chandler 1990). Perhaps the

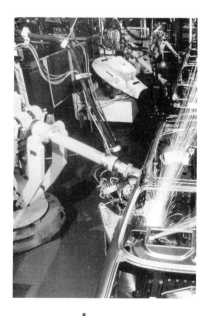

8
Robotics on the factory floor.

best example is in the recent triumphs of the Japanese automobile industry, which has made significant inroads into world markets by offering well-timed diversity, individuality, and reliability in its products (Burstein 1988).

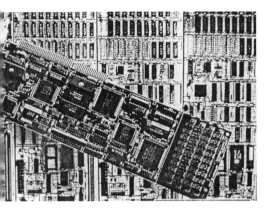

9
Products of Silicon Valley combined into information systems.

Another significant change occurred in the organization of production enterprises. Far more flexible arrangements were made with labor, in the form of higher levels of subcontracting as well as temporary and part-time labor pools. New, highly focused yet flexible production units also emerged as independent subcontractors able to respond to the increased demands for speedy compliance with other contractors' needs, and for a more diversified range of products. The computer industry is perhaps the best example of this phenomenon (figure 9), where many aspects of a complex system are jobbed out to smaller, independent units (Hall and Markusen 1985). The broad occupational category of research and development, so necessary for sustaining the modern technocracy, often followed the same organizational pattern. As a consequence, many new technical centers have emerged, such as Silicon Valley, no longer at traditional sites of business and industry. The resulting decentralized agglomerations of service industries dot the landscape of many metropolitan areas, largely tied to access and employee residential locations (Rowe 1991).

International mobility and procurement in both capital and labor have recently reached unprecedented levels, universalizing many business transactions. Inexpensive labor from one country is routinely purchased with capital obtained from another, the profits from which are invested in a third. Not only are multinational companies commonplace, but international joint ventures, even for specific projects, are no longer exceptional. Moreover, widespread deregulation has further allowed new corporate alliances to form and services to be diversified.

Finally, higher degrees of autonomy and responsibility seem to have returned to the workplace, although it remains far from its premodern, craft setting. Concepts like "co-responsibility" and "participative" forms of management have gained wide acceptance. The Volvo automobile company in Sweden is among the most celebrated examples of the former, while the corporate behemoths of Japanese business are most closely associated with the latter. At Volvo teams of skilled workers put complete cars together, work within a flexible time frame, and generally seem to have developed a much higher rapport with each other and with the products they produce. In the upper echelons of corporate management, the consensus-building practices of Japanese business are legendary. Compared to the brute force, speed, and power of the second industrial revolution, the new technological arrangements seem to have concentrated on quickness, agility, and endurance.

The Modern Technical Temperament

In spite of the episodic transformation that has taken place in modern technology as a way of engaging the world and shaping it to our own interests, a consistent outlook, orientation, or even ideology can be discerned hovering in the background. As Borgmann points out, modern science set the world within the matrix of scientific laws, and technology is concerned with changing conditions of the world largely in accordance with those laws (Borgmann 1984). Modern science makes the world apparent, as it were, and technology allows us to act upon those appearances; conversely, technological problems become questions for science to answer. Needless to say there is a similarity in the language and style of reasoning between the two domains. Knowing how to engage the world is closely tied to knowledge directly about that world. The strengths and limitations of one way of knowing, thus, are transformed to the other.

The evident achievements of modern technology obscure other important issues concerning its social reception. For some it is the way out of poverty, toil, and a marginal existence. For others it is the source of mindless drudgery, extreme socioeconomic disparities, and an overwhelming materialism that threatens to undermine the human spirit (figure 10). Almost all seem to agree, however, that technology is a pervasive presence in today's world. The philosopher Heidegger went so far as to claim technology as the culmination of western metaphysics, at the very foundation of our existence and independent of any other existence (Heidegger 1959 and 1971).

It is clear that most Enlightenment thinkers, at the very dawn of the industrial revolution, saw the prospect of technology in benign and munificent terms. For both Bacon and Descartes, for instance, understanding nature was a way of dominating it in the name of human reason and utility. Such domination was to be a concerted effort to release people from the debilitating privations of disease, hunger, and toil. It had, in effect, a teleology clearly marked by liberty and prosperity for all (Cassirer 1951). The more we knew about our world, the greater the understanding of our circumstances, and, therefore, the more reasoned and principled

10
The paradox of technological
time-saving devices.

our behavior would become, or so it could be argued. Emerging political movements in both the United States and continental Europe at the time clearly embraced these underlying ideas; freedom, liberty, and prosperity were readily married to science and technology.

In this relationship between technology and human causes, it has been the constant promise of technology, perhaps even more than its successes, that has been sustaining. Certainly a broad program for engaging the world needs to have successes in order to be sustained. Nevertheless technological developments have managed, largely through their promise, to (as one observer put it) "both guide and veil the shaping of the modern world" (Borgmann 1984, p. 39). Undoubtedly, this promise derives primarily from the continuity of the technological developments themselves. Almost by definition, they are to some extent always new, with all the hopefulness that goes with new creations. Moreover, developments occur both incrementally, in a more or less constant problem-resolving process, and by great leaps and bounds. If one course of action appears to be going nowhere another always holds out the prospect for success. The upshot is that we have a rather constant orientation toward the near future, in most technological matters, and toward what is promised there for us. It is precisely this "near future" orientation that often keeps present circumstances out of focus, so to speak, at least to the extent that the optimistic character of technology asserts its presence. As Borgmann points out, in this process the actual character of technology often remains in broad and ambiguous outline (Borgmann 1984, p. 39). It is easy to avoid direct confrontation with the social ills of a technological way of existence by reassuring ourselves that, with more development, situations will improve. With a reasonable record of success and this optimistic capacity to mask present difficulties, it is little wonder that a technological orientation is so persuasive.

There is another kind of ambiguity to technology that serves to reinforce the same orientation. According to the device paradigm of technology, those aspects or properties of a device "that provide an answer to the question: what is the device for?, constitute its commodity, and they remain relatively fixed. The other properties [of the device] are changeable and are changed, normally on the basis of scientific insight and engineering ingenuity, to make the commodity still more available" (Borgmann 1984, p. 43). In the example of the television set, the commodity is clearly the picture, its color, sharpness, and realism. All the rest of the set is of little consequence and, according to this paradigm, should be deemphasized for the viewer. Indeed, the miniaturization, electronic design, styling, and so on that have taken place over the years in television technology, by and large, bear out this emphasis on commodity. The better the technology, the more invisible it becomes. All we are presented with is the commodity in question, not the means of achieving it. It is this lack of visibility, or ambiguity, that masks the real character of technology, and the constant presentation of commodity that reinforces its optimistic acceptance (figure 11). Paradoxically, it is precisely when the means becomes an end that commodity is most available: when the technology becomes the commodity and the material device becomes the locus of our enjoyment.

Finally, in spite of its pervasive presence, there is a social anonymity to technology on at least three counts. First, as opposed to craft, it contains no real record of the human effort and aspirations involved in its making. There are an immediacy of availability, a remoteness of human involvement, and a generality to mass-produced products (figure 12) that are not found in craft, where waiting, expectation, imperfection, individuality,

11
Futurism and the visibility-invisibility of technology: *Twentieth-Century Traffic Arrest* by Jim Powers, 1956.

12
The technological genie at
work in and around the
home.

and the trace of the human hand are more salient characteristics. Second, with a thirst for facts and an underlying dispassionate reasoning similar to science, the technological orientation remains largely unaware of human moods, frailties, and, in any emotive sense, likes and dislikes. While the social science of management can certainly be practiced, there is always a degree of social anonymity involved that, in the end, amounts to a kind of ignorance. Third, in our day to day relationships with technology and technical devices we seldom understand how they work, how to repair them, let alone their histories or where they come from. Contrary to other human pursuits, like games, there is a gap between a function available to everyone and underlying rules or machinery known to virtually no one. Ironically, technology comes close to being magic, with much the same hold over us. Thus, the modern technical temperament emerges. It is more than simply a knowledge and a know-how. It involves fundamental beliefs and attitudes as well, not the least of which are little concern for the past, progressivism, a futuristic orientation toward liberation and material property, as well as a real preoccupation with what's new. Maybe Heidegger was correct in his metaphysical assessment.

Time, Space, and Technology

To be modern in the common usage of the word is to be situated in the present, the here and now, up to date. Thus to be thoroughly modern is to be entirely of the moment. Unlike being contemporary, which has the sense of simply being parallel in time ("Marc Antony was a contemporary of Julius Caesar"), to be modern has a sense of both immediacy and reality. Modernity, then, as we usually know of it, has a particular relationship with time and one that is inextricably bound up with contemporary ways of dealing with the world, namely with technology and its purposes. Moreover, this relationship defines the space-time continuum of our actions, including our architectural production.

Understandably, given the fundamental character of the concepts, relationships among space, time, and technology have received considerable attention over the years. Giedion's celebrated *Space, Time and Architecture*, originally published in 1941, forged a strong link between contemporary technological prospects, a new spatial conception based on an idea of space-time, and an architecture appropriate to the modern era. Perhaps of more fundamental import was Heidegger's *Being and Time* of 1927, which gave a profoundly new insight into our existence in a technological world. Later works, like Hall's *Hidden Dimension*, were more specialized, in this case dealing with the social meanings of both space and time within the technological setting of the modern world (Hall 1969). Toffler's *Future Shock* explicitly dwelt on the likelihood of an exaggerated compression of time and some of its future consequences (Toffler 1970). Conversely, Le Goff's backward-looking, historical account focused on the relationships between time, work, and culture in the Middle Ages (Le Goff 1980). Meyrowitz, in his *No Sense of Place*, concentrated on the spatiotemporal impact of one technology, namely electronic media, upon social behavior, while Relph's *Modern Urban Landscape* argued more broadly that it is the "internationalism" made possible by more rapid communication that shapes our contemporary environments (Meyrowitz 1985, Relph 1987). More recently still, David Harvey's account convincingly linked the political-economic transformation of twentieth-century capitalism, through the experience of space and time, to sweeping cultural changes (Harvey 1989).

Technology, as the characteristically modern way of engaging the world, has intervened and continues to intervene into time's relationship with space in a number of interesting ways. All largely involve rate changes, where the speed, sense of unfolding, and ultimately the meaning of spatial sequences are altered. For convenience, the following discussion is divided into four sectors each roughly corresponding to a kind of temporal experience: movement and communication time, event and task time, place time, and historical time.

Movement and Communication Time

From the beginning of the industrial revolution, modern production processes required large concentrations of workers at factory sites. In the absence of adequate public transportation, workers invariably lived as close as possible to where they were employed, often resulting in congestion and sometimes in extreme overcrowding (figure 13). Urbanization occurred on an unprecedented scale, and factories commingled with tenements and other establishments.

13
Conditions of extreme overcrowding: Mulberry Street in New York City in the 1880s. Photograph by Jacob Riis.

14
Overcoming the constraints
of distance in early urban
America: a trolley line in
Pasadena, California, c. 1900.

Toward the end of the nineteenth century, technology allowed the concentrated living conditions of industrial cities to be overcome through the use of streetcars and commuter railways. These transportation systems were quickly followed, in the early twentieth-century, by the automobile and extensive private automobile use. By the overcoming of distance through the speed of mass movement, earlier urban constraints could be relaxed (figure 14). Residential densities diminished considerably, especially on the urban periphery, and urban functions became redistributed in a more efficient manner. The resulting overall form of the city conformed to the monocentric or core-periphery model of spatial distribution, with a commercial core at the center surrounded by residential and mixed-use settings at decreasing density. Suburban sprawl emerged, and with it a spatial segregation of urban activities and a functional separation of uses. Spatial locations could now be rationalized according to several desirable characteristics, such as accessibility, elimination of nuisance from neighboring uses, and elimination of overcrowding, all without incurring prohibitive time costs for movement.

The same general process continued until a stage was reached, during the late 1960s in many American cities, at which several commercial and industrial centers began to emerge in dispersed, suburban locations. Rather than residences being located close to the firms where people worked, as in the early industrial revolution, the reverse happened: firms began locating closer to labor pools and markets. The result was a polynucleated city form with numerous centers of activity amid a nonhierarchical spatial realm of predominantly residential uses, of which Los Angeles and Houston are prime examples (figure 15). In parallel with new business alignments, urban populations and functions dispersed and reconcentrated to form a modern metropolis. Speed of travel was once again allowed to overcome space, resulting in a spatial arrangement with an even greater flexibility for accommodating a variety of human activities (Vance 1977, Muller 1981, Rowe 1991).

Quick movement through space also affected the way in which environments were routinely perceived and, consequently, the manner in which they were designed. The view of objects in a suburban landscape through the windshield of a car traveling at speed, for instance, was necessarily fleeting and often blurred. Detail was difficult to register and only bold outlines and forms were recognizable. Unfortunately, when design followed perception in such situations, the result ran the risk of becoming cartoonlike in its attempt to grasp essentials. Absent was the richness of detail and scale so necessary for establishing a varied, comfortable, and lasting relationship between building form and human scale.

Other technological developments have also resulted in an increased span of space in compressed time. Communications, together with information processing and media, have all radically altered our view of the spatial domains of the world. Especially during the last few decades, the increased access to and scope of communications, information processing, and the like have both speeded up and made global many socioeconomic transactions. With this globalization has come familiarity, and with familiarity has come a lessening of distinctions between one place and another. Not only has the space of our worlds expanded, it has also become more universal in its design and physical appearance. Modern commercial cities in all parts of the world now resemble each other. Consequently, a sense of place, that way by which we differentiate space in our minds and through our cultural activities, has become diminished. Furthermore, an emphasis on the speed and scope of communications unavoidably brings a concomitant emphasis on similarity rather than on distinction. As the use of technology continues to level spatial boundaries, many people from increasingly less different realms of existence can be brought together almost simultaneously.

A further aspect of simultaneity is the spatial juxtaposition that occurs when many different facets of experience are brought together at once. The resulting collapse of view, sense of movement, and transparency have long been celebrated in art. Cubism, for example, deliberately incorporated these concepts into its representational scheme (Stangos 1974, Blatt 1984). Duchamp, for one, clearly emphasized successive images of a single body in motion, in both the *Sad Young Man on a Train* of 1911 and in his definitive *Nude Descending a Staircase* of 1912 (figure 16). Consequently, the very way in which space can be represented and understood, especially vis-à-vis time, has changed appreciably. Indeed, the increasingly momentary and transitory aspects of life continually place new demands on the artist. As early as 1863, Baudelaire was to declare that the task of the painter of modern life was to capture "the ephemeral, contingent newness of the present" (Baudelaire 1964, p. 8).

15
Polynuclear form of urban development: Houston's City Post Oak area, 1970s.

16
Movement and transparency:
*Nude Descending a Staircase
No. 2* by Marcel Duchamp,
1912. Oil on canvas, 58 ×
35 in. Philadelphia Museum
of Art, Louise and Walter
Arensberg Collection.

Event and Task Time

With the onset of the second industrial revolution and its emphasis on time management, many actions in space have become defined as discrete spatiotemporal units with labels like "event," "task," and "activity." Generally a "task," for instance, has a finite beginning and end, together with a temporal sequence of actions in between. The important modern feature, however, is the increasing emphasis that has been placed on time within this spatiotemporal complex. Sequencing and other temporal arrangements like management have become important preoccupations. Taylor and other students of efficiency fundamentally helped change our conception of even the most mundane of daily activities. In place of earlier seasonal, diurnal, circadian, and even astronomical considerations of time, we now have an artificial matrix of increasing complexity and applicability at our disposal. Moreover, it is a temporal matrix that seems somehow controllable and not simply the result of external, natural forces. With sufficient attention there can even be a degree of predictability. If we adhere to a particular sequence of activities in a timely manner, for instance, then a certain outcome can reasonably be expected to happen. Furthermore, within the scope of this predictability, the relative merits of various courses of action, especially in terms of time and effort, can be defined clearly and then compared, thus establishing the central modern concept of efficiency.

During the course of everyday events, the mastery of time, or more specifically the control of activities according to time, is now pervasive. Appointment schedules become both a means for regulating social contexts and a way of allegedly extracting the most out of a day. Unfortunately, however, they can also impose unwanted social and psychological pressures. Adherence to schedules requires us to confront the world ready or not. Appointments made at some earlier time may or may not have the same relevance, yet the ritual often goes on. Improvisation and spontaneity give way to the formality of a known format for a known period. Time thus claims a degree of certainty in the spatial experience of our lives.

Work schedules, likewise, order aspects of our lives and largely subordinate the spatial context of our actions to temporal dictates. It would be quite unusual, for example, to order business meetings by distinctions in spatial context, as opposed to differences in daily time. But perhaps above all it is simple measures of efficiency, of accomplishing things in a certain span of time, that continually meter our daily lives. Efficiency is not simply a spatiotemporal measure; it becomes a good in itself, a state of being that once again shows a mastery of time, or rather of space with respect to time.

As early as 1927, the pervasiveness of these routines of modern life was eloquently depicted in Kracauer's concept of mass ornament (Kracauer 1977). For him the Tiller Girls (figure 17), an American dance troupe popular in the twenties, emulated the movements of industrial production lines with the geometric precision of their movements. The rhythmic tapping of their feet and the synchronized movement of their legs seemed to illustrate the joyous progress of rationalization. More generally, the decisive ornament in daily life was the mass itself and the movement of people going about their business. Through a strong convergence with capitalism, the mass became thoroughly rational and, in contrast to the ballet or to groups of people in, say, parades, it became an end in itself, standing for nothing else but itself. Nevertheless, according to Kracauer, when seen against the decrepit backdrop of the city, the mass became an ornament of modernity in motion (Frisby 1986, pp. 148f.).

17
Emulation of the movements
of mass production: the
Tiller Girls of the 1920s.

18
Abstraction and
standardization in the
architecture of the machine
age: housing at Im Bergfeld
in Römerstadt, Frankfurt,
1925–1930.

Another spatial tendency that derives from the routine of tasks is standardization. This was particularly apparent during the first and second industrial revolutions, in which industrialization and standardization were causally related. Simply put, mass production and assembly of standard components were perceived to be the path toward industrial efficiency. Much the same outlook was also applied to modern architecture, especially during the so-called machine age of the 1920s (Banham 1960). Here one consequence of standardization, however, was not only a sameness in appearance but also a degree of abstraction, as general rather than particular design conditions were anticipated (figure 18). Both characteristics can also be found in various standards of technical accountability that emerged at about the same time. Codified and standardized building practices, for instance, inevitably produced uniformity and at least some measure of removal from specific localized circumstances.

Not unexpectedly, planning emerged during the 1920s as a formal method for controlling and managing the application of material and other resources. With the predictability of events and various measures of performance like efficiency, hypothetical temporal sequences of tasks and events could be described along with likely outcomes or goals. Thus the future was pulled into the present, so to speak, and given a high degree of articulation and apparent reality. When set beside present realities, such future scenarios often held considerable appeal, extending promise and even hope while helping to mask present circumstances and removing their urgency. Plans could thus be resorted to as a way of living in the future and of helping to sustain the modern technical temperament's progressive optimism and interest in what was new.

Place Time

The nationalization and even globalization of work and of leisure activities have become exaggerated in recent years, usually resulting in periodic movement of people from place to place. A long-recognized exigency of the multinational corporation, for instance, is relatively high levels of employment mobility. For some time now the average length of residency in the United States without a move has been less than 5 years, unheard of in preindustrial or even early-industrial eras (figure 19). With this mobility, the long-term experience of one place is replaced by the contracted experience of several places. A sense of rootedness is thus loosened and spatial experience becomes metered by the time spent in any one locale. The remark "It depends when!" is now a familiar response to the question: "Where do you come from?" Furthermore, amid a spatially fragmented past, the hold of the present and future is usually reinforced.

Closer to home, the idea that a sense of community is necessarily tied to spatial proximity has been seriously questioned. Melvin Webber and others argue that with modern transportation and communications we find ourselves capable of maintaining a network of social and business contacts based more upon personal and individual affinities than upon geography and propinquity (Webber, Dyckman, and Foley 1964). We are more likely to live in what has been dubbed a "non-place urban realm" than we were in the past, when the travel frictions associated with getting from place to place were higher. The concept of time and daily movements has altered significantly, greatly reducing the need for geographically driven relationships (Webber 1964).

19
Coming to the neighborhood: *Moving Day, Los Angeles*, 1953, by J. R. Eyerman.

Spatial expansion of business and other influences also tend to produce a sameness in the prevailing architectural environment, but for reasons other than those noted earlier. Lynch's epithet "What time is this place?" is certainly applicable in many parts of the world where less and less concern has been shown for local variety and regional differences (Lynch 1972). Nowadays cities can be more readily identified by the times of major building booms than by local stylistic orientations, building materials, methods of construction, and so on. The sheer availability of building technology marks a place by its time, rather than the other way around. Consequently, there is a universality to modern urban space corresponding to the universality of modernity as a cultural experience (Relph 1987).

Recently, however, some of this uniformity has begun to recede. The pluralism that is evident in the new technological alignments of flexible production and individualized consumption is also evident in the urban landscape. Emerging entrepreneurs and old-style corporations alike want their signature, as it were, on the skyline. People in search of career flexibility and lifestyle, having found it, are anxious to maintain its ingredients, one of which is usually the peculiarly local flavor of the physical environment in which they find themselves. Likewise people tired of living entirely in the eternal present and contending with the leveling effects of a lack of difference seek out a foothold in the past and a sense of tradition. Consequently, the narrowness of early modernist architectural doctrines like "form follows function" is challenged, replaced by attempts to reinstate continuity with the past and a return to vernacular traditions. Parenthetically, the appealing aspect of vernacular building practices, in this situation, is that they are contemporary and yet retain the specificity of a local area or region. Thus the universalizing effect of time is cheated (figure 20), without resort to backward historical references.

Environmental appearance also affects a sense of place, changing with time in other ways. Modern urban development often results in rapid and wholesale alterations to city neighborhoods and districts. Obsolete structures are torn down and replaced by new buildings, typically much larger in size and functional scope. Furthermore, this process of renewal is usually widespread and not isolated to a single building or city block. During the 1980s about 80 new high-rise structures were built in Manhattan alone, approximately the equivalent of adding downtown Dallas to the New York skyline. Such dramatic changes not only affect investment portfolios and tax rolls, they also remove one sense of place and replace it with another. And a sense of place is inextricably interrelated with time and stability. If the new place does not live up to expectations and the

20
In a vernacular and time-honored tradition: housing for the Bricklayers' Union at the Charlestown Navy Yard, Boston, Massachusetts, by William Rawn, 1985.

21
Compensation for the real
thing: World Showcase,
Disney World, Florida, 1992.

comfortable familiarity of the old environment is gone forever, those who
made the old area a fundamental part of their lives are alienated, and thus
the city becomes for them a little less of a reality and more of a memory
(Hiss 1990). Environmental change is of course an old story, but the sheer
rapidity and scale of many contemporary changes is unique to the modern
era. Without doubt, the prevailing economic and technical exigencies of
development in many parts of the world have steadily increased project
scales and made the impacts more instantaneous. Consequently place
time—the period during which a unique area of a city can be enjoyed with
familiarity—is shortened dramatically. This ephemerality of a sense of
place can also lead to a form of compensation through all sorts of simulacra
(figure 21; Baudrillard 1983).

Finally, in most modern cities the sense of place also changes with the
social mobility of the inhabitants. Changes in individual socioeconomic

circumstances usually mean changes of abode, especially under conditions of functional separation to be found in most contemporary cities. For better or worse, people and firms of similar socioeconomic standing in the larger community reside close together. Progressive optimism promises an individual the hope of advancement; and the spatial component of socioeconomic mobility often results in a contracted and all too brief experience of several places, as people now empowered move to better their lot.

Historical Time

Historical time is concerned with the interpretation of events and their placement into a longitudinal frame of reference. It is the temporal frame we accept as our past, across which we tell stories of past events, and in which we look for evidence of our early beginnings. Sometimes it stretches back millennia and we use it to explain our anthropological origins. On other occasions, as with some avant-garde movements, we turn our back on its existence altogether.

Before the eighteenth century, history was regarded under classical doctrines as a story about the contingent aspects of human endeavor that needed to be sifted through, as it were, in order for the underlying truth to be finally revealed. Gradually this began to change, however, with the realization that these underlying truths and values themselves developed and acquired new meanings with the passage of historical time. Thus, the explanation for why Caesar crossed the Rubicon, for instance, might change from one era to the next, depending on prevailing attitudes toward power, the role of nonhuman agents in people's affairs, military tactics, and so on. Consequently for pioneers in the field of historiography, like von Ranke in the nineteenth century, a historian's task was twofold: first, to make an exhaustive examination of the facts; second, using this examination as a guide, to go beyond the facts and capture the essential spirit of the period concerned, knowing full well the relative nature of such speculation. For a later historian like Collingwood the task was similar, namely to move behind the facts to the "thought that lay behind the event" (Collingwood 1946, p. 15). Thus history, for Collingwood, involved a speculative reenactment of events in an attempt to capture them wholly in their own time. The idea of history as truth gave way to a "historicist" view that all sociocultural phenomena are historically determined and, furthermore, that all truths are relative to their positions in history.

From the direction of philosophy came a parallel although more metaphysical idea of historical development. German idealists saw both the world and human history as the objective expression of creative reason, from which some, like Fichte and Hegel, argued that reality is none other than the life of absolute reason. Furthermore, just as one person's history is their knowledge of the Absolute, so the "will of history," Hegel reasoned, would replace the "will of the [individual] historical subject." Thus a teleological process is set in motion implacably under the influence of the "world spirit," which replaces both God and nature (Copleston 1963, Löwith 1964).

This kind of philosophical attitude was also to find its way into the historiography of art and particularly into German developments in that field, roughly between the 1820s and the 1920s, under such prominent figures as Semper, Riegl, Wölfflin, Warburg, and Panofsky. Acknowledging an essential reciprocity between the search for historical facts and the development of artistic concepts, these art historians were most interested in aims and circumstances of the time that were inextricable from their expression in an art work (Podro 1982). For them, each era had its own thrust and underlying spirit, and works became shaped accordingly. Gothic architecture according to Panofsky, for instance, was shaped largely by the outlook and habits of mind of scholasticism (Panofsky 1967).

22
The avant-garde's sharp
break with the past: Villa à
Garches by Le Corbusier,
1927.

All these ideas, as Colquhoun partially points out, were central to modernity's concept of historical time, particular at the moment of the avant-garde's celebrated break with the past (figure 22). From historicism, or the relativistic view of history, came the idea that every artifact belongs to its own time (Colquhoun 1989). It was the domain in which it was shaped and ultimately had meaning. From Hegel, Riegl, and others came a progressively deterministic view of history and the *Zeitgeist* or "spirit of the times." There was, therefore, no real use for history and traditions of the past, reasoned members of the avant-garde, and as Walter Gropius was to put it, "modern man, who no longer dresses in historical garments but wears modern clothes, . . . needs a modern [architecture] appropriate to him and his time" (Conrads 1964, p. 95).

There was, however, another coincidence of ideas worth noting that also would have led modernists into a sharp break with the past and a radically discontinuous view of their own historical time. Indeed, as we saw earlier, a real change was going on in the world. The second industrial revolution was rapidly transforming the underlying material conditions of modernity, and material change provoked a powerful interest in the future. It was where the image of technology was the clearest and thus where the most promise lay. Furthermore, as technology became more available, so the temptation of this progressive orientation grew. A preoccupation not only with "the new" but with "the potential" was hard to avoid. The new conditions, the new facts, and the new methods all emerged from a technological revolution that was at hand. What remained for historicist philosophy was to provide an intellectual rationale.

Almost the opposite can be said about the underlying idea of historical time during the late 1960s and the early 1970s. Then the positivist inclinations of historicism were seriously questioned, and technological novelty held less fascination, in spite of the spectacular achievements of space exploration, electronics, and data processing. Historical time did not appear inevitably progressive in social terms, nor was the cloak of technocratic well-being quite so seamless. If anything, the events of May 1968 and the energy crisis of 1973 saw to that. The positive idealism that had carried almost all before it for over half a century was in decline as the underlying technocratic way of life underwent radical rearrangement. With the loosening of these underpinnings, modernity's attitude toward the past began to be rethought. Historical time had been compressed in such a way that traditions were difficult to form, let alone sustain. Constant novelty began to seem glaring and garish and, by its very constancy, difficult to keep up with, interpret, and understand. In architecture, the plastic arts, and elsewhere, there was a move away from modernity's positivist face and scorn for history.

Historical knowledge, however, requires both a knowledge of history and reasonably consistent societal ideas about history in order to sustain any broad meaning and influence on life. The difference, for instance, between "consensus" and "conflictual" versions of urban history affects the way in which we understand and place confidence in society's institutions. The consensus view, dominant in America during much of the corporate and technocratic era, gave considerable support to institutional due process. The recent conflictual view does not. Likewise, in the plastic arts and architecture, a knowledge of movements and periods of development is essential to the constructive use of historical knowledge at more than simply a superficial level.

Memory, on the other hand, is about personal experience and the things around us during the course of our lives. We recall places, events, and things, recreating, as it were, sights and other past senses in our minds (figure 23). According to Rossi, monuments, special places, or what he

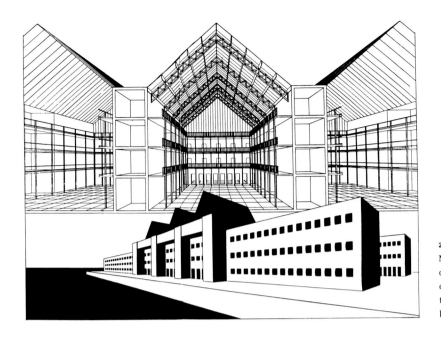

23
Memory and the ambiguous
condition of contemporary
civic government: project for
the Regional Hall at Trieste
by Aldo Rossi, 1974.

calls the "permanences" of a city are all repositories of collective memories (Rossi 1982). Similarly, places of "collective dreaming" also provide locations for release from the here and now, or ever present, partially by reminiscence but mostly by way of future hopes and aspirations (after Benjamin 1969). More technically in the domain of architecture, the idea of type has both the residue of past experience and a sense of present-day usefulness (Moneo 1978). It is a relational complex that has a comparatively timeless utility, fitting halfway between memory and historical knowledge. Through analogous features it allows present circumstances to be resolved by reference to past circumstances, configurations, and spatial organizations. Nevertheless, memory is probably best served, architecturally speaking, through a broad, heterogeneous palette of spatial experiences, drawing on an uneven knowledge and recollection of the place in question, but with an underlying familiarity that is likely to fit all comers.

When emerging from a period of historical amnesia it is not unexpected to find a real interest in past practices and an emphasis on learning and connoisseurship. Indeed, in the historically inclined branches of the so-called postmodern movement in architecture, that is precisely what happened. Of the two avenues to the past, however, memory would seem to be the more reliable and perhaps more interesting. By drawing on direct experience and locale it is likely to be less precise than historical knowledge, but also less abstract, universal, and potentially deadening. If Simmel was correct in asserting that a fundamental condition of modernity is the translation of the world of experience into an "inner world" largely of senses and emotions, then memory holds the key to this gateway and subsequent release into the outside world (Simmel 1968). Use of memories and especially of collective memories, therefore, is an important way of releasing the modern present from the stranglehold of the here and now. Furthermore, unlike various forms of traditionalism, such strategies possess this important capability without running the risk of refreezing a place, so to speak, in a particular past era.

Spatiotemporal Masks

So far in the discussion of the modern interaction between space and time, almost all of the emphasis has been placed on time and, specifically, on time's leveling effect on space and spatial distinctions. Territory no longer has the allure it once had during the era of the western frontier or that of sailing ships. Even the key to cosmic space, perhaps the last frontier, seems to go through time (Hawking 1988).

Nevertheless there are several occasions on which the spatial aspect has had an active and crucial role, especially in making up for perceived deficiencies and excesses in artifacts of contemporary production. In architecture, for example, we have just discussed the way in which a return to traditional forms, evoking the past, was used to break the hegemony of the here and now. Allusions to other times and other eras, amid contemporary circumstances, certainly blur the impact of the present, allowing notions of continuity to be reestablished and even traditional values to be reawakened. In the following chapter we shall get a fuller sense of this phenomenon, among European and American housing developments of the 1920s and early 1930s.

24
Streamlining of car and
home: Shult trailer, 1937.

Allusions, however, can also be made in the other direction as well. Again during the 1930s, for example, there was a preference, particularly in automobile design, for streamlining (figure 24). Moreover, as we have recently come to learn through wind-tunnel tests, it was a kind of streamlining that was as much about the idea of speed as it was a practical application that made vehicles go faster. Put another way, it was a spatial prefiguration of time and its subsequent effect on distance. The promise rather than the reality of greatly increased speed was being offered through the streamlined design. Similarly, in a less exaggerated fashion perhaps, the appearance of many avant-garde architectural processes was more

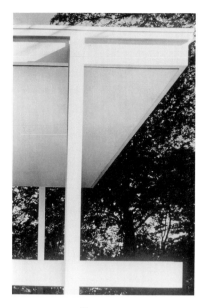

25
Column and beam assembly
in a modern handcrafted
tradition: the Farnsworth
House by Mies van der Rohe,
1946–1950.

about the temporal aspect of machine production and assembly than it
was the actual result of such processes. The column and beam assembly
of Mies van der Rohe's Farnsworth House, for instance (figure 25), was all
carefully handcrafted (Schulze 1985). Although this emulation of the machine world is well known, what is perhaps less clear was the role it
played in anticipating temporally based building practices like fabrication
time and job management (Banham 1960, Frampton 1980).

Less progressively, much of twentieth-century American architecture and
urban development can be seen as an interplay between a technological
orientation and a romantically inclined naturalism. The excesses of mass-
produced, standardized residential subdivisions were masked by spatial
allusions to bucolic settings and life in the countryside, away from the
hustle and bustle of business and the choking fumes of modern industry.
The houses themselves were usually efficiently planned with modern
layouts, yet the overall shape and appearance were often copied from a
bygone age (figure 26), usually in the colonial past. Similarly, corporate
offices, the very centers of modern technological proliferation, were often
developed like country estates, again from another era (Rowe 1991). Architecture and urbanism were not alone; in both American art and literature, usually for critical purposes, the juggernaut of technology and
modern civilization was cloaked in a natural or pastoral garb (Marx 1964,
Novak 1976). Moreover, the personal and emotional aspect of romanticism
was pitted squarely against modernity's proclivity toward homogenization
and detachment. Nevertheless, all these romantic allusions and attempts
to bolster technology's benign promise convey the feeling that the spatial
aspect of the space-time complex is the least consequential. It is the veneer
that is applied, when necessary, in order to make the more important
temporal features of modernity more palatable.

26
Modern pastoralism in the
American domestic
landscape.

Representation and Modern Forms of Rationality

With the decline of metaphysics during the eighteenth and nineteenth centuries, a shift occurred in philosophical outlook toward subject-centered reason (Habermas 1987). This was not simply the placement of the human subject at or near the center of things, as one would encounter in varieties of humanism (Thrall, Hubbard, and Holman 1960), but a full-fledged meditation on reason and rationality, including the irrational and mythical aspects of human experience. The shift in outlook was pursued independently in several disciplines. Karl Marx argued that social class and relations among classes determined beliefs and actions, thus limiting individual freedom and rationality. James G. Frazer, in the *Golden Bough* of 1890, demonstrated that myth and magic perform fundamental roles in providing the bases for taking action through the unconscious mind of cultures. Friedrich Nietzsche not only declared that God was dead but presented a compelling portrait of the antinomy of the Apollonian and Dionysian sides of human nature. Finally, Sigmund Freud raised the specter of the subconscious as the determinant not only of many of our actions but of our entire individual outlook on life. Thus, in all the fields that had become centrally concerned with human affairs during the latter part of the nineteenth century, nonrational, antihumanist positions were coming to the fore (Trilling 1961, Spears 1970).

This orientation was to continue well into the contemporary era. By then the relativism that was systematically introduced into modern thought bordered on nihilism. An underlying "philosophy of differences" emerged in which contraries such as rational and irrational, sane and mad, beautiful and ugly, merged or exchanged positions. Any foundational aspect of knowledge was seemingly stripped away forever, revealing, at the very least, a postmetaphysical modernism (Bernstein 1986, Vattimo 1988, Wellmer 1991). Somewhat less emphatic, perhaps, were other poststructuralist positions, although their vision of modernity also began with Nietzsche et al. and opened up discussions of modernity, rooted in Enlightenment values of reason and rationality, to critical reappraisal (Lyotard 1984, Huyssen 1986). Aesthetically, the prior documentary stance of modernism gave way, more and more, to autobiographical attitudes and experiential "texts" (Habermas 1981, Huyssen 1986). In spirit, anyway, this was not at all unlike surrealism's earlier odysseys in the mind (figure 27), which, as Adorno put it, "set aside the usual logic and rules of the game of empirical existence" (Adorno 1967, p. 29).

27
Setting aside the usual
rules of the game: *Object*
(Luncheon in Fur) by Meret
Oppenheim, 1936. Collection
The Museum of Modern Art,
New York, Purchase.

By contrast, the scaffolding of a scientific interpretation of people and their world, grounded in the Enlightenment, was also being erected at much the same time (Krimerman 1969, Bernstein 1976, Gadamer 1982). The aim of this position was to arrive at foundational theoretical propositions and laws about human behavior in a variety of settings (economic, social, psychological) in the manner of the natural sciences. On most occasions there was a positive, progressive orientation to these efforts aimed at improving the quality of life for individuals in society and, again like the established sciences, at being in a position to predict outcomes from certain social arrangements and courses of action. A technocracy quickly developed along the corridors of public power, populated by technical experts (Nelson 1982). Private corporations also enlisted technical experts, particularly in fields of management related to the emerging fields of sociology, psychology, and economics. In spite of many methodological problems, the results from the fledgling social sciences were often impressive and were quickly incorporated into many of society's institutions and practices. Thus practical rationality, together with closely correlated traits like efficiency and organization, became publicly regarded as desirable and the social role of planning became thoroughly ingrained.

There was no real merger of these two different aspects of modernity's complex intellectual terrain, yet the two are periodically interwoven. From the Frankfurt School, for instance, comes an affirmation of Enlightenment principles of reason and rationality, but with a nonfoundational concept of knowledge (Bernstein 1986, Habermas 1987, Wellmer 1991). Both sides have influenced modern architecture and the design of modern housing.

At certain moments a disinclination toward tradition essentially grounded in the metaphysical past, such as classicism, helps explain a reluctance to employ imitation as a mode of architectural expression. At other moments a counterreaction has set in, such as the recent concern for continuity with the past. Similarly, the strong modern relationship between architectural form and function receives considerable impetus and legitimacy from the positive orthodoxy of the social sciences, whereas its dissolution owes much to the poststructuralist critique of the same orthodoxy. Finally, high levels of abstraction expressed in many forms of modern architecture, from both the avant-garde and postmodern periods, arise not only from being cut off from the past but also from moments of disciplinary specialization, when the gaze, as it were, is inevitably directed inward. As Toulmin aptly put it, with reference to a folk dance, in most fields there are periods of "marching" and periods of "weaving" (Toulmin 1961). These were periods of weaving.

Imitation

According to Aristotelian poetics, imitation lies at the origin and is the very aim of all poetry. It is a form of expression, natural to people, enabling both learning and pleasurable experience of the world. Tragedy, for instance, is an imitation of incidents that arouse pity and fear, and from which moral insights can be gained about the human condition (Ross 1942, Kaplan 1958). In later classical theories, the timeless ideals of the works of antiquity themselves become the subject of imitation, as perceived reflections of mankind's perfectibility (Preminger 1965, Drabble 1985). Thus the classical orders, particularly of ancient Greece, formed a cornerstone of architectural expression for several centuries. In some later movements, such as romantic versions of naturalism, art remained imitative but was now seen to penetrate below surface realities to reveal the idea inherent in the object or scene under scrutiny (Barzun 1961). Although the work was usually a close approximation of the organic and "true to life," it was so less because of any desire for realistic expression than because of what Worringer referred to as empathy: an aroused feeling for the beauty of the form (Worringer 1967). Throughout, the driving force behind imitation was an extrinsic reality requiring depiction. In spite of internal stylistic and other technical considerations, poetic expression was essentially about something in an outside, external, natural world. Moreover, this was appropriate, given the confidence that could be placed, at the time, in a metaphysical reality.

At the beginning of the twentieth century this confidence was severely strained, as we saw, and in architecture the idealism of extrinsic natural reality was replaced by an exploration of the intrinsic world of forms, functions, and material properties. However, unlike the role of function in, say, romantic naturalism, where, according to Alison's theory, the senses were to be entranced by the sheer richness and profusion of embellishments, the modern functional doctrine concerned the stuff of architecture itself (Early 1965). Materials, fabrication methods, pure forms, and uses became the focus of attention, and characteristics such as honesty and intrinsic suitability of materials, simplicity of construction, parsimony of design, universality of space, and efficiency of use were sought after. The aphorism "form follows function" emerged, although function now had a meaning intrinsic to the artifactual nature of the objects being produced. Undoubtedly there was a corresponding loss of empathy, although more in kind than necessarily in magnitude. After all, modern works, particularly works of great beauty, could still be arresting to the senses.

Imitation also continued, however, but not the imitation of classical forms or of nature. Instead, the objects of imitation were drawn mainly from the contemporary technological environment close to intrinsic matters of makeup and function. It was mimesis in Auerbach's broad sense, where the reality being represented was the most fascinating at the time, namely technology, machines, and the unprecedented realism of the second industrial revolution (Auerbach 1953), as in Le Corbusier's celebration of ships, airplanes, and grain silos in the 1920s (Le Corbusier 1959) or the work of the Russian constructivists at about the same time. Chernikhov, for instance, in his manifesto and proposals of 1928 developed explicit ways of making and combining architectural forms—so-called constructive principles—that clearly emulated physical conjunctions in cross sections of factory machinery, tool dyes, and wiring boards (figure 28; Cooke 1983). Later analogies drawn by groups interested in "system" properties, like the metabolists, could also fall into this category. Indeed, the architectural imitation of technology and machines seems to have occurred in at least three different forms. First, buildings were made to perform like machines, as in Le Corbusier's famous aphorism about "machines to live in" (Le Corbusier 1975). Second, buildings were detailed to resemble machines and, third, buildings were analyzed and conceptualized like machine assemblies.

One early modern exception was Baudelaire's interest in the urban crowd as an important source of artistic inspiration. Although he saw it as very

28
Chernikhov's "constructive principle" of interpenetrating bodies and a selection of *Constructive Compositions*, 1920–1930.

much a contemporary phenomenon, by pointing to both its transitoriness and its eternal beauty he was also suggesting a more traditional mimetic sensibility. Similarly, Le Corbusier's work at La Tourette and at Ronchamp, although contemporary, owed much to earlier Romanesque architecture (Soltan 1988). In all cases, however, Aristotle's dual aspects of imitation have persisted, namely learning and the provision of pleasure. Machines and systems were of interest precisely for reasons of learning and understanding, and, to someone like Walter Gropius, real pleasure could be derived from modern artifacts for modern times (Conrads 1964). The clear difference, though, was a narrowing of focus to properties intrinsic to objects themselves and the almost total absence of a backward historical glance.

With the emergence of a philosophy of difference and other nonfoundational outlooks on life, the social, scientific, and orthodox modern architectural hold on our attention became weakened. There was a renewed quest to regain meaning, and the realm of architectural exploration was broadened accordingly (Rowe 1987). Depending on definitions, there were at least two versions of the quest. One was an attempt to extend the historical time frame of a work of architecture and reestablish contact with past traditions. This resulted in extensive use of historical forms, as well as a certain amount of eclecticism; it was an affirmative rather than a critical reaction, in which classical norms were seen to be worthy of emulation (Jencks 1980, 1987). The other followed prevailing nihilitic philosophical outlooks; it celebrated disorder, discontinuity, spatial areality, and so on. Ironically, perhaps, by attempting to find new form for a new age it shared much in common with the earlier avant-garde. The work of Peter Eisenman is noteworthy in these regards, especially when it came, as he put it, to "working on the language" (Eisenman 1978). Where it differed greatly, however, was in its critical dimension, which radically questioned the presuppositions linking avant-garde modernism to the mindset of modernization.

In between these positions lay a preference, as one author put it, "for mixing symbolic dimensions and codes, . . . [as well as] an appropriation of local vernaculars and regional traditions" (Huyssen 1986, p. 186). He went on to exploit Adorno's and Greenberg's difference between high culture and mass culture by arguing that artistic developments since the 1960s have tended to draw strongly on the latter rather than on the former (Clark 1982, Lunn 1982). Architecturally, this is particularly evident in Venturi's and others' gravitation toward pop sensibilities and the crossing or contradiction of one set of conventions with another (Venturi 1966; Venturi, Scott Brown, and Izenour 1972).

Abstraction

In both commonplace and technical uses of the term, abstraction means stripping away, separating out, and reducing to an essence. Etymologically, it also means drawing away, in the sense of becoming removed from reality. For a theorist like Worringer, the "urge to abstraction" is a kind of artistic volition that finds beauty "in all abstract law and necessity." In fact, geometric abstraction, the ultimate form of abstraction, allows a work to be "set free from all external connections with the world" (Worringer 1967, pp. 4, 35). This urge to abstraction arises from feelings of anguish and bewilderment at the instability and obscurity of the world, and reflects an instinctive necessity to turn inward in search of order.

Avant-garde architecture, shortly after the turn of the century, was certainly abstract. Indeed, abstraction is a feature of the movement that has received considerable prominence over the years, even though it is arguably a characteristic of all art (Giedion 1941, Stangos 1974, Blatt 1984). The spare outlines, primary color, and clear geometric forms of avant-garde buildings projected an unmistakably abstract appearance, especially when set against the natural conditions of their sites. The circumstances surrounding the initiation and development of avant-garde architecture also certainly match Worringer's definition. It was a period of considerable social change and, as we saw earlier, a moment at which the modern technical orientation was undergoing radical revision and realignment. At the same time there was also an emerging sense of cultural relativism and a growing drive toward persistent experimentalism in many walks of life. The "tradition of the new," to use Rosenberg's phrase, coupled with a decidedly adversarial stance toward the past, seemingly ensured high degrees of abstraction.

In addition, there also seems to have been a decided optimism amidst the inevitable uncertainty of the time. This was, after all, a veritable revolution, the beginning of a new age. Abstraction was clearly necessary in order to prepare the way, sift through the confusion, and get down to basic principles. Furthermore, it was a habit of mind entirely befitting the new era of technological progress. If the mode of positivist or logical-empirical thought was anything, it was abstract, inexorably in search of underlying laws and theoretical constructs. Nevertheless, what remained was clearly more than simply abstraction and a turning inward toward architecture itself. It was a new formalism that focused attention primarily on functional doctrines and the broad social benefits of a technologically advanced, utilitarian architecture. Le Corbusier's five points, for instance, clearly set out formal principles to be observed along those lines, although they were probably no more abstract than Alberti's tract written a number of centuries earlier.

Alternatively, it can be argued that abstraction inevitably leads to formalism, especially amid rapidly changing circumstances. After all, special languages have two characteristics in common. They are necessarily formal, in order to deal with an otherwise confused world, and they are abstract, precisely in order to arrive at an appropriate level of formalism. Moreover, for different reasons, the degree of abstraction is likely to be higher during early stages of formulation of a cultural language, as well as during much later stages of complete development. Early on, abstraction is necessary simply to establish basic principles and procedures. Later, especially when developmental efforts are nearly exhausted, increasing levels of abstraction usually become a last resort.

At least in broad outline, the ascent and decline of what is commonly referred to as modern architecture followed this trajectory. The architecture of the early avant-garde, especially of the Bauhaus, Le Corbusier, and De Stijl, was, by most people's reckoning, abstract yet formally compelling (figure 29). Like it or not, it was relatively clear what the architecture stood for. Matters became less clear in the high modern developments of the 1940s and 1950s, and the architecture that appeared much later in the same tradition, by architects such as the New York Five, was even more abstract and visually complex yet without the same broad-based, compelling formal appeal (Five Architects 1972). Principles were beginning to shift, even in the work of these selfsame architects, eventually requiring the development of new formalisms.

The connection between abstraction and imitation is immediately confronted in the recent breaks that have taken place with the earlier modern architectural orthodoxy. The use, for example, of historical forms and motifs, a return to the layout and other organizational principles of venerable building types, and so on, all clearly involve imitation. Less obviously, perhaps, so does the work of the so-called poststructuralists. In a manner analogous to the avant-garde, they are fashioning, within contemporary circumstances, a new architecture precisely imitative of those objective signs of a new age, often based upon literary models. Usually these explorations draw either from criticism or from interpretation of narrative works, such as Eisenman's speculation around the theme of Romeo and Juliet (Eisenman 1985). On other occasions they draw on analogies with spatial phenomena in mathematics and linguistics (figure 30). Again as in the 1910s and 1920s, there is considerable uncertainty and confusion amid the sociopolitical and technological rearrangements that are taking place in the contemporary world picture. Not only is it a time ripe for abstraction and experimentalism, but both appear to have been occurring rather prolifically. Recently, however, the impetus has been simultaneously a general drawing away from the historical present and an intensely speculative inward turn toward the autonomous confines of architecture itself. In short, both abstraction and imitation are processes of artistic production. Abstraction gives an indication of what is being withdrawn from a work, whereas imitation, to the extent that it persists, usually indicates the

29
Compelling modern architecture: the Gropius House in Lincoln, Massachusetts, by Walter Gropius and Marcel Breuer, 1938.

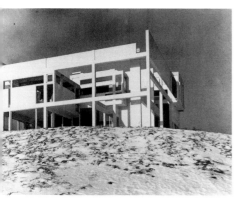

30
A house in the manner of
linguistic "deep structure":
House 11 by Peter Eisenman,
1972.

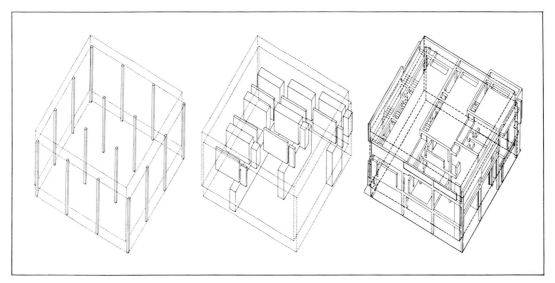

direction in which the abstraction is headed. Thus a machine aesthetic
may be devoid of conventional ornament but imbued with a strong sense
of material finish. Both processes, in architectural terms anyway, invariably evolve together into a particular formalism of design principles to be
followed.

Functionalism

The by now familiar modern functionalist doctrine in architecture consisted of four central considerations: material integrity and suitability, the
expression of contemporary building construction and fabrication techniques, efficient use and layout of buildings, and the propagation of a new
spatial order devoid of all references to the past. Summing up the central
role of functionalism as a manifestation of the *Zeitgeist*, Walter Gropius

declared that it was only "through constant contact with newly evolving techniques . . . new materials and new ways of putting things together . . . that the creative individual can learn to bring the design of objects into a living relationship with tradition and from that point to develop a new attitude toward design" (Conrads 1964, p. 95).

Needless to say there were several versions of the functionalist doctrine, without anything like total agreement. The similarities and differences between De Stijl and the Bauhaus, for instance, are well known. There can be little doubt, however, that the modern functionalist doctrine, with all its nuances, represented a new aesthetic order symbolizing a practical new realism. It was what became popularly known in Germany as *Zweckmässigkeit und die neue Sachlichkeit*, or functionalism and the new objectivity (Lane 1968, p. 131). Even exceptions, such as Le Corbusier, Terragni, and Leonidov, narrowed their historical awareness to the beginnings of other epochs, and thus exhibited an interest in the broad concept of cultural "newness" (Soltan 1988).

31
Plan Voisin by Le Corbusier,
1925.

A functionalist doctrine could also be seen at work in several early modern urban proposals. Major urban facilities, like dwellings and places of work, were segregated, each taking on a form uniquely suited to its inherent activities and related technological requirements. In Le Corbusier's Plan Voisin, for example (figure 31), commercial activities were located in cruciform towers uniformly distributed in a district of open landscape and roads. Dwellings were all placed much closer to the ground in slablike apartment blocks, each again surrounded by open space (Le Corbusier 1964). Transportation networks, principally automobile thoroughfares, also had a separate and distinct presence in the landscape. Unlike in the traditional city, however, they were not simply conformed by the space between continuous lines of buildings. They were released, as it were, from such constraints in order to be given a more independent and therefore precise functional form, better accommodated to the variable speeds, directions, and turning movements of motor vehicles. The surrounding open space assumed a generic character suited to the functions of providing adequate recreation space and clean air for the city to breathe. Earlier proposals, such as Ebenezer Howard's in *Garden Cities of Tomorrow* from the turn of the century, also had strong functional overtones, at least in their overall layout (Howard 1902).

Underlying and legitimating the modern functionalist doctrine, a scientific interpretation of people and their world could be discerned. There was also a certain euphoria in the promise of the second industrial revolution and its new materials and techniques. Despite an orientation abruptly cut off from the extrinsic reality of the past, substantiation and support were sought outside of architecture in the fledgling field of social science and in engineering technology. Le Corbusier, for one, explicitly enumerated questions to be answered by experts in these areas before the new architecture could be advanced (Le Corbusier 1964). For instance, apart from predictions from engineering and material science, the public health effects of different building environments were of interest, along with a better understanding of basic social relations affecting privacy and other spatial arrangements. In short, architecture was to have a firm scientific basis, but more than that, it was to take its inspiration from the rationalism and experimentation of the sciences. Colquhoun appropriately observed that functionalism replaced the earlier classical ideal as the transcendental characteristic of modern architecture (Colquhoun 1989). Perhaps one could go further and suggest that just as nature itself lay behind the ideal of classicism, so natural science and the world of technology lay behind the modern functionalist doctrine.

The import of the doctrine "form follows function" is well known. It was enthusiastically embraced by the Congrès Internationaux d'Architecture Moderne (CIAM) in their deliberations in both architecture and urbanism. It subsequently affected several generations of American architects under the mantle of the International Style and shortly after World War II was largely incorporated into the positions of Team 10. Parallel developments in the field of planning were probably even more far reaching, especially in the United Kingdom and North America. As we have seen, land uses were functionally described as separate units and functionally redistributed according to efficiencies of transportation, access to amenities, avoidance of pollution, and so on. Comprehensive plans, formulated along similar lines, became legislated. In addition, other aspects of public policy drew heavily on the emerging social sciences and translated them into instrumental action. Well before World War II, as the government presence in urban affairs became more prominent, a technocracy was forged around the central ideas of planning's functionalist doctrine (Boyer 1983).

By the early seventies, once its social scientific underpinnings began to loosen, the appeal of the modern functionalist doctrine began to wane. Gone were the heady early days of promise and forgivably exaggerated claims. Although by no means fully discredited, nor indeed found to be unimportant, it somehow failed to fully meet contemporary needs and lost its dominant role in architectural theory, if not practice. Other cultural priorities arose, not the least of which were attempts to recover some of modern architecture's perceived loss of meaning. In concert with congruent developments in other fields, including the rise of nonfoundational outlooks on contemporary life, an ideological pluralism emerged, reshaping architectural understanding. The functionalist doctrine was not lost. It simply became embedded in other orientations, or took its place alongside of them as a parallel program.

It is certainly clear, then, that a relative absence of imitation, a preference for abstraction, and a strong commitment to a functionalist doctrine were hallmarks of modern architecture, at least during and for some time after the avant-garde movement early in this century. Nevertheless, they are by no means decisive or definitive characteristics; all three existed, admittedly in different forms, during other eras. What were unique to at least avant-garde modernism were the nuances and the blend between them, and above all their interaction with modernist time that cut imitation off from the past and any extrinsic natural reality, focused attention inward on the constituent aspects of architecture itself, and necessitated both a functionalist doctrine and significantly high degrees of abstraction. Equally conspicuously, recent reactions to earlier modernism still focus attention inward but turn imitation in the direction of tradition and mass culture, largely abandon strict functionalist doctrines, and treat architecture with varying degrees of abstraction.

Normative Programs for Living

Although it is in large part a twentieth-century phenomenon, the modern process of normalizing residential environments in Europe and America began in earnest toward the end of the nineteenth century. At the outset, the process corresponded to a strong social reaction against the congestion and squalor of industrial cities. By 1879, for instance, in New York City some half a million people were housed in as few as 21,000 tenements (figure 32), rising ten years later to one million people in only 32,000 similar buildings (Schlesinger 1933, Bruner 1972). Early legislation in this regard included the English Public Health Act of 1875, the London Building Act of 1894, and similar German ordinances in places like Altona and Frankfurt-am-Main (Muthesius 1979, Goldberg and Horwood 1980). Such legislative activity represented an increasing governmental role in urban development, essentially aimed at stemming the debilitating excesses of laissez-faire economic growth.

At first there was a concentration on matters of public health and safety, such as adequate light and ventilation, together with vastly improved fire protection. The process then extended into matters of public welfare and the provision of adequate open space, residential support facilities, living space, and suitable layout. In most cases, the instruments of normalization were specific standards, typically in the form of quantitatively defined minima. Prescriptions of appropriate building practice were also used.

32
Turn of the century tenement
living in New York.

One role of the process was to establish order and consistency, as well as to minimize risks to both occupants and investors. Another was to promote social reform by improving the quality of urban life. In the American experience, around the turn of the century, this combination of conservative and progressive impetus was responsible for rallying broad support for housing standards (Fish 1979). In addition to buildings, the process of normalization and standard setting also extended to the spatial distribution of urban functions and public improvements. By the 1920s, after New York's ground-breaking legislation of 1916, the use of zoning and roadway standards had become reasonably common practices (Goldberg and Horwood 1980).

Another impetus behind the emergence of spatial norms, especially for housing, was the standardization necessary for mass production. With growing housing shortages and rising need for affordable units, mass production, in the manner of the automobile industry, appealed to many (Herbert 1984). Also, by offering the potential liberating effects of widespread and democratic use, this approach clearly found resonance with the positivist inclinations of the modern technical temperament.

In all, there were four types of normalizing process involved in defining appropriate living environments. The first and probably most common were building regulations and codes setting out to control the material substance and basic layout of all manner of buildings, including residences. Second, and almost as common, were zoning regulations prescribing the location, density, and character of uses anywhere within an urban area. The third were special space standards and similar requirements, usually as a condition of compliance with the terms of capital funds for building construction. Federal housing regulations and guidelines in the United States, for instance, were usually associated with specific government grants and loan-guarantee programs (National Housing Authority 1945). Finally, there were model housing projects that attempted to directly demonstrate the efficacy of certain ways of building and of providing good residential environments. This was a common practice among private home builders on both sides of the Atlantic (Mason 1982), although the Weissenhofsiedlung outside of Stuttgart, Germany (figure 33), is perhaps the most celebrated example. Open to the public between July and October of 1927, it was an exhibition of various kinds of dwellings. As many as 20,000 visitors per day made their way through the development (Lane 1968). In a similar vein, public display of urban proposals served to give onlookers a sense of what cities could be like in the future. Probably the most widely attended was Norman Bel Geddes's Futurama exhibit at the New York World's Fair of 1939 (Corn 1986).

Fundamentally, the very concept of such normative standards for living was made possible by the new scientific approach to human behavior. Rather than particular individuals, households, and institutions, living could now be studied in terms of population norms, means, and other measures of central tendency. As Gropius remarked, "on the whole, the necessities of life are the same for the majority of people. The home and its furnishings are mass consumer goods, and their design is more a matter of reason than of passion" (Conrads 1964, p. 95). Normalization of living standards also clearly befitted positivist attitudes of social progress through the rigorous application of scientific principles to human prob-

33
Weissenhofsiedlung in Stuttgart: apartment block by Mies van der Rohe on Am Weissenhof, 1925–1927.

lems. After all, as we shall see, most standards were highly quantitative and substantively grounded on the best available empirical evidence. Furthermore, standards began proliferating at about the time that management and control procedures found broad-scale application in industry and in the affairs of emerging corporations. It also occurred when direct connections could be made with confidence between harmful environmental organisms and public health effects. Bacteriology, for instance, was only pioneered by Koch and others in the late nineteenth century. Finally, standard setting and other normalizing processes clearly met the broad technological agenda of mass production and mass consumption. Under its aegis needs satisfaction virtually became a self-fulfilling prophecy.

Nineteenth-Century Crowds and Tenements

The growth of urban areas during the nineteenth century was dramatic, radically changing population distributions and the conditions under which people lived. Migration from rural areas occurred at high rates, as farmers and laborers flocked to the city to pursue the opportunities of industrial employment and the wider availability of consumer goods. Not all this migration was confined to urban areas within the country of an immigrant's origin. Especially toward the end of the century, many departed for overseas and the new world in search of better livelihoods.

In Europe, the number of cities with populations in excess of 100,000 increased from 42 in 1850 to 120 by 1895. Over the same period the proportion of the entire population that was urban almost tripled, from 3.8 percent to over 10 percent. Cities like London, the world's largest, grew in population from about 1 million in 1800 to over 4.2 million a century later. Berlin's population increased even more rapidly, from a paltry 173,000 people in 1800 to over 1.6 million by the century's end (Weber 1967). Even the population of Amsterdam, in a small country like the Netherlands, effectively doubled during the last thirty years of the last century (Ministry of Reconstruction and Housing 1953).

For the United States, the rate of urbanization was even more dramatic. Between 1800 and 1890, as the national population increased 12-fold, the urban population increased 87-fold, from much the same percentage of the total population as Europe in 1800 to well over 25 percent by 1900. New York's population growth exploded, especially between 1800 and 1850, at an astonishing rate of 47.3 percent, reaching over 2.7 million by the turn of the century. Even more remarkable was Chicago, which grew from its founding in the 1830s to be the second largest city in the United States by 1890, a thriving metropolis at the crossroads of major transportation routes, with a population of 1.1 million people (Weber 1967). Moreover, these two cities were not isolated instances of rapid urban growth. In 1910, fully fifty American cities had populations in excess of 100,000 people, compared to nine in 1860 (Bruner 1972). The principal differences between the United States and Europe were the timing and intensity of industrial development, as well as the overall extent and rapidity of the resulting urbanization. On all counts, the United States generally developed later and consequently progressed further in those developments than Europe. In his phase model of modernization, for example, the historian Black pegs the modern economic and social transformation of the United States to the period from 1865 to 1933, compared to the period 1832 to 1945 for the United Kingdom and 1848 to 1945 for France. Germany, the lone European exception, developed slightly quicker than the United States by achieving modern economic and social transformation between 1871 and 1933 (Black 1966).

The overall density of urban development exhibits a somewhat different pattern, however. By and large overall European urban densities were higher than those in the United States. For example, by the turn of the century the overall population density among a number of American cities was on the order of 15 people per acre, compared to over 25 people per acre in Germany and over 38 in England. Accounting for differences in patterns of settlement, where U.S. cities tended to be more diffusely settled, the differences were even more significant. In Germany, for instance, the urban density, purely as a function of building area, was 157 persons per acre, compared to only 22 in the United States (Weber 1967). Indeed, for cities like Berlin, dwelling densities for almost all the population were very high, relatively evenly distributed across the entire urban area.

New York was a significant exception to this trend. Although living environments varied widely within the city, the tenth ward on the Lower East Side was probably the densest district in the western world at the turn of the century, with the dubious distinction of having a population distribution of 523 people per acre (figure 34). For comparison, the densest districts in London and Paris at the time were 365 and 434 people per acre, respectively (Weber 1967). The Lower East Side as a whole had an average of 397 persons per acre, most of the population immigrants who had arrived during the period of 1880 to 1890, with further waves of immigration continuing into the early twentieth century (Weber 1967, Bruner 1972).

34
Cheek to jowl tenement
living in New York City,
c. 1900. Photograph by
Jacob Riis.

Dwelling densities (persons per housing unit) in New York City were also high, though, with the exception of places like the Lower East Side, they were less than in some European cities. Between 1890 and 1900 the overall dwelling density in New York was 18.5 persons per housing unit, compared to Berlin and Vienna at 28 persons, London at 20, and Paris at 14. Overall dwelling densities in other cities of the United States were considerably less. In Chicago, for instance, the figure stood at 8.6. The densities in rural dwelling conditions, by comparison were between two and three times less still (Weber 1967).

The effect of the high nineteenth-century urban dwelling densities on the quality of life, in both Europe and the United States, was both direct and, for the most part, alarming. Overcrowding, unsanitary conditions, and unsafe buildings were all too commonplace, in large measure due to public neglect and private greed. Suicide rates and the incidence of insanity in cities was much higher than in rural areas. Likewise, mortality rates, a significant measure of environmental quality, were almost twice as high in urban areas of the United States for infants, and 50 percent higher for people of all ages (Weber 1967). Fortunately, this was not a uniform condition. Some districts within cities were, in fact, better off than rural areas. In parts of Cleveland, for example, the overall mortality rate was more than a third less than in the countryside. High rents also often occurred, in spite of the poor living conditions, counterbalancing the advantages of generally lower-priced goods in urban areas. In some countries, like Germany, these higher rents and widespread conditions of overcrowding appeared to be due to a gross undersupply of housing, accounted for by an unwillingness on the part of landlords to manage working class dwellings (Weber 1967). Urban life for many of the nineteenth century was very hard indeed.

The most common forms of dwelling were tenements, especially within the inner areas of major nineteenth-century cities. Invariably, these buildings were stacked close together, occupying every available piece of land and forming a labyrinth of rooms available for rent. Sanitary facilities were usually scarce and rarely adequate, as was open space for light and ventilation. A particularly bad circumstance was Gotham Court in New York City, one of the infamous "railroad tenements" built for the purposes of maximizing rent (figure 35). Usually these tenements were arranged in narrow open spaces, often between alleys deep within regular city blocks. Frequently they were only about 18 feet wide, four to five stories in height, of flimsy construction, often of wood. Gotham Court was described by a building inspector of the time: "Twelve doors opened on to the wider of

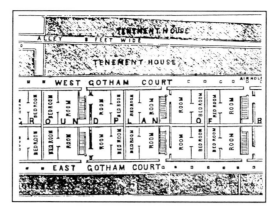

35
Gotham Court, New York
City, 1889.

the two alleys, and each door provided entry for ten families living in each section of the building—two families to a floor in identical 2-room apartments, with a main room about 15 by 9½ feet and a bedroom about 15 by 8½ feet. The structure housed around 500 people without provision for plumbing or heat. Ten years later a row of privies had been placed in the basement, but by then more than 800 people had crowded into the structure" (Glaab and Brown 1967, p. 161). This represented a dwelling density of something on the order of a shocking 4,000 people per acre and, for later comparison purposes, less than one quarter the floor space per person of early twentieth-century dwelling standards.

The majority of tenements in New York City were not as bad, although certainly intolerable by most norms. Under the Tenement House Act of 1879, so-called "dumbbell plan tenements" were routinely constructed five to six stories high, on 25 by 100–foot lots, usually over six rooms deep, housing four families to a floor. Light and air to internal rooms—all except for those on the front and back—came by way of narrow air shafts. In some cases, up to 25 to 30 rooms were served by an open shaft only 2 feet wide (Fish 1979). Needless to say living conditions within most units were appalling and eventually led, through a strong reformist movement, to the "new law" Tenement Act of 1901 (figure 36). Among other stipulations, this act required significant enlargement of open light and air courts, no habitable rooms without natural light and air, a 70 percent maximum level of site coverage, and a minimum lot size of 50 by 100

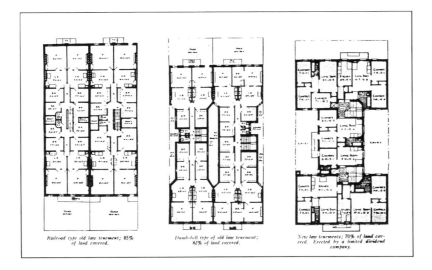

36
Progress in tenement
legislation: New York City,
1865–1901.

37
Berlin *Mietshäuser*:
Bayerische Platz, 1900.

feet. Furthermore, enforcement of the legislation, always a problem during the earlier laissez-faire period of development, was considerably more thorough. In fact, the 1901 new Tenement Law was to serve New York City well, even into the contemporary period (Veiller 1910, Fish 1979).

Inner-city housing in other large American cities was similarly dominated by tenements or rental flats. In both Baltimore and Chicago, for instance, dwellings were constructed with similar "through-floor" plans to those in New York, but not at quite the same high densities (Wright 1933). In Boston and Philadelphia, variants of the traditional row house formed the basic tenement stock, although in Boston an inner-suburban version emerged, referred to locally as the triple-decker, three stories in height with one and sometimes two flats per floor (Warner 1962). There can be little doubt, however, that by the turn of the century, the quality of inner-city housing in America's major cities was in desperate condition, so much so that the first Federal government action in housing was the 1892 survey titled "The Slums of Baltimore, Chicago, New York and Philadelphia" (Fish 1979).

In Europe the situation was little different, although there were some exceptions. The Berlin *Mietshaus*, or rent house, for example, was certainly crowded, with housing demand generally well in excess of supply (figure 37). Dwelling densities in specific locations were over 1,000 persons per acre, and by 1870 there was a 12 percent overall shortfall of units, reaching as high as 40 percent among lower socioeconomic groups. (Geist and Kürvers 1984). Nevertheless, many of the *Mietshäuser* were well constructed, with thick load-bearing masonry walls, and with gen-

38
Meyers Hof, Berlin, 1873–
1910.

erous (certainly by New York standards) open courtyards, or *Höfe*, between dwelling units. In one example, the Meyers Hof constructed in 1873 (figure 38), the open courts were more than 11 meters (35 feet) wide, providing light and ventilation to about 108 rooms. Many *Mietshäuser* of the period were built on narrow and very deep lots, with dwellings arranged in parallel blocks moving back from the street, each six stories high, with the courtyards in between. Meyers Hof, for example, was on a lot 25.6 meters wide and 135 meters deep, with six parallel housing units and five internal courts. There were also other common spatial organizations, although, in all cases, entire city blocks, regardless of shape and size, were covered throughout with buildings surrounding paved courtyards. Pedestrian and vehicular access was usually provided across the entire site by relatively wide openings between the courtyards, and many commercial activities were located in basement and ground-floor accommodations. Generally speaking, the *Mietshäuser* were constructed in a broad band around the old core of Berlin, with apartments on the street for the well-to-do and rooms in rear buildings for the working class and less fortunate members of society (Geist and Kürvers 1984). Again like New York, many buildings have been renovated over the years and still remain in use. Many now serve a contemporary immigrant group—the Turkish "guest workers."

In the Netherlands both conditions of overcrowding and substandard housing grew more and more acute toward the end of the nineteenth century. For men, the basic living conditions consisted of a single room with cupboard beds, a kitchen, and sometimes a WC. Almost 10 percent of the population of a city like Amsterdam lived in damp cellars (figure 39), many of which were only 1.7 meters, or 5.5 feet, in height. Even with some attempts at improvements by housing associations during the 1880s,

39
Nineteenth-century basement
dwelling in Amsterdam.

by century's end 59 percent of the nation's population lived in two-room tenement dwellings or less (Ministry of Reconstruction and Housing 1953).

Together with crowds, tenements and apartments formed a central cultural motif of the nineteenth and early twentieth centuries. Once regarded as ominous and threatening, the crowd also became celebrated as a source of modern artistic endeavor. From Baudelaire's *Painting of Modern Life* to Grosz's scenes of Friedrichstrasse in Berlin, the urban crowd acquired a character that symbolized both middle- and working-class life, another major feature of the modern era (figure 40). Far from being faceless, the crowd represented the frenetic hustle and bustle of the times, just as the tenements, in the hands of authors like Döblin and Dreiser, became the great catchment for the ebb and flow of human conditions. As Franz Biberkopf, one of Döblin's characters in Alexanderplatz, Berlin, was to observe: "House follows house along the streets. They are full of men and women from cellar to garret. . . . Outside everything was moving, but—back of it—there was nothing!" (Döblin 1931, p. 154).

Minimum Standards

The principal means for establishing regularities in everyday living environment were minimum dimensional standards covering a variety of building circumstances. The first such standards concentrated on public health and safety, almost to the exclusion of everything else. As Hermann Muthesius was to comment in 1904, "the most striking difference between the English and German building laws is that the English legislate basically on points of health and fire hazard and virtually ignore construction" (Muthesius 1979, p. 74). More specifically, the legislation in question, the London Building Act of 1894, covered access of light and air to buildings, height restrictions, light-well dimensions, room height restrictions, and regulations about refuse and sanitary facilities (Muthesius 1979). Contemporary standards in Germany and later standards for American housing, such as the 1901 New York Tenement Act, were similarly organized (Fish 1979). So was the 1901 Housing Law in the Netherlands that gave sweeping powers to local authorities (Ministry of Reconstruction and Housing 1948).

It wasn't really until the twentieth century that broader bases for housing standards began to appear. In fact, it was only as recently as 1939 in the United States that a first attempt was made to consolidate existing thinking on the matter of housing norms. At that time the National Association of

40

The urban crowd: *Friedrichstrasse* by George Grosz, 1918. Lithograph on paper, 24¼ × 19⁵⁄₁₆ in. Private collection, London.

Housing Officials and the American Public Health Association convened to produce "practical standards to modern housing in the face of vagueness and disagreement about housing standards throughout the U.S." (National Association of Housing Officials 1939, p. 1). All members of this joint committee quickly agreed that the standards in question "are believed to be fundamental minima required for the promotion of physical, mental, and social health, essential in low-rent, as well as high-cost housing, on the far as well as in the city dwelling" (American Public Health Association 1939, p. 112). In effect, they were universal guidelines encompassing the entire well-being of dwelling inhabitants.

More specifically, physiological needs extended to thermal comfort, light, air, and access to exercise space. Psychological needs included privacy, aesthetic satisfaction, maintenance of social standards, and a category titled "normalcy of family life," nebulous perhaps but an indicator of the importance of statistical measures of central tendency to the standards-setting process. Finally, social health covered topics ranging from protection against contagion through the water supply, for example, to public safety and personal injury. In all cases, medical evidence or some other scientifically based rationale was developed to support the standard in question. Physiological needs, for instance, such as thermal comfort and access to adequate light and air, were based on the medical performance of relevant bodily functions. All were aimed in the direction of establishing acceptable numerical or ordinal limits of performance (American Public Health Association 1939).

Earlier deliberations on an *Existenzminimum* at the second meeting of CIAM in 1929, in Frankfurt-am-Main, had a similar orientation. Conceptually the problem of the "minimum house" was seen to involve resolution of broad biological and psychological needs within the static system of the house itself. At issue was certainly something more than merely public health and safety. To paraphrase some of the participants: the minimum house was seen as a social tool indispensable to the new era and, in one of those remarkable turns of positivist rhetoric, it embodied "an appeal for scientific certainty to overcome customs of tradition" (Le Corbusier 1964, p. 33). Others, such as Ernst May, advanced concrete proposals (figure 41) based upon their own experimentation (Ernst and Sohn 1986).

Zoning practices for establishing norms for the spatial distribution of urban functions, as we saw earlier, proceeded along similar lines. A taxonomy of uses was established in precise categories, usually including numerical distinctions. Thus, the category of "residential," for instance,

41
Practical example of
Existenzminimum: Tornow II
complex in Frankfurt by
Ernst May, 1929–1931.

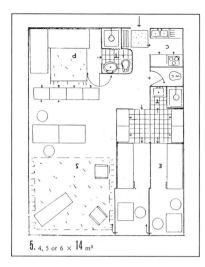

5. 4, 5 or 6 × **14** m²

42

Minimum standards, by
Le Corbusier, according to
"biological units," 1931.

was established for zones whose sole purpose was residential development, and a suffix like R-1 was appended to specify the limits of acceptable building density. The categories were also assigned to geographic areas according to underlying legal principles of public health, safety, and welfare. The resulting guidelines, in common with building standards, were seen to be universally binding for future development within the area of purview. The ordinance and its comprehensive plan were a broad normative prescription of a living environment, primarily embodying verifiable functional principles. More often than not, however, they were also a set of functional decisions that mixed a technical rationale with other socioeconomic and political motives of its framers. Protection of the status quo, for instance, was often uppermost in their minds (Babcock 1966, Boyer 1983).

Throughout, there appears to be substantial agreement on the values for basic dwelling space standards. Le Corbusier, in his deliberations on the matter in 1931 (figure 42), arrived at a value of 14 m² per person (140 sq. ft. per person) for what he referred to as the "biological unit" or "cell" (Le Corbusier 1964, p. 143). As we shall see in more detail later on, Ernst May's standards were similar in the Frankfurt housing estates, if slightly lower, and American standards for public housing were on the order of 12.5–13.0 m² per person (125–130 sq. ft. per person) of habitable space (Dreysse 1988, National Housing Authority 1945). In Le Corbusier's proposal the basic cell took the form of a well-designed bachelor apartment, with extrapolations, based on the 14 m² per person standard, all the way up to families with seven dependents. Similarly, the American standard ranged from one- to five-bedroom dwelling units. In a post–World War II study of dwelling units in fourteen European countries, similar values were again found. The average spatial occupancy rate was on the order of 12.5–13.5 m² per person (122–135 sq. ft. per person), across three reasonably dissimilar dwelling types (Blackshaw 1951). The amount of agreement, however, is less remarkable considering the common underlying concept of housing standards. All were acceptable minima and all were based on more or less the same empirically based technical logic. They were clearly intended for universal application, regardless of cultural differences. Moreover, the rationale was so strongly focused on human biological similarity that much else was almost entirely precluded.

Beginning in the mid-1960s to early 1970s, considerably more flexibility became evident in building, housing, and zoning standards. At this time other considerations, sometimes neglected in the past, assumed higher priority. The rigidity and exclusivity of many prescriptive residential zoning standards, for instance, were relaxed in favor of performance standards that could be satisfied in a variety of different ways (Krasnowiecki and Babcock 1965, Huntoon 1971). In something of a reversal of prior practice, the very technological progress ascribed to earlier standards was seen to be impeded. Prescriptive standards, it was argued, presumed a certain level and style of technological development that may have become obsolete (Rowe et al. 1978). Furthermore, again as we have already seen, the relativism that comes from a recognition of cultural heterogeneity was well on the rise by the late sixties, as was the expanded political power and proliferation of special interest groups (O'Neill 1971). Consequently, normative programs for living were forced to change and become more pluralistic.

At about the same time, facilities programming became considerably more sophisticated. An earlier naive functionalism gave way to increasingly more complicated culturally specific analyses of user needs and postoccupancy responses (Preiser 1978). In one of the most ambitious attempts to underpin design with an empirically verifiable behavioral base, Christopher Alexander embarked upon development of his "pattern language." Each "pattern," in effect, represented a normative situation and an appropriate design response. The extraordinary aspect was the comprehensiveness, rigor, and detail of the formulation (Alexander et al. 1977, Alexander 1979).

Standardization and Production

Another important role of normalization in the design and provision of housing was to promote efficient production. Indeed, it might well be argued that the technological imperatives of production pushed housing into a frame of reference in which the standardization of living accommodations became inevitable. It is clear, for instance, that a major consideration in the *Existenzminimum* discussion of the second CIAM conference was the application of mass production. In his address, Le Corbusier argued that "we must find and apply new methods, clear methods, allowing us to work out useful plans for the house, lending themselves naturally to standardization, industrialization, Taylorization, etc." (Le Corbusier 1964, p. 30). Just as clearly, the successes of the automobile industry, and Henry Ford in particular, were uppermost in people's minds. Walter Gropius, for example, pointed to the housing cost reductions that seemed possible for mass production with explicit reference to Ford's automobiles (Conrads 1964). Elsewhere, the logical and practical connec-

43
An early pilot project in industrialized building: construction of Forest Hills housing by Grosvenor Atterbury, 1910.

tion between standardization, mass production, and lower cost was being drawn and even demonstrated. The American architect Grosvenor Atterbury, for one, undertook a pilot project between 1910 and 1920 at Forest Hills, New York (figures 43, 44), in which his records showed a full 20 percent reduction in total costs (Atterbury 1936).

The distinguishing feature between these episodes and earlier uses of industrialized, prefabricated building technology was the strong emphasis that was placed on the social purpose of producing housing for lower-income residents (Herbert 1984). During the nineteenth century the mass production of decorative fretwork, for example, and a general use of precut technology enjoyed broad application (Wright 1981). Indeed, a widespread effect of technological improvements during the last part of the nineteenth century was a dramatic price deflation in the construction industry. Between 1870 and 1900 the overall price index for construction was reduced almost in half, declining from 128 to 68 (Bemis 1934). Nevertheless, attempts to explicitly develop mass-produced social housing were isolated, and largely confined to a very few experiments in Britain. The so-called heroic period of industrialized mass housing occurred much later in the 1920s and 1930s (Herbert 1984). It was only then that the idea of cultural democracy through mass production and the individually liberating effects of widespread affordability received more complete attention.

Beyond general agreement on the need and social aims of mass-produced housing, there was considerable debate over precisely what form this production should take and, therefore, what aspects of the building fabric needed standardization. Le Corbusier's Maison Domino, for example, was a proposal in which certain major elements of construction, such as floors and columns, were standardized, together with other components like doors and staircases. Considerable freedom was permitted, however, in achieving useful and varied interior arrangements through use of the so-called free plan. The relative independence of the exterior cladding of the building allowed further freedom of expression, orientation, and so on (Le Corbusier 1964). By contrast, Atterbury's system also consisted of components but assembly was more strongly guided toward specific house designs (see figure 44). In effect the process of making a particular house was radically rationalized, although the system of production remained essentially closed (Atterbury 1936). Gradually, two very different concepts emerged. One was essentially open-ended with respect to reference designs for the completed house, placing emphasis instead on small building components and efficient management of the construction process. The other was essentially closed with respect to reference design and concen-

44
Completed housing project at Forest Hills, New York, by Grosvenor Atterbury, 1911.

45
Concentration on economies
of scale from standardization
in modern housing.

trated on economies of scale from standardization and mass production
of large units of construction, achieving variety only through small building details (figure 45).

Recently, relatively high degrees of standardization have been achieved
in most building components, and, contrary to common perceptions, a
significant proportion of many houses in both Europe and the United
States have industrialized components (Eichler 1982, Mason 1982). However, unlike most mass-produced housing before and shortly after World
War II, flexibility and anonymity have asserted control of the basic technological outlook. Design options have replaced standards, in a manner
somewhat similar to the car industry, together with a relative independence between the outward appearance of a house and its technological
conformation. The role of housing types has also reemerged, providing a
technological middle ground by helping to center reference designs within
inherently open-ended, component systems of production. Contemporary
row houses, for example, may have numerous variations but remain basically similar. The result is that attempts to establish a monolithic connection between housing standards and production have become more
relaxed.

Standards and Distinctions

A profound influence of the modern technological orientation was the
importance of generic classifications. Mass production, for instance, virtually guaranteed uniformity in products, just as efficient throughput and
a well-functioning technocracy required precise and unchanging definition of task environments. In matters of building and physical planning,

as we have already seen, generic characterizations of occupant populations and their spatial requirements became widely accepted as both useful and appropriate. Indeed, when confronted with the growing need for mass construction and wholesale reorganization of cities, a strong argument could be made for generally attempting to reduce differences, concentrate on similarities, and develop standardization wherever possible. At the time, anyway, it certainly seemed like the only viable way of equitably tackling the large social problems left by nineteenth-century laissez-faire political doctrines. In effect, modern versions of functionalism and the normalization of building environments became two mutually reinforcing aspects of the same larger building enterprise.

Unfortunately, there were several largely unforeseen consequences. For one thing, a strong alignment developed between housing standards and socioeconomic class. Increasingly, minimum standards were identified with low-income housing. No doubt this was unavoidable to some extent. After all, a principal social aim of minimum standards was to ensure quality for those least able to afford housing. Nevertheless, housing that progressed in design no further than these standards of basic functional requirements took on a distinctive appearance. By now the fate of much of America's public housing is well known. Sturdy but sparse and characterless architecture (figure 46) effectively stigmatized residents as low-aid, down on their luck, racially dissimilar, or on the dole. The process of signification was also so strong that plain, functionally modern apart-

46

Alignment of socioeconomic
class and dwelling: public
housing in South Boston,
Massachusetts, 1990.

ment buildings almost automatically became identified with a social underclass (Rowe 1972). Unfortunately, in the long run, any broader appeal modern functional architecture might have had was thus sharply reduced.

Less obvious, perhaps, but just as potentially damaging was the practice of seeing the program for a living environment as housing rather than as urbanism. The result was an isolation of domestic space, together with the functional segregation of other urban functions and land uses. There is nothing intrinsically wrong with providing private, safe residential areas with considerable open-space amenity, provided that they don't also result in undue reinforcement of a separation in lifestyle. Otherwise the public realm is never encountered around housing and vice versa. Kracauer perceived this absence even more ominously. Writing about contemporary residential areas toward the outskirts of Berlin in the 1920s, he noted that "the streets are friendly and clean . . . [with] nice green trees before houses, and yet, there is an inexplicable angst . . . [for] they are neither inhabited by the proletariat nor are they witnesses to rebellion, . . . they cry out in emptiness" (Kracauer 1930, Frisby 1986, p. 142). Clearly Kracauer was mourning not so much a lack of the "scene of violence" as the lack of a truly public realm.

The functional segregation and efficient spatial distribution of interdependent urban functions, like home and workplace, almost seems to have dictated the need for a universal responsibility, on the part of city residents, for the resulting spatial order. Regardless of local situational differences, residents in remote locations are mutually accountable for their building and land use activities. Under uniform land use controls, deviations from established norms in one place require tacit approval of those in other places, regardless of any reciprocal effect. Vigilance on behalf of many virtually mandates this breadth of responsibility. Zoning ordinances, for instance, must be consistently upheld, requiring high degrees of uniform behavior according to generic categories of permissible land use. Once again, similarity and standardization, rather than difference and variation, seem to be most appreciated socially.

Unfortunately, normative programs of accommodations and spatial organization also run the risk of curtailing precisely those nonspecific spatial realms that seem to be the genius of truly well-functioning public places. For example, the layer of articulated public space around the edges of an old neoclassical railroad station forms what might be referred to as an "eddy space" of many but no particular functions, located outside the mainstream of the station proper. Moreover, these areas are often inviting precisely because they are tactile, small in scale, and possess a certain safe anonymity, again in contrast to the rest of the large-scale, very public building. A similar example is the *zócalo* in the traditional Hispanic town center (figure 47). Basically, it is a sophisticated layering of public open space, but all made within a relatively straightforward alignment of walls, paths, gardens, and paved spaces. To be sure a certain variety and spontaneity in the use of these places comes about independently of the spaces themselves, or because they are simply made to work, as it were, by the inhabitants. Nonetheless, the inviting and yet non–functionally specific character of the spaces also appears to play a significant role.

Finally, the very plurality of special needs, standards, and design guidelines, which seems to mount up with an increasing number of worthy special populations, can verge on becoming self-defeating. As we have seen, norms and standards are protections, guarantees, and purveyors of efficiency. They ensure health and safety, as well as minimum levels of environmental quality, and they allow production and management processes to be rationalized. In short, they are completely faithful to the modern technical orientation. Nonetheless, when the number of competing claims rises appreciably there is often no way of finding an appropriate reconciliation. Each functionally special case is special, and is pressed

47
A layering of public open space: the *zócalo* in Oaxaca, Mexico.

with virtually equal weight to all the others'. Moreover, the more we expand and tend to rely on the technical rationality of this process, the more out of touch we become with the realm of tacit conventions and understandings that do not lend themselves so easily to logical-empirical reduction. Broader questions of morality, for instance, often go unheeded in matters of city building. The final result can be a morass of regulation, requirements, financial expectations, and special group concessions. Moreover, this morass can go on to determine so much of a building, or a piece of a city, that little is left to other vital aspects of the cultural enterprise.

Orthodox and Post Modernity

Clear definitions are often difficult to sustain even in the best of circumstances, let alone among broad cultural categories that inevitably appear to be somewhat arbitrary. Recently, considerable effort has been made to distinguish postmodernity as a state of existence from modernity, its immediate forerunner. In a number of circles, a very definite break has been declared, along with pronouncements that we are now living in a new era (Vattimo 1988). By contrast, in other circles modernity continues to be seen as an "unfinished project" (Habermas 1981, 1987). In still others it is regarded as having become "modernism beyond utopianism, scientism and foundationalism, in short, a postmetaphysical modernism" (Wellmer 1991, p. viii). Certainly in architecture, where modernity tends to be closely associated with the orthodox inheritance of the avant-garde movements at the beginning of this century, at least two reactions have set in. There has been an attempt, first, to reestablish continuity with earlier architectural traditions, and, second, to expand the formal architectural repertoire without resorting to historical circumstances (figure 48). Nevertheless, both within architecture and more broadly, the postmodern condition generally appears to be identified with a reaction to specific

48
Two conditions of architectural postmodernity: Antigone at Montpellier by Ricardo Bofill, 1979–1983, and La Villette by Bernard Tschumi, 1987.

difficulties with modernism, rather than a completely new or different proposal (Habermas 1981, 1987, Colquhoun 1989). Moreover, as Huyssen astutely observes, more often than not postmodernism seems to assume a version of modernity only rooted in the high culture of the 1950s and 1960s, far removed from its earlier adversarial beginnings (Huyssen 1986). In this reactive stance alone, modernity would still seem to be exerting considerable influence. Rather than a definitive break or rupture, it seems that we may be confronting another shift in the grander scheme of things and the emergence of another version of modernity. The magnitude of the shift remains to be seen. So far it does not seem to be simply a next phase or obvious sequel.

Intellectual Conditions

Beyond an absence of metaphysical commitment, the intellectual condition of modernity has been defined mainly by specialization and antinomies related to subject-centered reason. For instance, without a broad framework to unite them, we are immediately confronted with sharp divisions among science, poetry, and morality, as well as the inherent opposition between a drive toward rationality, harmony, and the perfectibility of the human condition, on the one hand, and nihilism, discord, and acknowledgment of human limitations on the other. From one side of modernity comes the assertion that the logical-empirical orthodoxy of positive science lies at the very foundation of all knowledge. Furthermore, the fruits of this knowledge are progressive and their continual pursuit and application through technology is an essential and desirable aspect of the modern condition. It is a matter of freedom not only by helping to overcome the privations of toil, poverty, and disease, but by maintaining the future open. By contrast, from the other side comes a direct challenge to this authority through the assertion that there are other kinds of knowledge, such as "knowing how" and myths, that also provide real and legitimate frameworks for human action. Moreover, from this vantage point the alleged foundational aspect of scientific knowledge about human affairs is simply opinion, with corresponding elements of persuasion and rhetoric. This position also calls into question the efficacy of the positivist reliance on hypothetico-deductive methods of reasoning, replacing this mode of thinking with hermeneutic methods of analysis (Bernstein 1976, 1983). Throughout, the concept of what legitimately guides human action and what brings such a guideline into being are seriously questioned. Far from being only a contemporary occurrence, however, aspects of both sides extend well back into the nineteenth century. Even during the heyday of positive human science, alternative positions were already under discussion. As we have seen, the conditions of historical knowledge about human affairs also changed appreciably during the nineteenth century, as did disciplinary areas like anthropology, sociology, and psychology. Seemingly, for every step made in a foundational direction a charge of arbitrariness could be made with equal vigor from the other direction.

In the poetic realm conditions have been little different. Shortly after the beginning of the nineteenth century, if not before, the hegemony of the classical ideal and its working methods was strongly challenged on a number of points. The German poet Schiller's distinction, for instance, between the sentimental and the naive drew a strong line between methodical, almost arm's-length pursuit of formal ideals and the instinctive, natural, and emotive response of naive genius (Dilthey 1959, Schiller 1961). Later this was to become a significant concept in the emergence of romanticism. Indeed, in many modern definitions of classicism, beyond simply thematic and formal imitations of Greco-Roman models, a contrasting reference has been made to romanticism, and vice versa (Barzun 1961, Preminger 1965, Drabble 1985). Thus, in what amounted to definition by virtue of an antithesis, characteristics like objectivity, clarity, and idealistic imitation are juxtaposed against imaginative free play, originality, and functionally associative imagery. Well-known romantic and classical tendencies vied with each other in many forms of artistic expression throughout the nineteenth century, and architecture was no exception (Early 1965). Moreover, Poggioli's more recent division between "humanist" and "romantic" versions of modernism maintains the distinction well into the contemporary era (Poggioli 1968). Toward the end of the nineteenth century, classical ideals were also further challenged from another direction. Nietzsche, for example, interposed the Dionysian proclivities of hubris and excess against the Apollonian wisdom of moderation, self-knowledge, and self-control (Spears 1970). In so doing, he also remade the idea of an art work as a matter of experience as much as of judgment (Löwith 1964).

Given the antinomies and specialized character of modernity's intellectual terrain, invariably positions seemed to change. Progress is in the eye of the beholder, although we undoubtedly know more today than we did before, at least in different ways. If anything, the early relativism of the modern intellectual outlook has become confirmed further, and nonfoundational areas of knowledge have largely replaced a verified system of truths. Or, as Connor argues, postmodernism is an intellectual process of making distinctions and then resolving the differences thus created with new thinking. Inevitably it is inward-turning, and the constant process of renewal disturbs metanarratives dependent upon foundational truths (Connor 1989).

This does not, however, amount to a definitive break in the modern intellectual tradition. It simply represents, so to speak, another turn of the wheel, where one dominant outlook or process of modern sense making overcomes another. What seems to be distinctive about modernity is its variety expressed by conjunctions or amplifications of specific ideas. If we are willing to relax, for a moment, the shrillness of the voices from both positivism and historicism, then what we probably have, in architecture anyway, is another version of modernity and not, as many would have it, something entirely different.

Material Conditions

Technological advancement also appears to have resulted less in a monolithic pattern of development and behavior than in flexibility, a localization of interests, and a certain pluralism. Such an outcome probably stands to reason. We have already seen, for example, that technological advancement in the devices we use simultaneously liberates us from a consciousness of the technical effort involved. We can then focus on the commodities being produced and, therefore, on our own preferences in those regards. The result, naturally enough, is a strong tendency toward more specific requirements, distinctiveness, and individuality. The earlier, what might be called majoritarian phase of technological existence, with its strong emphasis on universal norms, mass production, and mass consumption, need no longer exist. The technological constraints have loosened and changed, resulting in what might be termed a pluralistic phase of existence, characterized by flexibility and localized distinctions. Nevertheless, throughout this transformation, the material aspect of everyday life has not changed state appreciably. Since about 1930, in most industrialized nations, the roads have been paved, houses have had electricity as well as indoor plumbing, and most families have driven cars. As already described in some detail, there have been dramatic changes in the way we conduct business, and yet the three basic sectors of industry, agriculture, and service have remained intact over the same time period. Again it is a matter of moving into a more advanced state of modernity rather than a sudden break with the immediate past altogether, although this, of course, also depends on how you draw the boundaries.

The generic form of cities themselves is a good illustration of this process of substantial transformation but without radical change. With the spatial transformation from the older monocentric to current polycentric forms of city development (figures 49 and 50), there also came changes in community attitudes toward service provision, for instance, and governance. Generally, there was a rise in both the number and diversity of special interest groups, and urban populations appeared to be more heterogeneous than ever before; moreover, protection of local interests was also on the rise. Nevertheless, the underlying modern capitalist system of property tenure, financing, and institutional provision of services, in keeping with other persistent features like automobile transportation, remained well intact. The facade of modernity may have changed, so to speak, but its basic structure was preserved.

49
A nineteenth-century quarter
of Amsterdam.

50
The spatial mosaic of a mid
to late twentieth-century city:
Framingham in the Boston
metropolitan area, 1978.

At this juncture we can return to the two moments in time that will form the basis for most of the subsequent discussion of the architecture of modern housing. To summarize, the first, between 1920 and 1930, coincided with a euphoric yet practical moment in the positivist and historicist development of modernity. It was a period that capitalized on the fruits of avant-gardism, prominently identified with a progressive confidence in the future, and made a substantive break with past traditions. It was a moment, we are often told, when time stood still somewhere between the ever present and the near future. New materials, new fabrication techniques, new social relations, or at the very least their promise, meant new forms for a new age, potentially one of great social progress.

This was also a moment that coincided with the early era of the second industrial revolution and its emphasis on big business, throughput, corporate management, and technocracy. Mass production brought ideas about operating efficiencies, organization, and standardization into every walk of life, not to mention a corresponding allowance and encouragement of mass consumption. Urbanism began to yield a more spatially compartmentalized environment for most people and a preference for suburban dwelling environments.

The second moment, between 1970 and 1980, more or less coincided with a time of almost universal uncertainty and potential instability. It was a period of postmodernism, or certainly of nonfoundational modernism, when second thoughts were being given to the lack of continuity with past traditions and it began to seem more important to respond to local contexts and cultural points of view. By contrast to earlier eras, the real temporal scope of activities had become dramatically shorter, and their effective spatial boundaries were drawn much wider. The result was a further reinforcement, if not original cause, of backward-looking, localized responses. Paradoxically perhaps, as one aspect of modernity's time frame became compressed, another, the sense of historical time, became elongated. Almost simultaneously the philosophical undermining of foundational positions about the world, the last of which could well have been embodied in the technological orientation of the second industrial revolution, greatly circumscribed the authority of prevailing aesthetic doctrines, inviting a search for other spatial and expressive orders.

This moment also coincided with new technological arrangements that were erasing the old rigidities of the second industrial revolution and taking the world into a new era of organizational flexibility, time responsiveness, and more individualized production and consumption. Centralized, hierarchically focused patterns of spatial organization and settlement were being replaced by dispersed, multiple concentrations of urban activity that were essentially nonhierarchical and distinct. In both the modern and the postmodern moments, however, what was decisive was time and the manner in which time was allowed to influence spatial conceptions, either literally or with reference to imagination and history. Thus, each modern housing project, usually in more ways than one, was very much in its own time, if not in its own place.

Surrounding and connecting the two episodes is a web of longer-term trends and influences. At the outset, the rise of modern housing had at least a rhetorical emphasis on the substance and spirit of a new age. The preceding and contemporary avant-garde emphasis was pushed productively toward new forms through a rationalized process of mass production. It was, nevertheless, also a time during which past sensibilities about settlement, especially in the form of small or manageable communities, were not abandoned but given a renewed emphasis. As we shall see, for housing the period from 1920 to 1930, and especially from 1925 to 1930 when general circumstances were relatively stable, was a synthesis, awkward at times, between a variety of planning and design influences, both traditional and new.

In the aftermath of this period, however, primarily in post–World War II housing developments in both Europe and the United States, the modern technical orientation, held artfully in check during the twenties and early thirties, took over almost completely, obliterating important spatial distinctions in the terrain of our daily lives. The result was often monotonous blocks of flats and towers, bereft of any immediate or local character, or, primarily in the case of the United States, row upon row of single-family detached tract housing with much the same lack of distinction. A misplaced faith in modern essentialism, reinforced as much as anything by the postwar tide of the technical temperament, reduced the frame of design reference for large amounts of housing to a bare caricature. Furthermore, the perceived scale and complexity of urban development increased substantially, again invited by apparent technical capacities for management. As time wore on, however, the upgrading of technical prowess failed to keep pace with unresolved problems and the entire edifice began to crumble.

Fortunately, realignment of the ideological landscapes during the seventies, if not before, began rejuvenating the circumstances of modern housing. In keeping with emerging postmodern attitudes born of uncertainty and senses of difference, the hegemony of entrenched, orthodox modern positions was challenged and upset. Conceptual processes of distinction and merger came into play; a historical condition began to be returned to housing, sometimes with a vengeance, and a renewed emphasis was placed upon localizing dwelling situations. The resulting pluralism of project forms and appearances underscores the apparent decline of a foundational narrative to architecture. In the broader interest of humanism, however, it reminds us of the need for a method of sustaining the design of good modern housing.

2 Modern Housing on the Rise, 1920–1930

The rise of modern housing coincided with the second industrial revolution, the demise of the old sociopolitical order, especially in Europe, and a new vision for community settlement. These three circumstances did not fully align simultaneously, however. The course of human events is rarely quite so tidy. Rather, they came together over a period of 25 to 30 years, beginning slightly before the turn of the century. Nevertheless, after the close of World War I, and certainly during a short prosperous span of years from 1925 to 1930, the die was cast, so to speak, and modern housing came of age.

51
Application of garden city
precepts at Letchworth by
Raymond Unwin and Barry
Parker, 1903–1919.

As we saw in chapter 1, prior to 1900 the production of housing was considerably industrialized in both the United States and Europe. Parts were manufactured in central locations and shipped to remote building sites for assembly into complete units. Industrialization was a way of making existing things quicker, more efficiently, and at greater profit. Nevertheless, the appearance and layout of houses went largely unaffected, still conforming to nineteenth-century neoclassical, romantic, and vernacular ideals.

This orientation was to change, however, when modern process management techniques, pioneered by Taylor and others in the second industrial revolution, were applied to housing. Suddenly the planning, physical layout, and shape of houses became subjects of rational technical scrutiny rather than simply following the cultural norms of Victorian, *Gründerzeit*, or Wilhelmine society. Moreover, the effect on housing of other concurrent technological developments of the second industrial revolution, such as private automobile transportation and electrification, also became highly consequential.

With World War I, the passing of the old aristocratic order in Europe was accompanied by the rise of numerous egalitarian and democratic political movements. At the outset many were to founder. In Germany, for example, there was a stormy period until the Weimar Republic came into its own shortly before the end of 1924. There and elsewhere, however, socialist causes became established, strongly focusing attention on the welfare of the working class and the poor, including housing. The late twenties were, nevertheless, a sober and more skeptical counterpart to the social ferment and optimism of the immediate postwar years (Friedrich 1972, Willett 1978).

Although the timing of the situation in the United States was somewhat different, here too there was a focus on mass housing. The period of pronounced social reform, usually referred to as the Progressive Era, dated from around the turn of the century and had almost run its course by 1917. Many other social reforms, including more universal suffrage, however, were to occur in the twenties, which by and large were a period of conservative prosperity.

The new vision of community settlement that emerged on both sides of the Atlantic primarily combined garden city precepts of physical planning and social organization with a freedom to explore architecturally the new technical opportunities of building. From Ebenezer Howard's *Tomorrow* of 1898 and the early garden city experiments at Letchworth (figure 51) and Welwyn by Raymond Unwin and Barry Parker, the idea developed of large satellite communities on the outskirts of existing cities, which were at once to be well-planned, largely self-sufficient, and perpetually ringed by green space.

Almost simultaneously, architecture, like other cultural fields at the time, became released from traditional iconographic responsibilities toward metaphysical foundations and could now be developed in exploration of a more autonomous existence. The spirit of *die neue Sachlichkeit* (the new objectivity, or realism) that emerged (figure 52) represented a dispassionate attempt to look at things as they were and to advance, practically speaking, avant-garde artistic ideas from preceding modern movements (Gay 1968, Willett 1978). Architects and planners immediately took advantage of the new freedoms of expression, and the fruits of their labors in modern housing quickly became evident.

52

The spirit of *die neue Sachlichkeit* at the Weissenhofsiedlung by J. J. P. Oud, 1925–1927.

Precursors and Contemporary Developments

Like the ingredients of a good mystery, the rise of modern housing required something akin to motive, opportunity, and means. The motive could be clearly seen in the appalling tenement dwelling conditions of the time. In most parts of Europe and to a lesser extent in the United States, the shortages due to World War I only exaggerated an already deplorable situation. The opportunity was equally clear. There were both the broad social mandate and the sponsorship necessary to create mass housing, as well as the technical opportunities offered by new materials and fabrication techniques. Many of the normalizing processes defining appropriate living environments, outlined earlier, also came into play. What remained was the means, and this quickly emerged from prototype developments for new houses and the restructuring of the housing industry that began shortly before World War I.

Technical Developments

By far the major emphasis in the prefabrication of buildings during the nineteenth century was on materials for new settlement. Several European nations had colonial outposts that required quick and easy expansion, especially where adequate building materials and skilled labor were in short supply. Similarly, emerging nations like the United States were rapidly developing and urbanization began to occur at numerous remote sites. The manufacture of housing was part of this trend, ranging from the crude corrugated iron and timber frame shelter used in British colonial territories like Australia, to the mass replication of Victorian ornament in the United States (figure 53; Herbert 1984, Archer 1987). In the Australian case, prefabricated components also had another purpose. They were routinely used as ballast in the sailing vessels that shipped agricultural goods on their return journey. Apart from the industry itself, the beneficiaries of these prefabrication efforts were the new settlers and especially the middle class: mass production required mass consumption. Only very scant attention was paid to industrial applications for relief of the mounting urban housing crisis.

Ironically, in Britain, the most prominent industrial center during the nineteenth century, the relationship between architecture and modernity up to the outbreak of World War I was standoffish at best. The arts and crafts movement and the influence of figures like Ruskin and Morris were strongly entrenched. Consequently, major architects, particularly in residential design like Voysey and Lutyens, staunchly followed traditional practices. Indeed, within the Victorian, neoclassical, and romantic scope of contemporary architecture there was little room for either new materials or new industrial fabrication techniques save for imitation of long-standing craft practices. Instead, both were often seen to belong exclusively to the engineer and to be appropriate for entirely new kinds of construction like railway stations. By contrast, for a later domestic architect like the American Frank Lloyd Wright, there was no real contradiction between the individual values of a home and mass production. Early on in his career he argued strongly for a diminution of drudgery through industrialization, and saw the outcome of a better life for everyone to be essential for a vital democratic culture (Brownell and Wright 1937, Wright 1945).

53
Prefabrication and mass replication of Victorian ornament in the United States.

It was in Germany slightly after the dawn of the new century that the first formal and lasting connection was made between industry and industrial processes on the one hand, and designers and particularly housing architects on the other (Heskett 1980, Herbert 1984). More precisely, in October of 1907 the Deutscher Werkbund was founded by Friedrich Naumann, Karl Schmidt, and Hermann Muthesius, among others, for the express purpose of "encouraging the fruitful cooperation of art, industry and craft" (Anderson 1968). Almost simultaneously, the architect Peter Behrens was appointed as the designer for the Allgemeine Elektrizitäts Gesellschaft (AEG) in Berlin, an enormously influential contemporary industrial corporation. A little later, Muthesius convened a meeting in Munich between a dozen artists, including several architects, and a dozen manufacturers involved in applied arts. The aim was to find more fruitful ways of producing products and, more important for us here, ones that avoided simply the mechanical production of craft products (Heskett 1980, Herbert 1984).

Clearly at stake in these efforts was recognition of the links between prosperity, mass production, standardization, and design (figure 54). In fact, during 1914 a debate erupted within the Werkbund over the establishment of a national culture around the unification of general taste. Muthesius argued strongly for an aesthetic means rooted in standard or typal industrial processes, whereas Henry Van de Velde was far less sanguine about the possibility of uniting art and industry for national economic advantage (Heskett 1980). As things turned out, it was precisely this kind of argument in favor of art for art's sake that was to blunt the Werkbund's subsequent effectiveness. Publications and exhibitions, however, were to continue well into 1916 and the remainder of World War I, although largely through the auspices of neutral countries such as the Netherlands.

Behrens for his part went further than Muthesius and his colleagues in rejecting any kind of arts and crafts basis for industrial production. For him standardization was the key. In his electric kettles of 1909, for instance, standardized parts were used interchangeably for the likes of spouts, tops, bodies, and handles to produce some 30 variations. As one author put it, "it was the exploitation of the possibilities of combining a limited number of standard components to provide a broad product range that made Behrens' work innovative, and distinguished him as one of the first industrial designers in the modern sense" (Heskett 1980, p. 70). Furthermore, he saw what he was doing to be rooted in the contemporary circumstances of industry and the life around him, rather than in the precepts of an earlier technological age (Anderson 1968).

54
Industrialized building processes incorporating mass production and standardization in design.

Walter Gropius, who entered Behrens's office in 1907 as an assistant, also saw the workshop and industrialization as a way of achieving a better architecture (Herbert 1984). For him it was a way of creating a progressive unity between art and technics, and something that was to be repeated with the founding of the Staatliches Bauhaus at Weimar in 1919 (Wingler 1969). Meanwhile, in 1910 Gropius prepared a significant memorandum for Walther Rathenau, the AEG head, concerning the potential merger between the construction industry and artistic principles. The memorandum was titled "Programm zur Gründung einer allgemeinen Hausbaugesellschaft auf künstlich einheitlicher Grundlage" (Program for the Founding of a General Housing Construction Company Following Artistically Uniform Principles), and in it Gropius emphasized the importance of standardization according to dimensional and architectural typological norms (Herbert 1984).

After resigning from the AEG in 1910, Gropius's first real application of this concept took place in the housing scheme for Törten-Dessau of 1926 to 1928 (figure 55). Here, reinforced concrete, cinder blocks, cross walls, beams, and so on were all standardized and manufactured on site. These components were then craned into place according to a rigorously planned organization of labor and materials (Herbert 1984). In fact, it was this on-site manufacture of houses according to efficient and well-coordinated operations that lay at the heart of Gropius's industrial process, and not exploration of the inherent variety to be found in parts and their combination. Moreover, the norms of the standardization within housing units were made the explicit subject of design. Broadly speaking, it was with the Dessau Bauhaus during the second half of the 1920s that the concept of "Art and Technology—a new unity" came to fruition (Wingler 1969).

Similar developments and an optimism about the role of architectural technology were also visible in the neighboring Netherlands. Here the idea of a unity of the arts, in keeping with Muthesius and the Werkbund, originated with H. P. Berlage and continued with the periodical *De Stijl* after its founding and first publication in October of 1917 (Groenendijk and Vollaard 1987). Berlage also endorsed industrial production and the sense of a whole building process, particularly for housing: "dwelling production must become mass production, which will thus mean that it must be possible to build very quickly and in addition very cheaply" (Grinberg 1982, p. 89).

It was J. J. P. Oud, however, whose article "Art and Machine" appeared in the January 1918 issue of *De Stijl*, who most clearly enunciated the potential relationship between the arts and the machine. As he put it, "for the modern artist the future line of development must lead inevitably to the machine. . . . Not only because the machine can give more determinate plastic expression than the hand; but also from the social point of view, from the economic standpoint, the machine is the best means of manufacturing products which will be of more benefit to the community than the art products of the present time, which really only reach the wealthy individual" (Grinberg 1982, p. 87). Moreover, during the Housing Congress conducted in Amsterdam during 1918, van der Waerder proposed standardization of all housing based on some nine floor plans (Grinberg 1982). From then on, in spite of controversy surrounding the curtailment of creative freedom, design of housing in the Netherlands became strongly influenced by technical and functional considerations of efficiency.

In several related and roughly parallel developments, technical standards became established at national levels as early as 1902 and the domestic environment itself underwent significant rationalization. In 1902 the British Engineering Standards Association was founded, followed in 1916 by the Deutsche Normen Ausschuss and, in 1918, by the American Standards Association (Heskett 1980). Usually standards were based upon best existing practice, as we saw earlier, and conformed to the manufacturing processes of large firms. They were, nevertheless, also usually a logical outcome of processes of standardization necessary for highly mechanized

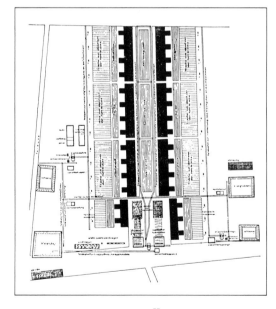

55
Application of
standardization and
typological norms at Törten-
Dessau by Walter Gropius,
1926.

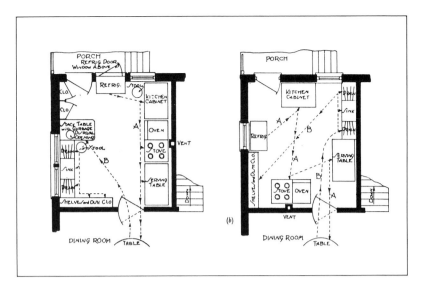

56
Application of Taylor's
principles of scientific
management to the domestic
environment.

production processes. By the 1920s, the period crucial to our story, the practice of standardization in order to achieve efficiency was almost fully accepted, with the standardization itself essentially coming from two sources—the dictates of mechanical production and rational consideration of function.

In this last regard, specific attempts to rationalize the domestic environment began at least as early as 1869 with Catherine Beecher and Harriet Beecher Stowe's publication *The American Women's Home* (Wright 1981, Hayden 1982). Within it, among other things, we find the reorganization and layout of kitchens thoroughly analyzed from a functional perspective and strongly based upon a ship's galley. In 1912, Christine Frederick applied Taylor's principles to the home and published her *Scientific Management of the Home* (figure 56). Furthermore, Hildegarde Kneeland in her 1929 address to the Tenth National Conference on Housing in the U.S. stressed the need for scientific planning (Fish 1979). Finally, in 1921 the German State Efficiency Board was organized to investigate and publicize more efficient means of production and procedure, including application to domestic circumstances. The RKW (Reichskuratorium für Wirtschaftlichkeit), as it was called, published several tracts containing specifications for household furniture and ways of planning or laying out domestic

84

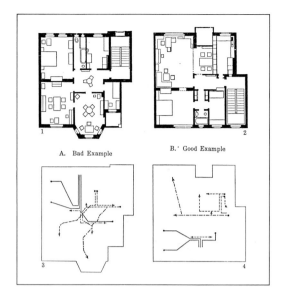

A. Bad Example   B. Good Example

57
Rational analysis of house
plans by Alexander Klein for
the Reichsforschungs-
gesellschaft, 1928.

space. Among these were *Household Work Made Easy* and *Standardization in the Home* (Heskett 1980). A little later on, in 1928, the architect Alexander Klein, working for an offshoot of the RKW called the Reichsforschungsgesellschaft, conducted extensive quasi-mathematical analyses of numerous house plans (figure 57), using principles from graph theory in order to determine the most efficient layouts. He then defined an array of typological plans for minimum housing requirements, ranging in size from 45.6 square meters to 73.5 square meters, with variations in both plan width and depth (Tafuri and Dal Co 1976, Benevolo 1984).

Probably the most comprehensive set of housing standards of the era directly effecting fabrication, however, was devised in Frankfurt-am-Main by Ernst May's staff. The *Frankfurter Normen* (Frankfurt standards), as they became known, covered a range of some 24 separate dwelling types, from one-family units up to multifamily apartment dwellings. Within these standards of house type, the dimensions of doorways, window openings, and built-in furnishings were also completely standardized. The *Frankfurter Normen* went still further, clearly defining practically all basic construction details. Moreover, through May's hegemony over practically all building in Frankfurt, they were rigidly enforced (Höpfner and Fischer 1986, Schaal, Pfister, and Scheibler 1990).

In contrast to the social Darwinism and laissez-faire business practices of the late nineteenth century, a substantial role for government intervention in urban affairs had been established by the 1920s, including the provision of housing. When confronted with the mounting crisis of the industrial city and the failure of a free-enterprise system to overcome market imperfections of congestion and blight, not to mention the raw social drama of poverty, crime, and vice, there was little alternative. Moreover, reform-minded electorates, including a burgeoning middle class, pressed their claims for better living standards and much higher degrees of government responsibility. Consequently, as the new century wore on, widespread use of government powers extended to building regulation, direct enablement of housing, and broad public powers to control, take, and develop property. All in some way affected housing and collectively established the modern institutional framework under which housing continues to be provided in most countries.

Building Regulation

The building regulations of note, as we saw, earlier, began at the beginning of this century with landmark public health and safety legislation in many countries. The New York Tenement Act was passed in 1901, for instance, setting a trend that was to continue in many American cities until almost all had such legislation by 1919 (Fish 1979). The Housing Law of 1901 in the Netherlands made similar provisions, regulating the minimum size, layout, and dimensions of dwellings; adequate supply of light and air; the prevention of fire hazards; and the adequate removal of residuals of production like sewage and smoke; as well as ensuring structural adequacy and sanitation (Ministry of Reconstruction and Housing 1948). Similar legislation was passed in the United Kingdom, a leader in the field, and in Germany.

In the United States the various tenement acts were usually based upon local surveys of blighted and poverty-stricken urban areas, as well upon federal government studies beginning in 1892. The New York Tenement Act, for instance, was based upon the findings of the Tenement Housing Commission of 1900, appointed by Governor Theodore Roosevelt, later to become President (Fish 1979). However, the real impetus behind the legislation came from the social reformers of the Progressive Era and writers like Laurence Veiller, Jacob Riis, Hamlin Garland, and Stephen Crane. Riis, for example, published his influential *The Battle with the Slum* in 1902, while Veiller issued his *Housing Reform: A Handbook for Practical*

Use in 1910, followed by his formulation of *A Model Housing Law* in 1914. The constituency and motives of the reformers were mixed, however, and the success of the Progressive Era was undoubtedly due to the widespread and diverse backgrounds of prominent reformers and reform groups. Most were genuinely interested in cleaning cities of crime, vice, and blight, although in many cases it was in their economic self-interest to do so. In short, morality, humanism, and self-interest commingled among a broad middle-class constituency to bring on lasting regulatory reform of housing (Fish 1979).

The situation in the Netherlands was little different, although the move toward reform came earlier. In 1853 the Royal Institute of Engineers Committee was appointed and in 1855 gave a "report to the King on requirements and planning of worker dwellings" (Ministry of Housing and Reconstruction 1953, p. 4). This was followed in 1873 by the Amsterdam survey of slum housing (figure 58) and culminated on June 12, 1901, with the nationwide Housing Law. Subsequent amendments to this law preserved and strengthened the health and safety regulations and also made provision, in 1912 for instance, for the control of the external appearance of houses (Ministry of Housing and Reconstruction 1953). In fact, the basic structure and statutes of the Dutch Housing Law have persisted into the contemporary era, whereas the more limited American tenement acts have largely been replaced by multiple-unit legislation, which again began in New York City around 1929. Nevertheless, by the 1920s the concept of a comprehensive set of minimum housing standards was widely and firmly in place. Moreover, as we have seen, the use of those standards as a basis for standardizing building practices and house types was also in effect.

58
Substandard housing in
Amsterdam, 1900.

Direct Enablement

Governmental enablement of housing production, the second major extension of powers, essentially took two forms: legal creation of cooperative housing ventures and direct financial subsidies. Once again it was the United Kingdom that took the lead in the creation of cooperative housing, beginning at least as early as the Rochdale Pioneers in 1844. By 1907 various cooperative housing societies in London had built on the order of 25,000 units (Bauer 1934).

In the United States, building societies began in Philadelphia during the first half of the nineteenth century, and the concept quickly spread to other cities (Jackson 1985, Clark 1986). Members of the building societies enjoyed the considerable advantage, at that time, of being able to take out fairly sizable, low-interest loans. Normally houses were paid for either by cash or through short-term general-purpose loans. The coming of age of a modern system of government-backed mortgages and long-term, relatively low-interest home loans was, however, still some distance in the future. In the United States it didn't transpire until 1934, during the Great Depression.

In the Netherlands, housing associations were first established in the nineteenth century by socially minded employers and by members of the middle class banding together (Ministry of Reconstruction and Housing 1953). Usually these were called "masters associations" of one kind or another, and were responsible for the construction of only a few thousand dwelling units throughout the nineteenth century. Later on, housing associations were established according to political and religious affiliations (*verzuiling*) with the express purpose of providing healthy workers' dwellings. Essentially, members of these denominational or political groups had access to cooperative housing, a method of housing delivery that was to become extremely successful, especially during the early decades of the twentieth century. In fact, between 1918 and 1920 as many as 743 new housing associations were sanctioned in the Netherlands, rising to 1,068 in 1935, of which 22 percent were Roman Catholic, 9 percent were Protestant, 4 percent belonged to professional groups, and the majority, 65 percent, were socialist (Ministry of Reconstruction and Housing, 1948).

The rapid growth in cooperative workers' housing in Germany was spurred on by the Compulsory Insurance Acts of 1883 and 1899, even though a strong sense of solidarity among workers for housing reforms had existed since the class struggles of 1848. Indeed, in Frankfurt-am-Main the Frank-furtergemeinnützige Baugesellschaft (Frankfurt Cooperative Building Society) was formed in 1860 (Gartenstadt 1935). Effectively, the 1883 and 1899 laws recognized cooperatives and limited-dividend societies, as a part of Bismarck's general reform of government activities and responsibilities (Aronovici 1914). By 1914 something on the order of 1,400 housing societies had been created in Germany, involving collective ownership of property and community facilities within housing estates, such as kindergartens, laundries, social rooms, and libraries. Also in the 1880s, legislation was created to allow pension funds to be used as a source of capital for house building (figure 59). Indeed, by the outbreak of hostilities in 1914 some $114 million had been loaned to housing cooperatives and trade union societies, making possible the construction of about 150,000 dwelling units (Bauer 1934).

In many respects an early model for direct public participation in housing was provided by the Austrians and especially the Social Democrats of the

59
Workingmen's housing in Frankfurt-am-Main.

Vienna City Council. Following quickly on the heels of a rent control law of 1917, parliament enacted taxing legislation, beginning in 1922, that turned the city of Vienna into the major provider of housing until the fascist regime of 1934 (Schlandt 1975, Tafuri 1980). The pressing need for public-sector provision was clear. Continual currency depreciations had all but obliterated the capital available for private industry, and stringent rent control provided an additional disincentive to private participation. In addition, the sheer demand for more housing grew appreciably, due to higher rates of household formation from the flurry of marriages after World War I and the declining state of the existing housing stock. In 1923 with the income from taxation, the city of Vienna commenced what would become an extensive building program, with the construction of 2,200 housing units. During the years that followed, production levels were usually in excess of 5,000 dwellings per annum, typically taking the form of multistory superblocks, or *Höfe,* built within existing urban districts well served by transportation networks (Schlandt 1975).

Direct public funding of housing in Germany began around 1901 with the creation of special governmental authorities. By 1909, over 50 percent of the larger German towns and municipalities were providing direct public assistance to low-rent housing (Bauer 1934). In an effort to stimulate production and overcome inequities produced by the high monetary inflationary period, a house rent tax (*Hauszinsteuer*) was levied in 1921. This applied to all buildings constructed before the First World War and presented owners with their property as free and clear equity. In return, taxes in the amount of 10 to 50 percent of prewar rents were collected, and administered by local municipalities through a revenue sharing program (Mullin 1975, Tafuri and Dal Co 1976). Between 1926 and 1932, $2.86 billion was raised, equivalent to double the income tax revenues of the same period, of which $1.25 billion was loaned back out in the form of mortgages to stimulate both the economy in general and housing production in particular (Bauer 1934). Indeed, this funding mechanism was to prove decisive in Germany's housing recovery of the 1920s.

A similar history of financial support can be found in the Netherlands. Between 1900 and 1914, for instance, full loans payable over 75 years were routinely issued to local authorities and to housing associations for improvements and even for the costs of public housing site acquisitions. By 1919 a housing subsidy arrangement had been worked out, providing for a 75 percent state share and a 25 percent local share. These funds were then deployed in both first and second mortgage arrangements for new housing construction, as well as rehabilitation of substandard dwellings.

A carrots and sticks approach was thus taken in the matter of housing reform, the Dutch government requiring house owners to rectify substandard dwellings under the regulatory provision of the 1901 Housing Law, and then also providing financial relief for this task. In all, something on the order of 89 percent of housing production undertaken before the Netherlands was overrun in 1940 was financially secured through these government subsidies (Ministry of Reconstruction and Housing 1948).

Control, Taking, and Development

Broader public powers to control, take, and develop property for public purposes including housing, the third major extension of government authority, also followed a similar historical trajectory. In Germany, for instance, the concept of *Kathedersozialismus*, or municipal capitalism, quickly followed in the wake of Bismarck's reforms during the 1880s, although the tradition goes much further back to the burghers of Augsburg and the medieval powers and responsibilities of towns. Moreover, many cities had received broad home rule powers as early as 1808 under the Stein reforms, named for Karl Freiherr von Stein who led the call for emancipation of Prussian peasantry (Cohn 1968, Mullin 1975). Simply put, in contrast to a governmental system that only does what is expressly required of it, under *Kathedersozialismus* a German municipality does everything except what is expressly forbidden from doing (Bauer 1934). Consequently, during the early years of the twentieth century, most German towns became aggressively involved in land acquisitions and public improvement projects. By 1902, for instance, half the larger towns owned land in excess of 60 square meters per capita—a considerable amount when we remember that the footprint of a modest house was on the order of 30 to 50 square meters (figure 60). Furthermore, land annexation powers and controlling authority over the uses of those lands were often in place by 1890, primarily aimed at stopping the adverse effects of land speculation in the wake of the rapid expansion of most German cities, occasioned by equally rapid industrialization. Indeed, the public capture of its share of improving property values was very much in evidence with the passage in 1911 of a universal land-value increment or transfer tax (Foulke 1911, Bauer 1934). Prior to that time the increment tax had been experimented with as early as 1898, with broad-scale municipal enactments beginning in 1902. Frankfurt-am-Main, for instance, adopted such a tax in 1904, and Berlin did likewise in 1910. In the former case, it followed passage of the "Lex Adickes" (literally Law of Adickes, the Mayor of Frankfurt) in 1902, which gave the city extraordinary expropriation powers (Foulke 1911, Mullin 1975).

60
Narrow building footprints and high dwelling densities in Frankfurt-am-Main.

A good example of *Kathedersozialismus* in action was to be found in Frankfurt prior to World War I. When the city adopted a property transfer tax, it immediately put the proceeds to good use. In 1898 it had purchased the mass transit system, immediately turning it into a modern and profitable enterprise. The city routinely undertook its own industrial operations, although usually in support of a bureaucratic or service function. Lithography, bookbinding, and general material supply, for example, became city-owned and operated functions in support of clerical activities. There was also a common practice of taking over enterprises that abused the public at large, for one reason or another, such as pawnbrokers and funeral homes. With regard to real estate, as a contemporary observer noted, the "city policy is constantly to increase the city holdings and to use the city funds and credit to advance the welfare of the community, especially in respect to dwellings" (Foulke 1911, p. ix). In addition to curbing land speculation, the city of Frankfurt also used its considerable land holdings, amounting to 21 percent of the total city area, as a grant-in-aid program to stimulate appropriate building activity. Under the *Erbau* system, for instance, building associations could rent land from the city at very reasonable rates and, in return, give up the improved property to the city after 60 to 70 years (Aronovici 1914). Although providing housing for many of its employees, the city stopped short of a more generally available worker housing program.

Public powers to regulate the uses of property expanded considerably, during the first quarter of this century. The year 1916 saw enactment in New York City of the first major American comprehensive zoning ordinance. Under this law a comprehensive plan was prepared for the city and the allowable uses in each area clearly designated (Fish 1979). This enactment was quickly followed, in 1920, by a Model Land Use Code, developed by the American Bar Association, for the purpose of achieving some procedural uniformity in the regulation of land uses within all American cities. In 1926 the U.S. Supreme Court upheld the government's right to zone, with its ruling in the landmark case of the Village of Euclid vs. Ambler Realty. From then on "as of right zoning," according to a comprehensive plan, became standard practice (Krasnowiecki 1965). However, unlike the German situation, the use of government powers to annex and take land for public housing purposes did not meet with the necessary constitutional approval until well after 1935, and direct provision of housing only became a reality with passage of the Federal Public Housing Act in 1937.

The general provisions of the Netherlands' far-sighted Housing Law of 1901 covered a broad range of governmental responsibilities. In summary, the law required passage and enforcement of local building bylaws. It empowered local authorities to require house owners to make necessary improvements to their property. It also allowed local authorities to condemn property and to expropriate land in the interest of providing housing. In addition, town planning was required and, as we have seen, substantial financial provisions were provided to enable local authorities to directly provide housing with state subsidies (Ministry of Reconstruction and Housing 1950). Planning and zoning procedures, however, didn't really come into full effect until about 1930, again paralleling the American experience, although larger-scale, regional plans were required as early as 1931.

The rise and rapid expansion of a governmental role and responsibility for housing and urban development, while a reaction to the crisis at hand, also closely paralleled the orientation of the second industrial revolution toward matters of procedure, management, and rational control. In a sense it was the public sector version of developments that were taking place, with such marked financial success, in private business. Among other things, it also allowed emerging bureaucracies to focus on specific topics of public concern, and upon a specialization of interest and expertise. Adequate housing thus became not only a matter of social conscience but also the subject of considerable technical discussion and advancement. Moreover, as outlined in chapter 1, housing requirements became explicitly normalized and standardized for one of the first times in history in an effort to exert comprehensive control and adequate provision. A felicitous conjunction was then established with design from a social perspective, reinforcing the technological conjunction with industry that was already emerging. A causal chain was thus established from a government's desire for improvement, to management of building activities, followed by establishment of norms, the creation of technical standards, and thence to opportunities for industrial production.

As for the broad domestic political climate of the last half of the 1920s, it could be characterized on both sides of the Atlantic as being practical in its orientation and primarily concerned with social welfare and, above all, with stability (Willett 1978, Blum et al. 1963). In all cases, there was utter fatigue with both the turbulent years of the First World War and its immediate aftermath. A return to normalcy was uppermost in most people's minds, together with an avoidance of unnecessary foreign entanglements and an effort to keep the far political left and right at bay (Allen 1959, Friedrich 1972, Willett 1978).

The merger between planning principles of the garden cities movement and the architecture of the "new realism" was at once bold and conservative, as well as innovatory and utilitarian. Paradoxical as it may seem, such a hybrid reflected the moods of the times and the different vantage points from which architectural positions were shaped. From the perspective of modern movements seen as an overlapping sequence of radical avant-gardes, the sobriety and matter-of-factness of the merger could be, and often was, regarded as socially uncritical, pragmatic, and without much novelty. Indeed, for someone like Kracauer on the political left, far too little emphasis was placed on the concrete realities of everyday life. Instead, the abstract beauty of the architecture and the clear forms of the overall plans obscured the brutality and alienation of everyday life in an industrial age (Friedrich 1972, Frisby 1986). By contrast, from the viewpoint of a professional mainstream and a general public unused to such sweeping planning efforts and basic building forms, the merger was liberating and shocking at best, while eliciting from conservative political factions charges of being dangerously unrepresentative of traditional values (Lane 1968, Friedrich 1972). In hindsight, the reality seems to lie somewhere in between. The new realism that emerged was a constructive vision, derived from principles developing in the technological arena but with a strong orientation toward real subjects, human needs, and righting the wrongs of past entrepreneurial excesses and public neglect. Far from turning its back on progress, this stance actively embraced discoveries from the modern movements and pressed them into effective community service (Willett 1978).

Garden Cities

The early precursors of the garden city movement and of suburban worker communities of high environmental quality were experiments like Port Sunlight of 1887, sponsored by the English soap magnate L. H. Lever, and Bournville Village, which also began in England around 1895 under the auspices of George and Richard Cadbury (Benevolo 1985). Both settlements offered their residents space, open air, and sunlight, in sharp comparison with the dreary squalor of English industrial cities. The spatial redistribution of urban population was, as one author put it, "another element in the search for an answer to the crises of the late Victorian City" (Cherry 1988, p. 64). Toward the nineteenth century's end, London was rife with ideas of relieving the pressures of industrial slums and moving working populations into the countryside. Like the parallel American reform experience, it was motivated by a conjunction of morality, humanitarianism, and self-interest.

In 1898 Ebenezer Howard brought things to a head with his *Tomorrow: A Peaceful Path to Real Reform* (revised in 1902 as *Garden Cities of Tomorrow*). Howard detailed an urban model of a constellation of ideal forms built as satellites to an existing conurbation, such as London. It was influenced, among other things, by Edward Bellamy's *Looking Backward* of 1888 and its vision of Boston as a communistic city.

In theory, Howard's Garden City would be surrounded by a belt of agricultural land and would be developed on land held in common by the community (figure 61). The profits of this development and the land appreciation would be turned back to the community and there would be no private gain. Furthermore, the close proximity of the satellite community to agricultural areas would offer new markets to a depressed sector of the economy. The planned satellite community would be limited to 30,000 inhabitants, ideally made up of 6,000-person wards, or small-scale environments, in which the anonymity of large settlements could be overcome readily (Kaplan 1973, Barnett 1986, Cherry 1988). Central to life within the community was a kind of town and country merger, in which "all the advantages of the most energetic and active town life, and all the beauty and delight of the country may be secured in combination" (Howard 1945, pp. 45–46). Finally, Howard was attempting to avoid the paternalism to be found in earlier factory settlements like Point Sunlight and Bournville. In its place he tried to foster self-sufficiency and a collective organizational spirit.

The first applications of Howard's ideas came with the town of Letchworth in England (figure 62) and then later with Welwyn. In 1903 the First Garden City Company was registered with Thomas Adams as Secretary Manager, and 4,000 acres of land purchased in the countryside of Hertfordshire north of London. A preliminary plan was accepted in 1904 from the hand of Raymond Unwin and his partner and cousin by marriage, R. Barry Parker. Construction began shortly thereafter (Day 1981).

The plan for Letchworth had few of the formal geometrical qualities of Howard's original diagrams. Instead, development was carefully related to the topography and the existing landscape, bringing with it, as one author put it, "an air of informality, . . . together with quadrangles, village greens and sites for detached houses" (Cherry 1988, p. 66). As might be expected from Unwin and Parker, two distinguished residential architects, design of the housing was very much within the English cottage vernacular tradition. In effect, Letchworth embodied Howard's social and general

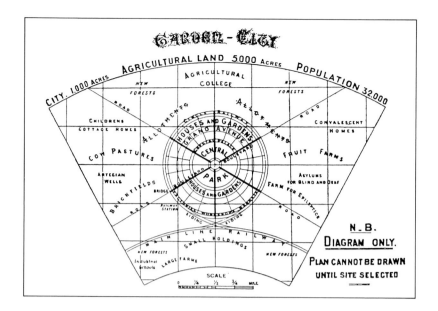

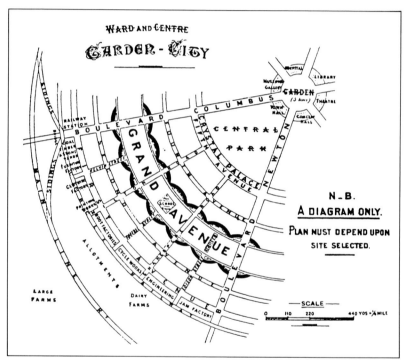

61
Diagrammatic representation
of "Garden City Principles"
by Ebenezer Howard, 1898.

physical organizational principles but architecturally projected the image of a picturesque, low-density country village.

Raymond Unwin was to continue to be a strong force in the years to come, particularly in English and American town planning circles. In 1909 he published one of the first major texts in the field, *Town Planning in Practice*, and around the same time became actively involved in the garden city movement, including propagation of garden city suburbs (Unwin 1911, Miller 1981). His Hampstead Garden Suburb of 1905–1907 (figure 63) was to become extremely influential, and within it one could find a full repertoire of Unwin's design ideas, such as quadrangle arrangements of housing, parks, and cul-de-sacs. Parenthetically, his interest in many of these spatial forms apparently derived from boyhood experiences growing up in Oxford (Cherry 1988).

From the turn of the century the spread of garden city ideas was rapid and diverse. The Garden City Association was founded in 1901 with Ralph Neville, a Liberal member of Parliament, as chairman. By 1903 membership had risen to 2,000, leading to formation of the International Garden City Association, which later became the International Housing and Town Planning Federation (Cherry 1988). In the United States, garden city ideas were well maintained between 1910 and 1930 by the Regional Planning Association in New York, a group formed to encourage area-wide planning. The membership of this association was to be quite influential, including Lewis Mumford, Stuart Chase, Catherine Bauer, Clarence Stein, and Henry Wright (Kaplan 1973). In fact Stein and Wright, together with Alexander M. Bing, were commissioned in 1923 by the Russell Sage Foundation to make a theoretical study for a possible American application of garden city principles (Wright 1933). One result was to be Sunny-

62
The Letchworth Garden City by Raymond Unwin and Barry Parker, 1903–1919.

63
The Hampstead Garden Suburb by Raymond Unwin, 1905.

64
Woodbourne: a garden city residential development in Boston, Massachusetts, by Alexander Pope, 1911.

side Gardens, New York. Many others also participated in the American Garden City movement (figure 64).

Continental European interest in Howard's Garden City proposal, even if less complete, was nevertheless quite strong. The Deutsche Gartenstadt-gesellschaft, for instance, was organized in Germany as early as 1902, and the first independent company for the building of a garden city was formed in 1908, resulting in the construction of Hellerau near Dresden. Garten-stadt Staaken followed shortly thereafter, between 1913 and 1917, in the Spandau district of Berlin. Designed by P. Schmitthenner, this housing estate incorporated some 2,400 housing units, of which over 60 percent were single-family (Berning, Braum, and Lütke-Daldrup 1990). In addition, Bruno Taut, who was to become an influential architect in Berlin's postwar modern housing, presented a paper at the 1914 Congress of the International Garden City and Town Planning Association. Also present at this meeting was Bruno Ahrends, another prominent architect of postwar German modern housing (International Garden Cities and Town Planning Association 1915).

At first the German garden city projects were not very effective as a housing solution for wage earners because of their high rents, although they were effective in eliminating excessive land speculation (Aronovici 1914). Following World War I, however, there was a general consistency between garden city principles and government policies for urban decentralization and rural resettlement. Even though the latter was to adhere to an increasingly conservative bias, particularly later under the National Socialists, urban decentralization was a hallmark of the Social Democrats' plans for Berlin under Martin Wagner, and for Frankfurt-am-Main under Ernst May. May was very strongly influenced by garden city principles, having worked in Raymond Unwin's English office between 1910 and 1912 (Risse 1984). Indeed, May himself candidly stated that his experience with Unwin was "the foundation on which the whole of my work is based" (Grinberg 1982, p. 63). Certainly Römerstadt and the other Nidda valley housing estates May created in Frankfurt, as we shall see, incorporated many garden city principles.

Although the influence was less complete in the Netherlands, probably because of the relative lack of widespread pessimism about the modern city, the idea did take hold of expanding the city following garden city principles (Grinberg 1982). H. P. Berlage, for instance, in his initial plans for Amsterdam South of 1900 to 1905 showed signs of this influence; with Vreewijk on the outskirts of Rotterdam, built between 1916 and 1919, the influence was unmistakable. Here a curvilinear, informal pattern of streets with low-density, single-family housing was developed in a countrylike, garden setting. Indeed, as one report put it, "when the garden city idea was put forward, Rotterdam was the first town on the continent where it was applied in practice and where it was later on developed" (Ministry of Reconstruction and Housing 1948, p. 15). By this time, however, the garden city idea had been diluted to mean simply dwelling in the countryside.

Later post–World War I criticism of the garden city movement in the Netherlands came from the political left and turned on the inappropriate congruence between the bourgeois one-family house and socialism's increasing popularity, as well as on the political symbolism of a traditional architectural style. The romantic bias of garden city aesthetics certainly did not coincide, for example, with the ideas of De Stijl. Nevertheless, Berlage's Vreewijk estate was a success, and certainly J. J. P. Oud's highly functionalist Kiefhoek project in Rotterdam, as we shall also see, shared with Vreewijk and the garden city movement the basic organizational concept of low-rise, one-family row housing, where each family has its own private parcel of land adjacent to its dwelling (Grinberg 1982).

Similarly, in Vienna there was considerable controversy surrounding the garden city movement, again divided along lines separating the broad political spectrum. The leftist city officials resisted pressure to expand housing on the urban periphery in the form of garden estates. Instead, they constructed large housing blocks enclosing the perimeter of sizable communal courtyards, in a modern version of a nineteenth-century urban housing type mentioned earlier (Tafuri 1980). The conservative opposition was critical of this program almost from its inception, because they, in turn, associated private ownership and houses in gardens with social stability. In fact the now familiar housing superblocks, primarily by the architect Karl Ehn, such as Strassenhof, Bekelhof, Rakenhof, and particularly Karl Marxhof (figure 65), did become the center of urban uprisings in early 1934. However, the extent to which the housing, mostly admired by its tenants, played a role in these events is difficult to fully estimate (Schlandt 1975).

The New Realism

The other side of the urban-architectural merger suggested above originated after World War I with a new realism—*die neue Sachlichkeit* (the "new objectivity") (figure 66). Dominant in Germany within many artistic and architectural circles from roughly 1924 until 1933, the new realism

65
Karl Marxhof in Vienna by
Karl Ehn, 1927–1930.

66
The new objectivity in
architecture: row houses at
the Weissenhofsiedlung by
J. J. P. Oud, 1925–1927.

also extended to several other European countries, most notably the Netherlands, Switzerland, Czechoslovakia, and France (Willett 1978). In the
Netherlands, for instance, it went under the name *Nieuwe Zakelijkheid*,
although it more generally coincided with the architects of the Nieuwe
Bouwen, including breakaways from De Stijl such as Oud, Rietveld, and
van Eesteren, as well as younger radicals like Duiker (Grinberg 1982). The
general sentiment of this international movement was toward practical
reality; recognition of circumstances for what they were, including new
opportunities presented by technology; and a reaction against egotistical,
individualistic, and romantic outlooks like expressionism. It was a concerted effort to apply the insights of earlier modern movements—such as
futurism, dadaism, and cubism—rather than to innovate for its own sake.
As Peter Gay and others have noted, it amounted to a liberation of the
modern movements, away from small cultural elites and toward a wider,
less personal level of community involvement (Gay 1968, Willett 1978).
The term *Sachlichkeit* conveyed a sense of objectivity in two senses. First,
it meant objectivity in reporting on what was literally around and about—
the circumstances of everyday life. Second, it meant to do so soberly,
neutrally, and in a matter-of-fact manner. In this last sense it also clearly
embraced concepts like functionalism, utility, and an absence of decoration (Willett 1978).

The phrase "die neue Sachlichkeit" was first coined by Dr. Gustav Hartlaub, an art gallery director, who mounted an extensive show with the same name at the Mannheim Kunsthalle in the middle of 1925 (Willett 1978). Hartlaub's exhibition catalog said that "the expression ought really to apply as a label to a new realism becoming a socialistic flavor. It is related to the general contemporary feeling in Germany of resignation and cynicism after a period of exuberant hopes. . . . Cynicism and resignation are the negative side of the New Objectivity; the positive side expresses itself in the enthusiasm for immediate reality" (Hartlaub 1925, p. 3; Friedrich 1972, p. 155). While certainly justification for a certain conservatism and retrenchment, it was also an affirmation of the economic and political stabilization of Germany under the socialist Gustav Stresemann, resulting from the simultaneous failure of both the far left and far right as well as from a new balancing of the international order after the Locarno Treaties of 1925 (Willett 1978).

By the "new objectivity" Hartlaub meant not simply realism but a change in national mood, although he did emphasize the contemporary inclination of many artists like Grosz, Dix, and Beckmann (figure 67) toward a more literal representation of their surroundings (Friedrich 1972). Between 1924 and 1925 Grosz's style, for instance, became less satirical and began, like Baudelaire's "modern painter," to capture transitory movements and everyday events (figure 68). Such works as *Gentlemen Dressing* (1925), *Street Scene, Berlin* (1925), and *In the Park* (1925–1926) were all realistic in their portrayals, commonplace in their themes, and considerably removed from the more extreme individualism of expressionism (Hess 1974).

Other exhibitions of the *neue Sachlichkeit* were to follow, including Hartlaub's production at Chemnitz and the 1927 show at Karl Neirendorf's Berlin gallery. Far from being a unified artistic field, however, the artists in the first Mannheim exhibition had little in common except for a strong figurative interest in their surroundings (Willett 1978).

In the United States, the realism of Charles Sheeler and the haunting depictions of Edward Hopper were strongly related to the *neue Sachlichkeit* in both urban, industrial content and objective distance (Fisher 1985). Emerging American architectural principles similarly stressed simplicity, honesty, and things natural (figure 69). Simplicity usually meant durability, functionality, and a parsimonious use of materials; for someone like Gustav Stickley, if a design was functional and used the least amount of material then it was beautiful (Stickley 1909). Honesty was a matter of

67
The new objectivity in art:
Die Dirnen auf der Strasse by
Otto Dix, 1925. Oil on
plywood, 37⅜ × 39⅜ in.
Private collection, Hamburg.

68
Life in the modern city:
Sunday Family Walk by
George Grosz, 1923. Collage,
pen, and watercolor on
paper, 11 × 8⅜ in. Marvin
and Janet Fishman,
Milwaukee, Wisconsin.

direct expression of the materials being used, while to be natural usually meant avoiding the contrived or artificial (Clark 1986). In the hands of an architect like Frank Lloyd Wright the three characteristics merged into an "organic architecture" that was ultimately fitted to its site, material, and social circumstances (Wright 1945).

Even in Hartlaub's mind, the *neue Sachlichkeit* probably applied most appropriately to architecture. As early as 1923 Otto Haesler undertook two radical projects, in the form of the Italienische Garten and the Georgsgarten *Siedlungen* at Celle (Taut 1979). It was in architecture that realism and objectivity could be directly translated into new materials, new technical conditions, and, most important, socially liberating effects. The *neue Sachlichkeit* certainly coincided with the concept of "Art and Technology—a new unity" that swept the Dessau Bauhaus in 1925, and the industrialized building systems able to provide affordable housing, espoused by the Nieuwe Bouwen in the Netherlands. Here Hartlaub's sense of "resignation" was probably a healthy disillusionment, accepting existing new conditions perhaps but ultimately making something constructive out of them.

Finally, the high levels of architectural abstraction that also emerged with the *neue Sachlichkeit* seemed to begin with the premise that in a truly enlightened, democratic, and modern society, traditional authoritarian and metaphysical powers no longer held sway. Logically speaking, then, the making of architecture should be about the very stuff of architecture and about the immediate circumstances that objectively bring it into existence. Consequently, a basic concern with fundamental spatial circumstances— like planes, lines, volumes, surface, and coloration—became primary and, at least initially, yielded an architecture necessarily sparse and abstract.

69
Architectural principles of simplicity, honesty, and things natural in the American bungalow.

Moreover, it was precisely in the essentialism of these socially directed new beginnings that abstraction became such a useful tool for revealing and poetically expressing the reality of contemporary circumstances. Similarly, again in the interest of broad social application, modern life was rendered without extraneous spatial distinctions that called attention to other eras. Thus time was unabashedly released to have a universalizing and democratizing influence on architectural space.

On the other hand, in the eventual mergers that took place between the new realism and garden city principles, the universality and contemporaneity of housing estates became greatly diminished, particularly when place-specific aspects of the broader landscape and historical time were expressively allowed to take over. Indeed, as we shall see in projects like Römerstadt, it appears reasonably clear that such a marriage of otherwise strange partners and such a blurring of spatiotemporal distinctions was intended for sociopolitical purposes.

In keeping with the political stability and economic prosperity of the time, the production of housing during most of the 1920s was unprecedentedly high in most western nations (see appendix B for details). The United States, for instance, reached an annual production rate of almost a million units in 1925, a level it would not achieve again until well after World War II. In the Netherlands, by contrast, housing production for the general period peaked in 1934, largely unaffected by the economic depression in other parts of the world. Generally, however, the profile of housing production was much the same in most places, rising up and then declining, largely in the form of a bell curve (figure 70).

The following discussion singles out housing production in three nations for analysis: the United States, Germany, and the Netherlands. These three were chosen largely because they are where major advancements took place in the development of modern housing estates. They also provide a useful international cross section in terms of population size and relative scales of urban development.

The United States

Between 1920 and 1930, over 7 million housing units were constructed in the United States, primarily in the form of single-family dwellings. Production started slowly after World War I, reaching 247,000 units annually by 1920 and then rising rapidly to a peak of 937,000 units in 1925, before declining to an all-time low of only 93,000 units during the depths of the depression in 1933 (U.S. Department of Commerce 1955). For a sustained period from 1922 to 1928 production was above 700,000 units annually.

Although the distribution of new dwelling units generally reflected the strong American preference for single-family living (figure 71), substantial numbers of multiple-family structures were also constructed during the boom years of the middle twenties. Statistically, the percentage of total housing production in single-family units declined from 82 percent in

1920 to around 61 percent by 1925 before increasing again to the 1920 level by 1933 (U.S. Department of Commerce 1954). Multiple-family structures of three or more units were constructed at over 200,000 per annum between 1925 and 1928, accounting for as much as 32 percent of the overall housing construction at a peak in 1927. Throughout the history of U.S. housing construction, booms in apartment construction have usually accompanied high levels of overall housing production, for at least two reasons. First, the incipient market demand for different types of units is greatly exaggerated during a general housing boom and, second, slightly higher market risks in apartment construction are more readily absorbed during a general boom.

The dynamics behind this period of housing production in the United States can be captured by examining population changes and capacities for both production and consumption of housing. Slightly before 1920, the United States statistically became an urban nation for the first time in its history. By 1920 the urban proportion of the total population stood at 51.2 percent, having risen from 39.1 percent only two decades earlier (U.S. Bureau of the Census 1950). The overall population increased 20.5 percent during the 1920s, from over 102 million to slightly above 123 million by 1930. This was not, however, a dramatic increase, particularly in comparison to the previous decades. Immigration during the twenties, for instance, was relatively low, accounting for just 24 percent of overall population growth, compared to nearly 70 percent during the previous decade with the early waves of European immigrants. The rate of urbanization, however, continued at almost the pace of the preceding years, rising by about another 5 percent of the total population between 1920 and 1930 (U.S. Bureau of the Census 1950). One reason for this sustained urban growth was undoubtedly the trend toward lower-density, garden-oriented suburban development that began to emerge even before the First World War.

Housing, like any other product, was strongly influenced by the character of prevailing business cycles and by shifts in applicable technologies. Business during the twenties was for the most part booming. After the depression of 1921, the hopeful improvements of 1922 quickly led to a revival of activity in 1923 and then a steady growth until the crash of 1929. The United States was a relatively prosperous nation at this time, not having sustained the war damage of Europe and possessing enormous natural and human resources, as well as a wide domestic market. The development of production techniques to a new high point of mechanical

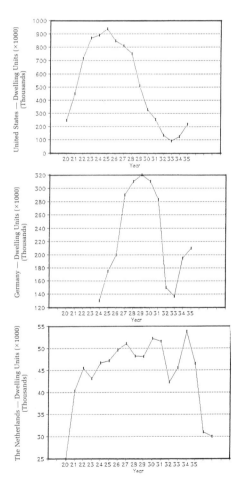

70

Housing production in the United States, Germany, and the Netherlands, 1920–1935.

71
Strong American preferences for single-family living.

and managerial efficiency also aided the business climate, as did the introduction of installment buying and credit (Allen 1959). In addition, transportation improvements and the availability of relatively inexpensive, serviceable land on the urban periphery sustained housing production at reasonable prices.

The general American population's capacity to consume during the 1920s was also at or near an all-time high, strongly driving the demand for housing. Per capita income, for instance, a reasonable indication of the capacity to consume, showed a rapid rise of 20 percent between 1920 and 1923, followed by a steady growth of some 12 percent from 1923 to 1930. The decline after that, during the Great Depression, was astonishing, with per capita income plummeting 52 percent in just two years and not recovering to World War I levels until 1936 (Vaile and Canoyer 1938).

Behind the financial well-being of most Americans during the twenties also lay dramatic shifts in occupation, as we saw in chapter 1, as well as substantial technological improvements in productivity. There was a continued decline in agricultural and manufacturing employment with a concomitant increase in the professional, service, and trade sectors. By 1929 the profile of the work force was considerably different from that of the turn of the century or even the end of World War I. Meanwhile technological improvements to production almost doubled the value added by manufacture per wage earner during the 1920s alone. This rapid improvement was largely due to the process improvements of the second industrial revolution and the increased use of electric-powered mechanical devices (Vaile and Canoyer 1938).

Germany

The overall profile of housing production in Germany and many of the dynamics were similar to those in the United States (see figure 70 and appendix B). Very little building occurred before about 1924, in the aftermath of World War I and the period of chronic currency destabilization. Housing construction then increased rapidly from around 124,000 units annually in 1924 to a peak of 320,000 units in 1929, before reverting to the 1924 level by 1933 (Benevolo 1984). As in the United States, declines in production were very dramatic during the economic depression of the thirties, dropping some 52 percent in only two years.

Again as in the United States, population growth in Germany during the 1920s was relatively steady, increasing to about 62 million persons by 1930. Urban development and housing production, however, were rapidly increasing due to continued urban immigration, the need to resettle workers living in appalling slum conditions, and emerging peripheral patterns of new settlement. There were also acute shortages of accommodations due to the prolonged curtailment of housing production around World War I (Benevolo 1984). The prosperity of Germans, particularly during the latter half of the 1920s, also rose quite dramatically. There was, for instance, a 20 percent increase in the levels of wages between 1925 and 1928, and in the latter year unemployment dipped to about 1 percent (Friedrich 1972).

In spite of acute demand, German housing production was at first stalled because of political instability, vicious inflationary cycles, and a destabilized currency. In November of 1923, for instance, at the height of the currency destabilization, the mark suffered a thousandfold devaluation against the dollar. Moreover before about 1924 building costs rose far faster than the general cost of living. Stability began to return with the Dawes Plan of 1924, under the Stresemann regime. Devised by the American banker Charles Dawes, this was the monetary doctrine under which Germany operated with its creditors until 1929, when the Hague agreements returned German control over its own economic circumstances (Friedrich 1972). It is small wonder, with such strong financial ties to other western markets, and especially to the United States, that the German economy suffered from the stock market crash of 1929 and the Great Depression. During this period, housing production slowed down considerably.

Unlike in the United States, government played a strong role in post–World War I German housing production. Apart from the tradition of municipal capitalism, this was spurred by the inflationary cycles of 1918 through 1924 and the industrial instability that followed, which necessitated heavy government intervention into all sectors of the economy. Also unlike the American situation over much the same time period, housing production in Germany did recover after the economic depression of the early 1930s, surpassing production rates of the twenties, to something approaching 400,000 units annually (Benevolo 1984). This recovery, however, was accomplished under an entirely different regime, that of the National Socialists.

Overall housing production in the Netherlands rose appreciably during the twenties and early thirties before rapidly declining to almost zero during the Nazi occupation between 1941 and 1945 (see figure 70 and appendix B). Before World War I, average levels of production were on the order of 20,000 units annually, declining to as low as 6,500 units in 1917. There followed the same kind of rapid rise in production that we saw in the United States and Germany, reaching 40,000 dwelling units annually by 1921 and a peak of 53,814 units in 1934. By the early 1930s production levels were erratic, although nowhere near the decline that took place after 1935. It should be noted that the period from 1920 to 1930 was also a time of declining need against available housing stock, from a gap of some 85,000 units to approximately 4,000 units. Nevertheless, these statistics do not take full account of the housing replacement needs, largely due to unsuitable extant conditions (Ministry of Reconstruction and Housing 1950, 1953, Ministry of Housing and Building 1964).

Besides the need to replace dilapidated and substandard dwellings, another reason for the high levels of production during the 1920s was a population boom. Between 1920 and 1930, population increased by 14 percent from 6.9 million to 7.9 million persons, a rate of increase greater than those in France, the United Kingdom, Belgium, and Denmark across the same period (Ministry of Reconstruction and Housing 1950), though considerably less than the population growth in the United States.

As in Germany, the period of housing recovery in the early twenties was due to strong municipal involvement and to the continuing efforts of semipublic housing associations. Indeed, by 1928 the Netherlands was spending 8.3 percent of its national budget on housing, compared to about 6 percent for Germany (Bauer 1934). Between 1917 and 1920 over 50 percent of all housing was produced by public and semipublic organizations, rising to as high as 80.4 percent in 1919. From then on their role dwindled, with over 88 percent of the housing produced during the peak year of 1934 coming from the private sector (Ministry of Reconstruction and Housing 1953). Also as in Germany, the 1920s was a period of urban resettlement and of improving the quality of available urban housing stock (figure 72). In 1900, for instance, over 25 percent of all dwellings had only one room. By 1930 this proportion was less than 4 percent, with most of the larger, better equipped housing units being built during the 1920s (Ministry of Reconstruction and Housing 1950, 1953).

Improvement of available
urban housing stock between
the wars in Amsterdam.

During the period of recovery after World War I, as in the United States, there was a marked preference for single-family dwellings, although many were actually built in a row house configuration. As one report put it, "thus we may consider the customary type of dwelling in the Netherlands to be the one-family house which is frequently adjudged best suited to the individualistic character of the Dutch people and not only as arising from historical conservation" (Ministry of Reconstruction and Housing 1948, p. 15). The latter remark refers to a preponderance of older housing stock in the form of attached single houses. By 1939 fully 72 percent of the housing stock was single-family, a proportion close to that in the United States (Ministry of Reconstruction and Housing 1948).

Among the three nations the overall level of housing production during the twenties was the highest in the United States, on a normalized basis, at 5.7 dwelling units annually per 1,000 population, followed closely by the Netherlands at 5.3 units per 1,000 and then Germany with 4.8 (see appendix B). Given the lags in high levels of production and especially Germany's slow start, these production rates are reasonably comparable, and, in comparison to what had gone on before, they were high.

More specifically, German peak housing production during the Weimar Republic lagged behind that of the United States by about four years, and the rate of increase after World War I in the United States was much more rapid at 190 percent over two years, compared to Germany's 140 percent over five years. High levels of production in the Netherlands more closely matched the American profile, although they were sustained far longer, well into the second half of the 1930s. Peak levels of production were also highest in the United States at 8.2 units per 1,000 population in 1925, compared to 6.7 units per 1,000 population in the Netherlands for 1927 and 5.1 units per 1,000 population in Germany for 1929. However, the reverse also holds. The decline in housing production during the depression years in the United States was both longer and a sharper than that experienced in Germany. Statistically the United States suffered an 88 percent production decline between 1928 and 1933, compared to a 52 percent decline in Germany a few years later, between 1931 and 1933. Germany's housing production was also able to bounce back, under the National Socialist regime, much faster than production rates in either the Netherlands or the United States. Although higher, housing production in the United States appears to have been generally more volatile, probably due to the comparative lack of a stabilizing government influence. Nevertheless, the broad profile of housing production across all three nations was one of relatively quick recovery after the First World War, a period of boom certainly between 1925 and 1930, the time of our specific interest, followed by very rapid declines in production with some recovery before World War II.

Among the suppliers of housing units, there was a far greater disparity between the United States and the European countries. Almost all of the American housing production came from the private sector, typically in the form of small, decentralized construction firms. In fact, between 1920 and 1933 less than 1 percent of all housing units constructed in the United

States involved government funding (Bauer 1934, Mason 1982). Direct provision of almost any sort had to wait, as noted earlier, until after the 1937 public housing legislation.

While the majority of housing units over the same period were privately produced in both Germany and the Netherlands, public involvement either in the form of direct production or financial assistance was far higher. In Germany, for example, 10 percent of the housing produced between 1919 and 1933 was provided directly by public agencies, 34 percent through government-assisted building societies, and 56 percent by the private sector. The distribution of production in the Netherlands was much the same, again with 56 percent of all units being supplied by the private sector (Bauer 1934). If we were to include government-sponsored mortgage assistance of all types, then the public sector involvement in the Netherlands would be much higher, at around 60 percent (Ministry of Reconstruction and Housing 1948). As noted earlier, one strong reason for higher levels of German and Dutch public and quasi-public participation in housing, political attitudes aside, was the scarcity of available capital, especially during the early twenties. The United States, by contrast, was in an economically much more solvent position, especially within its private institutions (Allen 1959).

Cost comparisons in construction are often difficult at the best of times, let alone with sketchy historical data. According to Catherine Bauer's analysis, the capital or "first costs" of a modest American house in the early 1930s amounted to about $7,500, of which 22 percent was attributed to the developed lot, 60 percent to construction of the unit, and 18 percent to "carrying costs." Typically, such an investment would have required a first mortgage with a 10 percent down payment and interest rates up to 6 percent over a 10-year period (Bauer 1934, Clark 1986). By comparison, the "first cost" of a modest German apartment at much the same time was $2,750; under a scheme of maximum public support, 4 percent of this total went for raw land, 5 percent to development, and 91 percent to actual construction. Financing typically involved substantial state support, leaving the amount of owner or tenant equity in the property at a very low level in comparison to American circumstances. On a normalized basis, however, accounting for disparities in property size (the typical American unit was almost twice the size of the German apartment), the "first costs" were roughly comparable at $3.75 per square foot for the United States and $3.8 per square foot in Germany. Furthermore, annual charges on a similar normalized basis were also comparable, at 11.3 percent of "first costs" for the United States and 11.6 percent in Germany (Wright 1933,

Bauer 1934). Admittedly this is only one set of rather carefully constructed data. Similar data from Henry Wright and others, however, do bear out much of Bauer's analysis (Wright 1933, Bemis 1934). Moreover, data available for the Netherlands suggest a comparable profile of costs (Ministry of Reconstruction and Housing 1948). Overall housing construction costs, therefore, were probably roughly comparable during the second half of the 1920s among the three nations. The advantages of higher levels of mass production, particularly in Germany, probably had more to do with the speed and scale of certain projects than with overall cost. Generally, it also appears that standards of construction in Germany and the Netherlands, especially on publicly assisted housing, led to more durable housing than in the United States (Bauer 1934).

Finally, the housing industry in the United States and the Netherlands essentially consisted of a large number of small-sized firms operating in a relatively fragmented and decentralized manner, a profile that persists today (Ministry of Reconstruction and Housing 1950, Mason 1982). In the Netherlands, for example, during 1938 there were 22,200 firms operating, 83 percent of which were of one to five persons in staff size, 16 percent of from 6 to 50 persons, and only 1 percent of more than 50 persons. Furthermore, the client base in the form of housing associations and building and loan associations, as well as private entrepreneurs, also tended to be numerous and dispersed. As we saw, in both the United States and Germany, growth in the number of housing or loan associations was very rapid from well back into the nineteenth century.

In Germany there were also certain similarities, with the exception of certain major centers like Berlin and Frankfurt-am-Main. There centralized, large-scale, multipurpose housing entities were deliberately established in order to effectively tackle the housing problem. In Berlin the most notable of these organizations was the GEHAG (Gemeinnützige-Heimstätten-Spar-und-Bau), a building society founded in 1924 by Martin Wagner, who later became the chief architect for Berlin (figure 73). An expert at forming effective cooperatives, Wagner, a former engineer and Socialist Party member, created the GEHAG primarily to produce low-rent housing mainly in large-scale housing estates, such as the Britz on the outskirts of Berlin, and roughly in accord with garden city principles of decentralization. The GEHAG was staffed principally by socialists and was well financed through trade unions. By providing an overall umbrella for all aspects of housing production, including closely coordinated design-build operations, the GEHAG, together with another major building society, provided 63 percent of the housing or 63,924 dwellings in Berlin between 1925 and 1929. This compares to 36,898 units in the same period by private enterprise and effectively none by the city (Bauer 1934, Willett 1978). Parenthetically, this compares favorably to public production levels in Vienna, where the city also had a strong influence, producing 63,754 units or 70 percent of the housing between 1922 and 1934 (Schlandt 1975). Of the total production in Berlin, however, only 20 percent, or around 20,000 units, were designed by modern architects such as Taut, Häring, Ahrends, and Gropius. Moreover, building operations as well as development activities were not well coordinated on a city-wide basis (Willett 1978).

In Frankfurt, by contrast, housing projects and city-wide planning were closely coordinated through a centralized authority of overlapping agencies created by Ernst May, in a unique model of social democratic planning and politics often referred to as the *das Neue Frankfurt* (the New Frankfurt) (figure 74). Taking a cue from the Viennese experience under Ehn, as well as his prior experiences as the planner for Breslau, May consolidated and coordinated all offices dealing with planning, construction, and financing, of which housing was a part (Risse 1984). He was able to do this under a compact reached in 1924 by a SPD (socialist)–Democrat–Center Party

73
The Berlin Britz housing
estate by Bruno Taut et al.,
built by the GEHAG,
1925–1933.

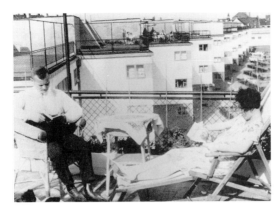

74
Das Neue Frankfurt:
Bruchfeldstrasse housing by
Ernst May, 1926.

coalition headed by Dr. Ludwig Landmann, who brought May to Frankfurt in 1925 (Höpfner and Fischer 1986). This new arrangement gave May's newly created bureaucracy sweeping powers, including compulsory land purchase in the name of the public good. Without much preparation, a 10-year plan was drawn up in 1925, an express purpose of which was to eliminate the housing shortage, especially for low-rent units. Between 1926 and 1930, May and his organization completed some 15,174 units in and around Frankfurt, predominantly in the form of peripheral estates of row housing, effectively rehousing 11 percent of Frankfurt's population (Willett 1978, Risse 1984). A similar centralization of production also occurred in Rotterdam under J. J. P. Oud as chief architect, without, however, nearly the same sweeping powers and production capabilities (Groenendijk and Vollaard 1987).

Three Projects in Three Cities

Within these three nations three modern housing projects stand out: Sunnyside Gardens, including the Phipps Garden Apartments, in New York, Römerstadt in Frankfurt-am-Main, and the Kiefhoek estate in Rotterdam. Each, to a greater or lesser extent, represented a merger between new design and planning principles. Furthermore, each was a large project, especially in its context, thus throwing interesting light on housing as a part of a broader city-building process. Finally, all three projects, either singly or in combination with other very similar schemes from the same locale and era, have proven to be architecturally significant. From both a typological and a historical perspective any mention of early modern housing usually includes the *Siedlung*, the garden apartment, and the urban housing terrace.

Sunnyside Gardens in New York

Between 1924 and 1928, Sunnyside Gardens (figure 75) was developed by the City Housing Corporation to provide, as they put it, "better homes for wage earners" (City Housing Corporation 1927a, p. 2). Essentially, Sunnyside Gardens was an attempt to provide an alternative to the post–World War I resurgence of tenement overcrowding that was taking place locally in New York, and part of a broader national attempt to create an American garden city. By the time that the "old law" tenements in New York City were declared unfit for habitation in 1909, around 51,000 of them stood empty. Unfortunately this trend was to become drastically reversed, with 19,000 tenement units still vacant in 1919 and only 1,366 vacant in 1923 (City Housing Corporation 1924a). Contemporary developments were little better. Speculative housing developments began to burgeon near the outskirts of the city, including vacant lands in the borough of Queens, with row upon row of monotonous treeless streets and tract houses standing close together (Wright 1933).

During the summer of 1923, members of the newly formed Regional Planning Association were commissioned by the Russell Sage Foundation to make a theoretical study of the application of garden city principles to the American urban context. A site in South Brooklyn formed the basis of the

case study, including detailed analyses of various medium-density residential lot layouts (Wright 1933). Shortly thereafter, in 1924, Alexander M. Bing, one of the members of the study team and a successful real estate developer in New York City for over a quarter of a century, founded the City Housing Corporation. Advisors to the original board of the corporation also included two other members of the study team: the planner Henry Wright and the architect Clarence S. Stein. In the years to come, their partnership was to be one of the most fruitful collaborations in American community planning history. Other members of the City Housing Corporation Board included luminaries like Eleanor Roosevelt and Felix Adler, one of the framers of the new law Tenement Act of 1901 (City Housing Corporation 1924a).

In essence, the City Housing Corporation was organized as a limited-dividend corporation "to build better homes and communities and, by careful experiment, to improve house, block and community planning" (City Housing Corporation 1927b). Its more specific aims included the building of low-priced houses as first-class homes for lower-income dwellers (figure 76) and development of cooperative methods of home ownership. It was also charged with developing better methods for home building and "to demonstrate the advantage of the large-scale purchase of land and the quantity production of houses" (City Housing Corporation 1924a, p. 7). Further, in keeping with its garden city roots, the corporation was to demonstrate the value of ample outdoor play space and "to arouse public social obligation towards decent homes for all" (City Housing Corporation 1924a, p. 7).

Financially, the City Housing Corporation issued stock to stockholders and, in return, guaranteed a 6 percent annual return on their investment. Each share cost one hundred dollars and, by 1927, there were something on the order of 520 stockholders in the corporation (City Housing Corporation 1927a, 1927d). The limited annual dividends payable to stockholders effectively meant that any surplus was immediately reinvested in the corporation's building activities, thus enabling high-quality housing to be delivered at moderate prices. In practice these financial arrangements proved to be most successful. Housing at Sunnyside was maintained at moderate prices of around $10 to $12 per room per month, including utilities, and the City Housing Corporation did manage to provide uninterrupted 6 percent dividends to investors, as well as a $300,000 cash surplus (City Housing Corporation 1927a, 1927b, 1927d).

Early in 1924, the City Housing Corporation purchased 77 acres of land from the Long Island Railroad, of which 55.82 acres was used to create Sunnyside Gardens. The purchase price for the project was about 48 cents per square foot of land, substantially more than the value of 3½ cents per square foot that would have been asked slightly before the turn of the century. Although these lands in Long Island City had been out of agricultural production for some 30 to 35 years, rising land values were a relatively recent phenomenon, primarily due to the real estate boom that was taking place across the East River. Land values at Sunnyside Gardens continued to rise more than threefold during the four-year construction period of the project (City Housing Corporation 1927a, Stein 1966).

The site location of Sunnyside Gardens also had other advantages (figure 77). It was situated adjacent to the Bliss Street station on the Corona subway line, only 15 minutes' ride from 42nd Street on Manhattan and easily accessible to most other parts of New York (City Housing Corporation 1927a). City services also extended to the edge of the property, making timely development a straightforward proposition. However, much to the disappointment of the planners, they could not spatially organize the development around the highly efficient concept of superblocks. Instead the Queens borough officials insisted they stay within the confines of 12 preplotted streets, most of which were laid out in a gridiron plan, with blocks 120 to 200 feet wide and from 600 to 900 feet long (Wright 1933). In the words of one of the project's architects, they had to "fit buildings to blocks rather than blocks to the living conditions" (Stein 1966, p. 24).

76
An early aerial view of Sunnyside Gardens, New York, by Clarence Stein and Henry Wright, 1924–1928.

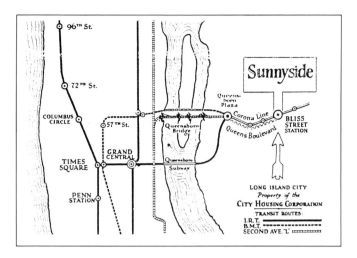

77
The location of Sunnyside
Gardens in relation to
Manhattan and the New York
transit system.

Physical development of Sunnyside Gardens, which took place over almost five years from 1924 through 1928 (figure 78), was divided into three phases, each corresponding with the distribution of particular housing types. The principal planner for the project was Henry Wright, originally from St. Louis and the Chairman of the Town Planning Committee of the American Institute of Architects. The principal architect was his partner Clarence S. Stein, the former Chairman of the New York State Commission on Housing and Regional Planning. Another architect, Frederick L. Ackerman, was responsible for many of the housing unit designers, and Marjorie S. Cautley was the landscape architect for the project (City Housing Corporation 1927a, Stein 1966).

The first phase or section of development commenced in 1924 and carried through the following year, with occupancy occurring as early as October of 1924. All told, over 350 dwelling units were constructed, primarily in the long blocks along Carolin and Gosman streets, between Spillman and Foster avenues. This was the part of the site nearest to the public transit, as well as to neighborhood schools and stores (City Housing Corporation 1924b). Parking garages were built on a remote location north of Middleburg Avenue (see figure 78), in order to establish and preserve a strong pedestrian character to the development and to allow the centers of blocks, often otherwise used for parking cars, to be developed as communal garden spaces. Stores were also constructed as a part of the development, adjacent to the transit line, in order to augment available neighborhood services (City Housing Corporation 1924b).

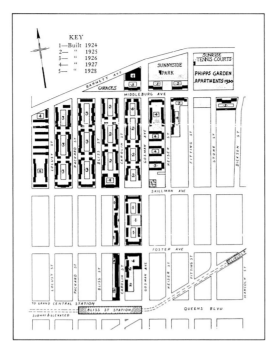

78
Physical development of
Sunnyside Gardens between
1924 and 1928.

A total of three basic house types were constructed in this first phase, with nine variations across those types (figure 79). Sizes ranged from 550 square feet for a cooperative garden apartment to 1,400 square feet for a one-family attached house. More specifically, there were two sizes of one-family house (designated as types N-1 and P-1); five arrangements of two-family houses (types A, B, C, D, and G), varying only slightly from four to five rooms per family; and two kinds of cooperative garden apartments, again in four- and five-room configurations (City Housing Corporation 1924b).

The site layout of housing units was concentrated around the perimeter of the long city blocks (see figure 76), with the garden apartments concentrated around playing fields and playgrounds toward the center of the development. The one- and two-family units were organized around semi-enclosed garden areas, primarily toward the ends of the long blocks. In total, something on the order of 90 to 100 units were accommodated in each block at a density of 27 dwelling units per acre. One of the most remarkable features of the development, however, especially at the time,

was the minimal 30 percent ground coverage by buildings (City Housing Corporation 1924b). Contemporary modern apartments, such as those built quite close to Sunnyside Gardens by the Metropolitan Life Insurance Company, also made garden improvements but covered over 50 percent of the land area with buildings and were constructed at densities of around 117 dwelling units per acre. Earlier tenement blocks in the Bronx, as another comparison, covered 73 percent of a site with building and had densities of around 150 families per acre (City Housing Corporation 1924a). There was, therefore, in the evolution of the garden apartment housing type a considerable progression away from congestion, toward what might be described as a suburban prototype for medium-density dwelling, and one that, parenthetically, was to have considerable future influence throughout the United States.

The intention behind the grouping of buildings around the perimeter of city blocks with gardens in between (figure 80) was to give a sense of a separate community (Stein 1966). At the time there was considerable concern, on the part of the architects and planners of Sunnyside Gardens, for the blighting effects of encroaching outside development. Wright made a point of deriding the monotonous rows of nearby tract housing and took pains to develop building types and arrangements of dwelling units that could more effectively insulate Sunnyside Gardens from unwanted outside influence (Wright 1933).

During the second phase of construction, effectively spanning sections 3 and 4 in the plan from 1926 through 1927, lessons learned from the initial construction were incorporated into the development. For instance, play-

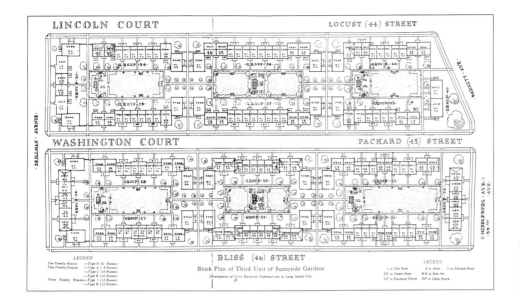

81

Lincoln and Washington
Court developments at
Sunnyside Gardens.

grounds at the center of the blocks were found to be noisy and annoying to those who dwelt around them. Moreover, the semienclosed common garden areas, running almost the length of a city block, were found to be too large and impersonal. Consequently, during this second phase of development, blocks were subdivided more tightly into smaller quadrangles, well scaled to the surrounding two-story dwellings.

Three relatively separate garden courts emerged per block in this new arrangement, spanning a width of 120 feet from building to building, of which a depth of 30 feet on each side was devoted to private gardens for adjacent units. The central common garden area, much like those in the first phase, occupied the remaining 60-foot width and included various garden structures. Throughout, extensive tree planting took place, both along streets and within the communal gardens, and all utilities were located out of sight underground (figure 81). In 1926, Sunnyside Park was constructed (figure 82), a 3.5-acre preserve on the northern edge of the overall development, largely to replace the smaller active recreational areas formerly located within the housing blocks. This park was fully equipped, including construction of a meeting hall, with management falling to the Sunnyside Community Association (Stein 1966).

During the second phase of construction there was also some scaling back of garden apartment construction. During 1926, for instance, the third section of the development included no garden apartments (City Housing Corporation 1927d). Nevertheless, one-, two-, and now three-family houses

82

Children's play at Sunnyside
Park in Sunnyside Gardens.

continued to be deployed in perimeter court arrangements, with variations within each basic house type. By now all one-family units consisted of 6 rooms. Two-family units, of which there were three types (designated types A, C, and K), varied in size from 8 to 10 rooms apiece, and the two versions of the three-family units (types J and H) contained 12 rooms each. Within this ensemble, the three-family units were set back further from the street alignment in order to create the three semiseparate courtyards mentioned earlier. Throughout, the paths and gardens (figure 83) were well laid out and established (City Housing Corporation 1927c). As the historian Lewis Mumford, a resident at Sunnyside for some eleven years, was to remark some years later, the development "has been framed to the human scale and its gardens and courts have kept that friendly air as, year by year, the newcomers improved the art of gardens and the plane trees and poplars continue to grow" (Stein 1966, p. 27). Juridically speaking, the communal gardens were reserved for community use as 40-year easements, with such restrictions extending roughly from 1924 to 1965 and beyond (City Housing Corporation 1927d).

In 1927, apartments were built as revenue-producing ventures for the first time (i.e., as rental units), and not for ownership. Sunnyside Park began to experience relatively high levels of attendance at about 100 children and adults per day, as well as 600 persons per day on holidays. In 1926 a kindergarten and play school were organized by mothers living in the development, held in space donated for the purpose by the City Housing

83
Pedestrian pathway system and gardens separating pedestrian from vehicular movement at Sunnyside Gardens.

Corporation. Together with a heavy emphasis on communal gardening, cooperative activities figured prominently in life at Sunnyside Gardens (City Housing Corporation 1927d).

The third phase of construction, according to changes in building type, essentially took place during 1927 and 1928, across sections 4 and 5 of the overall development. Introduced late in 1926, a U-shaped grouping of dwelling units was developed, with 16 units fronting onto a long rectangular entrance court, with the open end of the grouping facing toward the street and gabled at each end. This form of development served to finish off the development, so to speak, and by turning its back to the outside, insulate Sunnyside Gardens from unwanted visual intrusions. These units proved to be most popular and continued the tradition of both communal and private gardens, with the latter located to each side of a U-shaped grouping (City Housing Corporation 1927d).

During the five-year period of construction between 1924 and 1928, a total of 1,202 dwelling units were constructed at Sunnyside Gardens, plus several stores, parking garages, and extensive recreational facilities. Development began relatively slowly, with 128 units in 1924, 226 units in 1925, 287 in 1926, and a peak of 401 in 1927. During the final year, 1928, 160 units were constructed, primarily of the U-shaped form just mentioned (City Housing Corporation 1927d, Stein 1966). One constraint on the pace of development was maintenance of a sufficient flow of capital. On the other hand, construction of anything more than the 250-odd units per annum would probably have posed a considerable nuisance to existing residents.

Architecturally the housing consisted of standardized units, all of two stories above a basement, and all no more than two rooms deep in order to maximize cross ventilation and light (figure 84). A standard dimension of 28 feet 4 inches was established for the houses, based primarily upon stock framing lengths. This was increased to 28- and 34-foot widths for the garden apartments. Throughout, use was made of common brick. Roofs were a mix of flat and simple gables, with some upper-level porches set back into the gable pitches. Many of the flat roofs were also occupiable as additional outdoor space. Porches were located on both the backs and fronts of units, invariably of timber construction and generally traditional in styling with relatively ornate balustrades (City Housing Corporation 1928). In contrast to the uniform brick exterior finish of the units, the porches appeared to have been added on, and with a resemblance closer

to the garden structures outside, they rather effectively mediated between the external and internal space of the complex (figure 85).

As some commentators have already noted, there is a notational quality to the architecture of Sunnyside Gardens in which the subtle manipulation of building setbacks and porches creates identifiable outdoor precincts (Kwartler and Havlicek 1984). Well-composed facades, at the level of each unit, also expressed subdivision of housing rows into individual and paired units. It was neither a continuous ribbon line of building nor a unitary expression. Traditional elements in the architecture, such as chimneys, roofs, and cornice lines in the brickwork and lattice work on porches and balconies, combined with the articulated housing rows to give a familiar and suburban residential feeling. Overt modernism, in the sense of "new realism," was largely confined to many aspects of the overall planning and site layout, as well as to the built-in furnishings and functional layouts of the dwelling units. Most of these units were designed without any corridor space, compactly arranged around vertical stairways partially separating units along the front of each housing row. In keeping with the basic garden apartment type, all units were set back from the street with paired sidewalks and grassy nature strips in front (figure 86).

In spite of a traditional appearance, the building technology of Sunnyside Gardens was advanced in many respects, in order to achieve as many cost savings as possible. Dimensions were often determined based upon standard increments of construction. The pace of development was deliberately pushed toward achieving economies of scale, and building materials were purchased in bulk for similar reasons (City Housing Corporation 1927a). Indeed, in its report of 1927 the City Housing Corporation specifically made the claim that Sunnyside "has demonstrated that the economies of large scale operations are just as substantial in this field [housing]

86
Garden apartment units set
back from the street at
Sunnyside Gardens.

as in other industries, and *further* it has proved that scientific planning
can provide such essentials as garden and park spaces, even in communities intended for families of limited means" (City Housing Corporation
1927b, p. 3). In addition, actual construction at Sunnyside was done
primarily during the fall and the winter of each year, thereby lessening
seasonal idleness in the building trades, and simultaneously taking advantage of more plentiful supplies of both labor and materials (City Housing Corporation 1927d). Finally, the sheer standardization and repetition
of units also undoubtedly achieved cost savings.

As mentioned before, a considerable emphasis was placed on cooperative
homeowner and tenant activities during the early days at Sunnyside. In
fact, tenants and owners had an equal voice in community undertakings,
and the neighborhood unit idea, as a social model, received considerable
attention. Initially, the Sunnyside Community Association was formed as
a voluntary group to help sponsor and organize community activities and
to safeguard the general welfare of the Sunnyside community. The constitution and influence of the community association was to change during
the following years, but at the outset Sunnyside was a community in the
true sense of the word, and a heterogeneous community into the bargain.
In a 1927 survey approximately 66 percent of the population were white-
collar workers, although nonprofessionals outnumbered professional

workers by about four to one (City Housing Corporation 1927c, Stein 1966). This proportion changed little before the Great Depression (Kwartler and Havlicek 1984). Income distributions in the same survey indicated that a little over 50 percent of the families had incomes between $2,000 and $3,000 per annum, with only a very small percentage with incomes below $2,000 per annum. Those in the $3,000 to $4,000 bracket numbered about 19 percent, with 18 percent earning over $4,500 annually (City Housing Corporation 1927c). For the majority, the cost of housing at Sunnyside Gardens represented about 25 to 30 percent of their income, basically within affordable limits. This was fortunate, because about 50 percent of the first residents came from the tenements of Manhattan's East Side (Kwartler and Havlicek 1984).

Like many other entrepreneurial ventures, Sunnyside Gardens fell on hard times during the Great Depression that followed the stock market crash in 1929. Indeed, the City Housing Corporation went bankrupt shortly after 1930. During the Depression, Eleanor Roosevelt, one of the City Housing Corporation board of directors, successfully led protests by residents, who formed what became known as the Homeowners Mortgage Committee to conduct rent and mortgage strikes. The economic circumstances of the times were so bad that 40 percent of the Sunnyside residents became unemployed between 1928 and 1933, resulting in a 50 percent loss of income. An organization called the United Trustees replaced the City Housing Corporation board when it went bankrupt, with representatives from each residential court within the complex (Kwartler and Havlicek 1984).

During the 1940s, Sunnyside continued to maintain its varied social population, although it became a haven for young couples. By the 1960s it had become a moderate-income community but remained ethnically heterogeneous, with Irish, German, Jewish, as well as other residents. At the same time, a large number of the original residents were replaced by newcomers, unfortunately with little or no understanding or sympathy for Sunnyside's social goals. This social change, coupled with the cessation of the 40-year common easements that governed use of the community garden space, quickly led to the disassembling of this community property into private landholdings. The United Trustees, as the formal community association, was disbanded in 1965 largely due to desperate financial straits (Kwartler and Havlicek 1984). Moreover, there seems to have been a generational dispute over the use of the common garden courts. The younger generation saw them as gardens to be fenced off as children's play areas, whereas the older generation clung to the early idea of them as tranquil, serene, and well-maintained gardens.

87
Recapturing of Sunnyside's community space during the 1970s.

By 1974 the press called attention to the so-called fencing wars at Sunnyside, resulting in some protection of the original plan under the auspices of a Planned Community Preservation District. More recently, during the 1980s, there has been some constructive effort to recapture Sunnyside's community space (figure 87). However, by 1985 only 6 of the 15 courts had been returned to something near their original configuration and land tenure (Kwartler and Havlicek 1984). This recent history clearly stands as a testament to the difficulty of successfully organizing and sustaining communal open spaces in contemporary residential circumstances.

As an adjunct though separate development to Sunnyside Gardens, the Phipps Garden Apartments complex was developed on adjoining property during 1931 (see figure 78). Designed by Clarence Stein, the development was financed by the society of Phipps Houses, formed by the steel magnate Henry Phipps "to provide housing accommodation for the working classes" (Stein 1966, p. 87). Located on a site purchased from the City Housing Corporation in the northeast corner of the Sunnyside complex, the block of land for the Phipps apartment complex was almost square, at about 40 feet on a side. The overall organization of the apartment complex took the form of a perimeter plan of six elevator-serviced six-story units concentrated at the center of the block along the street, with 16 walk-up units distributed in between, partially enclosing the interior garden court (figure 88). The six-story units were constructed on a T plan, with the leg of the T extending into the interior court, effectively subdividing it into smaller garden precincts in the corners. The dominant idea behind the scheme was to balance the density needed to adequately distribute land

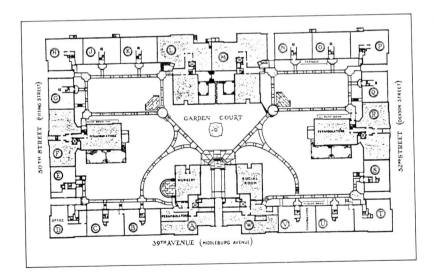

88
Plan of the Phipps Garden Apartments complex adjacent to Sunnyside Gardens, by Clarence Stein, 1931.

costs and a desire to provide a large, attractive, open garden area (figure 89). In this latter regard, the landscape architect, Marjorie S. Cautley, did an admirable job by providing a rich and varied garden, well tailored to the sloping terrain.

Both in concept and in practical application, Sunnyside Gardens was influential and the direct forerunner of other developments like Radburn, New Jersey (figure 90), and the greenbelt new towns of the 1930s. Seen less in the light of garden city principles, Sunnyside also helped popularize the suburban garden apartment complex, which was to become a fixture in most American cities during the years to come. More immediately, Sunnyside served as one of the primary models for the 1926 enactment of a state Housing Law in New York, and Henry Wright exhibited drawings and photographs of the development in Vienna, during the conference of the then-influential International Federation for Town and City Planning (City Housing Corporation 1926, 1927c).

89
Garden court at the Phipps Garden Apartments complex.

90
An aerial view of a portion of Radburn, New Jersey, by Clarence Stein and Henry Wright, 1928.

In Frankfurt-am-Main, having assumed the position of Stadtbaurat (municipal architect) and Dezernent für Bauwesen (overseer of city planning), a post especially created for him, Ernst May had almost absolute power over building and urban design in the city from early in 1925 until mid-1930. So great was his power over architecture that critics accused him of perpetuating a *Stildiktator* (aesthetic dictatorship). Nevertheless, at that time Frankfurt was, in the words of one historian, "extremely cosmopolitan, liberal, relatively well-to-do, and receptive to social reform," and this was not lost on a native son (Lane 1986, p. 287). Moreover, May had the strong support of the mayor, Ludwig Landmann, and the city treasurer, Bruno Asch, and took a free hand in assembling his staff. The architect Martin Elsässer became building inspector, Max Bromme, a noted landscape architect, became director of garden construction, and Ferdinand Kramer became head of an organization for setting standards, which would eventually result in the *Frankfurter Normen* described earlier. Herbert Boehm, May's colleague from Breslau, was named city planner, and Adolf Meyer became building advisor. Many others soon joined May, either as members of various city organizations like the architect H. C. Rudloff, or as consultants on a part-time basis, like Walter Gropius. Having completely restructured the Siedlungsamt (office of housing estates), May then set about in earnest to resolve Frankfurt's mounting housing shortage. Throughout, he was a member of both Der Ring and the Deutsche Werkbund and also had close ties with avant-garde intellectual circles, including the art school where Max Beckmann, a prominent *neue Sachlichkeit* artist, taught (Risse 1984, Schaal, Pfister, and Scheibler 1990).

One of May's first initiatives was to conduct a comprehensive survey of Frankfurt's housing stock and available sites for new development. Results of the survey quickly revealed that the only areas available for immediate development, including housing construction, were located in open areas on the city's fringes (figure 91). Inevitably, survey results also showed an overwhelming demand for new housing, due primarily to the privations of war, indiscriminant rent control, inflation, and large population immigration into the city. Interestingly, the survey also showed that existing housing was poorly utilized because it did not meet emerging family needs. Especially for two-person families, existing apartments were often too large and therefore costly (Mullin 1975). In other situations, generational conflicts of extended family living pushed up the demand for modest dwelling units. In fact, over 50 percent of the subsequent housing came to be designed for relatively small families with modest means (Dreysse 1988).

91
A master plan for the
development of Frankfurt-
am-Main by Ernst May and
his staff, March 1930.

In the subsequent master planning activities that followed in 1925, 1926, and then in 1928, May and his staff clearly adopted what became known as the *Trabantenprinzip* (satellite planning principle), whereby Frankfurt would become ringed by semiautonomous, predominantly residential communities (Lane 1968, Mullin 1975, Tafuri and Dal Co 1976). No doubt May was led in this direction by several circumstantial factors such as the availability of cheap land, the physical need to decentralize the heavily congested city core, and a pressing desire, characteristic of the time, to avoid any further speculative pressures on existing urban areas. The direction was also ideological and a matter of experience, however. Very much in keeping with the sobriety of this stage of the Weimar Republic, Ernst May, like Martin Wagner in Berlin, was interested in establishing and preserving social stability. He also had a predisposition, as we have seen, toward the garden city movement and, by implication, the concept of satellite communities (Risse 1984, Lauer 1988). At Breslau in the early 1920s, he had already created satellite residential communities, 12 to 18 kilometers from the city center, replete with architecture having a strong picturesque, English influence (Buekschmitt 1963, Tafuri and Dal Co 1976).

In practice, however, May's satellites were not made to be economically autonomous and did not incorporate Ebenezer Howard's idea of urban centers full of cultural and civic activities. The satellites in Frankfurt were attached to already existing communities, such as Praunheim and Heddernheim in the northwest. This was done for both technical and psychological reasons (Risse 1984). For instance, it allowed needed housing to be constructed quickly in areas where nonresidential facilities were already in place. It also allowed inhabitants of the entirely new settlements some connection with the city as they already knew it.

Satellite growth was restricted by May in keeping with the spirit of Howard's original theoretical proposal. Unfortunately, however, this did not preclude Frankfurt's general outward sprawl from continuing. In 1926, May affirmed his commitment to the satellite community concept by ordering the construction of Höhenblick and Bruchfeldstrasse (figure 92), two small and, one might say, experimental housing estates.

By 1928, May and Boehm had more carefully worked out Frankfurt's general plan. In addition to the satellite communities, expansion of the old city was planned to the north and east as a contiguous form of development. Also considered was dispersal of urban functions within this matrix of expanding core and satellites, in order to reduce commuting distances and hence congestion as well as to create an environment that was close to that of a small town. May coined the term *daughter town* for bedroom communities to be located next to industrial complexes, especially along the river Main (Mullin 1975, Risse 1984, Höpfner and Fischer 1986). "The general plan of the city," he wrote, "attempts to eliminate the old-style large city development. The inner city will be districted according to its natural borders and the expansion districts will be bedded in as separated settlement complexes in the open landscape. An interconnected system of green space will also be made available to the inhabitants of the inner city. Good public transportation connections . . . will serve the need for travel between satellites and the central city. The open spaces between the expansion districts should eventually serve various economic purposes, as well as purposes of recreation. Sports areas and playgrounds are to alternate with areas for agriculture or intensive garden cultivation" (Risse 1984, p. 17). Herre it should be stressed that rapid expansion of the *Strassenbahn* (streetcar) system was an important key to the day-to-day functional success of the satellite communities. On these two points—the satellites and the public transit system—May and his patron Landmann were completely in accord (Mullin 1975, Tafuri and Dal Co 1976, Lane 1986).

A strong influence in the new Frankfurt was the old demand of the working classes for home ownership and individual accommodations for small families (Dreysse 1988). Together with rigorous economic demands on any mass production of housing, including the need for decentralization, an ambition emerged among May and his staff for creation of a *neue Wohnkultur* (new dwelling culture) in the fullest sense of the term (Banham 1960, Mullin 1975). Central to this idea of a new *Wohnkultur* was the use of both planning and architecture as active vehicles for changing social values (figure 93). Indeed, May had a deeply seated belief that environments could challenge and shape the behavior of inhabitants, and that this could be accomplished toward socially progressive ends (Bahrdt 1968). Furthermore, May and his colleagues eagerly embraced *Existenzminimum* (the minimal dwelling) in this spirit of renewal. In addition to being a response to economic necessity and the area of most pressing housing need, minimal dwellings were seen as part of a "spiritual revolution" ushered in by a return to basics and essential qualities (Lane 1986). As Bruno Taut, one of May's counterparts in Berlin, was to put it, "only in freedom from disorder can the personality develop freely." Simplicity in building would "produce a new mental attitude, more flexible, simpler and more joyful" (Taut 1979, Lane 1986, p. 293). For May himself in somewhat more epochal terms, "architecture now recognizes the laws of form appropriate to our time. . . . The altered spiritual attitude . . . has resulted in a new dwelling form . . . an architecture that is specifically expressive of the twentieth century" (May 1926, pp. 2f.).

Befitting the new realism of the time, there was, however, another side to May's new *Wohnkultur,* and one with far more conservative design and planning implications. Throughout the Frankfurt housing program May and his staff constantly preferred the single-family house to apartment blocks. The gardens associated with these homes, as well as the nearby allotment gardens for apartment dwellers, were seen as a place to recuperate from daily labors. This repose, in turn, contributed to subsequent productivity and eventually to social stabilization. In May's social-economic terms, *Siedlungen*, or satellite communities of small individual homes, effectively ameliorated the effects of increasing industrialization by returning people to nature, as it were, and went a long way to ensuring political stability (Risse 1984). Again, the effect on May of the utter turmoil in Germany of the previous ten years should not be underestimated.

On a more practical level, May brilliantly organized for the production of housing within the *Siedlungen* on a largely unprecedented scale. Throughout, there was an emphasis on cooperation and communalization. Municipal building services were created, based upon institutions already in place and the trend for municipalities to own their own raw materials and means of transportation. A *Bauhütte* movement was also started, with self-organized building firms formed by previously unemployed workers (Dreysse 1988). This proved to be highly conservative of valuable human resources, as it capitalized on the skill and experience already accumulated in the building trades. The Frankfurt Panel Factory (figure 94) was also established in a trade fair hall and at the east harbor along the Main, in order to supply prefabricated wall units, floor units, and beams. Insistence on use of the *Frankfurter Normen* (building standards), which by now covered a wide variety of situations for dwelling unit types through to the dimensions and fabric of interior furnishings, reinforced this industrialized building process. At its peak, the daily output of each factory was on the order of 2½ terraced houses, with a minimum of excess labor (Dreysse 1988). More specifically, the prefabrication system consisted primarily of planks made from precast slag concrete 3.00 meters by 1.10 meters and weighing 1,250 kilograms. When used at Praunheim, one of the first applications, it became a multipurpose system, with planks going together something like a jigsaw puzzle, forming walls, floors, and flat roofs. Usually the system was combined with standard cinder block construction (Buekschmitt 1963).

The stage was now set for creation of the housing estates of the New Frankfurt and, in particular, of those that collectively were to form the Niddatal, located along the Nidda River, a northern tributary of the Main—namely Praunheim, Römerstadt, Westhausen, and Höhenblick (figure 95). After May's initial survey, the site for this development was determined by a quick process of elimination. The east and west of the city were devoted primarily to industry along the Main, whereas southerly development was blocked by the large Stadtwald (city forest). The only available

94
The Frankfurt Panel Factory
in an existing trade hall
along the Main River.

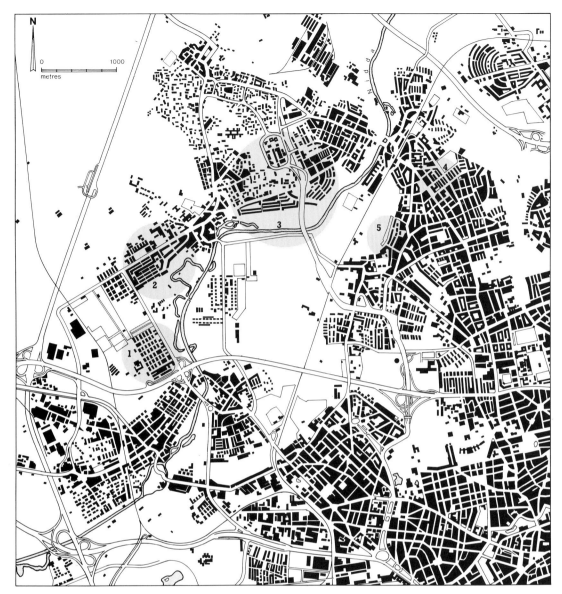

95
Plan of Frankfurt-am-Main
showing the housing estates
of the Niddatal region: *1*,
Westhausen; *2*, Praunheim; *3*,
Römerstadt; *4*, Lindenbaum;
5, Höhenblick.

Three Projects in Three Cities

large and inexpensive plots of land were to be found in the northwest toward the Taunus Mountains (Mullin 1975).

Höhenblick (figure 96), the first phase of the development, was constructed between 1926 and 1927 on a hill overlooking the Nidda valley and the Taunus Mountains beyond, on the southwest side of the Nidda, opposite the eventual Römerstadt estate. Consisting of 76 one-family units and 100 small apartments, Höhenblick was built contiguously with existing development. In what was to become a repetitive pattern of development, all homes had gardens, including allotment gardens along the Nidda River (Risse 1984).

Praunheim was considerably larger, eventually containing 1,441 housing units. As the first major *Siedlung*, Praunheim was controlled directly through the Hochbauamt (central building office) of May's organization. Both May and Boehm were primarily responsible for planning, with May sharing architectural responsibilities with Kaufman and Brenner. Again like Höhenblick and the other *Siedlungen* to follow, Praunheim was closely associated with an existing community, the old town of Praunheim to the west.

Development at Westhausen (figure 97), to the west of Praunheim, occurred later between 1929 and 1931 and was one of the last *Siedlungen* in which May was directly involved. By this time the German economy had deteriorated, requiring very small units and a sparse physical layout of dwellings. In all 1,116 units were completed (Dreysse 1988).

Römerstadt, located 8 kilometers from the center of Frankfurt, is regarded by many as epitomizing May's housing efforts (Banham 1960, Lane 1968, Mullin 1975, Risse 1984). Located between the new section of Praunheim

96
Housing at the Höhenblick estate in Frankfurt-am-Main by Ernst May et al., 1926–1927.

97
Housing development at Westhausen in Frankfurt-am-Main, 1929–1931.

98
An aerial view of Römerstadt
on the Nidda River in
Frankfurt-am-Main by Ernst
May et al., 1925–1935.

to the west and the existing town of Heddernheim to the east, Römerstadt
was constructed on very cheap land of little agricultural value that was
initially swampy and flood-prone (figure 98). In fact, all the Niddatal
development was accompanied by an extensive flood control and land
management scheme for the Nidda valley, largely conceptualized and
executed by Max Bromme.

As early as 1914 a plan had been drawn up to control flooding along the
Nidda. Two subsequent floods in quick succession, one in 1920 and the
other in 1926, prompted the city to action, especially in view of May's
decentralization policy. Bromme's plan, carried out between 1928 and
1930, called for selective straightening and lining of the Nidda, with
extensive meadowland management and some tree planting adjacent to
the river's course. Stream meanders, separated into semiisolated water
bodies because of the stream rectification, were incorporated into specially
designed recreational areas. The beach and pool at Praunheim and near
Römerstadt are good examples of this practice (Risse 1984).

Development of Römerstadt was the responsibility of Gartenstadt AG, also
known as Meitheim AG, a cooperative, limited-dividend building organization, similar in many respects to Sunnyside's City Housing Corporation (Gartenstadt 1935, Lane 1968). Unlike the City Housing Corporation,
however, Gartenstadt AG had substantial public involvement and was
responsible, over about a 10-year period from 1925 to 1935, for construct-
ing some 4,500 housing units across ten or twelve separate communities.
Partially an outgrowth of the Frankfurtergemeinnützige Baugesellschaft of
1860, Gartenstadt AG or Meitheim AG also became known later as the
Aktienbaugesellschaft für Kleine Wohnungen (the organization for building small houses) and a part of May's extensive influence (Gartenstadt
1935, Dreysse 1988). As with most of May's housing projects, the primary
source of capital for Römerstadt was secured by way of the *Hauszinsteuer*
outlined earlier, a tax on real estate income for buildings built prior to
World War I. In fact, between 1924 and 1929, Frankfurt was to spend
some 118 million marks on residential projects, of which approximately
half was advanced in the form of loans to building societies and cooperative organizations, as well as, minimally, to the private sector (Tafuri and
Dal Co 1976).

Römerstadt was planned by May, Boehm, and Wolfgang Bangert, as a
relatively low-density settlement in a garden setting (figure 99). To this
end, the topography of the site was carefully reflected in the curving road
system and terracing of housing units and gardens. A nominally 3-meter

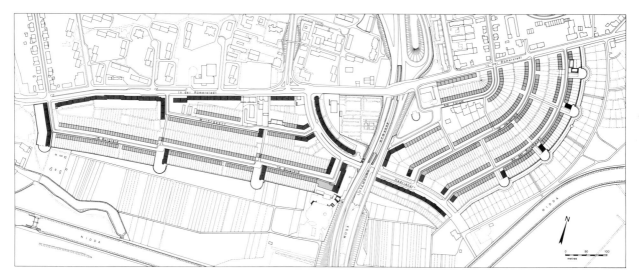

99
General plan of Römerstadt
in Frankfurt-am-Main,
showing the relative layout
and density of dwelling units
within the pattern of existing
development, 1985.

100
Retaining walls facing
building platforms, private
gardens, and belvedere at
Römerstadt.

high retaining wall was created along the southern perimeter with the
Nidda River valley, clearly raising the settlement above flood-prone areas
(see figure 98) and also providing a sequence of public viewing platforms,
or belvederes (figure 100), in what became known as the bastion wall
(Dreysse 1988). The development stretched some 1.5 kilometers along In
der Römerstadt, the major road linking Heddernheim to the east with
Praunheim to the west (see figures 95 and 99). The overall site area,
including extensive gardens and an existing cemetery, is about 47 hectares
or around 116 acres (Gartenstadt 1935). With close to 1,200 housing units,
the gross density is 10.5 dwellings per acre; allowing for open areas, the
net residential density is comparable to that at Sunnyside, at around 25
units per acre. The single major exception to the topographical alignment
of the street network was Hadrianstrasse, which cut through the geographical center of the development and around which nonresidential facilities
were concentrated (see figure 99).

The architecture of Römerstadt was also a collaborative venture. The ring
of dwellings around the outer, bastionlike perimeter was primarily the
responsibility of Gustav Schaupp, a consulting architect to May's organization. May himself, together with C. H. Rudloff, Albert Winter, and Karl
Blattner, took responsibility for most of the housing, especially in the Am

Heidenfeld area (figure 101). The southern portions of Hadrianstrasse, on the perimeter and forming a link with the Nidda River, were designed by Franz Schuster, another consulting architect, and the so-called "leberwurst block" of 20–44 Hadrianstrasse, with its familiar rounded corners and shiplike architectural motifs, was the responsibility of Rudloff (Dreysse 1988).

In aerial extent, most of the housing was provided in the form of two-story, primarily one-family dwellings, with some two-family structures incorporated, particularly toward the end of long terrace rows (figure 102). Four-story apartments were concentrated in a perimeter line along In der Römerstadt at the northern edge of the development. This, however, does not seem to have been May's intent. Instead, apartment buildings were to have lined both sides of In der Römerstadt, forming a high spine, as it were, or city street, and lower-density development was to have continued on the other side of the road (Risse 1984, Dreysse 1988).

Although 1,220 units were originally planned, 1,182 were constructed, of which 581 (49 percent) were one-family houses, mostly with four or more rooms. In addition there were 50 units (4 percent) in two-family homes, with from two to four rooms each, and 551 (47 percent) flats of from two to three rooms each, primarily in the form of four-story apartment buildings. All units were centrally heated and supplied with electricity, had radio connections, and included kitchens and baths. In fact, Römerstadt was the first such community in Frankfurt to be fully electrified (Gartenstadt 1935, Risse 1984, Dreysse 1988).

At the building level, the one- and two-family homes were arranged in long terraces of row houses, each with a private garden (figures 103 and 104). Cross sections through buildings across internal streets, such as Im

101
Housing along Am Heidenfeld at Römerstadt, by Ernst May et al.

102
A typical terrace of row housing at Römerstadt in the Im Bergfeld area.

103
Row house with private
garden at Römerstadt.

Bergfeld and Im Heidenfeld, were arranged to maximize solar orientation to dwelling unit. Consequently, the terraces on the north side were set back from the street with a communal garden in between (see figure 110). The total width of the street, plus this common area, was around 18 meters (59 feet), compared to the width of houses without the private gardens of usually a little less than 9 meters (29½ feet), dimensionally comparable to many of the similar units at Sunnyside. As Leberecht Migge, the landscape architect for the project, was to note, "it is the task of the gardens in the streets . . . to provide refreshing vegetation, and they are intended to intensify and add color to the street scene" (Risse 1984, p. 275). The private gardens directly attached to each single-family unit were even up to 20 meters in length (65½ feet), about twice the size of the gardens at Sunnyside, and running the full width of each unit, normally 5.5 to 6 meters (18 to 19½ feet) These private gardens were separated, in turn, by neat hedgerows and usually incorporated a paved patio adjacent to the house and a small vegetable garden to the rear of the lot (Gartenstadt 1935, Dreysse 1988).

The single- and two-family housing units essentially followed May and Kramer's elaborate and predetermined scheme of spatial organization

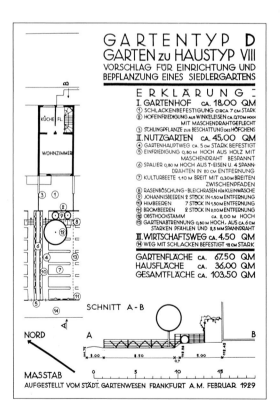

104
Plan and sectional layout for
typical private garden plots
at Römerstadt.

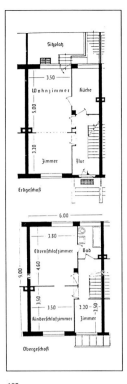

105

Typical first- and second-
floor plans for dwellings at
Römerstadt.

106

The essentialism of *neue
Sachlichkeit* architecture in
the Am Forum area of
Römerstadt.

where, in principle, units could range anywhere from 43 square meters (430 square ft.) to 144 square meters (1,440 square ft.) in area. All were only two rooms deep (figure 105), thus ensuring adequate light and ventilation (Höpfner and Fischer 1986). In the case of Römerstadt, most one-family units were on the order of 80 to 87 square meters in area, with side entries and upper floors given over to bedrooms. Among the multifamily units, roughly half had three rooms or less and were around 43 to 65 square meters in area (430 to 650 square feet), somewhat smaller than comparable units at Sunnyside. Indeed, fully 64.5 percent of all units constructed at Römerstadt were relatively small, at three rooms or less (Gartenstadt 1935).

Architecturally, housing at Römerstadt clearly reflected the essentialism of the *neue Sachlichkeit*. Roofs were flat (figure 106) and walls were sheer, although punctuated with well-composed arrangements of doorways and window openings. Front doors with simple flat-roofed entrance verandas were usually paired, further diminishing the individuality of each unit within the terrace row (figure 107). Unlike at Praunheim, building construction was primarily of cinder block with a wooden roofing structure (Risse 1984). Horizontal bands of windows were also used, especially among the multifamily units and apartment buildings. Against the predominantly white facades, brightly colored finishes, usually in primary colors, were used for window frames and doors. Interiors of rooms were also colorful and well finished, with an unusual emphasis on built-in furniture, foldaway beds, and so on. As the economic situation began to deteriorate, this aspect of May's housing became even more apparent, in efforts to save space and preserve the efficiency and spaciousness of units (Lane 1986).

Of particular interest in this regard was the well-known *Frankfurter Küche* (Frankfurt kitchen) (figure 108) and its only slightly less remarkable companion, the *Frankfurter Bad* (Frankfurt bath). Designed by the Austrian architect Grete Schülte-Lihotsky, a member of May's team, the kitchen's intention was to liberate housewives through Taylor-like efficiency. Indeed, Christine Frederick's scientific kitchen planning served as a model. Largely prefabricated, the pullman or galley type kitchen measured 1.87 meters in width (6 feet 2 inches) by 3.44 meters in length (11 feet 4 inches), with 0.86 meters (2 feet 10 inches) free space between the horizontal work surfaces that lined each side (Kramer 1986). Design of the kitchen within this basic framework was highly specialized by function. Literally, it was a kitchen in the form of a laboratory, with specific types of work surfaces, drawers, and cabinets for specific functions and utensils (Lane 1986, Kramer 1986). Ironically, it was precisely this high level of specialization that

107
Flat-roofed verandas and
pairing of doorways at
Römerstadt.

108
The *Frankfurter Küche* by
Grete Schülte-Lihotksy.

was to render the kitchen obsolete (Lauer 1988). The *Frankfurter Bad* was similarly partially prefabricated and carefully designed in an ergonometric fashion (Braun and Heimel 1977).

Architecturally, the most exceptional housing to be found at Römerstadt is Rudloff's northern Hadrianstrasse block, with its strong sculptural and somewhat expressionistic elements, reminiscent of Mendelsohn's work (figure 109). Here the shops on the ground floor were spaciously defined by individual facades that were pulled away from the main facade of the building, with a suggestion of Jugendstil detailing. It was, however, the only housing block that readily lent itself to perception as a single object. The remainder of the housing, while always presenting strong wall-like facades, was ultimately well integrated into surrounding gardens and other site works. This singular quality for the Hadrianstrasse block was, nevertheless, not inappropriate, given its prominent and exceptional position within the overall plan and its peculiarly mixed-use function.

In addition to designing models for the private gardens, Leberecht Migge, the landscape architect, also laid out on a large scale many allotment gardens just outside the bastion retaining wall, with communal gardens in between. As the landscape architect for several large housing estates in Berlin under Taut and Wagner, such as the Onkel Tom Siedlung of 1926 and 1928 and Siemenstadt of 1929 to 1931, Migge was also a follower of Rudolf Damasche, an early twentieth-century land reformer (Lane 1986, Risse and Rödel 1987). According to Damasche there was economic value to be gained by families growing much of their own food, as well as a sense of having a stake in property and its continued productivity and healthfulness for future generations. These latter qualities were soon to be of considerable interest to the National Socialists, forming part of their *Blut und Boden* doctrine (Lane 1968, 1986). At Römerstadt, Migge and May also set aside, as a landscaped preserve, a swath of land leading down to the Nidda from In der Römerstadt (see figure 99). This was then used as a sheepfold, sharpening, as the historian Lane carefully noted, "the tensions and ambiguities inherent in May's 'new architecture' for a 'new Frankfurt'" (Lane 1986, p. 294).

109
The Hadrianstrasse block at Römerstadt by C. H. Rudloff, 1927.

Even today a certain "tension and ambiguity" as Lane put it, or a certain "symmetry and asymmetry" as Dreysse put it, surrounds the ensemble of buildings and landscape at Römerstadt (Lane 1986, Dreysse 1988, p. 5). Moreover, it is one of the real strong points of the project. The housing appears highly composed, static, explicit, and yet autonomous, without any particular local character. The surrounding landscape, on the other hand, was and remains somehow dynamic and open in its rhythms, sequences, and vistas. Practically all the exceptions to the building rules at Römerstadt, such as asymmetrical street alignments, pedestrian paths and passageways, the belvederes mentioned earlier, and so on, seem to come from the site through the landscape (figure 110). The result is always interesting and usually vibrant. Furthermore, it is here that the influence of Raymond Unwin is perhaps clearest. Like at Letchworth, there is a clear adaptation of the terrace housing to topography and the general landscape. There is also a consideration of solar orientation, and the capacity to mix housing types in order to better locate the project in its site.

After completion in 1928, Römerstadt was inhabited by a relatively homogeneous population of white-collar workers and a few craftsmen. Rents were determined according to economic and social criteria and, much to the dismay of the architects and planners, they were relatively high. A 1970 breakdown of tenant occupations showed that fully 78 percent were white-collar workers, 15 percent were blue-collar workers, and 7 percent were self-employed. Given that about two-thirds of the prewar tenants had moved back, these figures give a fairly good estimate of Römerstadt's original social composition (Lauer 1988). Together with the distance from the city center and the feeling of being pioneers, this social homogeneity also greatly strengthened the feeling of community. By and large the residents of Römerstadt maintained a positive image of modernity, unlike the working-class inhabitants of Praunheim a kilometer or so down the road. In particular, ample use was made of the extensive outdoor realm at Römerstadt and residents seem to have shaken off the negative epithet of "new Morocco" directed toward them as an expression of the perceived strangeness of the housing complex, a condition that should not be underestimated. Soon, however, Römerstadt was accepted, at least by the middle class, as an expression of modernity (Lane 1986, Lauer 1988).

Later in 1928, residents of Römerstadt formed the Interessenverband Römerstadt, a tenants' association interested in protecting residents' rights and, particularly, in reducing rents. By 1932 they had achieved some success, although they were quickly dissolved by the National Socialists in 1933 and didn't emerge again, informally, until after the war. In the face of

110
Asymmetrical setback of gardens along Im Heidenfeld at Römerstadt.

worsening financial circumstances, there were also some conversions of one-family houses to two-family units during this period. Throughout, however, demand for housing at Römerstadt remained high (Dreysse 1988, Lauer 1988).

The cumulative effect of May's short tenure in Frankfurt was substantial. With 1,200 housing units planned for in 1926, fully 2,200 were completed, followed by 2,865 units in 1927 and 3,259 in 1928. In spite of these efforts the housing shortage seemed to keep pace with supply, prompting May and his colleagues, in 1928, to revamp their program toward a target of 4,000 units annually. With the market collapse in 1929, difficulties were encountered in getting credit, although 3,460 units were reportedly completed during that year, followed by 3,200 in 1930, by which time economic and political conditions were in disarray. Finally, the dizzying rise in building costs in late 1929 and 1930, which ran as high as 190 percent of prewar costs, brought production to a halt (Tafuri and Dal Co 1976, Risse 1984). A remarkable total of some 15,000 units were completed in the comparatively short space of five years, accounting for 90 percent of Frankfurt's housing production during that period and the rehousing of up to 11 percent of the city's population (Mullin 1975, Risse 1984).

Overall, 25 percent of the production was undertaken by town authorities directly, 30 percent by municipal companies such as Gartenstadt AG, and 45 percent by housing cooperatives and private firms combined. In very broad terms financing involved 20 percent equity capital and 80 percent either in the form of special loans or more conventional mortgages (Dreysse 1988).

Between 1926 and 1930, May with F. Wichert edited a magazine titled *Das Neue Frankfurt,* more or less as the official organ of the new housing and city building program. Topics ranging from regional planning to house finishings were covered (Höpfner and Fischer 1986). In both this comprehensiveness and specificity, May's vision of the city differed from his counterpart Wagner's in Berlin. May seems to have firmly believed in the perfectibility of the modern city and of its ordering according to rational, evolutionary principles. Wagner, though equally rational, saw planmaking in more ameliorative terms. For him the planner constantly confronted the indefinite growth of a metropolis and attempted to correct social and economic distortions (Tafuri and Dal Co 1976). Both, nevertheless, deliberately used architecture and planning to push for social change rather than vice versa.

Around the middle of 1930, Ernst May and a number of his colleagues abruptly left Frankfurt for Moscow, living there for a few years before moving on. City officials like Landmann and Asch left shortly thereafter, Asch living in exile from the National Socialists in Holland. Others, like Taut and Wagner from Berlin, also quickly departed from the scene, emigrating to Istanbul in 1938 (Höpfner and Kuhn 1988). Effectively, by 1933, if not before, the bold promise of *das Neue Frankfurt* had come to an abrupt end, to be followed by a period of brutal repudiation under the National Socialists (Lane 1968).

As for Römerstadt, during the war it suffered some damage and several homes were destroyed. Between 1945 and 1948 the housing estate was commandeered for American army families, displacing the original tenants. By 1956 over two-thirds had moved back and began to reorganize the tenant association once more, although it would never fully regain its earlier authority (Lauer 1988). During the late 1950s up until 1967, they fought unsuccessfully to resist the completion of the Rosa-Luxemburg Strasse, a four-lane highway cutting through the center of the development, causing considerable loss of property (Dreysse 1988, Lauer 1988). Ironically, this road was part of another much later satellite development, the Nordweststadt, reaching further out on Frankfurt's periphery. During the 1960s, additional one-family houses were erected on land not originally acquired as part of the development, compensating somewhat for the highway intrusion. Finally, in 1972 Römerstadt was placed under a preservation order and in 1985 plans were drawn up to extend and refurbish some of the open spaces. The Aktienbaugesellschaft für Kleine Wohnungen still retains control over the estate and it continues to be in popular demand (Dreysse 1988). When recently asked about the disadvantages of living at Römerstadt, residents had some complaints about their houses and apartments, such as bad insulation, little room to put objects and furniture, as well as outmoded equipment. In the interior, many had closed off doorways to enlarge the surface wall area of rooms and modified interior finishings to make the units more cozy. On the exterior, however, Römerstadt has continued to thrive, even though many communal spaces have essentially become privatized (Mullin 1975, Lauer 1988).

Kiefhoek in Rotterdam

The Kiefhoek housing estate in Rotterdam, by Jacobus Johannes Pieter Oud, was relatively small in comparison to either Römerstadt or Sunnyside Gardens. Its scale was nevertheless fairly typical of developments in

111

Housing along a side street
at Kiefhoek in Rotterdam by
J. J. P. Oud, 1925–1930.

Rotterdam earlier this century, which tended to be piecemeal, relatively self-contained, and incremental in the way in which they made up a district. The architecture of Kiefhoek, on the other hand (figure 111), was highly refined and more sophisticated in its modernity than anything at either Römerstadt or Sunnyside Gardens.

City Expansion

Early in the twentieth century, if not before, the economic vitality of Rotterdam paralleled developments in the port facilities that lined the river Maas. Before World War I some 10 million tons were transshipped annually, doubling to as much as 20 million tons in 1925 before declining during the depression years. The social effects of port expansions, prior to more complete mechanization, were also magnified because of the high levels of manual labor required. Population in Rotterdam, for example, increased dramatically from 312,000 people in 1900 to well over 500,000 by 1920 (Department of Housing 1950).

In order to keep pace with these development pressures, physical expansion of the city was guided from 1906 onward by broad plans, the first of which was proposed by G. J. de Jongh. New development, however, proved to be an expensive proposition because of problems with drainage and the inadequacy of many building foundations (Department of Housing 1950). Private sector resistance to expropriation laws was noticeably low in view of these expenses, and a common practice ensued whereby the municipality would service and make expropriated land suitable for development and then sell significant portions back to the private sector (Tafuri and Dal Co 1976). Public works known as *wetering* were carried out, creating a series of linear drainage canals with green spaces and roadways on either side. First proposed by Rose, the town architect during the mid-nineteenth century, this practice provided both open-space relief in Rotterdam's relatively dense fabric of buildings and, later, the rights-of-way for needed highway expansions (Department of Housing 1950).

As elsewhere in Europe, there was a severe housing shortage in Rotterdam in the aftermath of World War I. Furthermore, the number of privately built dwellings decreased dramatically from about 100 percent of all production in 1912 to only 12 percent in 1918. Again as elsewhere, public housing efforts had to be mounted in response to the shortages. A 1916 municipal resolution, for example, provided direct financial support to both housing associations and firms in the private sector. It also instituted a municipal housing agency to provide for direct government provision. In the period between 1916 and 1923 some 18,000 new dwellings were constructed in Rotterdam of which 39 percent were provided by housing associations, 37 percent by the municipality itself, and 24 percent by the private sector. There was, nevertheless, an alarmingly large overall deficit at the end of this period of some 10,000 dwellings (Department of Housing 1950).

The year 1916 also marked the time at which the new building codes, stemming from the original 1901 Housing Law, became fully effective. With a vigorous stress on expanding the size and particularly the public health aspects of dwelling units, the quality of housing in Rotterdam improved significantly. A typical house, however, still had a large multi-purpose living room with bedroom alcoves adjoining it: a form of housing that was only really discontinued during the 1920s. At this time the first modern houses, especially among the lower middle class, were built, with separate rooms for functions like sleeping, cooking, living, and so on (figure 112). Certainly by 1925 all rooms in newly constructed houses were adequately ventilated and well lit. In fact, most were built as we just saw, by local authorities or by housing associations with direct government support (Department of Housing of the Municipality of Rotterdam 1950). There was, however, no overall plan to these efforts, as there was in say Frankfurt-am-Main or in Vienna at much the same time.

During the 1920s, the one area of the city in which direct public provision of housing was very strong was in the south, on the left bank of the Maas. In fact, until 1900 this area was almost entirely rural and the municipality of Rotterdam owned considerable preserves, including many potential building sites. One reason for this lack of development was that vested interests, fearing property value declines on the other, northern side of

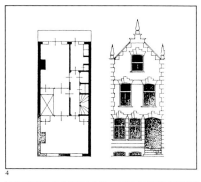

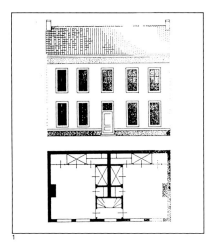

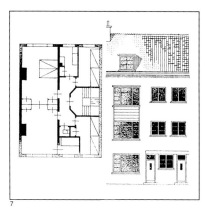

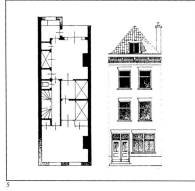

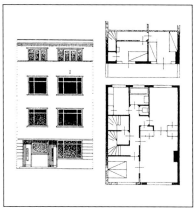

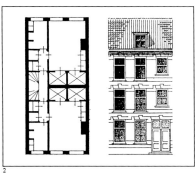

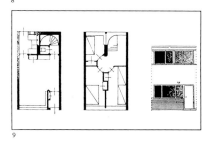

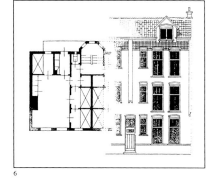

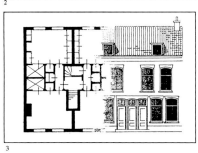

112
Evolution of house plans in
Rotterdam: 1, 1865; 2, 1875;
3, 1885; 4, 1895; 5, 1905; 6,
1915; 7, 1925; 8, 1935; 9,
Kiefhoek.

the river, did what they could to hinder southern development of the city. But geological conditions in the south were generally better and it was, therefore, less expensive for building houses. Improved access was also provided through the construction of new bridges, further helping to overcome a reluctance of Rotterdam residents to live in the south (Department of Housing 1950).

Using its expropriation powers, the city of Rotterdam acquired 73 acres of land in 1918 on the south side, between what is now Lange Hilleweg and the Hilledijk. The latter, as its name suggests, was a polder, and Lange Hilleweg was one of the *wetering* (drainage canal) improvements mentioned earlier. Within this general zone, the city then established sites for what it termed garden villages (Department of Housing 1950). This was perhaps not surprising, given that Vreewijk, one of the Netherlands' first garden city communities, was established on the other side of Hilledijk in 1913, designed by Berlage. The eventual site for the Kiefhoek housing estate, in the same general context of single-family dwelling, ran between Lange Hilleweg and Hilledijk, immediately to the south of Hillevliet (which paralleled yet another drainage canal improvement).

Architectural Influences

At much the same time that these acquisitions were taking place, J. J. P. Oud became the city architect of Rotterdam, a post he apparently took on the advice of Berlage at the relatively young age of 28 years (Stamm 1978b, Groenendijk and Vollaard 1987). Upon taking office Oud immediately established a strong commitment to low-cost and working-class housing, a direction that befitted both the strong need for public intervention to end rising shortages and the local socialist government's rise to power. Until that time, his early experience with housing had been confined to the Leidendorp worker housing project of 1914 and the experimental proposal for the Ocean Boulevard apartments of 1917. The latter scheme, in retrospect, proved to be something of an indication of things to come, as Oud began displaying his considerable penchant for abstraction and a repetitive use of building volumes (Stamm 1978a, 1978b).

The first projects Oud constructed as city architect were in the Spangen estate, a westward expansion of the old city on the northern side of the river. In all, Oud was responsible for four large blocks in the overall development, of which Blocks I and II were built in 1918 and Blocks VIII and IX in 1919 (figure 113). Another project of note in the estate was Michiel Brinkman's block, with double maisonette construction and gallery access to the upper units (Groenendijk and Vollaard 1987). All were

113
Block IX in the Spangen
District of Rotterdam by
J. J. P. Oud, 1919–1920.

closed-block apartment dwellings, with the building mass evenly distributed around the perimeter and an open court in the center. Spangen was quickly followed by the Tusschendijken estate in 1920, with architectural advancements being made by Oud in both the street corner details of the closed block arrangements and the layout of the interior communal courts (Stamm 1978b).

The design of both the Spangen and Tusschendijken estates showed the strong influence of Berlage and especially his belief in the mass dwelling on the street. Drawing on the urbanistic theory of Camillo Sitte, Berlage strongly argued that "modern city planning strives towards the individualizing of the city view, not towards that of each house. [Therefore, it is] the rhythmical stringing of houses together, the 'blockfront' [that] forms the spatial element of modern city architecture" (Grinberg 1982, p. 90). Moreover, for him "repetition of the same motif [namely a housing unit] is a primary aesthetic function." Clearly in his Rotterdam housing estates, Oud shared such ideas. Indeed, symmetry, repetition, and standardization, not to mention the residential block as a fundamental element of city design, could be found in varying degrees throughout Oud's work (Polano 1977).

A little later on, first in the Oud-Mathenesse estate of 1922 (figure 114) and then in the incomparable Hoek van Holland estate of 1924, J. J. P. Oud began to find his own form of architectural expression (Fischer 1965, Stamm 1978b). In both layouts, there was a strong simple overall form made up of standardized, repetitive housing units. Also in both there were subtle realignments within this strong overall form that conveyed considerable visual complexity. At Oud-Mathenesse, for example, rows of houses near the apex of the overall triangle plan form of the estate were placed out of a strict alignment (Oud 1984). In addition, both estates contained single dwellings, attached as rows, or in two terraces as at Hoek van Holland. Architecturally, both projects were pure in line and severe in detail, although housing as Oud-Mathenesse was capped by simple gable roofs, whereas at Hoek van Holland a "new objectivity" was very much in evidence (figure 115). Also in the latter project the implication of infinite extension, by repetition of basic housing forms, was arrested by semicircular, streamlined corners, primarily made of glass and containing several local stores.

The Project
Oud began designing the Kiefhoek housing estate in 1925, although it wasn't constructed until some years later, between 1928 and 1930 (Stamm 1978a, 1978b). In fact, quite a political struggle preceded the building of this development. In 1926 the Rotterdam city council passed a motion approving the scheme and initiating construction. However, subsequent increases in the production of rental dwellings for the middle class, and hence an easing of the overall housing shortage, gave rise to an argument that the very poor could now occupy homes left behind by more affluent families moving into better quarters. This argument probably would have held sway if it had not also been recognized that over 150 houseboats

were grossly deteriorated and nearing demolition, adding further to shortages, especially among poorer segments of society. On the basis of this new evidence the project went ahead, although with a bare minimum of financial support (Department of Housing 1950).

The physical plan of Kiefhoek incorporated 300 housing units in uniform rows of two-story duplexes, each with individual gardens (figure 116). Also included was a church—the Hersteld Apostolische church—several playgrounds, and two shops (Tafuri and Dal Co 1976, Barbieri 1986). The entire development was situated inside the subdistrict of Rotterdam described earlier, bounded by Hillevliet, Hilledijk, Meerdervoortstraat, and Lange Hilleweg (figure 117). In fact, except for the church on Hillevliet, no portion of the estate was actually on one of the bounding main streets. Instead, the entire development was built at least half a block in from those streets, surrounded by traditional forms of predominantly row house development (Barbieri 1986). Indeed, organization of the plan itself continues this physical isolation within the subdistrict, through internal street network with few points of entry or exit. Inside the estate, three streets run in parallel, roughly in an east-west direction, with two shorter streets, oriented north and south, producing an orthogonal grid of long rectangular blocks. With certain allowances for scale, this internal arrangement of the housing estate, encompassed by a perimeter of higher-density development, remains similar to the closed-block apartments designed earlier by Oud at Spangen and in the tradition of Berlage. The social purpose behind this inward orientation was undoubtedly to foster a strong collective sense of community.

Concern for the integrity of the street or block front, another of Berlage's preoccupations, was clearly evident within the development in a number of ways. First, any recognition of individual dwelling units within the facade of the row house terraces was almost entirely suppressed, except for the pairing of doorways at the ground level. Instead, the linear uniformity of the facades was amplified by the continuity of the ribbon of windows just below the roof lines, and by the equally continuous stuccoed wall surfaces that run the full length of each street (see figure 111). The standardization and repetition of units was thus elegantly unified into a collective whole.

The integrity of the residential block was also recognized in Oud's skillful architectural resolution of corner conditions, especially at the junction of several streets around one of the entrances to the estate where two shops

116

Aerial view of the Kiefhoek
housing estate in Rotterdam.

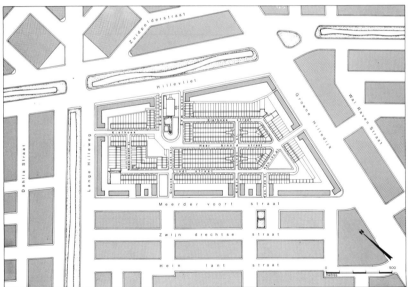

117
General plan of the Kiefhoek
housing estate in Rotterdam.

118
Architectural resolution
of corner conditions at
Kiefhoek.

were located (figure 118). Although Oud reportedly struggled with many
De Stijl versions for the rounded facades, he finally settled on the present
highly simplified, elegant, and one might say streamlined solution (Stamm
1978b). Less apparent corner resolutions of the otherwise continuous residential facades can also be found, primarily in the form of rounded
balconies that project onto the front margins of each block. Here a certain
ambiguity, or transition, in Oud's work can also be felt between Berlage's
sense of unified space, or *Raum*, on the one hand, and a more modern
universal sense of space on the other (Banham 1960).

Finally, the singular importance of the residential block was also made
apparent in the sense of closure that was provided on all sides, and
particularly by the location of shared facilities at the otherwise open ends
of each block (see figure 117). Although the blocks of row houses were far
more open than Oud's earlier higher-density schemes at Spangen, in comparison to the same building type at either Römerstadt or Sunnyside
Gardens the blocks remained relatively closed. Very clear distinctions
were thus maintained between the social realm of each residential block,
the realm of the estate itself, and the larger context of the city district to
which it belonged. Again this reflected a by now traditional attitude toward town planning. Indeed, one consistent criticism of Oud's work has
been the limits of his urban design perspective. There was never an
attempt to reach out on his part, as it were, and engage the surrounding
context. Consequently, each project remained largely isolated within its
own design terms of reference (Tafuri and Dal Co 1976, Benevolo 1984).

Within each residential block at Kiefhoek there was room for the personalization of dwelling space, in spite of what seemed to be deliberate
attempt to establish a collective image and, as one critic put it, "an aes-

thetic intent . . . to equalize the front and rear" (Grinberg 1982, p. 98). In keeping with the duplex arrangement of the row house type, there was a definite front and back to each unit, further reinforced by the private garden space in the rear (figure 119), which over time became the locus of individual expressions. Grinberg's earlier observation notwithstanding, it was as if the sheer neutrality of the relatively blank garden facade of each terrace was intentional. Oud certainly understood the spatial dualities involved with the row house type. His later work in the Weissenhofsiedlung in Stuttgart, for instance, was ample testament to that fact (see figures 52 and 66). What he seemed to be offering the residents of Kiefhoek

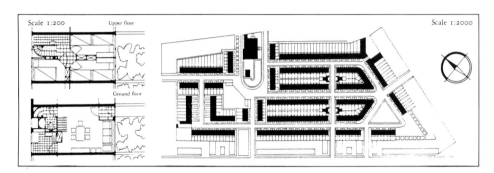

119
Floor plans and private garden space at Kiefhoek.

was a basic building framework against which their own individual modifications could take place. In common with his conservative attitude toward town planning and urban design, there was the sense, in Kiefhoek, of a limit to how far architecture could go in predetermining private dwelling spaces. This openness to the potential for personalization of space, the overall low density of the development, and the relative abundance of garden space were also very much in evidence within nearby garden city communities mentioned earlier.

Another related aspect of the residential blocks at Kiefhoek concerns the refinement and purity of the design (figure 120). As Benevolo points out, "the passion with which all the details were worked out went beyond pure technique and was a basic, one might almost say moral feature . . . of Oud's architecture" (Benevolo 1984, p. 461). The continuity of building volume and the planar character of all wall surfaces suggested a prototypical rather than a unique solution, further reinforced by the homogeneous coherence of the glass and stucco material finishes (Grinberg 1982). Clearly modern materials and building techniques appealed to Oud, as we saw in his article "Art and Machine," and what seemed to appeal most were "the horizontal spreads of considerable dimensions, and the possibility of co-ordinating pure planes and masses" (Banham 1960, p. 161). At root, both the symmetries and material properties of Oud's work from this period convey an illusion of weightlessness and an almost classical sense of refinement and order. As he himself seems to have been well aware, "the development of the art of building goes toward an architecture more bound to matter than ever before, . . . [an architecture] brought to purity of proportion and colour, organic clarity of form; an architecture that, in its freedom from inessentialism could surpass even classical purity" (Banham 1960, p. 162). Like most other architects working within the "new objectivity" of the time, Oud was never a pure functionalist and was always guided by an aesthetic intention.

120
Refinement and purity of
modern design at Kiefhoek.

The dwelling units at Kiefhoek were primarily of one type: a two-level arrangement, with living room, kitchen, and wc on the ground floor and three small bedrooms on a second floor. At least four other variations were also employed, but only in the special circumstances of unusual corner conditions within the residential blocks (Barbieri 1986). The units were small but spacious in layout, with direct access to light and air from each room. At 4.1 meters (13 feet 6 inches) in width and 7.5 meters (24 feet 7 inches) in overall depth, the floor area per family was less than at either Römerstadt or Sunnyside for comparable units, and very close to Le Corbusier's *Existenzminimum*. Indeed, an express intention behind the building of Kiefhoek was to build full-fledged minimum dwellings of the highest possible quality. Unfortunately, a lack of funds meant that fairly basic facilities such as a shower, wash basins, and laundry facilities had to be abandoned, at least initially. Space, nevertheless, was provided for later installation. In addition to the back garden, a small private yard was also located at the front of each unit, with separating low brick parapet walls and metal railings (figure 121).

Social Circumstances

From the outset the social circumstances of the Kiefhoek estate were oriented toward large, poor families. The dwelling units were expressly designed for families with five or more persons (Tafuri and Dal Co 1976). Most if not all early inhabitants were working-class, primarily from the labor pool for the nearby port. Many had probably moved from substandard living conditions in older and dilapidated sections of Rotterdam. Oud's commitment to higher-quality low-cost housing was apparent from his own statement: "How serious this was to me is especially demonstrated by the settlement Kiefhoek. They were the smallest, cheapest houses possible . . . [yet] they satisfy all requirements—good living, mass production, and so on. There was variety in their appearance, although use was made of only one type" (Polano 1977, p. 308).

121
The Kiefhoek housing estate in context, showing a typical front facade with low garden walls.

Children also figured prominently in the design of the housing estate, with several large areas, raised slightly above street level, set aside explicitly for children's play (see figures 117 and 121). Furthermore, the discontinuous pattern of roads and the narrowness of streets within the community greatly enhanced pedestrian safety, as well as the almost suburban serenity of the scheme. Oud designed the neighborhood church, another important community facility, at his own expense, specifically to preserve the integrity of the overall project (Stamm 1978a).

Today the housing estate remains in intensive use. Maintenance over the years appears to have been high, especially given the cheapness of the original buildings, further testament to Oud's skill in architecturally detailing with new materials. Gardens have grown up, including planting in public areas around the Hersteld church and the playgrounds, understandably softening the pristine architectural qualities of the buildings. Planting also appears around entries within the small front years of each unit. Socially speaking, the development appears to remain working-class with a mixture of age groups, although there is less evidence of large young families. Unfortunately, the two stores with the rounded corners, which made such a striking entrance to Kiefhoek from Heer Arnold Straat, are no longer in use, and much of the original glazing has been replaced by a continuous wall (see figure 118). Loss of such commercial activity is understandable, however, given the dramatic changes in merchandising that have occurred over the past quarter century. A similar abandonment of local stores can also be found, for instance, in many of the Frankfurt housing estates described earlier.

Public housing circumstances began to deteriorate in Rotterdam even during the construction of Kiefhoek. A strong conservative shift in the local government during 1929 slowed major planning activities and direct public involvement with housing. From then until well after World War II there were constant decreases in subsidies for public housing. Production itself did not decline quite so rapidly, however, for housing starts remained high at least until after 1935. At that time unemployment in Rotterdam became almost epidemic, as the privations of the world economic recession became fully felt (Department of Housing 1950). Amid this retrenchment of public responsibility, J. J. P. Oud, resigned his position as city architect of Rotterdam, undertaking no further large housing projects, although he was to continue to practice architecture well into the 1950s (Stamm 1978b).

A Modern Approach to Housing

From the period between 1920 and 1930, and especially between 1925 and 1930, there emerged a characteristically modern approach to housing. By contrast to the earlier piecemeal and largely private provision of dwellings, there were higher levels of public concern and involvement, as well as strong interests in cooperative and community-wide activities. In short, the domestic environment was consciously shaped in the interests of broad social welfare.

Behind the mass housing experiments of the period there was a belief that environment and social betterment were directly linked. If you improved housing conditions, for instance, there would be a noticeable decline in social pathology. On the larger scale, confidence grew in the perfectibility of cities, especially away from the squalid and poverty-stricken conditions of the nineteenth century. Moreover, modern, scientific planning principles, together with a rationalization of architecture around new materials and techniques of construction, were available and equal to the task.

These sentiments of the modern period were not, however, universally held, nor unanimous in their reception. Even among the initiated there was considerable disagreement, as we have seen, over strategies and the importance of specific objectives. Rather, it was a loose international confederation of planning, architectural, and building interests. Furthermore, while distinctly modern architectural influences were clearly apparent in some places, in many others they were not. Often the immediate effect of modernism on housing was erratic, and during some subsequent periods modern principles were vigorously repudiated. In the longer term, however, the modern influence became more pervasive as it became less strident. By the post–World War II housing booms, modern approaches to the planning, design, or construction of housing were rapidly and almost universally assimilated.

Organization and High Public Involvement

The fruits of housing reform and new levels of government bureaucracy resulted in much higher levels of public involvement in the design and provision of mass housing. The influence of Taylor, Ford, and other contributors to the second industrial revolution extended not only to big business but to the expanding activities of government as well. To be sure, the rebalancing of powers was born of necessity, among other things in order to address the crisis of the nineteenth-century city. It was, nevertheless, a clear reflection of a modern emphasis on organization, specialization of function, division of labor, and comprehensiveness of scale. Like any good production system, the necessary controls, checks, and balances were required, together with leadership and direction. In Frankfurt-am-Main, for instance, the level of public involvement in housing was almost total, somewhat less in Rotterdam and still less in the expansion of New York. In all cases, however, the guiding hands of government bureaucracies were much more present than they had been during previous eras.

Contrary to some interpretations of the modern period, the interest in housing aimed more at achieving social stability than at radical reform. This was a period when practical idealism began to take up where the earlier avant-garde fervor had left off. Ernst May, for instance, although clearly embracing a radical architectural stance toward housing, was primarily interested in getting the job done. The same can be said for J. J. P. Oud and for Henry Wright and Clarence Stein. Strong links were also established through these pragmatic interests with earlier reformers such as Howard, Unwin, and Geddes (Tafuri and Dal Co 1976).

On a more specific level, there was a heavy emphasis on various forms of cooperative or communal action in the provision of housing (figure 122). Although varying in both degrees and realm of influence, there was a consistent interest in a sense of community that went well beyond the usual traditions of the public realm. It was inherent in the theoretical

122
Cooperative construction of housing at the Praunheim estate in Frankfurt-am-Main by Ernst May et al., 1927–1930.

ideas of the garden city movement about neighborhoods and communities, as well as in the satellite communities of Ernst May and Martin Wagner. In these latter examples, it was often the relative isolation of the development and the shared sense of a pioneering spirit among inhabitants that sustained strong feelings of community. At Sunnyside Gardens, considerable effort was invested in development and maintenance of community gardens and open-court spaces between housing units. Here another layer of property tenure and responsibility was introduced between the traditional public and private domestic realms. Even the production and financing of housing was effected by a communitarian spirit. In many places, cooperative housing associations and development corporations were formed with limited profit motives. Labor organizations and construction companies were also formed around shared community interests.

At least within the spatial realm of housing, however, the emphasis on communal areas and facilities proved difficult to sustain. In many cases, communal areas became increasingly privatized, especially after the original inhabitants of housing complexes began to leave and when various statutes of limitation began to run out. At Sunnyside Gardens, the so-called fencing wars of the 1960s all but obliterated the original community garden courts. In both Römerstadt and Kiefhoek there was also a substantial diminution of interest in maintaining communal spaces over time.

In spite of obvious interests in social welfare and particularly the plight of the working class, modern public involvement in housing was hardly democratic in the contemporary user-oriented sense. On the contrary, public involvement was, if anything, paternalistic, with professional elites, who presumably knew best, placed in positions to provide housing more widely. User preferences were usually of marginal consideration and, clearly in the case of Frankfurt-am-Main, a deliberate attempt was made, through the housing architecture, even to reeducate the working classes (Risse 1984, Lane 1986). More generally, this paternalism took two forms, both of which were consistent with the emerging roles of both business and government in the life of citizenry. The first form epitomized by Frankfurt and only to a lesser extent by Rotterdam, involved public patronage. The second, characterized by the City Housing Corporation at Sunnyside, New York, was private or semipublic. In most places, a mix of public and private interests predominated, roughly coinciding with the intermediate community organizational level mentioned earlier.

Finally, the increased level of public involvement in many places had a shared sense of a common enemy. Principally this took the form of the blight of existing slums and tenement dwellings, as well as the specter of excessive property speculation caused by modern urban expansion. The effects of the latter phenomenon had already proved ruinous in many European and American cities. Consequently, modern-day planners, architects, and city officials went out of their way to safeguard broader public interests through city development strategies and increased police powers. Many of these efforts, however, proved to be less effective than first imagined, as economic recoveries continued to fund urban sprawl. Several later observers were probably correct when they attributed the relative lack of success in curbing speculation to an overemphasis on one or only a small number of urban initiatives like housing (Tafuri and Dal Co 1976, Benevolo 1984).

Rationalization and the Perfectible World

The second very broad characteristic of modern housing was the rationalization of almost all the activities involved and a simultaneous belief in a perfectible world. There was, as we saw, an inherent optimism and confidence in the modern technical temperament. Rational approaches, which represented substantial breaks with tradition, were introduced into architecture and, only to a slightly lesser extent, into planning. Throughout there was an emphasis on solving the problems at hand and in obtaining results in the near future. A close alignment was struck between social causes like housing and the wherewithal of technical progress.

A confidence in the perfectibility of urban areas in crisis, and the making of plans, manifested itself in a distinctly "organic" concept of housing within a city (Tafuri and Dal Co 1976, Benevolo 1984). Basic dwelling units could be conceptualized largely from first principles, and then organized and arranged to address local circumstances. This 'bottom-up' yet hierarchical approach was typified, as we saw, by the *Frankfurter Normen*, which evolved into a range of dwelling unit types and were then arranged into *Siedlungen* to make up subregional plans, such as the Nidda valley development. It was, nevertheless, a view of the city that remained largely incomplete and, except in the broadest of generalities, did not move above the district planning level (Tafuri and Dal Co 1976, Benevolo 1984). In this respect it can be contrasted, for instance, with Ludwig Hilberseimer's *Grosstadtarchitektur* of 1927, in which city functions were implacably integrated, producing a more anonymous, compact, and singular theoretical model than the interdependent yet decentralized views of either May or Wagner (Tafuri and Dal Co 1976). The "almost deductive process of assemblage," as Benevolo calls it, closely mirrored the prevailing scientific idea of order in the physical world (Benevolo 1984, p. 514). Nature was known in its parts, but not as a whole. Similarly, urban functions could be identified and improved, according to the management principles of Ford and Taylor, and then effectively reorganized in time and space.

In this process of rationalization, we also saw a very strong merger between planning and architecture. Indeed, in the persons of May, Oud, and Henry Wright, both disciplines were practiced simultaneously and often interchangeably. There was a direct connection in their minds between the standard dwelling unit and a city's physical form as a whole, even if they chose to operate largely at or below the district level. Generic standards and organizational norms were introduced into the architecture of housing, and the physical properties of efficient spatial assemblage were introduced into planning. Among the latter was the concept of the superblock or *Zeilenbau*, whereby large tracks of land were appropriated at once for the independent planning of housing units. Unfortunately, this was sometimes accomplished with little relationship to surrounding developments. By and large, however, the merger seems to have been a productive one. This modern period was one of those unfortunately too rare occasions on which design of buildings informed the development of larger environments, and vice versa.

Finally, most conspicuous in the prevailing rationalism were the relationships among functionalism, form, and a fascination with abstraction. Again in keeping with the modern technical temperament, there was an evident delight in the idea of thinking in essential terms and from first principles. Concepts like *Existenzminimum* were not only possible, but achievements to be embraced and diffused throughout the world with enthusiasm. Only by moving away from the distortions of past practices could a design situation be seen freshly and appropriately. At once new materials and building techniques provided an underlying logic for architectural form, stripped of superfluous features. The formalism of Der Ring, the Bauhaus, and of the new realism forthrightly displayed bold, cubic forms, plain surfaces, and an absence of decoration. The "figure" of the house, to borrow a rhetorical analogy, became its "form." Here, among the examples discussed, Oud's Kiefhoek was certainly the most architecturally refined. Moreover, there was a real confidence in the social relevance and intellectual integrity of this stance. At least for those concerned it was obvious and could be applied to almost any design situation.

favor of more selective area improvements. A building condition survey of 1971 found there to be 1.25 million slum units, of which only 723,000 (58 percent) were within feasible clearance areas. Moreover, at that time and for a short period thereafter, the annual rate of slum clearance was only on the order of 80,000–90,000 units annually, hardly enough to keep pace with the obsolescence of aging stock. Consequently, the Housing Act of 1974, with the Labour Party back in power, did not project blanket redevelopment as a remedy for poor housing conditions. Instead, efforts were refocused on infill housing, rehabilitation, pedestrian systems, and other community services that could be designed to fit within predominantly low-rise, high-density environments, typical of the bylaw flat milieu of inner suburban areas. In this regard, earlier experimental projects, such as the Rye Hill General Improvement Area in Newcastle upon Tyne from the mid-1960s, served as useful models (Burns 1964, Pepper 1975).

Rebuilding of housing in Italy did not stimulate the reorganization of comprehensive planning and development activities, and public subsidies played a diminishing role in the provision of housing. The economic expansion of 1958 to 1963, in particular, spurred on private-sector development (Garavini 1975, Benevolo 1984). This became very evident in housing, where home ownership was seen as an obvious hedge against poor financial circumstances. Indeed, by 1975 Italy had the highest proportion of home ownership within the European Common Market, in spite of the lowest average income level (Garavini 1975). Similarly, the level of publicly provided housing in Spain dropped off sharply in the 1960s as private sector production soared. Here, public housing construction had been used as a simple means to absorb surplus labor. When this strategy was no longer necessary, housing provision increasingly devolved to the private sector (Bohigas 1975).

Germany also quickly recovered to production rates of more than 300,000 units per year by the 1950s, as its *Wirtschaftswunder* (economic miracle) came into effect, and the neighboring Netherlands recovered even quicker (Ministry of Housing and Building 1964, Benevolo 1984). In both cases, strenuous efforts were made to stimulate housing production and simultaneously to protect low-income households already occupying dwellings. German subsidies, for example, sought to make housing an attractive venue for consumer expenditure, producer activity, and capital investment. Consequently, government activity was directed toward channeling large amounts of private capital into housing as it became available, largely through a complex tax incentive system. Rents were decontrolled in 1960, but only in places where the shortage of dwellings was less than 3 percent.

By 1967, however, rent controls were lifted in 75 percent of German towns and cities (Welfeld 1972).

High Production Levels

The level of housing production in the United States in 1945 was only 209,000 units. However, it quickly exceeded prewar levels, rising to 1,025,000 units in 1949 and as high as 2,379,000 units in 1972, before sharply declining to 1,172,000 dwellings in 1975 (see appendix B for details). On a normalized basis, production levels during the 1950s, 1960s, and early 1970s were equally impressive, remaining above 7 dwelling units per 1,000 population throughout this period and reaching a peak of 11.4 in 1972 (U.S. Department of Commerce 1955, 1976). Similarly, in the Netherlands a prewar production high of 53,814 units per annum was consistently exceeded from 1951 onward, with normalized rates around 7 dwellings per 1,000 population here too (Ministry of Housing and Building 1964). Much the same occurred in Germany, where the 1949 production level of around 100,000 dwellings grew rapidly to 300,000 units annually during the first half of the 1950s before peaking at 605,000 units in 1966, at a normalized rate of over 10 dwellings per 1,000 people of population. By 1970, however, overall production had declined to around 448,000 units annually and a normalized rate of 7.3 dwellings per 1,000 population (Welfeld 1972). Likewise, Italy experienced a very rapid postwar growth in housing investment, exceeding 20 percent in annual growth from 1950 to 1955. Subsequent growth continued but at a much slower pace, followed by declines during the economic recession of the middle sixties and early seventies, with the exception of a peak year of production in 1969 (Garavini 1975). For Britain sustained recovery was slower. Apart from a surge in production during the early 1950s, prewar annual levels were not consistently reached until 1964 (see appendix B for details). In that year 373,676 units were produced, at a normalized rate of close to 8 dwellings per 1,000 population. After 1968, however, production began to decline, dwindling to well below prewar levels by 1973 (Barr 1958, Pepper 1975). Similarly, Spain experienced a housing boom during the 1960s, consistently above 8 units per 1,000 population, although largely due to private speculation (Bohigas 1975).

The type of housing produced varied from place to place, primarily according to available resources, accessibility to housing sites, and local customs. In the United States, for example, by far the most units built were for single households (figure 136). This was particularly apparent during the height of the postwar suburban boom during the late forties and fifties, when roadway transportation improvements quickly made

136
Postwar mass production of single-family homes in the United States. Copyright William Garnett, 1955.

numerous sites readily accessible. At a peak in 1955, almost 90 percent of the annual production was for single-family houses, exceeding even the prewar high of 82 percent. By contrast, during the sixties and early seventies, there was a general decline in this proportion, reaching as low as 54 to 55 percent between 1969 and 1973, periods of high overall housing production (U.S. Department of Commerce 1976). Reasons for this decline are hard to pinpoint. By the 1960s, however, the pent-up housing demand from the war years had subsided. Furthermore, production on the urban periphery became less convenient, and as the housing market expanded so, naturally enough, did the demand for different types of dwelling units. During the early 1950s a significant proportion of the non–single family units produced were for low-cost housing or as part of urban renewal programs. This practice was also to continue more intensively into the 1960s.

In Europe, housing densities were almost uniformly higher, conditioned among other things by land availability and accessibility. In Britain for example, a major provider of urban housing like the London County Council built residential estates at between 25 and 50 dwelling units per net acre (figure 137), ranging between row house configurations and high-rise apartment towers. Similarly in continental Europe, where densities were often even greater, multistory slab blocks and apartment towers served as a predominant form of abode.

Finally, postwar increases in housing production were usually accompanied by significantly higher levels of private-sector participation. At least partially this was a consequence of policies aimed at shifting the burden of provision from one sector to the other. In Italy, for example, over 25 percent of the housing investment in the early fifties came from the public sector, declining over time to only 3.3 percent in 1972. During the same period, high production was usually accompanied by relatively low public involvement, such as the peak production year of 1969 when public investment only represented 5 percent of the total (Garavini 1975). As indicated earlier, Spain's housing boom was precisely because of speculative private-sector participation during the 1960s and early 1970s, when public involvement was less than 9 percent (Bohigas 1975). Similarly in Britain, there was a general trend from 85 percent public involvement in the early 1950s down to 37 percent by 1973; during the peak periods of British production during the middle to late sixties, private investment was well over 50 percent (Barr 1958, Pepper 1975). The same sort of trend can be found for Germany. Between 1950 and 1970 the level of direct government subsidy dropped appreciably, from 43.9 percent to

137
High-density, high-rise
postwar dwelling in Britain.

only 7.6 percent, although the *Bausparkassen* (building and loan associations) made up much of the difference, rising from a negligible share in 1950, when little private capital was available, to 34 percent in 1970 (Welfeld 1972). The production profile in the Netherlands is less clear, although again there was a general decline in direct public-sector involvement from 41 percent in 1951 to as low as 14 percent in 1962. Nevertheless, the magnitude of subsidized housing from all sources remained impressively high (Ministry of Housing and Building 1964, Welfeld 1972). Finally, in the United States, for the reasons already outlined, direct public provision has never been very high, although here again there was a gradual decline during the postwar period from 3 to 4 percent in the early 1950s to almost nothing in the 1970s, while total production climbed from around one million units annually to above two million (U.S. Department of Commerce 1976).

Boxes, Big and Small

Postwar housing took advantage of conceptual and technical developments in architecture and planning, most of which also became established during the interwar years of the twenties and thirties. Innovations in practice occurred at two levels of spatial concern. One was in the organization and architecture of dwelling units themselves, including the development of several new housing types. The other was in the aggregation of dwelling units according to various principles of functional and social organization. Throughout, one or more of the presumed advantages of higher-intensity development were actively pursued, including cost-efficient construction, a better relationship to recreational open space, and greater opportunities for functional integration.

Towers and Slabs

The development of modern tall residential buildings began in earnest during the later part of the 1920s, both as an outgrowth of theoretical speculations and as a response to rising urban demands for higher densities. Between 1928 and 1931 Walter Gropius made a number of studies about the future of modern housing, particularly in relationship to needs for recreational open space, adequate sunlight, and ventilation (figure 138). In addition to single-family housing, he argued that high-rise dwelling principles should be established. The open space between buildings could be increased appreciably, for instance, with higher-intensity residential developments. Furthermore, infrastructural and support service costs could be simultaneously decreased through high-density building prac-

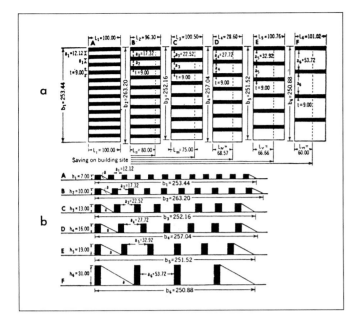

Studies by Walter Gropius of
building height, density, and
sunlight under a *Zeilenbau*
organization, 1928–1931.

tices, sufficient to offset increased costs for additional structural support
and elevators. Consequently, he saw the usual practice of building three-
to five-story apartment buildings as irrational, for it offered none of the
flexibility and independence of a single-family house nor any of the consolidated amenity and community services of high-rise living (Benevolo
1984). The upshot of his investigations was an optimum height, for Germany anyway, of 10 to 12 stories, distributed in narrow slab blocks following a strict north-south orientation. The alternating strips of building
development and open space were then distributed in the form of a *Zeilenbau* or superblock, resulting in only a 15 percent land coverage (Plunz
1990).

Gropius made two specific proposals incorporating tall residential buildings, both in Berlin. One was for the Spandau Haselhorst district in 1929
(figure 139), the other for the Wannsee district in 1931 (Tafuri and Dal Co
1976, Benevolo 1984). In many respects the narrow slablike apartment
buildings were similar to Marcel Breuer's 1924 theoretical proposal for
low-cost housing, in the form of a seven-story block with reinforced concrete floor slabs supported on columns and braced by an elevator and stair
structure at the ends. The general spatial and poetic model, however,
followed "tower and slab in the park" principles, probably first articulated
by Auguste Perret in 1922 and then taken up in modern form by Le
Corbusier in his Ville Contemporaine of 1927 (Plunz 1990).

High-rise slab blocks for the
Wannsee district in Berlin by
Walter Gropius, 1931.

140
Hybrid apartment buildings:
the Beresford Apartments in
New York City by Emery
Roth, 1928–1930.

In the United States, New York City's 1929 Multiple Dwelling Law mandated building bulk and height restrictions for high-rise housing, primarily in response to real estate pressures for higher-density development on Manhattan Island. Under this legislation towers could rise three times the adjacent street width, provided the building footprints were no greater than 20 percent of the lot area. The lower portion of what effectively became hybrid buildings, incorporating courtyard apartment blocks with towers, could rise to a height of one and three-quarters of the street width. In short, structures covering a substantial portion of a city block and rising to a height of some 30 stories were permissible. Perhaps the most notable results of this legislation were the apartment towers that began to line Central Park and, in particular, those by Emery Roth such as the Beresford Apartments of 1928 and 1930 (figure 140) and the San Remo of more or less the same time period (Fish 1979, Ruttenbaum 1986, Plunz 1990).

At much the same time and in a similar manner, Les Gratte-Ciel de Villeurbanne (figure 141) were being constructed at the center of a planned expansion of the French city of Lyons (Urbanisme 1933, Roche 1934). The brainchild of Lazare Goujon, the socialist head of the municipality, Villeurbanne was seen as a semiautonomous district on the eastern periphery, the center of which was to include a town hall, public administrative offices (Le Palais de Travail), and high-density, high-rise housing. The architect for the last portion of the project was Môrice Leroux, who immediately set out to exemplify the modern, progressive spirit of the entire undertaking with a bold, four-block housing scheme, axially centered around a broad boulevard, terminating at the town hall. With the adoption of a stepped-back profile for the high-rise housing and a steel-frame technology similar to those of Roth, Raymond Hood, and others, the skyscrapers of Villeurbanne, as they became known, quickly took on a distinctly

141
The skyscrapers of
Villeurbanne in Lyons, by
Môrice Leroux, 1930–1934.

142

Stepped setback of a high-
rise apartment away from
the central boulevard at
Villeurbanne in Lyons.

American image of modernity. The integration of building components, and the sweep of building volumes away from two symmetrically placed 20-story towers at the end of the complex, also showed the strong influence of Sant'Elia and the futurists (Delfante, Meuret, and Lagier 1984). Designed and constructed between 1930 and 1934, 1,500 dwelling units were provided in four large and highly articulated hybrid buildings. In general, the plan of each was a narrow rectangle, conforming to a city block bounded by streets and avenues. A typical building cross section (figure 142) consisted of an 8-story rise above the central boulevard, followed by a stair-stepped setback to a height of 11 to 13 stories, forming a high spine to the overall building complex. The ground floor and lower levels were zoned for shops and other nonresidential functions, while upper portions of the building were devoted to apartments of various sizes, each with its own balcony or private outdoor space (Clémonçon, Curt-Patat, and Lagier 1988). Overall, the project has proved to be both desirable and remarkably civic.

The first modern American proposal, along the lines of Gropius's slab blocks, was made by the firm of Howe and Lescaze between 1931 and 1932 for the Chrystie-Forsyth Street housing project on New York's Lower East Side (figure 143). Designed primarily by William Lescaze, who had joined the firm in 1929, the project incorporated a number of L-shaped high-rise slab blocks raised above the ground plane on pilotis. The long side of the L-shaped blocks ran parallel with the main streets of Chrystie

143

The Chrystie-Forsyth housing
proposal by William Lescaze
of Howe and Lescaze on New
York's Lower East Side,
1931–1932.

144

The Bergpolder project by J. A. Brinkman, L. C. van der Vlugt, and W. van Tijen in Rotterdam, 1932–1934.

and Forsyth, with the overall project spanning between East Houston and Canal streets in the other direction. Although never built, the project did advance the idea of high-density development with low building coverage and ample open space for recreation. Each tower was to have been from 10 to 11 stories in height, with gallery access to a regular arrangement of apartments on each floor. Exhibited in the International Style Exhibition at the Museum of Modern Art in New York, the project showed a strong European influence, as well as some of the characteristics of Richard Neutra's Rush City Reformed proposal for Los Angeles of 1923 to 1925 (Architectural Record 1932, Tafuri and Dal Co 1976, Plunz 1990).

Practical application of Gropius's high-rise apartment building occurred between 1932 and 1934 with the Bergpolder project on Borgesiusstraat (figure 144), in a working-class area of Rotterdam, by J. A. Brinkman, L. C. van der Vlugt, and W. van Tijen. Surrounded by three- to four-story apartments, this single 10-story linear block faces ample open garden space and incorporates a low-rise building volume along the street, in order to harmonize the overall scale of the project with its surroundings. Structurally the building has a steel frame, with horizontal partitions, doors, and windows made of wood. Identical apartments for families of four lined each floor, with screened balconies to the west and gallery access to each unit along the east. Stairs and an elevator were located at one end, near the street, with the spacious elevator operating on a skip-stop principle of opening at every second floor. In total there were nine levels of housing, with eight apartments per floor. Each apartment measured 6 meters wide by 8 meters deep and was zoned across its width into two unequal parts: a narrow zone for bedrooms and a wider zone for the living room, kitchen, and bathroom. Community facilities such as a laundry, storage facilities, and a nursery were located on the ground floor. Although several earlier attempts had been made to construct high-rise apartments in Amsterdam they had proven to be financial disasters. At the Bergpolder, by contrast, standardized means of production and a low-cost structural system enabled a reasonably economical building to be constructed. Subsequently the small apartments have been adapted, taking advantage of the partition wall configuration (Benevolo 1984, Groenendijk and Vollaard 1987).

Another similar building was constructed in 1932 on the Plaslaan Estate, this time for higher-income tenants. Designed by van Tijen and H. A. Maaskant, the apartment block was also 10 stories in height, but now with stairs at each end. The relationship between each apartment unit and its adjacent balcony of private open space was also accentuated, blurring the usual distinction between indoors and outdoors (Casabella 1938a). Aimed at a similar income bracket, high-rise apartment blocks began to appear in prominent locations in other European cities at about the same time. A three-tower project, for example, was proposed in 1938 by Luigi Carlo Damian for Genoa's waterfront (Casabella 1938b). Meanwhile, the point tower, with its compact and centralized floor plan, emerged in 1933 at the Cité de la Muette in Drancy, France, by the architects Eugène Beaudoin and Marcel Lods (destroyed in 1976). Here, five towers, each 16 stories in height, were located at the end of a series of streets lined by lower-rise, four-story apartment blocks. Although each apartment tower faced a broad expanse of park, the overall arrangement of buildings was not in the garden city tradition, verging much closer to the modern tower in the park. In a manner similar to the Bergpolder and the Plaslaan Estate, the high-rise buildings were constructed of steel with prefabricated infill panels (Tafuri and Dal Co 1976, Benevolo 1984).

Many immediate postwar developments in high-rise housing took place in the United States, there as elsewhere largely serving two groups at either end of the socioeconomic spectrum. Mies van der Rohe, who along with other members of the Deutscher Werkbund and Bauhaus migrated to the United States shortly before World War II, quickly established highly refined and almost open-ended principles for high-rise development. His design for the Promontory Apartments in Chicago in 1946, for instance, featured a continuous reinforced-concrete frame, strongly expressed on the exterior of the building and seemingly extending unconstrained outward into the surrounding space (figure 145). Within the gridwork of this frame were masonry infill panels with glazing above, thus allowing Mies to maintain a semblance of human scale, regardless of the actual expanse of the facade (Benevolo 1984). Although only some 20 stories in height and eight bays wide, Promontory Apartments were almost double the size of the earlier Bergpolder project and provided direction for many slab-block apartment projects to come, especially those with notable views and for people of means.

In the Lake Shore Drive Apartments of 1949 through 1951, for example, again on Chicago's lakefront, Mies refined these principles of extension and scale still further. Two freestanding, compact rectangular towers, each some 26 stories in height, were arranged perpendicular to one another (figure 146). Each was five bays by three bays in overall plan dimension, with elevators, stairs, and services located at the center, in a manner similar to commercial office towers. The layout of the apartments within each floor was according to principles of the free plan, and the articulated steel frame with a glass curtain wall also echoed office building practice

145

The Commonwealth Promenade Apartments in Chicago by Ludwig Mies van der Rohe, 1953–1956.

and the simplification of poetic formulas within the emerging International Style (Tafuri and Dal Co 1976). Furthermore, the artful arrangement of the buildings on their site, although recognizing the diagonal orientation of the grid of the city at that point and a certain tensile relationship between the two towers themselves, remained largely oblivious of a surrounding architectural context.

During the 1950s and 1960s, residential towers and slabs figured prominently in many American urban renewal schemes, especially in areas where the requirements for density were relatively high. The North Harlem public housing project of 1951, by the office of Skidmore, Owings and Merrill, for example, featured eight identical International Style tower blocks, very similar in many respects to Mies's Promontory Apartments. The three towers of the celebrated Society Hill renewal project in Philadelphia of the early 1960s, by I. M. Pei, followed a direction similar to that outlined by Mies with the Lake Shore Apartments some ten years earlier. Unfortunately, however, as we shall see in more detail later on, numerous low-income public housing and urban renewal projects also included high-rise residential towers, but of vastly inferior architectural quality.

Tracts

A roughly parallel historical development took place in the mass production of single-family detached housing. In the United States in particular, but also in parts of Europe, development of housing estates consisting of groupings of single dwellings, each on its own lot, had been common practice from well before the turn of the century. Most of these estates, on the periphery of towns and cities, were for the well to do and conformed in both appearance and layout to prevailing aesthetic orthodoxies of the day. Later, with the advent of the garden city movement, such peripheral development also became available to some of the working classes (figure 147). In fact, this form of residential development had become so popular in the United States that the Chicago City Club was prompted in 1913 to hold a competition for the design of a typical Chicago square gridiron subdivision tract of 160 acres (a quarter section). Here the 33 entries could be grouped roughly into three themes: the city beautiful, with a strong emphasis on symmetry and classical composition of site layouts; the garden city; and romantic naturalism, something of a holdover from the nineteenth century (Yeomans 1916). In spite of these efforts, however, most speculative residential subdevelopments of the teens and twenties were straightforward, rectilinear block layouts, within an overall gridiron pattern of roads.

146
The Lake Shore Drive Apartments on Chicago's lakefront by Ludwig Mies van der Rohe, 1949–1951.

147
American working-class
housing under the garden
city movement: Woodbourne,
Boston, by Alexander Pope,
1911–1919.

By the 1930s, however, these uncomplicated rectilinear gridiron layouts were becoming problematic. First, in many places there was a scarcity of regular land parcels. Second, with the rising use of automobiles it was discovered that gridiron plans encouraged through traffic and therefore diminished the public safety of residential streets. Finally, the undifferentiated appearance of many subdivisions seemed monotonous, even to the most hard-nosed developer (Tunnard and Pushkarev 1963, Rowe 1991). Furthermore, with a strong governmental presence in the housing industry, standards became imposed and guidelines were developed for efficiency, safety, and amenity in residential neighborhoods. The Land Planning Division of the Federal Housing Administration, for instance, under the direction of Seward Mott, began distinguishing different types of traffic within a typical 160-acre quarter section tract development, tailoring roads accordingly (figure 148). The result recommended elimination of through streets, pushing traffic toward external arterial roads located at half-mile intervals. Traffic safety internal to the development was also improved through the elimination of control points and the use of T and Y intersections. Finally, a park or similar recreational space was placed at the center of the subdivision for use by neighborhood residents (Mott 1941, Rowe 1991). The FHA also wielded considerable influence with its minimum housing standards, including 5,000-square-foot lots and setbacks, arising out of deliberations that concluded in 1939. Shortly before the war, well over 50 percent of the total volume of housing starts were subject to the administration's scrutiny (Scott 1969, U.S. Department

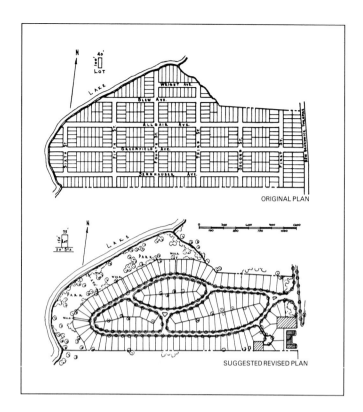

148
Redevelopment of a quarter
section tract development
according to Federal Housing
Administration principles.

149
Motor court cul-de-sac
arrangement at Radburn,
New Jersey.

of Commerce 1955). Similar regulations were also developed in Britain, through local provisions of the 1932 Town Planning Law. Enforcement through the speculative booms of the 1930s was, however, less than stringent (Barr 1958, Benevolo 1984).

One radical model of single-housing subdevelopment was proposed and partially constructed at Radburn, New Jersey, from 1928 onward, well in advance of the Federal Housing Administration's standards. Designed by much the same team as Sunnyside Gardens, including Clarence Stein, Henry Wright, and Frederick Ackerman, and for the same client (the City Housing Corporation), Radburn followed at least five basic design principles. First, superblocks of roughly 250 acres were defined, bounded on three sides by high-capacity traffic arteries and on the fourth by a major street, along which were concentrated commercial activities and higher-density housing. Each superblock became the basic spatial unit within which neighborhood planning took place. Second, all roads, streets, and even footpaths were defined and specialized according to their function. Of particular note were the motor courts in the form of cul-de-sacs (figure 149), around which the individual homes were tightly grouped. On the other side of the houses was an elaborate system of pathways leading past private yards and gardens to larger-scale green spaces. Third, all pedestrian and vehicular traffic were separated. The division between motor court and pedestrian path was a case in point (figure 150). Fourth, a large continuous system of parks and public open spaces became the backbone of the community. Finally, schools and other community functions were located toward the center of the superblock adjacent to a main road, well within the community and well within comfortable walking distance, up to one-half mile, from each residence along the pedestrian pathways (Wright 1935, Stein 1966). Unfortunately, only two superblocks were partially completed when the City Housing Corporation failed in 1933. Con-

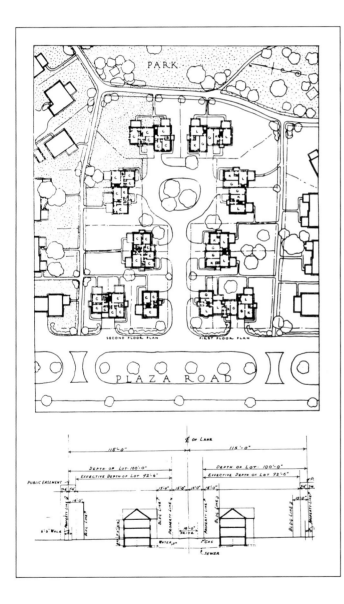

150
Residential development at Radburn and the division between pedestrian paths and motor courts.

cepts similar to those at Radburn, however, were incorporated in other community planning guidelines. In 1929, for instance, the County of Los Angeles proposed a similar cul-de-sac form of motor court (figure 151; Rowe 1991).

During the post–World War II era, FHA and other more local residential guidelines changed. Gone were motor courts and long cul-de-sacs, as they proved to be impractical for service vehicles. In their place curvilinear patterns of loop roads were proposed, preserving the private character of residential streets. Parks or other public facilities at the center of the developments were also abandoned, for lack of consistent community attention (Scott 1969, Rowe 1991).

Two residential developments that above all epitomized this period of single-family home construction, at least in the United States, were Levittown in New York, begun in 1949, and the community of the same name in Pennsylvania, begun a year later in 1950 (figure 152). Both communities take their name from the brothers Abraham, Alfred, and William Levitt, who had begun building high-priced housing in the 1930s, followed by defense housing in Norfolk, Virginia, during the war. Having moved to

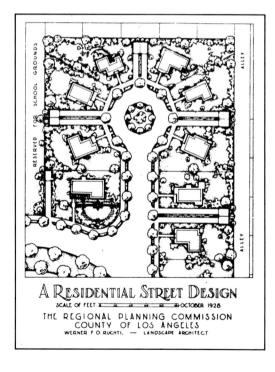

151
Motor court proposal by the County of Los Angeles, 1929.

152
General view of Levittown, New York, by the Levitt Brothers, 1949.

153
The standard model of Cape Cod housing at Levittown, New York, 1950s.

Hempstead, Long Island, an outlying area of New York, in 1949, they began construction of Levittown following by then a more or less standard pattern of curvilinear residential streets defining blocks that were subdivided into relatively small lots, on which could be placed inexpensive housing. The standard house model (figure 153), sometimes called a Cape Cod, was one and a half stories high, with a very compact and simple floor plan. Heavily financed by the Federal Housing Administration and the Veterans Administration, homeowners could obtain a house for as low as a $90 down payment, with $58 monthly payments spread over 25 years (Wright 1981). In a word, houses were inexpensive, and they proved to be popular with prospective homeowners and profitable for the developers. Most were sold as quickly as they became available, even with a production rate of some 150 houses per week (Rowe 1991).

Levittown, Pennsylvania, also proved to be successful and was more highly planned. Eight master blocks were established on a site of some 5,000 acres of rolling countryside, each centered on a school or major public facility. These master blocks were then subdivided into three or four residential neighborhoods each, providing housing for 60,000–70,000 residents. Not unlike at Radburn, the master blocks were defined primarily by major roadway arterials, with a curvilinear street pattern inside each block. A 250-acre forest reserve was also provided inside the neighborhood (Levitt and Sons 1951, Wright 1981).

Other communities by different developers quickly followed, such as Daly City in California, and many were constructed along similar lines, such as Sharpstown in Houston, Texas, which was begun by Frank W. Sharp in 1954 (figure 154). Indeed, Sharpstown was lavish in its scope, covering 6,500 acres of land and, after 1961, accommodating a large enclosed regional mall, together with high-rise offices and residential condominiums at its center. The development was basically divided into four quadrants, at the center of each of which was located a major recreation amenity or nonresidential use. As at Levittown, all housing was heavily financed by the Federal Housing Administration, and usually took the form of a single-story, single-family home with three bedrooms (figure 155), built on a standard residential lot (Papademetriou 1972, McComb 1981, Rowe 1991).

Technical developments in single house construction were episodic and evolutionary. Generally speaking, the housing industry in the United States was decentralized, relatively fragmented, and low in technological sophistication. No firms were truly national in scope and even sizable firms, other than truly large firms like the Levitts, only produced on the order of 100 to 500 units per year (Mason 1982). Standard construction practice, using a timber stud wall or balloon frame system mounted on a slab poured at grade, provided flexibility and required relatively low-skilled labor and an economic use of building materials.

During the late 1930s construction of such housing units began to become more highly industrialized, with the aggregation of pieces into preconstructed components and the precutting of materials into standard sizes. With the war years, and particularly the defense housing efforts, production lines became streamlined and new management techniques were introduced. The Levitts, Sharp, and several other prominent postwar housing developers were heavily engaged in these wartime efforts. The 1940s and early 1950s saw extensive application of wartime process management techniques, the coordination of labor and materials at the site, and the integrated coordination of various trades. The single-family housing industry quickly evolved into what became known known as the assembly line in reverse, with crews and materials moved from building site to site by the product under construction, rather than the product being moved down the line (Eichler 1982, Mason 1982). In addition, more intensive use was made of prefabricated components, precut materials, and power tools. Innovations in floor slab construction, plumbing trees, and other technical components also took place.

154
An aerial view of
Sharpstown, Texas, by
Frank W. Sharp, 1954.

155
A typical single-family home
in Sharpstown, Texas.

The late fifties and the sixties, in contrast to the immediate postwar period, were a time for the refinement of existing practice and a relative absence of significant technical innovations. Throughout, technical progress was made in order for the shape and appearance of the house to remain the same. Unlike in the *neue Sachlichkeit,* no real attempt was made to overtly express the rather considerable technical development that had taken place. Contrary to some widely held opinions of monotony, conformity, and rigidity, however, the low-technological standard form of single-house construction proved to be flexible and an almost endless source of opportunities for individual creativity on the part of homeowners. Relatively easy to modify, expand, and reshape, the tract house has accommodated changes both in American family size and in lifestyle (Gans 1962, Rowe 1991).

Submultiples

Underlying most comprehensive modern housing proposals were definitions of an integrated dwelling environment at levels below that of the district, an environment that represented, as Benevolo put it, "submultiples of housing and community services," where each was no longer seen as a separate function (Benevolo 1984, p. 732). These spatial concepts, in turn, were at least partially supported by models of social interaction, which stressed the priority and centrality of certain functions over others. Primary schools, for example, often played a major role in defining the center of a residential neighborhood. And while the quest for an appropriate "submultiple" was not unique to the modern era, its importance was certainly magnified by prevailing technocratic preoccupations with control, management, and functional interdependence. Moreover, as projects increased in size they were also regarded as being inherently more complicated, requiring very special attention to the way in which individual dwellings were aggregated together to form meaningful communities (figure 156).

In the previous discussion, a prominent form of subdistrict definition was that of the so-called neighborhood unit, variously conceived of as "a scheme of arrangement for the family-life community" (Perry 1939, p. 11). As a basis for aggregating housing units together, the neighborhood unit idea had fascinated architects and planners for many years and was strongly evident in Ebenezer Howard's and others' garden city proposals. At the core was the idea of a cohesive community that was large enough to support and enjoy transactions over a local array of community services and nonresidential functions, and yet small enough for inhabitants to have

156
A modern version of the neighborhood unit: Parklawn, Milwaukee, Wisconsin, by DeGelleke, 1937.

a real sense of belonging to a particular neighborhood. In addition to size, functional composition, and mix, however, there were also considerations of the manner in which particular spatial arrangements of dwellings and other uses could support the community idea.

Generally speaking, the neighborhood unit idea has had a strong association with the garden city movement, both in the United States and abroad. In fact, it became one of the backbones of British new town planning shortly after World War II and strongly influenced the conceptual planning activities of many local authorities (Abercrombie 1959). Continental European communities were also often influenced by the idea. The overall plan of Römerstadt, for instance, while not literally following English neighborhood models, was certainly centered around local community facilities, such as a school, and around services, such as shops. In the United States the neighborhood unit idea was inherent in the conceptual thinking of many members of the Regional Planning Association, and later in the guidelines of the Federal Housing Administration, as well as the building practices of several postwar developers like the Levitts and Sharp. In short, the neighborhood unit has been a pervasive part of Anglo-American community planning and, to only a slightly lesser extent, of planning in Europe and Scandinavia more generally.

A common version of the neighborhood unit idea followed several basic principles, each concerned with the physical layout of a residential neighborhood. First, residential development should be sufficient to support one elementary school, usually meaning a population on the order of 1,000 to 1,600 people. Second, the school and other related community facilities, such as day care and special recreational venues, should be grouped at a central point in the neighborhood and within walking distance of all residences. Third, open-space preserves should form a recreational focus for the community, and, in the typical 160-acre quarter section, should amount to a land area of some 16 acres. Fourth, local shops should be placed at the perimeter of the neighborhood, preferably at traffic junctions and adjacent to the local shops serving other neighborhoods. Finally, the street network should be specialized to meet specific functional needs, and through traffic should be avoided at all cost. Obviously for today's needs the centrality of an elementary school might be called into question, together with the underlying bias of the neighborhood unit idea in favor of traditional nuclear families. Nevertheless at the time when these particular standards were in vogue (they were often cited before World War II and were strongly based, in the United States, on the earlier Regional Plan for New York and its Environs of 1922), such a social emphasis was not misplaced. Furthermore, as Perry and others clearly showed, the neighborhood unit should not be regarded as the exclusive domain of low-density, single-family dwelling. It can be applied equally, in principle, to higher-density residential communities, as demonstrated by many Public Works Administration projects like the Williamsburg Houses of 1937 to 1938 described earlier (figure 157; Perry 1939, Plunz 1990).

Another spatial concept often, although not exclusively, associated with the neighborhood unit was the superblock. As the name suggests, it was often an aggregation of a number of normal urban blocks forming a sufficiently large territory for efficient and flexible planning to take place. In theory, anyway, a superblock should be sufficiently large to allow the geometry of a residential layout to be dictated by dwelling unit designs and their aggregation, rather than by the often arbitrary dimensions of city blocks. As we have seen, the superblock was also strongly associated with the tower or slab in the park idea, and, in the case of Gropius's *Zeilenbau*, the dimensions were derived from an appropriate repetitive spacing of apartment blocks and interstitial open space. The superblock was also commonly adopted in many urban renewal projects as the basic unit of planning and often coincided exactly with the neighborhood unit idea in many residential subdevelopment activities, as well as in government-sponsored housing projects on both sides of the Atlantic. In short, again in an attempt to better and more comprehensively manage residential development and city-making activities, architects and planners sought a broader territory for their experiments.

As we have seen, the superblock was not confined to either high-density or single-family residential developments. Radburn, New Jersey, for example, was fundamentally constructed on the superimposition of a neightborhood unit within a superblock of mainly residential streets and open space. Hillside Homes of 1933 (figure 158), by essentially the same design team, incorporated the same ideas, only this time for higher-density dwelling (Stein 1966). In a more complex and functionally integrated version, the so-called Green Milan scheme for the Sempione-Fiera zone of the city, by F. Albini, I. Gardella, G. Minoletti, et al., of 1938, incorporated the superblock idea on at least two levels. First, the basic layout of residential and other functional areas within the plan combined several typical Milanese city blocks together. Second, the overall proposal itself had more than a sufficient sense of formal and functional coherence to be interpreted as a singular entity (figure 159). Moreover, it was generally bounded on

157
General layout of the Williamsburg Houses in Brooklyn, New York, by Richard Shreve, 1937–1938.

158
The superblock arrangement at Hillside Homes in New York by Clarence Stein and Henry Wright et al., 1933.

the north and south by major thoroughfares (Casabella 1938c, Tafuri and Dal Co 1976).

Apart from urban renewal projects, perhaps the most notable postwar examples of the superblock were associated with new town developments and extensions to existing communities. From 1948 onward, for instance, the firm of van der Broek and Bakema developed a number of projects to help rehouse the Dutch population on new sites. Their proposal for the Klein Driene quarter of Hengelo of 1955 to 1968 employed a superblock configuration of low- to mid-rise residential slab blocks, organized around private yards, community gardens, and public facilities. Similarly, in their scheme for expanding Leeuwarden of 1958, a repetitive organization of mixed residential development was bounded on all four sides by major roads. Other projects like the Alexanderpolder of 1953 to 1956 also had similar characteristics (Benevolo 1985).

The capitals at Chandigarh in India and Brasília in Brazil also stand out among superblock developments, particularly in the more radical modern tradition. Begun in 1950 as the new capital of the Punjab, Le Corbusier's plan for Chandigarh called for the creation of a gridiron of major thoroughfares, defining large "sections" or superblocks of some 100 hectares, or 250 acres, in area. Within each section, high- and medium-density residential development was grouped largely according to a caste system of socioeconomic class (Benevolo 1984). Local community facilities, commercial shops, and recreational resources were also incorporated. Similarly, in Lucio Costa's plan for Brasília, commenced in 1957, residential

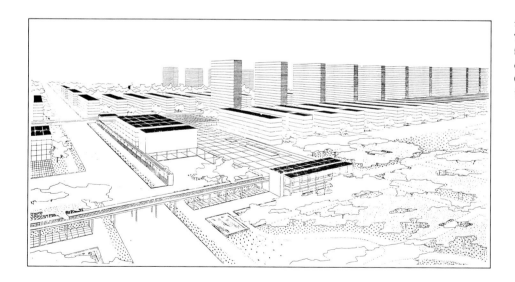

159
The Green Milan proposal for the Sempione-Fiera zone of Milan by F. Albini, I. Gardella, G. Minoletti, et al., 1938.

zones were defined by *supercuadras* (figure 160) comparable in size and
layout to the superblocks in Chandigarh (Tafuri and Dal Co 1976). Interestingly, many superblock proposals were of a very similar size if not scale
of development. Those at Chandigarh, Brasília, and Radburn, for example,
are almost of the same area, at 250 acres, about half as big again as the
typical American 160-acre quarter section. These similarities are probably
not surprising, however, given the underlying social models at work and
a need to be able to conceptualize the physical layout of each superblock.

Finally, Le Corbusier provided another definition of a subdistrict, or submultiple, with the *unité d'habitation* (figure 161). Although not exactly
conceived of as a vertical neighborhood, the *unité d'habitation* was of
sufficient size and did contain within a single high-rise building all the
local shops, services, and recreational opportunities for a community of
some 1,200 to 1,500 people. At 400 dwelling units, the population of the
unité d'habitation was roughly comparable to that of the neighborhood
unit centered on a primary school, or, historically speaking, to those of
Fourier's Phalanstère and Robert Owen's "parallelogram." Indeed, for Le
Corbusier, the *unité* was the "basic cell" of the new city, in much the same
way as the minimum dwelling unit had been the cell of housing (von
Moos 1979). Furthermore, as a single building and plastic entity, the *unité*
promised to make the formation of subdistricts within a city architecturally tractable.

Le Corbusier commenced work on the *unité* concept in 1944, with proposals for the *unités d'habitation transitoires,* or emergency housing, although many of the ideas embodied draw on his earlier work, including
the 1922 *immeuble-villas* (von Moos 1979). In 1946 the newly created
Ministry of Reconstruction and Town Planning in France provided an

opportunity for a trial application of the *unité* at Marseilles. Completed in 1952, the project drew considerable attention, although it was without adequate community shops and services. Originally they were to be located halfway up the building between the seventh and eighth floors. Shortly thereafter a second project was built at Nantes-Reze between 1953 and 1955, for a private corporation, and a third in Berlin in 1957 as a part of the Interbau enterprise (Architecture d'Aujourd'hui 1956, von Moos 1979). Finally a fourth *unité d'habitation de grandeur conforme* was constructed at Briey-en-Forêt. At 365 dwelling units it was slightly smaller than the nominal size of 400 units. It did, however, house the community and commercial facilities at the ground floor, overcoming some of the earlier problems with the location of these services halfway up the building. In fact, a persistent criticism of such a deterministic approach toward community formation is the simple observation that just because 400 dwelling units is sufficient to support a particular facility does not mean that all people in those dwellings will actually use the facility. On the contrary, the more isolated it is from other similar facilities the less likely it is to survive (Benevolo 1984). Several other *unités* were also designed and built by others in France, including the Unité de Voisinage at Bron Pouilly, by Bourdeix, Gages, and Grimal (Architecture d'Aujourd'hui 1956).

Finally, Fernand Pouillon's *unité* for 800 dwelling units, in the new town of Climat de France at Oued Korine in Algeria, also warrants special comment. Constructed in 1957, the *unité* is organized in the form of a fully enclosed rectangular perimeter block, with a monumental peristyle surrounding the Place Ben el Aghlab, also known as the "place of the 200 columns" (Querrien 1984). The entire edifice is large, at 260 meters in length and 65 meters in width, and is located laterally across a hillside, with a monumental entry up steps on the downhill side (figure 162). Each apartment, largely of a conventional plan, spans through the entire building, from the interior courtyard to the exterior walls facing the outside streets. With a resulting overall building thickness of some 12.5 meters, the totally paved monumental court is very ample, at 235 meters by 40 meters, forming a major center for the entire community. All told the building rises some seven stories above the street, with the interior peristyle of rectangular columns, running to a height of five stories. The exterior facades, of masonry construction throughout, are well composed, with an overall symmentrical order of screens and small asymmetrically placed windows. Shops and other community facilities are located at the ground floor, together with entrances to the apartments above. Indeed, the peristyle fulfills its traditional role of mediation between the very public

162
Perimeter block around the
Place Ben al Aghlab in
Climat de France at Oued
Korine, Algeria, by Fernand
Pouillon, 1957.

court on the outside and the private precincts on the inside of the complex (figure 163). It also forms something of a street and a climatic relief from the hot Algerian sun. For perhaps the first time in the modern era, homage was paid to the idea of a palace for the people (Querrien 1984).

Later on, other European projects followed the essential idea of the *unité*, although on an even larger scale. The Corviale project in Rome, for instance, was designed to house some 6,000 residents (figure 164). Begun in 1974, the enormous linear complex is located on the Via Portuense in a then-peripheral area of southwest Rome, with commercial facilities located beneath horizontal slabs of apartment dwellings, punctuated at more or less equal intervals by elevators and stair towers. The project was coordinated by Mario Fiorentino and, with a certain architectural directness, reflects its elongated site, program of accommodations, and material composition.

Urban Growth and Integrated Systems

As the boom of postwar urban development wore on, changes in the spatial structure of metropolitan regions began to emerge and, in the minds of many architects, planners, and public officials, there was an increasing need for yet higher levels of coordination and functional integration among various urban activities and facilities. From their efforts emerged new architectural forms expressive of relationships between spaces and activities and systems approaches to the definition and management of urban areas.

163
Peristyle of 200 columns
mediating between public
courtyard and private
dwellings at Climat de
France.

164
The extensive linear complex
at Corviale in Rome by Mario
Fiorentino et al., 1974

Changes in the spatial structure of urban areas, and especially of metropolitan regions, were primarily directed by the advancement and proliferation of movement technologies. First, as roads and transit lines from central cities improved and became cheaper to use, accessibility also improved, allowing more people to live farther from central areas. The result, often termed "suburban sprawl" or "ribbon development," usually vastly increased the area of metropolitan development, particularly at lower densities around the urbanized periphery (figure 165). The result was the so-called monocentric model for the spatial distribution of urban activities, with a concentration of nonresidential functions at the center, surrounded by rings of residential development at declining densities. Second, as much higher-capacity and faster roads were introduced, linking farms and metropolitan areas together, patterns of accessibility and therefore potential development intensities changed yet again. Early on, especially in the United States, introduction of high-speed, limited-access, high-capacity radial expressways and circumferential ring roads radically altered patterns of transportation accessibility and the relative economic advantage of sites within a metropolitan area. This was particularly evident along peripheral ring roads. In one of the first examples, the circumferential Route 128 was introduced into the Boston region in 1949, accompanied by several high-speed, high-capacity radials, such as the Massachusetts Turnpike a little later on in the mid-1950s. The resulting redistribution of employment facilities was both large and almost immediate. Within a short span of years, some 70 firms formerly located within or close to downtown Boston moved to the urban periphery along Route 128 (Wilbur Smith and Associates 1961). Nationally, by 1973 the amount of employment provided in the suburbs overtook the amount in the cities (Muller 1981). Furthermore, with increasing aggregation of many traditional inner-city functions within peripheral sites, metropolitan regions began to assume not one but several centers of intense commercial activity. The result was the so-called polynucleated model of urban development, now epitomized by places like the Los Angeles region and Houston (Rowe 1991).

Not long afterward, similar developments began to take place in many European cities. Barcelona in Spain, for example, currently has a city population close to 2 million but a metropolitan population of some 5 million. Lyons, the third city of France, has a similar distribution between a distinctly centralized urban population and a broader metropolitan population. Moreover, significant concentrations of commercial activities within once-peripheral areas are also emerging along the lines of the American phenomenon. This is most apparent at junctures along the high-

165
Horizontal mobility, accessibility, and the transformation of the American metropolitan structure.

speed roads stretching east from Lyons toward the mountains. While the timing of transportation improvements has varied, producing different scales and forms of development, the influence of essentially the same underlying technological paradigm of urban growth is by now very clear. During the past 40 years it has been the template used for organizing metropolitan space in a manner largely independent of local circumstances.

Certainly by the late 1950s and the 1960s, if not before, the development of metropolitan areas was generally regarded as a dynamic, interactive sequence of events. In the relationship between land use and transportation, for example, a change in one dimension quickly resulted in a change in the other. Architectural and urban space was clearly a dimension of this interaction but one that could be molded readily to contemporary purposes. By and large, as we began to see in chapter 1, urban space was considered to be ubiquitous and not culturally specific. Frequently, at the urban level anyway, abstract qualities of time-distance and surface area were given more emphasis in urban design and planning than the presence of unique features or the historical results of prior developments. Above all, time's intrusion on space, through this dynamic and interactive formulation of urban development, was pervasive.

One consequence of this predominant view of cities was a general trend toward mixed developments and then toward integrated systems approaches toward urban architecture. "Mixed development," at least as expressed within British housing practice of the 1950s, was aimed at a balanced development based on the variety of types and sizes of dwelling units suited to household needs. As initially expressed in the Dudley Report of 1944, there was "a need for mixed development of family houses with blocks of flats for smaller households intermingled" (Dudley 1944, Barr 1958, p. 35). Also of consequence was the deliberate use of architectural variety in producing a more satisfactory layout and the introduction of nonresidential, or "mixed," uses. Four distinct advantages were to be seen from mixed development. First, it produced a variety of accommodations. Second, a pleasing variety of architectural form could be obtained, replete with visual excitement and contrast. Third, satisfactory outdoor amenities could be created readily incorporating a variety of open spaces. Finally, an economic balance could be achieved by using high-rise, mid-rise, and low-rise forms of development. Out of this mixing certain economies of scale could also be obtained, especially when the housing estates were large enough. Arrayed against these advantages were the problems of creating order out of an inherent housing variety, of ensuring good scale relationships among various forms of development, of avoiding overlooking from one residential block to another, and of providing a reasonably equitable distribution of private outdoor space among otherwise disparate dwelling unit types. In practice, most mixed developments were built at densities ranging from 20 to 40 dwelling units per acre, well in excess of the garden city idea of 12 to the acre but less than inner areas of say London with densities on the order of 70–80 dwelling units per acre (Dudley 1944, Barr 1958).

A fervent practitioner of the philosophy behind mixed development was the London County Council (figure 166). It was also a producer of housing on a grand scale, certainly comparable, in size if not scope, to Ernst May's Frankfurt administration before the war, and to the later Urban Development Corporation of the State of New York. In a period of seven to ten years during the 1950s the London County Council was responsible for building some 10,000 housing units, primarily in the form of estates ranging in density from 25 to 40 dwellings per net acre. The Abbey Wood Estate in Woolwich, of 1956 to 1959, at 2,566 units and 143 dwelling units to the acre, was among the largest and most dense, whereas the Fitzhugh Estate in Wardsworth, of 1953 to 1955, with 213 units at 34 units per acre, was about the smallest and least dense (Barr 1958).

Among the many London County Council estates, Roehampton stands out because of its size, quality, and epitomizing of the mixed development idea (figure 167). This extensive estate was constructed in several phases between 1951 and 1959. The architect to the Council until 1956 was J. L. Martin, to be succeeded by Hugh Bennett. The principal housing architect throughout was Whitfield Lewis. In fact, this design team was widely responsible for a large amount of the London County Council's work (Barr 1958).

The Roehampton estate on Clarence Avenue occupied a site of 100 acres and included 1,875 dwelling units at an overall density of 28 units per acre, or roughly 100 persons per acre. A simple majority of the dwellings, or 55 percent, were contained within high-rise apartment buildings, 33 percent were in four-story maisonettes, and the remaining 12 percent were in single-family dwellings. Developed on relatively open and wooded land adjacent to an existing village, Roehampton's plan incorporated five 11-story apartment slab blocks containing maisonette apartments in a line along Clarence Avenue, with fine views over an extensive meadow to the eastern side of which was a grouping of point blocks. Terrace housing extended out from the village, in keeping with the relatively low scale of

166
The London County Council's philosophy of mixed development at work in a housing estate.

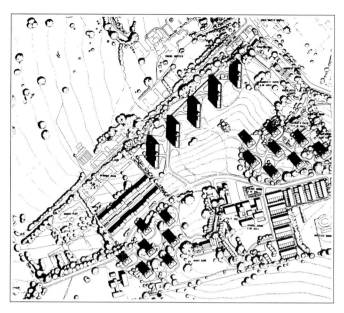

167
The overall layout of
Roehampton by the London
County Council, 1951.

development. The open landscape between buildings (see figures 166 and
167) and the relationship of buildings to one another created highly varied
scenes of considerable visual interest. In another phase along Portsmouth
Road, 737 dwellings were included on a 25-acre site, bringing the overall
total to around 2,500 units. Again the majority (60 percent) were high-
rise, principally in the form of 11-story point blocks, followed by 30
percent in four-story maisonette apartments and 10 percent in terrace
houses. Throughout, the same close attention was given to integrating
buildings within the open landscape, again with picturesque results (Barr
1958, Benevolo 1985).

Parallel and similar kinds of housing development can also be found in
other parts of Europe. Hansaviertel, for example, was first proposed by
the Berlin Senate in 1953 as an international exposition of modern architecture and urban thinking (figure 168). Planned by G. Jobst and W. Kreuer,
it became the site of the Interbau exposition in 1957, with buildings,
including nonresidential buildings, by numerous well-known architects,
including TAC and Gropius. In layout, however, Hansaviertel was a mixed
development in the spatial sense as well, with high-, medium-, and low-
rise structures loosely aggregated within an overall free field of informally
organized landscape (Benevolo 1984).

The next stage in the evolution of mixing housing densities, uses, and types of buildings came with the work of Team 10, among others. Formed in 1956 on the occasion of the CIAM conference in Dubrovnik, Team 10 was a group of architects and planners who called for a new humanism in the built environment and an end to the sectoral zoning and other strongly deterministic functional doctrines of CIAM. Instead, renewed emphasis was placed on relational spaces, such as from streets to dwellings, and upon multipurpose buildings. Specific urban-architectural developments included suspended streets, a continuity of movement and of service networks in general, a rationalization and expression of different support systems within a building or urban complex, and prolific employment of multiple-use spaces. Among the group there was also a preoccupation with promoting or facilitating urban growth, change, and interaction, as well as making productive allowances for chance in the plan-making process (Smithson 1968, Tafuri and Dal Co 1976, Benevolo 1984).

Drawing on strong organic analogies, members of Team 10 created architectural concretizations of the idea of the city as a highly integrated yet dynamic system, in which housing played a major role. Early to the fore were the Smithsons' "continuous structures" in their Golden Lane housing estate proposal of 1952 and later in their Hauptstadt plan for Berlin of 1957 to 1958. Also included must be "the labyrinthian clarity" of van Eyck, together with the "spine and district" proposals of van der Broek and Bakema, especially for the development of eastern Amsterdam in 1965 (Tafuri and Dal Co 1976, p. 342, Benevolo 1985). Above all, the "stems, spines and networks" of the firm of Candilis, Josic, and Woods downplayed the architectural rhetoric of the systems approach while giving full freedom to its organizational possibilities (Woods 1975). Their scheme for Toulouse Le Mirail of 1961, for example, incorporated a latticelike structure of residential blocks, retail uses, and community facilities embedded in multilevel transportation corridors, all organized next to each other in plan at 120-degree angles (figures 169 and 170). Their 1962 scheme for the Freie Universität in Dahlem, a suburb of Berlin, was similarly organized, although this time in the overall form of a grid. A basic motivation behind the design of each scheme was to define and clearly establish an infrastructure of movement and services, around which a dependent structure of urban (or in the case of the university, institutional) uses could form. Managing the dynamics, so to speak, of an interactive set of activities was clearly of importance (Candilis, Josic, and Woods 1975, Candilis 1977). Finally, work of the Japanese metabolists of the 1960s and the utopian projects of Archigram, during much the same period, followed a similar organic and dynamic impetus.

168
Mixed development at Hansaviertel in Berlin by G. Jobst, W. Kreuer, et al., 1953–1957.

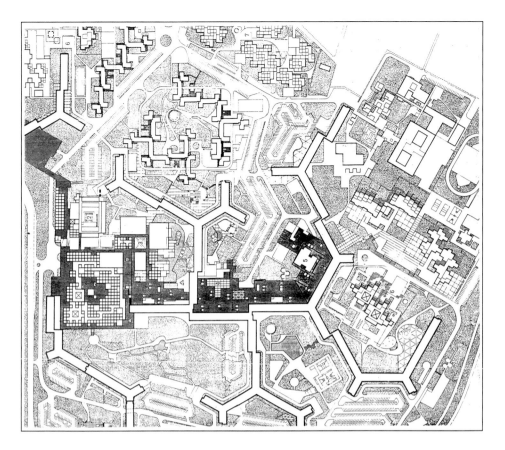

169
The stems and spines of
Toulouse Le Mirail by
Candilis, Josic, and Woods,
1961.

Another broad consequence of a predominant view of cities as changing
and interrelated sequences of events was felt in the public policy arena.
Omnibus bills, within a specific area of governmental interest such as
housing, began to be replaced by a more comprehensive and inclusive
management of urban affairs. Once again a strong motivation appears to
have been the desire to control, rationalize, and integrate areas of government activity. Moreover, in the continued development of comprehensive,
integrated policies there was a sense of curing the ills of past legislative
actions and of overcoming prior misunderstandings. Rarely if ever was
the more general capacity for such complete management questioned,
given enough resources and time.

In the United States, for instance, the war on poverty and the urban
renewal legislation of 1949 and the 1950s was relatively quickly repudiated as being, in the words of Patrick Moynihan, "the maximum feasible
misunderstanding" (Moynihan 1969). In 1966 it was replaced by the Model
Cities Program, which was explicitly aimed at directly involving com-

munity organizations in planning, rather than relying on either advocates or plans, as it were, "from on high." Promising though this step was to be, it was curtailed prematurely in 1969 by President Nixon with a drastic cut in funding (Krueckeberg 1983). The Housing and Urban Development Act of 1968, under the Johnson administration, merged otherwise separate government initiatives concerned with urban areas; the omnibus bills of special areas of interest gave way to a more singular form of comprehensive legislation. Similar reorientations occurred in Britain and other parts of Europe as the perceived task of urban government became more complex and widespread. The search for a new comprehensiveness was at once geographic, by focusing on interlocal contracts and relationships; functional, by focusing on the integration of aid across various disciplinary or thematic boundaries; and pluralistic, by focusing on the inclusion of more and more constituencies.

Evidence of a dynamic systems-oriented view of cities, resulting from a merger of the physical and the policy dimensions, can be found in efforts to contain and manage peripheral development, as well as, in some places, to effect large-scale regional decentralization of economic activities. The creation of complete satellite communities on metropolitan fringes, a basic component of many nations' urban policy during the 1950s and 1960s, was both a physical and political accomplishment of some importance. In hindsight, however, this perceived capacity to create urbanity *de novo* was also probably a major conceit of the time.

In Britain, as we saw, the new town movement started following efforts to reduce development pressures around London and to redistribute economic activity more equally among the regions, especially to the north. The New Town Act of 1946 called for the development of balanced, if not self-contained, communities of from 20,000 to 60,000 inhabitants (Clawson and Hall 1973). The first eight communities, later known as the Mark I New Towns, were built around the outskirts of London and strongly embodied neighborhood unit principles. Harlow, for example, was built in 1952 and located 20 to 25 miles northeast of London, while Stevenage, developed in 1954, was located about 10 miles farther away from London's center. Both communities thrived, exceeding their population targets in a relatively short time. There was, however, something of a contradiction between these new housing facilities and efforts to redevelop blighted inner-city areas (Alderson 1962). By 1952 the New Town Act was amended so as to encourage the development of already existing towns into larger communities.

170
Housing, commerce, and multilevel transportation corridors at Toulouse Le Mirail.

171
The Town Center Housing complex at Runcorn by James Stirling and Michael Wilford, 1968–1974.

In the years following, over 35 new communities were constructed in several different generations of development, ranging from Mark I to Mark IV. A gradual interest in the integration of urban systems can be found, especially in the new town centers and higher-density residential areas of towns like Cumbernauld, planned by Hugh Wilson between 1958 and 1960. Here the possibility of megastructures was experimented with in earnest, although with little lasting success. Later, even more sophisticated proposals were developed for larger-scale towns, such as Milton Keynes by Llewelyn Davies, which was scheduled to house 250,000 people (Benevolo 1985). Runcorn, planned by Arthur Lang between 1964 and 1965 and built several years later, incorporates a strong interest in the definition, integration, and articulation of urban subsystems, especially in its architecture and urban design. Situated between Liverpool and Manchester, the primary purpose of Runcorn was to relieve unemployment and nineteenth-century slum housing in those two urban centers. The overall form of the town center, with its characteristic figure eight plan, was almost totally dictated by movement technologies and the integration and separation of various subsystems. The resulting architecture of skeleton frames and panels, while not forming a megastructure in quite the same sense of Cumbernauld, evinced a strong interest in flexibility and the possibilities of urban growth and change.

The Town Center Housing at Runcorn (figure 171) is also instructive because it clearly marks the transference of similar attitudes and emphases on urban systems into the realm of housing. Designed by James Stirling

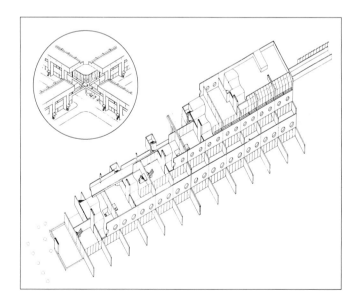

172
General arrangement of housing units at the Runcorn Town Center Housing complex.

and Partners with Michael Wilford as the partner-in-charge, the housing complex was constructed between 1968 and 1974, to house some 6,000 people in 1,500 dwelling units, all within a 2- to 5-minute walk from the town center. Essentially an exercise in low-rise, high-density residential development, 30 percent of its units were two- to three-person flats, 30 percent were four-person maisonettes, and the remainder were five- to six-person houses. The overall density was 117 persons per acre, comparable to the earlier London County Council developments, and the different dwelling unit types were deliberately dispersed throughout the project in order to avoid concentrations of particular household types. Within a typical cross section of the housing (figure 172), the two- to three-person flats were located at the top, with the larger units for five to six persons located at the ground level, where advantage could be taken of private gardens at grade. The four-person maisonettes were sandwiched in between, also with their own outdoor space and direct access to the horizontal pedestrian system, effectively located at the second-floor level running throughout the complex. All garage space was located at grade, with 1.5 cars per dwelling (Pepper 1975).

In plan, the overall complex basically conforms to a grid made of L-shaped housing blocks (figure 173). In many respects it is similar in concept to

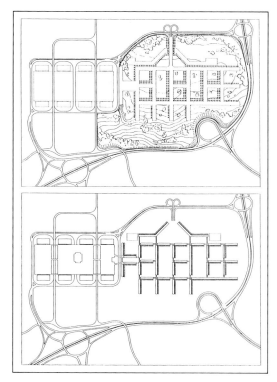

173
General layout of the
Runcorn Town Center
Housing complex.

Berlin's Freie Universität, with the same preoccupations with flexibility and change. The public footways at the second level enclose spacious garden squares for use by adjacent families for recreation (see figure 172). Some shops and pubs are also located along the footway. The systems interest was also carried through to the architecture, which almost exclusively uses an industrialized precast system of construction employing repetitive units. Nevertheless, the overall appearance of the housing remains at the level of the L-shaped buildings around the garden squares.

During the 1950s and 1960s the French government pursued a similar policy of urban and regional deconcentration and reconcentration. A number of ZUPs (Priority Zones of Urbanization) were formed, beginning in 1958, both to relieve development pressure from around Paris and to channel economic activity into the provinces (Strong 1971). The town of Toulouse Le Mirail was a consequence of this policy, again demonstrating a strong interest in the systematic development and exploitation of various urban subsystems. Scandinavia had similar programs, especially in Sweden and Finland, while the United States was much slower to adopt a new communities policy. Columbia, Maryland, Reston, Virginia, and later The Woodlands, Texas, were prominent new towns of the late 1960s and early 1970s, most receiving support from federal government entitlements in the form of loan guarantees.

Form, Identity, and a Crisis of Meaning

In spite of all the increased efforts to broaden and deepen the scope of environmental management in general, and to provide adequate dwelling environments in particular, most western nations' housing policies were either abandoned or in considerable disarray by the early to middle 1970s. Except for some relatively isolated peaks, production levels for housing systematically began to dwindle, and, as time went on, the long hoped for improvements in quality proved even more difficult to obtain. In Britain, for instance, the earlier comprehensive policies of new production and redevelopment were virtually discontinued by 1974, amid chronic downturns in output. Moreover, over 10 percent of the housing in the Netherlands still remained designated as slums, in spite of massive postwar improvement efforts, and in 1972 fully 20 percent of all dwellings still lacked adequate bathroom facilities (Welfeld 1972). In the United States, there was a dramatic 50 percent curtailment in housing production between 1972 and 1975, although it should also be noted that the period from 1970 to 1974 saw an unprecedentedly high production. Nevertheless, as one noted American industry representative put it, "by late 1973 the whole system of housing had virtually spun out of control. The situation was one of extremely tight money compounded by soaring inflation, the energy crisis, material shortages, and a severe crisis in consumer confidence" (Eichler 1982, p. 221). Similarly, in Italy the recession of the mid-1970s saw the Gross Natural Product fall for the first time in 30 years, followed by the emergence of a black market with the submerged economy of firms. Housing production, like everything else, was adversely affected, especially in the public sector. Even in Germany, where the postwar economic recovery seemed to be robust and lasting, housing production dwindled from 605,000 units in 1966 to 448,000 in 1970, a 26 percent downturn. Admittedly this might also be interpreted as a natural fallback from peak levels of production. However, it was accompanied, as in the Netherlands, by an almost chronic inability to improve the quality of housing conditions. By 1972, for instance, 20 percent of all dwellings were still without adequate indoor plumbing facilities, 32 percent were without showers or baths, and 20 percent were considered old and obsolete (Welfeld 1972). In a quite remarkable statement that summarized for many the plight of American and European housing policy, Lord Goodman, the Chairman of the Housing Corporation, said at the Town and County Planning Association meeting of 1973: "It is only in a society where we have a government working day and night on our behalf that the housing problems are insoluble" (Ward 1974, p. 7).

Extrapolation and Loss of Meaning

Accompanying the expansion of modern urban management techniques and housing policies, almost to the breaking point, was a corresponding extrapolation of prewar housing design and planning principles under conditions of high demand, rising scale, and substantial bureaucratic encroachment. Typical annual production rates were almost double prewar levels, and yet the central paradigm for making housing was little changed. Almost by necessity, with each increase in size and complexity the focus shifted, becoming more and more abstract and far less concerned with an attention to detail and the particularities of local circumstances. Production levels and other vital statistics seemed to matter more than the physical suitedness of specific dwelling environments. Consequently, these environments became increasingly similar, as the leveling effects and arbitrariness of abstract formulas took over. Unfortunately, the results of this development by rote was bland, architecturally reduced, and socially unresponsive housing (see figure 174).

Nowhere was the development by rote more visible than in the peripheries of American and European cities, including development in transition areas closer to traditional neighborhoods. In the United States, for example, the early suburban dreams of Sharp and the Levitts, let alone Stein and Wright, deteriorated into mile after mile of monotonous housing tract developments. Increasingly, instead of embodying ideals of home and hearth, the house, and particularly the single-family house, was seen merely as a product or even more pessimistically as a token of trade. The commodification of housing, to borrow an economic term, quickly accompanied postwar rises in affluence and corresponding rises in owner occupancy. In 1930, for instance, the American level of home ownership was less than 50 percent; it had risen to 55 percent by 1950, with subsequent steady increases to around 65 percent by 1970 (U.S. Bureau of the Census 1950–1970). Although ownership levels have remained relatively constant since then, much of this can be attributed to the practice of trading up from a modest dwelling to something more commodious, and to the second home market. For those under 30 years of age, the primary postwar home buyers for instance, there has been a substantial decline in home ownership rates, currently down to a level of only about 35 percent.

174
Generational development of ghetto-specific norms: Robert Taylor Homes in Chicago.

By contrast, home ownership rates for older segments of American society have risen appreciably (Joint Center for Housing Studies of Harvard University 1985–1991). Not surprisingly, the commodification of tract housing was also accompanied by the common practice of building to minimum standards. Under the dictates of economies of scale, the tolerance for experimentation was narrowed considerably. Moreover, as the cost of the actual house itself, in relationship to the composite of total housing costs, declined, attention was shifted to other nonspatial aspects of the housing industry. In 1949, for instance, the labor and material or "shell costs" of an American single-family house amounted to 69 percent of the total. By 1974 it had declined to around 48 percent (U.S. Department of Commerce 1976).

The other aspect of the United States' mass housing efforts unfortunately faired far worse. At the low end of the economic spectrum the promise of an adequate home for every family deteriorated into at best a holding pattern of tenement living and at worst a downward spiral of abject poverty, crime, and social destruction. Especially in areas like Chicago's so-called black belt of poverty, located in a transition zone between the suburbs and the city center, the consequence of almost total isolation without much hope of escape was the generational development of ghetto-specific norms, many of which had little resemblance to the world outside. In Robert Taylor Homes, for example (figure 174), a 95-acre complex of 4,312 dwelling units formed by 28 16-story towers, almost all the families were and still are below the poverty line. Infant mortality there is three times the national average, and levels of substance abuse are well beyond the alarming rates for the population as a whole (Bowly 1978). Columbia Point in Boston (figure 175), another example, was constructed in 1951 under the 1947 Federal Act for low-rent housing and was hailed at the time as a significant step toward obliterating poverty. Although less dense than Robert Taylor Homes, with some 1,500 families occupying a site of 40 acres, sadly the results of physical and social isolation were much the same. The complex consisted of 75 seven-story apartment buildings and 12 three-story structures, all placed at almost equal intervals in a bland and undistinguished landscape. The commercial and community facilities that were originally intended to accompany the project were never built, and the sheer physical isolation on a spit of land that was an old refuse dump continued to be exacerbated by a lack of public transportation. By 1978 only 30 percent of the units were occupied, as the project slipped further and further into disrepair. The project, now called Harbor Point, has undergone substantial redevelopment, as a target of a mixed-income housing strategy (figure 176). However, the social damage done during the intervening 30 or so years remains incalculable.

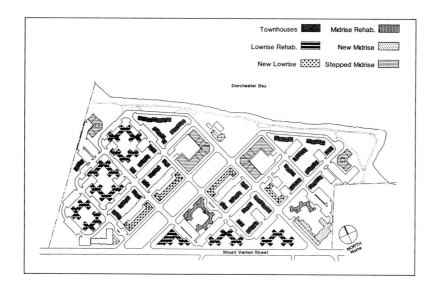

Townhouses Midrise Rehab.
Lowrise Rehab. New Midrise
New Lowrise Stepped Midrise

Dorchester Bay

Mount Vernon Street

NORTH

175
Columbia Point in Boston
by the Boston Housing
Authority, 1951.

176
Transformation and
redevelopment of Columbia
Point into Harbor Point, by
Goody and Clancy et al.,
1983.

Many peripheral housing developments in Europe suffered similar albeit less exaggerated outcomes. Row upon row of multistory slab blocks were often constructed, at or below minimum standards during periodic speculative booms. Services were almost invariably never adequately provided, and they often lacked viable open space and nearby places of employment. Today many European cities have large areas that have become bedroom communities with only the most basic form of tenement living. The *polyganos* of Barcelona, for instance, or the point towers outside of Milan have become symbols of the failure of modern housing development.

Together with the obvious problems of the architectural reduction of dwelling environments, functional and social isolation also played a significant role in these failures. In Naples, for example, the Istituto Case Popolari drew up a well-intentioned housing agenda, during the middle 1960s, for the northern and southern expansion of the city, primarily in the form of two affordable housing districts, named Secondigliano and Ponticelli respectively (Mariani 1982). The development of Secondigliano was very ambitious, calling for full development of a 130-hectare site in the form of dense, functionalist architecture, to house some 64,000 inhabitants. Today, however, the project remains unfinished, although it houses over 10,000 inhabitants. Tragically, the project remained without adequate schools, markets, and public transportation, isolated some 10 kilometers from a viable town center. Streets and roads remained often impaired, and inhabitants dwell within the bare megastructural concrete skeleton of largely unfinished buildings. In a response to the rising crisis in production and undersupply, squatting and underpaying movements also became rampant in Italy during the late 1960s, adding further to the separation between the dwellers and dwelling providers (Garavini 1975).

In addition to functional and social isolation, the modernist concept of the space between buildings did little to alleviate the immediate sense of separation between individual dwellings and the larger communities to which they belonged. Especially under exaggerated conditions of bigness in scale, reductions in budget, and a lack of coordination among representative service agencies, the space between buildings in housing estates too often became a no-man's land of disputed territory or of neglect. With little to guide development beyond modern axioms regarding open space and hygiene, it is little wonder that the so-called public realm of housing fell into disrepute. Taken together with a shape and appearance of buildings that did little to deflect from the most expedient sense of contemporaneity, with no real attachments to either the past or local conditions, these underdefined zones inevitably proved inhospitable and alienating. The earlier promises of an architectural new realism and of garden city principles were reduced to a mere caricature through a combination of neglect, misunderstanding, and application well beyond reasonably available means. When it came to the matter of housing, the modern technical orientation collapsed, as it were, under its own weight.

Pluralism and the Need for User Autonomy

Simultaneously with the rising crisis of meaning in the architecture of modern housing and the failure of many production policies, the very idea of a normative program of accommodations became increasingly questioned. With rising consumer expectations and many earlier goals already satisfied, housing norms and standards, the benchmarks of mass production and control, were often seen as unnecessarily limiting and inflexible. Conversely, as public policies attempted to reach further down into and across the socioeconomic spectrum, differences in housing wants and needs began to emerge. These moves toward pluralism and greater autonomy for specific users, understandably perhaps, came with almost equal force both from outside and from within the discipline of architecture.

From outside, deep structural changes were occurring in the demographic makeup of urban areas that were to strongly challenge, if not render obsolete, many earlier assumptions about housing. In the United States, for example, where a strong equation had been repeatedly forged between the idea of the nation, the family, and the home, the concept of the nuclear family, which lay at the heart of this equation, was severely shaken. Families of married couples, mostly with children, ceased to be an overwhelming majority, declining from fully 75 percent of the number of households in 1960 to just 56 percent today (table 2). Conversely the number of singles without children rose from 22 percent to 36 percent during the same period, and the number of single-parent families doubled, from 3.4 percent in 1960 to 7.4 percent in 1990. Overall, average household size in the United States shrank from 4.3 persons in the 1920s to 3.4 person in 1960, and down still further to the present level of 2.6 (Masnick and Bane 1980, Joint Center for Housing Studies 1985). Given reasonable expectations of a match between household types and housing types, these changes were profound indeed. Furthermore, as far as this account is concerned, there was a period of accelerated change during the 1970s, following the socially tumultuous era of the sixties. Similar changes also occurred within many European nations, albeit with slightly less force. Clearly a contemporary condition of the world has been the rise of heterogeneous populations, at least with respect to household type.

A second feature of population change was also at work, although in this case it harked back to the turbulent growth in urban populations around the turn of the century. An increasing international mobility led to an emerging pool of world labor markets, which gravitated toward centers of capital and employment. The result, as we quickly recognize today in both

Table 2

Changes in Household Types for the United States, 1960–1990

Household Types	1960			1975			1990		
	number (in millions)	%	subtotal of preceding types (%)	number (in millions)	%	subtotal of preceding types (%)	number (in millions)	%	subtotal of preceding types (%)
Married couples—1 child	7.0	13.6		7.5	10.8		10.0	11.3	
Married couples—2 or 3 children	11.0	21.4		12.0	17.2		12.5	14.2	
Married couples—4 or more children	3.0	5.8	40.8	1.9	2.7	30.7	2.2	2.5	28.0
Married couples—no children	17.5	34.0	74.8	24.5	35.2	65.9	25.0	28.3	56.3
Male head, single—no children	1.8	3.5		3.0	4.3		5.8	6.6	
Male head, previously married—no children	2.2	4.3		3.8	5.5		7.0	7.9	
Female head, single—no children	1.5	2.9		2.7	3.9		4.2	4.8	
Female head, previously married—no children	5.7	11.1	21.8	10.1	14.5	28.2	15.0	17.0	36.3
Male head, previously married—children	0.3	0.6		0.4	0.6		0.6	0.7	
Female head, previously married—children	1.4	2.6		3.1	4.4		5.0	5.7	
Female head, single—children	0.1	0.2	3.4	0.7	0.9	5.9	1.0	1.0	7.4

Source: Masnick and Bane 1980, Joint Center for Housing Studies 1991.

Europe and North America, is a multicultural mix of urban populations of almost unparalleled extremes. The guest workers in Germany and Switzerland, the colonial immigrants in Britain and France, the Hispanic and Asian influxes to the United States, quickly brought with them cultural as well as social differences, many requiring reflection in the shaping of contemporary housing. Although immigration in the United States, for instance, has not been inordinately high during the period from 1960 to the present, immigration seen as a proportion of total population growth rose dramatically from just 14 percent in 1960 to 30 percent in 1990 (U.S. Bureau of the Census, 1960–1990). With near-zero population growth among national populations, similar impacts also began to register in Europe, especially during the 1970s. If anything these trends have only intensified since then.

Unlike other earlier periods of urban population flux, however, the social pressures exerted toward the leveling of cultural difference have no longer remained so intense. On the contrary, many contemporary attitudes reflect the opposite impetus toward the celebration of cultural difference. In many places in Europe and North America, the melting pot has been replaced by cultural mosaics. Although the precise impact of these shifts in cultural attitudes is not yet certain, if anything the concept of housing seems likely to be broadened both in kind and in the extent of user autonomy.

Finally, through a combination of demographic changes, socioeconomic hardships, and above all a rising bureaucratic sense of differences among various groups in society, the housing of special populations began to emerge as one of the watchwords of contemporary policy. This has been particularly evident in many developed nations, such as France, Great Britain, and the United States, as well as, parenthetically, in the recent economic superpower of Japan. Specialized views inevitably seem to result from an increasingly modern technocratic perception of urban affairs. One consequence of such a managerial attitude is the targeting of special populations in order to solve general problems. Another, as Nelson insightfully pointed out in his general treatment of bureaucracies, can be a process of political self-perpetuation around special interests (Nelson 1982). In either event, today's current housing focus on the elderly, the handicapped, and the economically disenfranchised marks a sharp break with earlier, more normative practices. Moreover, it is a break that occurred with the widespread urban demographic, cultural, and managerial shifts that began at least in the late sixties and have continued forward into the present era.

From within the discipline of architecture, recognition of the pluralistic needs of society was strongly registered in a desire to better understand the relationship between environment and behavior, as well as in finding practical ways to open up and democratize the building process. Again in keeping with the coping behavior of the modern technical temperament, increased information about urban functions was assumed to bring increased understanding and a concomitant betterment of dwelling environments. Nowhere was this better exemplified than in the landmark works of Christopher Alexander. In his *Notes on the Synthesis of Form*, published in 1964, Alexander presented a sophisticated, quasi-scientific case for a fit between function and form across a broad range of largely anthropological considerations. Unlike the earlier orthodox modernists' functionalist arguments, where form making and function in the final analysis remained separate, Alexander saw appropriate physical form as virtually materializing from function and its surrounding environmental circumstances. Moreover, the anthropological approach, with its emphasis on user sovereignty, and a kind of local vernacular determination, clearly broke away from traditional architectural briefs and programs. Indeed, in Alexander's and others' eyes, the reformation of architecture lay in the subversion of conventional facility programs and in the direction of a much more thoroughgoing analysis and identification of user needs (Alexander 1964, Rapaport 1969).

Shortly afterward, Alexander and his colleagues took another step toward what they regarded as the despecialization of building environments and the empowerment of everyday users. The "pattern languages" that emerged attempted to chart graphically an entire building operation, from the smallest detail through to the most large-scale and basic locational decisions (figure 177). Once again there was a strong behavioral agenda at work and a belief that behavior, correctly described, could generate the most appropriate physical circumstances of our constructed environments. If there was to be a failure in this process, it was from our inability to probe deeply enough into the relationship between environment and behavior and not from the inherent limitations of this view as such. Additions and refinements were made to this approach over more than a decade (Alexander, Ishikawa, and Silverstein 1968, Alexander et al. 1977, Alexander 1979). In addition to Alexander's work there was a strong emergence into architecture of a variety of social sciences, ranging from anthropology to environmental psychology, through which the role of users and their specific requirements was forcefully projected. Today this approach still has an impact, although it is far less a part of the architectural mainstream than it was some 20 years ago.

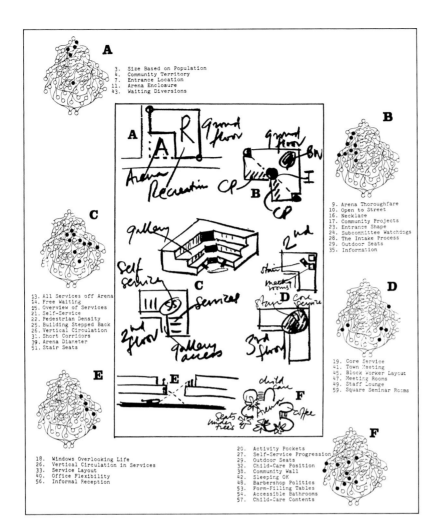

3. Size Based on Population
4. Community Territory
7. Entrance Location
11. Arena Enclosure
43. Waiting Diversions

9. Arena Thoroughfare
10. Open to Street
16. Necklace
17. Community Projects
23. Entrance Shape
24. Subcommittee Watchdogs
28. The Intake Process
29. Outdoor Seats
35. Information

13. All Services off Arena
14. Free Waiting
15. Overview of Services
21. Self-Service
22. Pedestrian Density
25. Building Stepped Back
26. Vertical Circulation
31. Short Corridors
39. Arena Diameter
51. Stair Seats

19. Core Service
41. Town Meeting
45. Block Worker Layout
47. Meeting Rooms
49. Staff Lounge
59. Square Seminar Rooms

18. Windows Overlooking Life
26. Vertical Circulation in Services
33. Service Layout
40. Office Flexibility
56. Informal Reception

20. Activity Pockets
27. Self-Service Progression
29. Outdoor Seats
32. Child-Care Position
38. Community Wall
42. Sleeping OK
48. Barbershop Politics
53. Form-Filling Tables
54. Accessible Bathrooms
57. Child-Care Contents

177
Alexander's "pattern language."

Of a related yet more practical import was the roughly concurrent interest in informal processes of building, squatter settlements, and evolutionary vernacular practices. Most of this grew out of a shift in focus toward the housing and other needs of the so-called developing world, although they also reflected an analogous sense of the needs of blighted inner-city neighborhoods in the developed world. This was particularly apparent in attempts to adopt and develop social and political practices that would both empower user groups as well as aid localized processes of building. Suddenly, otherwise remote deliberations on the third world crossed over into the first world (Turner 1972). Consequently concepts like self-help, participation, and alternative technology made their way into mainstream architectural discussions, as an emphasis on users' rights, autonomy, and a pluralistic perspective on housing began to make an indelible impression.

178
Spontaneous settlements
called *ranchos* on the
hillsides of Caracas,
Venezuela.

At the forefront of the third world deliberations were the painstaking
investigations of John F. C. Turner and William Manguin into the processes
of informal or spontaneous settlement (figure 178), particularly in Latin
America. Beginning around 1968 detailed accounts began emerging about
owner-builders in the *barriadas* of Peru, the *barrios* and *colonias prole-
tarias* of Mexico, and the *favelas* of Brazil (Manguin and Turner 1968,
Manguin 1970). Shortly thereafter a general theory of user control and
production of housing was formulated, one that was to have a far-flung
effect on subsequent efforts by the World Bank and others to adequately
house a substantial proportion of the world's population (Turner 1972,
Turner 1976). At much the same time activists, like Colin Ward in Britain,
advocated an anarchist position toward housing that ran virtually tangen-
tial to traditional approaches from either the political left or the right
(Ward 1976). Generally speaking, such an approach sought a nonauthori-

tarian, self-organizing approach to housing in which the direct users had full control and autonomy. In one such proposal Ward advocated the tenant takeover of municipal housing as the only real means of constructively addressing Britain's debilitating housing problem (Ward 1974). From a fundamental belief in dweller control, the anarchist position quickly advanced arguments toward cooperative ownership of property and away from traditional forms of tenure, as well as emphasizing processes of self-help, self-building, and user participation. Ultimately the position argued that the most satisfactory dwelling environments were those where matters of shape, location, and appearance were aimed at in an unselfconscious, evolutionary manner. Significantly, the examples most often cited were the spontaneous settlements of Latin America, Africa, and the Middle East (Ward 1990).

The Road to Recovery

After what can now only be described as the general housing crises of the late 1960s and early 1970s, when centralized, modern, technocratic housing programs either fell under their own weight or were voluntarily discontinued, the road to recovery ran along two tracks leading in roughly the same direction, essentially in tandem. The first involved local determination and provision of housing, and the second an attempt to expressively recover architectural meaning and appropriateness. Both tracks, to continue the metaphor, ran away from an orthodox modernist position of absolutes, abstractions, generality, and certitude, toward the other side of modernity described in chapter 1, tempered by cultural relativism, an interest in differences, specificity, and localism.

Generally, local determination and provision of housing was often pursued on at least four fronts. The first and most obvious involved local rather than central forms and lines of authority. Housing activities were often dispersed into neighborhoods or, better still, fostered to spontaneously develop and grow there, independent of higher levels of control. Second, local provision invariably involved specific users and user groups, as distinct from abstract, institutional user categories. Housing was to be built around real clients involving their direct participation and requirements. Indeed, many government regulations expressly mandated such participation. Third, housing in many projects was designed for and allocated among heterogeneous groups rather than a singular monolithic constituency. In order to overcome the stereotyping of conventional public housing, for instance, several local programs in the United States and

228

elsewhere required mixed-income occupancy. Finally, local provision often involved a shared responsibility between the public and private sectors in the form of joint developments. With central pools of resources either discontinued or in disarray, many local authorities had to turn to other nongovernmental sources for needed financial support. Often, special-purpose quasi-public authorities, as well as nonprofit private entities, were created in order to fill the growing institutional gaps among housing providers.

Experiences during the late 1960s and most of the 1970s in both the state and city of New York graphically chronicle this devolution of housing responsibility from national to local authorities. As early as 1966 the newly elected Mayor Lindsay embarked upon a major reorganization of New York City's government, out of which emerged a superagency in the field of housing and urbanism called the Housing Development Administration. Invested with wide powers of coordination, this agency primarily set out in the area of housing to tackle the problems of redeveloping public housing projects, particularly from the now infamous days of urban renewal. Not long after, in late 1968, the state of New York legislatively created a special authority with a similar purpose. The Urban Development Corporation, as it was, had sweeping powers and considerable fiscal and operational independence. Both agencies quickly replaced, or rather rechanneled, the traditional federal role in housing. In fact, when President Nixon announced his housing moratorium in early 1973, the Urban Development Corporation had truly become the leader of publicly sponsored housing in New York. Among its many projects the Corporation was responsible, in 1969, for commissioning a plan for an "In-Town New Town" on Roosevelt Island from the firm of Johnson and Burgee. As a part of this project several innovative high-density housing complexes were completed, including the river-facing units of Sert, Jackson and Associates in 1976 (figure 179). Later in 1975 a competition was sponsored, again looking for innovative housing ideas. It was won by Robert A. M. Stern and John S. Hagmann. Also of considerable design interest was the Urban Development Corporation's collaboration with the Institute for Architecture and Urban Studies, and David Todd and Associates, on Marcus Garvey Park Village in Brooklyn (figure 180; Plunz 1990).

Unfortunately, the Urban Development Corporation lost funding and was abolished in 1976, largely ending the era of local yet comprehensive special housing authorities in New York. Similar events occurred in other parts of the United States and, as private interests began to take over, smaller and even more local community development corporations began

179

Roosevelt Island development by the Urban Development Corporation, including river-facing housing by Sert, Jackson and Associates, 1969–1976.

3 Modern Housing in Crisis and Transition, 1970–1980

180
The Marcus Garvey Park Village in Brooklyn, New York, by the Institute for Architecture and Urban Studies with David Todd and Associates, 1975.

to emerge. Operating at or near the grass roots level, these nonprofit organizations acted as conduits for scarce housing resources and provided considerable expertise in coordinating as well as in qualifying local communities for support. Mixtures of public and private sponsorship also began to emerge. What had begun almost a century earlier as either a private or a public responsibility was now vested in a local and, at times, fragile merger. A similar devolution also occurred in several European countries, including Britain and Germany as well as the Netherlands.

The second aspect of recovery from the crisis, involving attempts to recover expressive meaning in the architecture of contemporary housing, took several different forms. At the core of the entire enterprise lay a lack of complete confidence in any one particular expressive direction and a willingness on the part of many either to entertain multiple perspectives or, at the very least, to recognize the limitations of overly privileged positions. Certainly the overriding hegemony of orthodox modernism, in any form, was almost completely dismissed.

One form of expression placed emphasis on the process by which housing was defined, developed, and implemented. In many ways it was an extension of the work by Alexander and others in which local distinction was striven for through local participation. By closely reflecting local forms of construction, habits of dwelling, and other related social mores, bland and reduced forms of modern living could be replaced by a commonplace vitality. In the hands of skillful architects like Lucien Kroll and Ralph Erskine, an almost literal expression of building process could also bring considerable distinction to local housing environments.

A second form of expression placed emphasis on historical contexts and past architectural traditions. Here the aim was to eliminate the modern leveling of spatial distinctions among places by reinforcing local traditions and by providing expressive continuity with past building practices. At the forefront of this movement were to be found neoclassical and similar forms of architectural postmodernism. In the case of the recent IBA projects in Berlin (figure 181), under the supervision of Josef Paul Kleiheus, traditional building and urban block types were adopted and the neoclassicism of architects such as Rob Krier used to establish ties with the past (Kleiheus and Klotz 1986). Similar efforts can readily be found elsewhere, including Britain and France. Indeed, much of the housing in New York's Battery Park City has a similar expressive inclination. At once it conjures up images from past heroic eras, replete with neoclassical iconographic references.

Finally, rationalism in the pursuit of architectural autonomy was used in an attempt to set architecture apart from other influences and, therefore, to reestablish housing in a broader historical context. Rather than being new and simply a reflection of the times, contemporary housing was to reflect, for instance, the time-honored tradition of housing types and the continuing development of longstanding and yet essentially architectural design problems. The work of Aldo Rossi and of Alvaro Siza, as we shall see, admirably reflect these preoccupations.

181
Residential development as a part of the IBA project supervised by Josef Paul Kleiheus in Berlin, 1975–present.

Three Projects in Three Places

Three notable projects represent these various facets of modern housing in transition from the reductive excesses of orthodox modernism. These are the Byker Redevelopment at Newcastle upon Tyne, in the United Kingdom; Villa Victoria in the United States city of Boston; and the Malagueira Quarter in the town of Evora, Portugal. Each is a large project and reflects a significant attempt to deal with the new demands of a rising social pluralism and the expressive needs of local communities. Each is interesting for its architectural distinction, set against the sameness of many other contemporary examples. Furthermore, all three projects have proven to be significant and have materially helped to reestablish a vital role for modern housing.

The Byker Redevelopment in the United Kingdom

The Byker Redevelopment Project, by Ralph Erskine and his many associates, is a bold, sprawling, yet well-composed urban project that proposes a strong sense of community identity in the design of public housing and an architecture based on the *process* of habitation (figure 182). Located approximately one and a half miles from the center of Newcastle upon Tyne, in the north of England, the project occupies about 200 acres (81 hectares) of what was once a deteriorated neighborhood, adjacent to a subway station and a major shopping district (figure 183). The current population of about 6,300 people is housed in some 2,000 dwelling units, ranging in accommodations from one to six residents each. A distinctive architectural feature of the project is housing in the form of an "inhabitable wall"—affectionately known as the Byker Wall—that rises up to eight stories along the northern perimeter of the site, adjacent to the railroad right-of-way and what was once to be an extensive motorway, leading in an easterly direction out of Newcastle. The remaining units, and indeed the majority, are in the form of low-rise terrace and courtyard housing on the downhill slopes of the south-facing site (figure 184), overlooking the River Tyne and downtown Newcastle (Rowe 1988).

In addition to Erskine's own work in Swedish towns like Barberanen and Brittgarden, the architecture of the Byker Redevelopment Project derives

182
General view toward the perimeter block from inside the Byker Redevelopment Project at Newcastle upon Tyne by Ralph Erskine and his associates, 1969–1982.

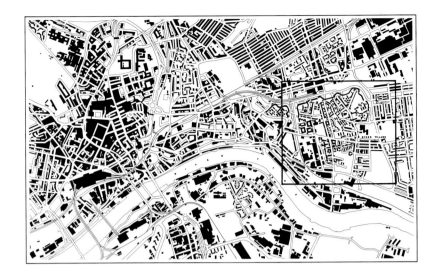

183
Plan of Newcastle upon Tyne
showing the location of the
Byker Redevelopment
Project, 1969–1982.

from several sources, all in one way or another concerned with the expressive potential of processes of habitation. First, there is a clear affinity with the spirit of the garden city, recalling both Howard and more particularly Patrick Geddes. This is particularly apparent in the organic quality of the relationship between dwellings and open space. Second, there is something of Cullen's "Townscape" in many aspects of the open-space design, as well as a certain "off-the-shelf green housery," as one author puts it (Dunster 1979, p. 70). Finally, ideas of building systems, popular as we saw during the 1960s, as well as a changing decorative program that seems to invite modification, play a clear role in the Byker's architectural expression. The work, nevertheless, is far from derivative, remaining distinctive, coherent and, above all, locally responsive. It is, as one commentator said, "one example in England of an architectural response carefully considered and predicated upon the idea that architecture can improve people's lives" (Dunster 1979, p. 72).

The Community and Redevelopment

Originally Byker was a tiny settlement set in a rural area largely owned by the Lawson family since about the seventeenth century. During the early nineteenth century, the settlement both expanded rapidly and was swallowed up by the expanding growth of Newcastle caused by the nearby coal and heavy industries. As the Lawson family sold off plots to local developers, row upon row of small one- and two-story, cold-water terrace houses were constructed (figure 185) at high densities. By the 1880s, Byker was subdivided by a gridiron of lots and steep streets down the hillside, bisected by the main thoroughfare of Raby Street running north-south

184
A variety of housing types on
the hillside at the Byker
Redevelopment Project,
Newcastle upon Tyne.

down the slope to Walker Road near the River Tyne to the south. Significantly overcrowded, the hundreds of four-room dwellings were rented by Tyneside workers, primarily employed in the nearby shipyards and engineering factories. By 1900 the area had five schools, a good variety of shops, including corner stores, and a well-developed network of community facilities (City of Newcastle upon Tyne 1981).

As a community, Byker had no real physical center. It was, instead, a community based upon a street, or a few streets, accumulating into a fabric of associations. With increased development and urbanization, Shields Road, to the northern edge of Byker, became a major shopping and commercial area, a position it maintains today. In fact, between 1950 and 1960 some 200 commercial firms located there, making it a strong local rival to central Newcastle. Historically, most residents of Byker—or Geordies as they are often called—worked and lived in essentially the same environment, while their children went to school nearby and played just around the corner (figure 186). It was, in a phrase, a long-lived and homogeneous community, which in itself was not unique within Britain except perhaps for its persistence and sheer spirit. Among the circumstances that reinforced this prevailing sense of community were undoubtedly a camaraderie fostered by neglect, a large number of older people in the community maintaining social traditions, a congenital neighborly willingness to help one another, and no real generation gap. In this last regard the pattern of life for both young and old was much the same, and from this similarity of experiences and problems sprang mutual companionship and trust (City of Newcastle upon Tyne 1981).

Redevelopment of Byker dates back at least to 1951 when the city of Newcastle upon Tyne, like many other British towns and cities, produced its first development plan around the theme of providing a decent home for every Newcastle family. At the core of the plan was a policy to relieve housing stress by reducing residential densities to at or below 80 people per acre. At that time much of Byker, for instance, had a residential density of 120 people per acre, although even higher densities could be found on Newcastle's poorer west side. The plan of 1951 was followed in 1953 by a local medical and sanitary officers' report citing 10,000 dwelling units in Newcastle as unfit for human occupation, of which 1,175 units were located in the older sections of Byker (City of Newcastle upon Tyne 1981). More specifically, the 1951 census showed that 33 percent of all Newcastle households were without a bath and only 59 percent of all households had exclusive use of all five basic facilities (i.e., fixed bath, piped water, WC, kitchen sink, and cooking stove). Overcrowding was also a severe

185
Row upon row of one- and two-story flats in the old Byker at Newcastle upon Tyne.

186

A street party in Solway
Street in the old Byker, 1918.

problem, even in the aggregate, with 73 percent of larger families living in overcrowded conditions (Burns 1964). In keeping with general British policy at the time, relief from overcrowding and inadequate facilities was to be accomplished through slum clearance and redevelopment, beginning among the worst conditions like Rye Hill and Elswick on the western side of the city center along the River Tyne.

Between 1959 and 1963, Byker came under concerted redevelopment scrutiny, with compulsory purchase orders confirmed in 1963, by which residential and other property was condemned for clearance and redevelopment. Clearance eventually began in the mid-1960s and continued until 1979, although fortunately during the intervening time Newcastle's housing policy, again as elsewhere, was to change quite radically. Instead of a piecemeal approach to slum clearance and redevelopment based solely on characteristics of sanitation and the adequacy of light and ventilation, a 20-year comprehensive approach was formulated to housing policy, resulting in the 1963 development plan. The country's first independent planning department was also formed at much the same time, under a single City Planning Officer. In addition to slum clearance and new building, a key component of the new housing policy was environmental improvement and rehabilitation, marking, as we saw earlier, a turn away from earlier urban renewal programs (Burns 1964, City of Newcastle upon Tyne 1981).

In 1966 the Planning Department produced the document "Byker Neighborhood: Guidelines for Development," making explicit for the first time the intent to demolish and replace or, at the very least, renew all the houses in Byker, commencing somewhere between 1969 and 1971. As with other old areas in Newcastle, the housing stock of Byker had become too small and obsolete for its population due to both rising expectations and increases in household size. Many of the housing units were also too dilapidated to save. Indeed, revitalization was considered but quickly rejected in favor of clearance and redevelopment, primarily because of substandard space standards, inadequate possibilities for proper daylighting, and very poor housing conditions.

Another issue that compounded the task of redeveloping Byker was the planned right-of-way clearance and improvement for a motorway along the northern edge (figure 187), near and roughly parallel to Shields Road. This motorway was seen as a part of the emerging modern plan for Newcastle and required demolition of between 3,000 and 4,000 dwelling units, whose families were displaced to other parts of the city. The problem of vehicle noise along the periphery of the motorway was resolved in 1967 with the suggestion by the Housing Architect of the Housing Committee, the unit of government overseeing redevelopment, that a physical barrier be built to screen the noise. Sadly, given the social displacement that took place, the motorway was never built, the right-of-way later being used instead for a subway. In 1969, Ralph Erskine was appointed as planning consultant for Byker and he and the client, the Newcastle upon Tyne Metropolitan District Housing Committee, quickly confirmed a commitment to "Byker for the Byker People" (figure 188). As we shall see, Erskine also quickly turned the disadvantages of the motorway right-of-way into the renowned Byker Wall, a residential complex and noise barrier combined (City of Newcastle upon Tyne 1981).

The Program and Project

The expressed aims of the Byker Redevelopment Project were fivefold. The first was to produce housing at the "lowest possible cost" and in the "most intimate collaboration" with residents in order to build an integrated living environment in the broadest possible sense. Second, every attempt was to be made to maintain "valued traditions and characteristics

key
A. pilot scheme (Janet Square), south end of site
B. perimeter block, stage 1
C. Grace Street flats
D. Grace Street (low-rise)
E. Kendall Street housing
F. Gordon Road housing
G. Chirton Street housing
H. Dunn Terrace housing

1. St. Michael's Church (existing), center
2. Raby Street school (existing)
3. Bolam Street school (existing)
4. waterworks (existing)
5. Shipley Street baths (existing)
6. Shields Road shopping area
7. proposed bridge link to Shields Road

187
An early plan of the Byker Redevelopment Project showing the proposed Shields Road motorway.

188
A participatory process
embodied in "Byker for the
Byker People."

of the neighborhood," including its relationships with the rest of New-castle. Third, Byker residents were to be rehoused without "breaking family ties and other valued associations or patterns of life." Fourth, the physical features of the site were to be exploited, especially the slope to the south with its fine views and sunny aspect. Finally, the redevelopment project was to be provided with a recognizable form, within which the local individuality of each group of houses could be expressed (Erskine 1968, p. 3)

With these aims in mind a plan of intent was formally prepared by Erskine and his group in 1970 and approved by the city council. Essentially, the plan took the form of a flexible policy document, as distinct from a fixed master plan, and described a "rolling programme" of clearance and re-building with minimal displacement of population at any one time. Under this program the normal size of clearance areas was reduced from 1,000–1,500 dwellings at a time down to 250, enabling most residents to continue to reside in Byker should they wish to do so. The smaller increment of housing also allowed many existing neighborly relationships and other attachments to be preserved (City of Newcastle upon Tyne 1981). At much the same time as planning got under way, a pilot project was produced at Janet Square, in the southeast section of the overall site, to test the housing design ideas. Terrace housing consisting of 46 units was arranged around an open courtyard, in what would become a familiar pattern throughout Byker (figure 189). Intensive contacts and design consultations with pro-spective tenants took place during this pilot phase, lessening the need during later stages of redevelopment. In many respects, Janet Square em-ulated Erskine's earlier Swedish housing projects, as well as aspects of the Studlands Park project in Newmarket, England, of 1969. Here, tightly and loosely defined courtyards provided considerable spatial variety and

189
Terrace housing around open
courtyards within a network
of pedestrian circulation at
the Byker Redevelopment.

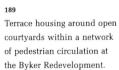

pedestrian zones, surrounded by patio housing. In fact, Erskine's group was not unknown to the Newcastle authorities, having successfully entered a limited competition for Killingworth, a satellite town of Newcastle, in 1969 (Collymore 1983).

Throughout, design and development of Byker was a collaborative effort. Led by Ralph Erskine's Swedish office, the British office at Byker was run by Vernon Gracie and Roger Tillotson from 1969 to 1979, and by Tillotson alone from 1979 until the early 1980s. The Swedish office at Drottningholm included Bengt Ahlquist, Erskine's collaborator on the earlier Killingworth project, Mike Lunett, Nils Viking, and Pet Hederus, among others. The landscape architecture, at least in large measure, was designed by Par Gustavson, Gery Kemp, Arne Nilsson, and Derek Smith. All components of the design team, together with representatives of the Housing Committee, worked on site, out of an office in an old funeral parlor (figure 190), allowing ready and constant contact with prospective tenants. A liaison committee was also established with an open forum chaired by the Byker residents and with representatives of both the institutional client and the design team. More than anything else, this strong presence and connection to the ultimate users helped to significantly demystify the redevelopment process (Rowe 1988).

Actual construction of Byker was divided into six stages, with stages one through five built between 1970 and 1975. The remaining parts of the

190
The old funeral parlor that
served as a site office for the
Byker Redevelopment
Project.

project were then completed between 1975 and 1982. Following the pilot scheme at Janet Square, large sections of the perimeter block (figure 191) were completed, containing 212 dwelling units, with an additional 165 units in the Grace Street section. The Kendall Street complex came next with 214 dwellings (figure 192), followed by the Grace Street low-rise, in the northeastern corner of the site, and the Gordon Road complex, with a total of 239 units. Dunn Terrace (figure 193), providing special housing for the elderly and others, formed the sixth stage, with 264 dwellings, as well as Awondale Road at 135 units. With the scheduled but not constructed Clydesdale and Harbottle portions of the project, the total unit count would have stood at 2,216 dwellings, at an overall density in built-up portions of the site of about 100 people per acre, or roughly 30 dwelling units per acre. All dwellings were provided as rental units, available through the District Housing Committee. Overall, 80 percent of the housing was in the form of low-rise dwellings, and unit plans ranged from one-person efficiencies to six-person apartments. All family units were located at ground level with direct access to exterior gardens and play space (Rowe 1988).

The overall layout of the plan for Byker was defined precisely by the enclosing, undulating wall of housing to the north and the pattern of

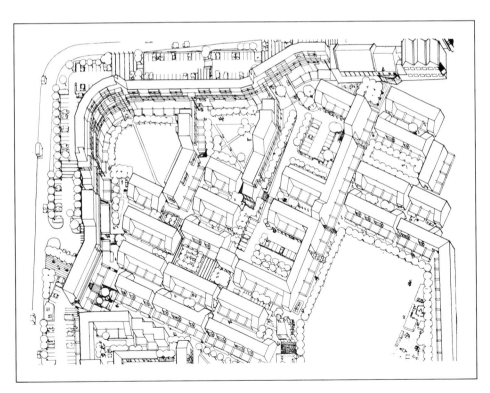

192

The Kendall Street complex
in the Byker Redevelopment
Project.

traditional streets, such as Raby Street, running north to south down the slope. Within this loose matrix a more intricate network of pedestrian pathways was defined, linking adjacent neighborhoods together (see figure 187). All told, housing was divided among 12 residential neighborhoods, each with its local character and range of community facilities. Areas between neighborhoods were also defined by irregularly shaped open spaces, providing ample opportunities for more extensive outdoor recreation. The basic residential component of each neighborhood consisted of either courtyard arrangements of low-rise houses, each with its own garden, or linear terraces of similar units. Some neighborhoods, such as Ayton toward the center of the project, consisted of both configurations. Raby Street, running through Raby Gate, formed the main spine of the project and also provided the principal link from Byker to the Metro and then to the nearby Shields Road commercial center.

Housing at Byker took three specific forms (figure 194). They were the predominant low-rise development, the perimeter block, and the "link blocks" in between (figure 195). Generally, the low-rise housing was arranged either in linear rows of dwellings terraced into the steeper slopes or in courtyard groupings of similar units on flatter areas. Almost uniformly, the low-rise housing had a simple low-pitched roof (figure 196)

193
Dunn Terrace, special housing for elderly and others at the Byker Redevelopment Project.

194
Plans and sections of perimeter, link, and terrace housing within the Byker Redevelopment Project.

and clapboard or sheet siding. Windows were generally organized with respect to internal functional requirements, and extensive use was made of clerestory lighting under the eaves. Balconies, doorways, and pergolas extended the building structure into the otherwise open courtyard space, which was usually paved and generously planted. All family units were two stories in height, organized in a traditional manner, with living spaces on the ground floor and bedroom suites above. All the low-rise housing was built to take advantage of solar orientation, views down the slope toward the Tyne, and the provision of pedestrian circulation without steep slopes for ease of walking, especially during harsh northern winters. Formal variety was also achieved through punctuation of the matrix of low-rise housing with higher-rise apartment blocks, such as the Chevron.

Although it constitutes only about 15 percent of the project's dwelling units, the perimeter block, or Byker Wall, forms the recognizable symbol of the community. From the north, outside of Byker, the wall appears as a continuous, undulating, multicolored patterned brick edifice, punctuated by small windows coinciding with bathrooms, kitchens, and stairways on the interior. The intensity of the brick patterns also increases to mark entries to the site from the adjacent roadway. The territory between the wall and the metro right-of-way is occupied by heavily landscaped

196
Inside the Byker Wall near
the Raby Gate.

car parks. Appropriately, the wall swells out at points where pedestrian crossing is required, such as at the Raby Gate, in order to minimize walking distances to surrounding areas. Apart from forming a sound barrier to the north, the wall also provides a splendid microclimate along its southern aspect, thus turning an environmental problem into a distinct residential asset. Elevators with generous lobbies, stairways, and balconies (figure 197) serve the access needs of residents and provide a complex architectural surface to the southern aspect, greatly helping to reduce the eight-story scale to human proportions. Interlocking maisonette units in the flats of the wall allow bedrooms and living rooms to be located either above or below access balconies, ensuring both privacy and unencumbered views. As mentioned, larger family units are all located on the ground level with generous private garden spaces. Other high-rise buildings in the complex were also constructed at Dunn Terrace, under a distinctive shed roof. These dwellings, however, serve the needs of special population, such as elderly housing.

The link blocks occur where the low-rise housing meets the wall; they consist of maisonettes and flats coming down in scale from four and five stories to two. The link blocks share circulation with the wall through stairs, bridges, and elevators. They also serve to further reduce the apparent scale of the wall from the important southern side, by subdividing it into clear segments along its horizontal length and associating each segment with a sheltered area of low-rise housing, recreational amenity, and open space. Again the facades of the link blocks have an air of informal composition, and yet they are rigorously organized (figure 198).

One of the most remarkable features of Byker is the extent and variety of the open space (figure 199), ranging from large common areas with irregular boundaries to the much smaller private gardens of almost every dwelling. The common areas, in particular, exude a robust, unkempt quality, consistent with walking in the country or playing football. Less successful are the overtly public spaces, such as the paved plaza areas in front of the gates to the wall. By contrast, local seating areas, dispersed throughout the terrace housing, are considerably more effective. As a part of the general strategy of user autonomy, all tenants were encouraged to make their own gardens. Extensive reuse was also made of old elements of the former Byker landscape, such as curbs, carved stonework, flags, and granite (Buchanan 1981).

Finally, community facilities are abundant and, in many cases, preserve existing institutions, with all their local cultural attachments, in place.

197
A generous network of lobbies, elevators, stairways, and balconies at the Byker Redevelopment Project.

There are, for instance, four churches, a YWCA, four schools including day nurseries, two geriatric units, a library, a central community center, and numerous smaller dispersed clubs and similar social facilities. The most prominent facility is the Shipley Street Baths with its tall smoke-stacks and saw-toothed, partially glazed roof (see figure 191). Refurbished back to its prior glory, the baths further reinforce traditional patterns of life, as well as providing a ready source of heat for large portions of the project. The facile incorporation of the baths into the perimeter block also helps to ameliorate the generic quality of the "habitable wall."

An Architecture of Process

To a considerable extent the Byker Redevelopment Project is based on both literal and metaphorical processes of urban habitation. First and foremost, the design of Byker was a participatory process in which the ultimate users' sovereignty was clearly emphasized. It was also a collaborative process among designers and other technical experts, including members of the housing authority. Through weekly meetings of the Byker Officers Group a smooth process of redevelopment was ensured. Extensive on-site design work also greatly assisted efforts toward creative collaboration (see figure 188).

User autonomy, though by no means absolute, received considerable constructive attention. Forward allocation of housing units was made, for instance, six months in advance of completion, thus allowing residents to

198
Informality yet rigorous formal organization of the link blocks at the Byker Redevelopment Project.

199
A variety of open spaces at
the Byker Redevelopment
Project.

make necessary moving plans. Moreover, the allocation process also allowed tenants to pick and choose their units and, therefore, their neighbors. Also, each increment of the allocation process concerned only twelve dwellings at a time, ensuring careful consideration and attention. Once shown where their unit would be located, usually through large axonometric drawings, tenants had ten days to accept or refuse the proposal. Erskine also insisted from the outset that small community associations be organized to look after communal areas, play spaces, common facilities, and so on (Dunster 1979). A "tree bank" was also established in 1973 to further this community function and to provide plants for individual gardens, with significant savings in cost, as well as to foster the initial impact of mature vegetation on subsequent development phases.

On a more metaphorical level, the low-technological, "kit of parts" character of much of the architectural detailing (figure 200) strongly suggested that there was room for modification, and that personal upkeep of property was possible. Even though little has in fact changed (even the original bright color scheme remains), this appearance of a capacity for change was both expressive of the populist ambitions of the project and an open invitation to keep the habitation process going. Moreover the off-the-shelf technology can be associated immediately with the scale of the individual, rather than either the scale of the entire community or the level of some

200
The organic architectural
language of the Byker
Redevelopment Project.

other entity. The resulting part-functional and part-decorative detailing of balustrades, balconies, bridges, window boxes, etc. has clearly sustained, as one author put, "a metaphor of human occupation" (Dunster 1979, p. 67). The organic architectural language of the Byker, without strong boundaries and full of blurred distinctions between buildings and landscape, also makes a strong link with analogous, unselfconscious processes of human settlement. Moreover, the self-help aspect of gardening and outdoor maintenance further blurs usual distinctions between professionals and tenants (Buchanan 1981). Far from being orderless, the loose arrangement and hierarchy of spaces within the project derive unique meaning from numerous special places preserved from the Byker of old. In this manner the process of habitation is provided with necessary continuity to the past but, consistent with the organic analogy, only under terms that are relevant in today's world. Even the habitable wall enhances the process of habitation by providing the icon of distinction for what was already a community that thought of itself in distinctive terms.

Villa Victoria in the United States

Villa Victoria, in Boston's South End, raises interesting questions regarding ideas of architecture and historical contexts. Unlike the formula designs of nearby public housing projects from an earlier era, a deliberate attempt was made to fashion a scheme for a specific group of residents and a place in the city, a scheme that provided continuity with the past, sometimes in unusual ways. Like the Byker redevelopment project, Villa Victoria also involved a broad and well-defined participatory design process, as well as a high degree of user determination. Indeed, it was the first renewal project in Boston to be granted resident control (Schmertz 1978).

Begun in 1969, the present stage of Villa Victoria's development was completed in 1982, under the direction of project architect John Sharratt. The site, in an urban renewal area close to downtown Boston, covers 19 acres of contiguous city blocks, bounded on the north by Tremont Street, a major traffic artery leading out of the city toward the suburbs (figure 201). So far, a total of 736 dwelling units have been constructed, together with a range of office and retail commercial establishments. Today, Villa Victoria is a well-maintained, thriving, and vibrant Puerto Rican community and one that significantly helped establish a new and more sensitive attitude toward urban residential development in Boston.

South End Developments

Like much of Boston, the South End was constructed on filled land, expanding southeastwardly the narrow neck of what was then called the Shawmut Peninsula. Developing slowly during the early nineteenth century, it grew rapidly in the 1850s "into a region of symmetrical blocks and high-shouldered, comfortable red brick or brownstone houses, bow-fronted, high-stooped and with mansard roofs" (Whitehill 1959, p. 122). The area, however, never fulfilled its promise of becoming a well-to-do location within the city, in spite of much solid and handsome building (figure 202). It went into decline even while relatively new, losing out as a fashionable address to the later, adjacent landfill project of the Back Bay. In the 1850s the Roman Catholic church brought institutional development to the South End, where its cathedral still stands today, close by to Villa Victoria. The Boston City Hospital also located nearby in 1861 on a seven-acre tract of land (Whitehill 1959).

In 1960, Mayor Collins founded Boston's Development Program in an attempt to pull the city out of an economic slump that had lasted since 1954, during which only about 5,000 residential units had been constructed. Although the city of Boston continued to lose population, particularly from around the city core, some 26,000 additional housing units

201
Villa Victoria in the general
urban context of Boston.

were built between 1960 and 1966. The low-cost housing inventory, however, was severely depleted from demolitions that had occurred since 1960, and, in spite of promises to place an accent on neighborhood rehabilitation rather than clearance, the federal Department of Housing and Urban Development's plan for the South End Urban Renewal Area of 1965 called for almost total demolition and redevelopment. In fact, almost all the low-income housing was intended to be replaced by upper-income housing and institutional uses. Drastic though this action may seem to be, from the prevailing managerial perspective of the day it was not without justification. By 1960, housing vacancy in the South End, at 11.5 percent of all units, was the highest of any of the federally assisted urban renewal areas in the city, and was almost double the renewal area's average of 5.5 percent. In addition some 55 percent of all dwellings in the South End were considered substandard, again the highest level among the federally aided urban renewal areas. Furthermore, population was declining, even more rapidly than prevailing rates of demolition (Boston Redevelopment Authority 1967).

Over much the same period, a relatively large group of rural Puerto Ricans moved to Boston and settled in the South End, attracted by cheap rents, the state's good welfare benefits, and low-skilled jobs, as well as proximity to others with similar cultural backgrounds (Schmertz 1978). Thus the South End (figure 203), and particularly its urban renewal areas, became a typical port of entry for an immigrant population, as many other areas of Boston had been in prior eras. The North End and East Boston, for instance, had seen successive waves of Irish, Jewish, and Italian immigrants dating well back into the nineteenth century. Even today the pattern continues in several parts of Boston, for similar reasons, although now the immigrants are from the Caribbean, Central America, and Southeast Asia.

In 1968 the plight of the Puerto Rican residents of the South End, in the face of clearance and urban renewal, was taken up by the Episcopalian Church. At first they invited representatives from the nearby Lower Roxbury Community Corporation, by then a well-organized tenant group, to share their experiences in resisting large institutional takeovers of their residences. John Sharratt, the eventual architect for Villa Victoria, was working at that time with the Lower Roxbury group on what would later become the Madison Park project. Sharratt then began working as an architect and advocacy planner for the South End residents, providing both technical assistance and design support (Sharratt 1980).

202
Boston bowfront row housing, 1860s.

203
Aerial view of general development within Boston's South End.

To begin with, Sharratt returned to the 1965 Urban Renewal Plan for the South End, regathering and remapping information on building conditions, land use, ownership, tenancy, employment, and traffic. Based on this new information he then challenged assumptions of the Urban Renewal Plan and the basic argument of use for upper-income and institutional purposes, which was largely based on the close proximity to the downtown. Although the debate revolved around questions of use, the real underlying issue was one of local control and ownership, which the Boston Redevelopment Authority was not ready to accept (Sharratt 1980, 1991).

About the time of Sharratt's initial investigations, residents became organized into a representative group, called the Emergency Tenants Association, later to become the Inquilinos Boricuas en Accion. A plan was then prepared for a 19-acre site in the devastated center of the South End's Urban Renewal Area, covering 11 separate though contiguous redevelopment parcels. The plan consisted of mixed-income housing, some commercial uses, and a public plaza recalling outdoor gathering spaces in Puerto Rico (figure 204). Support for the plan was also elicited from numerous organizations and political figures, many of whom were impressed by its sensitivity to the needs of local residents and the idea of on-site relocation instead of the displacement of past renewal projects. In 1970, after numerous attempts, the Emergency Tenants Association finally received approval for their plan, as well as control and majority ownership of the property. By this time, the political climate had also changed. Mayor White, among others, was clearly mindful of winning votes and treated community leaders as housing advocates in a time of new sensitivity toward resident groups. Today, the residents manage the entire project, including 300 units owned by the Boston Housing Authority, and employ a full-time staff of some 50 residents within a neighborhood priority hiring program (Sharratt 1980, 1991).

A clear influence on the political change, however, was the practicality of the proposed project and its federal and state support. Among the incentives for housing were the ownership of land, under the urban renewal program, the availability of sizable financial grants from the Department of Housing and Urban Development, and the effective reduction of a financial equity proportion to about one percent. This latter incentive was also increased by a prevailing tax law that enabled equity partners to fully deduct 100 percent of their project costs, if the project was for low-income housing. Indeed, each phase of Villa Victoria's development involved sizable government grants and the formation of limited public-private partnerships (Sharratt 1991).

204
Aerial view of Villa Victoria
in its immediate urban
context within Boston's
South End.

The Project

The most significant planning feature of Villa Victoria is the looping of existing streets within the boundaries of the project (figure 205), minimizing through traffic and enabling a pedestrian spine to extend from the community plaza on one end to the large playground on the other. Within the outer edges of Tremont Street, West Dedham Street, Shawmut Avenue, and West Newton Street, the project is relatively introverted. Except for portions of a single block, redevelopment along the busy Tremont Street edge took place within existing structures, with the new development located behind. An urban street structure was still preserved, however, with the front door of every housing unit facing onto a city street (figure 206).

The form and organization of residential blocks owe something to the surrounding context, as well as to a general mandate to provide adequate outdoor open space, especially for families with children. The result is a virtual encirclement of the street edges by row houses, with passages in between leading to ample semipublic areas in the rear, structured primarily as children's play space. Each dwelling unit, as we shall see further, also has its own private outdoor space within this configuration. Initially, Sharratt's block plans for Villa Victoria were criticized by the Boston Redevelopment Authority and others as being too dense for the South End. Admittedly units were small, given cost and assisted-housing requirements, and yet the overall density was only on the order of 40 units

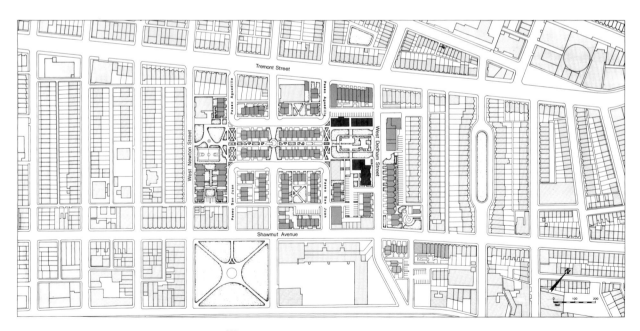

205
General plan of Villa Victoria
in Boston by John Sharratt,
1969–1982.

206
Typical row house
development at Villa
Victoria.

per acre, compared to some surrounding areas where densities reached as high as 70 units per acre (Sharratt 1991).

Planning occurred in six stages, each coinciding with a specific area and type of redevelopment. As at the Byker redevelopment project, on-site relocation of residents was a high priority, and so development phases were relatively concise and incremental. During phase one, 17 apartment units were constructed for low-income tenants, together with 54 other units, through HUD section 221(d)3 funding and the support of a local bank. In phase two the Torre Unidad was constructed (figure 207), an 18-story apartment building primarily for elderly residents, the ground and second floors of which were used for shops and recreational facilities. This was financed through Massachusetts Housing and sold to the Boston Housing Authority. Vivendas La Victoria (see figure 212), a mid-rise residential structure, and some 181 units of townhouses were completed during phase three, along with additional commercial space. Finally, Casas Borinquen, the renovation of nine existing townhouses into 36 apartment units under HUD's Section 8, was completed in 1977 (Schmertz 1978). Subsequently, two additional phases of activity have been completed to round out the residential development to slightly less than 750 units. Of these, 19 percent are studios, 62 percent one- and two-bedroom apartments, and the remainder distributed among larger dwellings, upward to five-bedroom units (John Sharratt Associates 1991).

The three-story row house units that make up most of the project consist of three-, four-, or six-bedroom duplex units arranged over one- or two-bedroom flats on the ground floor. A prominent stoop (figure 208), remi-

207
The high-rise Torre Unidad
in the context of row houses
and a neighborhood park at
Villa Victoria.

208
Prominent front stoops and entry stairs to row houses at Villa Victoria.

niscent of nearby townhouses from the nineteenth century, provides access to the larger upper units, with two units located side by side sharing a single stoop. Front yards in this scheme are assigned to the smaller ground-floor units, while the yards in the rear are linked, again by stairs, to the upper units (figure 209). The ground-floor units, however, do have visual access to these gardens. Beyond the private yards at the center of each block, a common garden and play area was provided. In the case of the row houses on either side of the pedestrian spine down the center of the project, this common space was somewhat more public, taking the form of a linear park. Sometime after completion of this portion of the project, however, the pedestrian link was closed by a series of iron gates and the open space reverted to a common area serving adjacent households, as in other parts of the project (see figure 211).

Construction of the row houses employed light-weight steel frames in combination with masonry load-bearing walls. Stucco exterior surfaces on the upper levels were usually painted in a bright palette of colors and roofs were pitched in a way that depicted individual dwellings, rather than the terrace row as a whole. Finally, the internal organization of each row house unit was around a centrally located wet core of kitchen and bathroom facilities. To the street side of this arrangement was the living room, and to the garden side were the bedrooms. Undoubtedly, this standardization and the relatively small size of units accounted for appreciable cost savings (Sharratt 1980).

Both the Torre Unidad apartment tower and the lower-rise Vivendas la Victoria slab block were clad in dark purple-brown brickwork, with rea-

209
Plan of row house units at Villa Victoria showing the relationship to outdoor garden space.

210
Loggia and gallery access to
housing along one edge of
Plaza Betances at Villa
Victoria.

sonably well-composed facades of window openings and spandrel panels.
Neither structure, though large, appears too bulky for its surroundings,
and the tower provides a point of focus to the community, especially from
the outside. The most significant aspect of this building complex, however,
is the plaza between the buildings, called Plaza Betances. Organized according to traditional Puerto Rican principles, the plaza is paved and has
a central seating area sheltered by trees. Vivid ceramic murals cover surrounding walls, and the outside rim of the plaza is almost fully lined by
a pedestrian arcade under the taller buildings. The shops that line West
Dedham Street at one edge of the plaza (figure 210) also form gallery
access to the townhouses above, in an unusual though successful hybrid
building. During the evening and at other times of the day, the Plaza
Betances is an active and popular space among residents.

An Architecture of Context

The urban design and architecture of Villa Victoria raise several interesting
questions regarding the uses both of history and of surrounding context
in the design of housing. One commentator, for instance, praised the
project for its social and political accomplishments, while simultaneously
criticizing its apparent lack of similarity to what was seen as a cohesive
nearby fabric of nineteenth-century townhouses (Lyndon 1982). In fact,
Villa Victoria is distinctively different in appearance from adjacent residential developments, although it preserves a relatively typical lot and
block layout. Moreover, this difference is hardly casual, nor the result of
a lack of architectural awareness about surrounding areas (see figure 206).
It is, in fact, a work about vernacular tradition and context—though it
rather pointedly raises questions about which context and whose vernac-

211
Row house in a distinctly suburban manner at Villa Victoria.

212
The Vivendas la Victoria and the Plaza Betances offer a cultural double reading at Villa Victoria.

ular. In doing so, it also adheres closely to the original goal of the project, which was, in Sharratt's words "to maintain the individual human dignity of residents" (Sharratt 1980, p. 28).

First, in the choice of context, the design of Villa Victoria can be seen as at least transitional between an urban residential landscape and a suburban model, if not strongly in favor of a more suburban experience. While residential development is dense and in the form of row houses, the figure of each house is articulated in a distinctly suburban manner, with an emphasis on individuality and a sense of private space (figure 211). The appropriateness of this choice lies not in the typical historical dimension of existing surrounding circumstances, but in the aims and aspirations of the residents and their role as a recent immigrant group. Clearly, like many other Americans, the residents of Villa Victoria aspire, at least in part, to the suburban American dream, a physical context of which also exists not many miles away. They are also interested, we should assume, in making their own place in Boston's urban history, much as other immigrant groups have done.

We should also quickly recognize that the South End never really did have a singular, cohesive, urban context of buildings, as Whitehill has observed in describing the almost immediate decline of the South End shortly after its first development (Whitehill 1959). Furthermore, in a contemporary sense, it is difficult to point clearly at any one physical context in the South End as being somehow most appropriate. Rather, the area is a patchwork quilt of more or less distinctive developments rather than a coherent fabric.

Second, the choice of whose vernacular was again decided in favor of the residents' cultural background and contemporary aspirations. In a kind of double reading, we are presented with clear recollections of Puerto Rico alongside the vernacular of a modern American lifestyle (figure 212). As described earlier, the Plaza Betances, the community hub of the scheme, is overtly Puerto Rican in spatial and architectural character. Although not now used, so was the pedestrian *paseo* leading down the center of the project. Contemporary America, by contrast, is reflected in the individuality of houses and private spaces and the general suburban feel of much of the residential neighborhood. Again the issue of appropriateness can certainly be raised. At the time of construction, these aspects of Villa Victoria were no doubt viewed as defiant and vehemently distinctive. Today, amid increasing multicultural tolerance, such a sociopolitical resistance to prescribed images is more likely to be comfortably accepted.

The interesting quality of Villa Victoria is that it raised those questions and maintains that resistance, while simultaneously still performing a useful traditional urban role within the city.

The Malagueira Quarter in Portugal

The Malagueira Quarter housing project, by Alvaro Siza Vieira, provides us with a subtle and complex example of locally responsive architectural rationalism. On the one hand the project is reminiscent of the German *Siedlungen*, in addition to sharing similarities with the work of the Dutch modernist J. J. P. Oud. On the other, at Malagueira there are numerous references to a rich local architectural tradition, historical precedents, and a vernacular heritage. In the end, the Malagueira Quarter has an enigmatic quality that vacillates between modern and locally traditional.

213
The Malagueira Quarter housing project on the periphery of Evora, Portugal, by Alvaro Siza, 1977–present.

Located on the periphery of the provincial Portuguese town of Evora, 140 kilometers (88 miles) east of Lisbon, the project comprises an extensive residential district situated among farmland, informal settlements, and high-rise towers of public housing (figure 213). The site of 27 hectares (67 acres), formerly an agricultural estate, slopes gently down the side of a large hill toward the main road to Lisbon. The development is being constructed in multiple phases and now has close to 1,200 low-cost, single-family units. Individual houses are aggregated into blocks of residential streets, making up several neighborhoods, with units available for either ownership or rental through a housing cooperative (Rowe 1988).

The Context of Evora

A settlement of about 30,000–40,000 inhabitants, Evora dates back to the second century and the time of Roman conquest. Strategically located on a major route across the Iberian peninsula, the early settlement assumed the characteristic *castrum* plan. Over time several major public buildings were constructed, at least one of which survives today. Moorish occupation followed, as well as the royal courts of early Portuguese dynasties. From at least the sixteenth century onward, Evora exercised regional authority (figure 214). Indeed, its perimeter wall dates from the fourteenth century and the town as a whole represents a composite and temporally stratified order, each layer corresponding to an important era in Evora's history. Though having some trade and commerce (figure 215), Evora has remained a predominantly rural community at the center of the Alentejo region (Testa 1984).

214
The old town of Evora,
Portugal: the Praça do
Geraldo.

215
The town of Evora in the
Alentejo region of Portugal,
showing the old wall and a
system of viaducts.

On 25 April 1974 a military-led, bloodless left-wing coup ended 48 years of dictatorship in Portugal and ushered in a new era of development, of which the Malagueira Quarter was to become an integral part. The reasons for the revolution were at least threefold. First, it was a reaction against Portugal's colonial policy, especially on the part of the armed forces and particularly with regard to the African colonies. Second, there was a desperate need for a better life. Portugal was by far the least developed country in western Europe. It had the lowest per capital income, the highest illiteracy rate at around 30 to 35 percent of the adult population, and an infant mortality rate four times that of Sweden. Finally, both agricultural and industrial production were under virtual monopoly control and workers were harshly exploited. Indeed, overall, a handful of powerful groups controlled four-fifths of the nation's wealth (Green 1976).

It was in agriculture, however, that some of the most egregious underdevelopment and exploitation were to be found. With farmers accounting for 40 percent of the work force, significant numbers owned no land. In fact, under the semifeudal latifundia system of land tenure, only 3 percent of the landowners held more acreage than the other 97 percent (figure 216); "many of the huge estates belonged to absentee dukes and barons, or were in the hands of banks, insurance companies and corporations, and were largely uncultivated. The wheat yield per acre, for instance, was 50 percent that of the remainder of Europe" (Green 1976, p. 19). In fact, the Malagueira estate was a part of this system of land tenure until it was

216
An estate in the vicinity of
Evora forming part of the
semifeudal latifundia system.

taken over by revolutionary political forces in 1975 as a part of a widespread land reform. The Alentejo, with its predominant rural base and
strong Popular Communist Party following, was in the vanguard of this
movement.

As one might imagine against this backdrop, both rural and urban housing
conditions in Portugal were often appalling. The infamous *ilha*, or island,
settlements in cities like Oporto were desperate tenement slums. Clandestine or squatter settlements had become a common occurrence in rural
areas, especially close by towns and other sources of employment. Overall,
only 40 percent of Portuguese homes had their own water supply, and
only about 17 percent of the urban population was served by a public
sewage system (Green 1976). Consequently housing reform quickly followed in the wake of the political revolution, starting in the urban slums
but rapidly spreading to rural areas and smaller municipalities like Evora.
At the center of these efforts were the SAAL experiments, described in
chapter 4, which engaged many architects, like Alvaro Siza, working
closely alongside brigades of workers and community groups. The numerous projects that resulted undoubtedly helped establish a new frame
of reference for further housing reform. After the initial euphoria, however,
progress was to be slow and socially painful.

In 1975 the newly elected left-wing government of Evora embarked upon
a plan to integrate the town's peripheral developments into a more co-

herent and rational settlement. Under former regimes, residential, industrial, and agricultural development had sprung up around major roads leading out into the countryside, and on parcels of land in and around the latifundia system. The local area around the Malagueira estate, for example, was a patchwork of disparate residential developments, ranging from unsuccessful seven-story public housing blocks, through clandestine settlements, to an upper middle-class suburb of villas. Also interspersed were small factories along the Lisbon Road, and community facilities such as a large swimming complex (see figure 213). In concert with the public takeover of large agricultural estates (several, for instance, were converted into tourist hotels), the Malagueira Quarter was requisitioned for low-income housing development. Strategically this seemed to be appropriate, given the general direction of peripheral growth out of Evora toward Lisbon. Shortly afterward, in 1977, Alvaro Siza was engaged as the architect and work on the project commenced.

The Project

Instead of having an internally consistent master plan, the spatial organization of the Malagueira Quarter conformed to a seemingly ad hoc arrangement of residential neighborhoods, each focused on immediate local circumstances (figure 217). Moreover, at least initially, the community was deliberately incomplete with respect to its nonresidential functions. Instead, Siza anticipated an evolutionary process of urban growth and change, by which the "fissures," as he called them, between the housing blocks would gradually become filled in over time, "fracturing

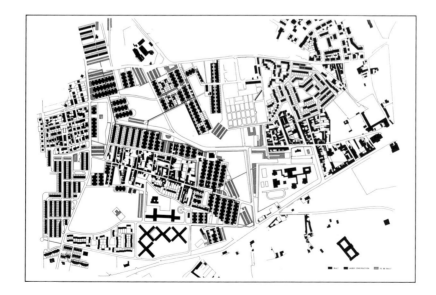

217
Plan of the Malagueira Quarter housing project showing its relationship to the immediate context of existing development.

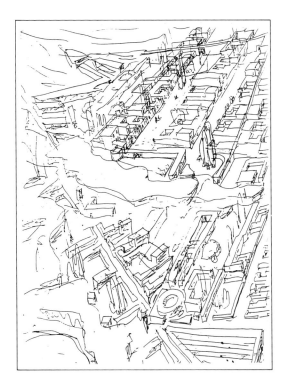

218
Drawings by Alvaro Siza
depicting the evolutionary
process of urban
development at the
Malagueira Quarter housing
project.

the tissue" of the housing in very particular ways (figure 218). "Rome was not built in a day," Siza constantly reminds us. Furthermore, the very idea of instant monuments and special places is a contradiction in terms (Siza 1988). To the extent that overall organizing patterns were at work, an east-west axis was developed within the community, extending an existing roadway leading out from the old town of Evora. A long parallel residential block structure also lent the project an aura of consistency.

Another major spatially organizing device was the monumental two-story masonry structure that channels utilities and forms both a literal and a metaphorical backdrop for the individual dwelling units (figure 219). Clearly reminiscent of the aqueducts that crisscross the neighboring countryside from prior epochs of Evora's development (figure 220), these channels provided a consistent civic presence throughout the project that was greater than could be achieved by housing alone, and provided it with an immediate cultural setting. Furthermore, as others have noted, placement of this structure as the virtual spine around which housing development evolves conveyed a sense of "founding ritual" and a distinct "urban cadastre" for the project (Rayon 1982). This latter point should not be underestimated, given the former use of the Malagueira estate and the

219
Monumental masonry
channels, or viaducts, form a
literal and metaphorical
backdrop to housing at the
Malagueira Quarter.

contemporary need to legitimize an entirely different form of development in the hands of a housing cooperative.

At its edges, where the project meets surrounding developments, Siza has found numerous opportunities to relax the otherwise uncompromising geometry of the long housing blocks. In some places, for example, he has created the opportunity for establishing small neighborhood vegetable gardens and lines of fruit trees. This is particularly apparent along the boundary with the adjacent clandestine settlement. In another instance, a gently curving gravel pathway, which has become such a lyrical motif in Siza's work, runs as a visual counterpoint to the strong rectilinear geometry of the housing blocks, fashioning an edge that also functions simultaneously as a seam with the existing nearby neighborhood.

Approximately 100 dwelling units compose each neighborhood of the project, within which housing is strictly organized into relatively narrow linear blocks with parallel streets. It is not a regular gridiron; neighborhood streets, 6 meters in width, lead on to broader roadways that essentially crisscross the community in both east-west and north-south directions, providing immediate and obvious connections with surrounding areas. Whenever the topography allowed, streets were placed in a manner that enhanced a sense of spatial enclosure and of residential scale. By aligning the streets across the site's undulating landscape, for instance, a slightly bow-shaped cross section was achieved, giving the usually horizontal street surface a slightly upward cant at each end and a strong sense of enclosure (figure 221). This apparently fragmentary approach toward neighborhood development also had the advantage of adapting to the uncertain institutional support for the project likely from an undercapitalized economy. By settling on small neighborhood-sized groupings rather than a grand overall plan, specific site conditions could be immediately addressed in a way that embroidered the overall design. It also allowed the evolutionary pace of development to be met without the appearance of large and obvious vacant areas between uncompleted phases (Rowe 1988).

Siza's innovative use of courtyards facing the street and of second-level patios (figure 222) also contributed to a sense of community space. The latter devices facilitated a more personal manifestation of street life by bringing the house out onto the street, as it were, and vice versa. From the upper vantage point of the second-level patio, neighbors have the opportunity to chat with one another across the street or down into adjoining courtyards, unhampered by what is happening in between and

220
Integration of viaduct and housing within the old town of Evora, Portugal.

221
An enhanced sense of
enclosure from integrating
housing within the local
topography.

outside. At a more detailed level, the Dutch door arrangement that provides access from the street, by opening at the top, also allows free exchange from house to street while still controlling entry and egress. Raising the courtyard slightly above street level architecturally enhanced the modest scale of the housing, and also allowed ready management of storm water from not infrequent downpours. Like much of the Malagueira project, the housing and street cross section provides a basic spatial framework appropriate for day-to-day activity yet allows considerable room for transformation and individual elaboration.

All housing within the project consists of terrace or row house units of one or two stories in height (figure 223). Each residential plot is uniform, measuring 12 meters by 8 meters (39.4 feet by 26.2 feet), producing a net residential density of some 30 dwelling units per acre. Each housing unit is of either of two basic courtyard configurations: one with the courtyard adjacent to the street, the other with the courtyard in the back of the unit. The organization of rooms within each dwelling generally reflects the public and private zones of a house, with living quarters on the ground floor and bedrooms on the second floor. It also reflects prevailing Portuguese rural-urban customs, with the kitchen and its characteristic wood-burning fireplace placed toward the front of the house (figure 224) and a spare room on the ground floor for nonresidential, business-related activities. Architecturally, the housing represents a stark and yet traditionally consistent residential landscape of cobblestone streets, white stucco walls, broad stone steps, sparse fenestration, and pronounced doorways. Against this backdrop, individual expression is usually registered in the paint work of specific houses, shutters, and decoration around windows, as well

222
Two-level patios within
housing units facilitate
community interaction
within the Malagueira
Quarter.

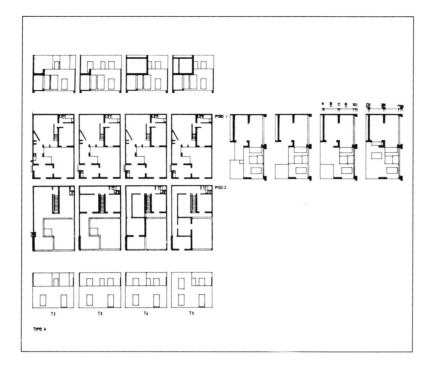

223
Unit plans for courtyard
housing at the Malagueira
Quarter.

as the presence of grape arbors and other planting within the courtyards
and patios. Unlike either the Byker or Villa Victoria, the figural expression
of the housing is almost entirely mute, save embellishments by inhabitants. Formally speaking, however, the project is almost uncompromising
in the rigor with which it presents blank surfaces and strong cubic volumes
(see figure 221).

Nonresidential facilities, such as corner stores, community facilities and
public institutions, are generally located in the spaces between the housing
blocks, usually adjacent to main roads. Typically these facilities are also
located at the edges of residential areas, thus providing easy access from
within each neighborhood and an appropriate meeting ground between
them. This location outside of the stricter orthogonal system of residential
blocks also provides needed flexibility (figure 225). Indeed, again in keeping with a general distinction between the public and private realms of
the community, these facilities are often spatially counterposed to the
matrix of repetitive residential units (Testa 1984).

Unfortunately, construction and management of the Malagueira Quarter
has not been without difficulties. Political infighting, for example, dis-
rupted the process of building and at least one building contractor de-

224
Interior view of a dwelling at
the Malagueira Quarter,
showing a traditional wood-
burning fireplace.

faulted on adequate performance of services, causing further delays and the need for substantial reconstruction. Chronic undercapitalization has also hampered the project, in spite of its extremely low-cost and technologically modest form of construction. In fact, these latter characteristics, when coupled with mismanagement and construction defaults, have in places also hastened the material deterioration of the project (Rowe 1988).

An Architecture of Locally Inspired Rationalism

A remarkable aspect of the Malagueira project is its simultaneous evocation of high architectural modernism and local tradition. A resemblance to the German *Siedlungen* of the 1920s is unmistakable (see figure 221), especially at the scale and in the housing type of many of Ernst May's projects. Adolf Loos's Lido house has also been indicated as a source of inspiration by at least one commentator, and J. J. P. Oud's unbuilt Scheveningen Project of 1917 has similarities, especially in the alternating expression of strong cubic volumes across the face of the housing blocks (Frampton 1982, 1986). In addition, the simple courtyard arrangement and entry condition at Malagueira bears some resemblance to Oud's Weissenhofsiedlung project, with its towerlike blocks arranged orthogonally to the line of the street (see figure 52). Apart from these overt references, design of the Malagueira Quarter also continued Siza's strongly rationalist ap-

225

Spatial variation in the orthogonal arrangement of residential blocks at the Malagueira Quarter.

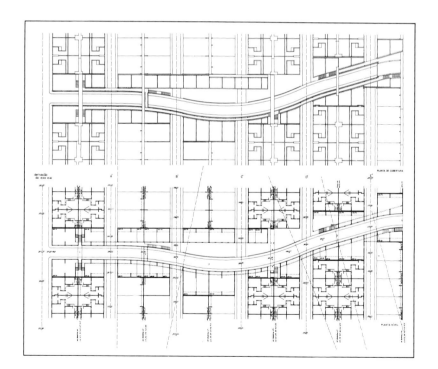

proach from earlier Portuguese projects for the SAAL, such as the collective housing for the Associaçao de Moradores Da Bouça of 1973 through 1978, and the San Victor project in Oporto of 1974 to 1977.

By contrast, the project, though modern, unequivocally reflects the urban architecture of Evora and its region, with its narrow, stone-paved streets lined with stucco walls punctuated by doorways, small openings to gardens, and carefully positioned windows. The Travessa da Caraça, for example, a well-known street in the old town, has much the same character as the Malagueira, including the presence of the aqueduct framing the view down the street (figure 226). There also appears to be a kind of intentional consistency between the traditional townscape of Evora and Siza's obvious invitation to residents of the Malagueira Quarter to elaborate and transform the initial blank walls of the project. In addition, the scale and many details of the project are consistent with adjacent clandestine settlements, not to mention the overt local references in the masonry utility channel to historical nearby aqueducts. The 8 meter by 12 meter lot size, for instance, is close to those of the clandestine settlements, as is the preference for the single-house form.

There is, however, an essentialism at work that goes well beyond matters of style and architectural reference. As several authors have pointed out, Siza seems to draw upon universal and timeless sources in his design of the Malagueira. Reference to Roman town building, the *insulae*, and courtyard houses in the Greco-Roman tradition have been used to trace the antecedents of the Malagueira Quarter back well beyond orthodox modernism (Rayon 1982, Testa 1984). Even without result to these historical analogies there is the feeling at Malagueira of dwelling, so to speak, "in the first instance": of essentially attempting to find a rational and parsimonious basis for community formation. In the end, there is a basic, constitutional quality to the proposal that transcends both the universal impetus of modern architecture and the localism of a vernacular tradition.

At a more practical level, this constitutional quality to the housing serves as background amenable to both domestic and civic life. The residential streets, for example, serve as multipurpose reservoirs of activity, where people go to and from work, children play, men and women gossip, and residents park their cars. The invitation for individual elaborations on the basic design is already evident in the wide palette of window details, shutters, arbors, door details, planters, and decorative tile work that has emerged throughout the project. Clear correspondences were also struck with the old town of Evora, although never by simple repetition. In both,

226
The Travessa da Caraça in the old town of Evora.

227
A time-honored orthogonal pattern of long rectangular blocks establishes a constituent quality to housing at the Malagueira Quarter.

dwellings face narrow streets and use a similar palette of materials, but with very different cross sections. A pattern of long rectangular blocks persists in both cases, although the orthogonal form is far more rigorous in the Malagueira Quarter (figure 227). Views are frequently framed by elements of public building, although at Malagueira it was invariably in the direction of Evora itself as the traditional civic locus of the overall community. Nowhere was the hierarchy confused between city and suburb, or between town center and community place. Moreover, like all good constitutions, Malagueira's has yielded a development both seemingly complete and yet full of promise for future amendments and elaborations.

Finally, unlike many of its modernist counterparts, Siza's scheme for the Malagueira Quarter resists all totalizing influences that would tend to artificially cohere the project into any kind of singular whole. It is clearly recognizable as a place, but simply as a segment of the town rather than something set apart. In place of the more usual overriding sense of spatial organization, specific neighborhoods take cues from their immediate context, avoiding the projectlike label of many other forms of publicly sponsored housing. Over time, and certainly given the companion capacity for civic and institutional elaboration, segments of the project seem likely to become even more distinct and localized in their specific environmental and social circumstances. So much the better; in addition to a semblance of coherence, the power, once again, of a good constitution is the pluralism of expression it can foster. At Malagueira it is the underlying relational structure of regulating themes that is of significance and not the surface manifestations of style or embellishment.

Reformed Modernism

By the beginning of the decade of the 1970s, if not before, the modern system of housing provision envisaged some fifty years earlier had collapsed. In one western country after another, despite obvious national differences and concepts of dwelling, the result was much the same. The modern experiment with housing, largely based on the fruits of the second industrial revolution, had reached a dead end. Although not a failure in the sense of a sharp rending of the social fabric, it was a failure nevertheless, as a profound lack of confidence set in regarding the ability to comprehensively manage urban affairs and to plot the course of future events.

In the architecture of modern housing two rather substantial shifts in orientation began to occur. First, the universality and constancy of earlier modernism's progressive vision of the world was altered dramatically in favor of a discourse about the very process of change itself, which in turn could lead in the direction of more heterogeneous future possibilities. Essentially, the stasis of the modern progressive projection of a living environment as an agent of change gave way to a concern for the process through which other less well articulated alternatives might be reached. Second, there was a fundamental shift in thinking about the scope of reasonable housing provision. This was not so much a lowering of expectations, although that often happened also, as it was a more realistic reckoning with the sheer complexity of the issues involved. There was, for instance, a clear and unequivocal withdrawal from omnibus approaches under which large areas of cities and large segments of urban affairs were depicted and managed. In a kind of back to basics movement, a strong preference was voiced for local initiatives and specific projects.

This reformation of modernism, for it can probably be called that, produced an architecture (as demonstrated at least partially in the last three projects) that seemed simultaneously to recognize new aspects of the space-time dimension of dwelling environments and the not unrelated need for user autonomy. Indeed, one could even say that self-determination and housing for people were embodied in the very architectural substance and expressive capacity of a reformed modernism: an architecture in which what was being depicted took on a renewed importance.

228
The promise of change in the Byker's kit of parts.

More specifically, two emphases or directions emerged, as alluded to above. The first was an interest in the representation of change and the concomitant possibilities of difference that could be wrought. The second was an interest in place, locale, and context, primarily as means of establishing a stronger sense of cultural continuity with the past.

As we saw in the last three examples, the representation of change as the subject of architectural speculation could take on several different complexions. At the Byker Redevelopment, for instance, the very promise of change was clearly represented by an architectural kit of parts (figure 228). Even if the kit of parts was not actually operable, the depiction could certainly have the effect of turning general discussion toward notions of change and, by implication, toward the crucial question of self-determination. Moreover, it entertained the prospect of such change both at the level of the collective and at the level of the individual home occupant. By almost direct contrast, the architecture of the Malagueira Quarter presented a blank canvas, so to speak, a necessary framework that seemed to invite embellishment and transformation (figure 229). Throughout, there

229
The Malagueira's blank canvas inviting embellishment.

appears to have been an underlying assumption that whatever the future shape and appearance of the residential neighborhoods might be, they would certainly differ from the original form. Somewhat less obviously, perhaps, the architecture of Villa Victoria presented a dialectical set of images that pointed in the direction of social change. Local row house vernacular and allusions to suburbia combined to both address present aspirations on the part of inhabitants and suggest a continued pattern of social mobility within the mainstream of American life (figure 230). In all three cases, a preoccupation can be seen with articulating the *process* of changing the community, and hence with providing a sense of local empowerment.

A concern for the substance and representation of change, in lieu of the projection of some future vision of the world, is also clearly evident in the indeterminacy of the projects. In at least two cases, the Malagueira and the Byker, incompletion, especially of the more public realm, was a deliberate strategy. Room was set aside within and between the dwelling environments for future accommodation of public facilities, community areas, and needed sections of infrastructure. At work was also a clear recognition that the temporal frame of reference for the public realm is usually larger than for individual private developments, where far less consensus and deliberation are required. The provision of such room for renegotiating can have the effect of empowering inhabitants through the prospect of future change in their dwelling circumstances, and making possible a sense of solidarity from having arrived at such decisions. In neither case, however, was the prospect of future change left unbounded. A broad frame of reference was provided by initial stages of development. To do otherwise would have run the risk of conceptually aligning the prospect of change with the far more disquieting conditions of uncertainty, disorientation, and alienation.

A reemphasis of place can also be seen in these examples that clearly departs from earlier modernist doctrine. The architecture of Villa Victoria, especially in its row house form, prominent front stoops, and extensive brickwork, clearly established a link to the modern context of Boston's South End. Within the project there was also an attempt made to create around the main plaza a sense of place specifically related to the culture of the residents. At Byker, the extensive preservation of long-time institutions and institutional settings instantaneously established a matrix of places with special significance, even though the remainder of the project was almost entirely new. The steadfast resistance to social displacement and the deliberate maintenance of neighborhood ties and attachments during the relocation process also helped to quickly cohere a familiar sense of belonging, if not of place in the literal sense of the word. Finally, at the Malagueira, although less literally than in the other two examples, constant references were made to the traditional form and environs of Evora.

These examples suggest two general approaches to providing a sense of place. One is by way of direct reference to past institutions or elements of the local context, for example by actually maintaining the institutions in place, or by the deployment of iconographic references to a particularly significant local epoch. The other and perhaps more robust approach is the use of a heterogeneous text of local references. Here the diversity seems to offer an increased likelihood of a sympathetic reception. It also allows any invidious and perhaps unforeseen symbolic distinctions between particular temporal and spatial references to be conveniently blurred.

The results of this reformation of modernism have the potential for a thoroughgoing reaffirmation of tradition in its most culturally productive sense. It is no longer the strictly bioptical view of tradition seen solely by virtue of, or by contrast with, a new vision of the future. The inherent notion of *bringing across*, so crucial to tradition as a form of guidance, no longer relies upon the contrast between past and present practices and those of some different set of conditions, whether the latter are rooted in the past or in the future. Such a use of tradition is essentially open-ended, allowing the character of future habitable environments to remain indeterminate and, therefore, subject to later sustained negotiation by users. It is also less universal by remaining firmly anchored, so to speak, in a specific place and prevailing cultural circumstances.

230
Villa Victoria: row house tradition yet allusion to suburbia.

4   Situating Modern Housing Architecturally

The universality of modernity is undeniable. What were once insurmountable barriers of custom, creed, natural surroundings, and superstition are now readily transgressed by television images, flights in jetliners, and the contents of soft-drink machines. Being convincingly in one particular place for any length of time is becoming difficult. Conversely, however, the full import of cultural and geographical differences was probably never fully realized until well into the modern era. Understandably, it was in the attempt to breach sociocultural barriers that the real nature of those differences became clearer to us. Moreover, in spite of considerable alleviation of human need, at least for some, the effort to bring people closer together and to treat them similarly has had a reverse effect. Most have clung tenaciously to their traditions, striving to identify more precisely those attributes that make them distinctive yet also allow them to reap the benefits of the modern world. Not surprisingly, contemporary housing reflects both faces of modernity: an inherent facility for uniform provision and a renewed call for diversity. Of primary importance, however, is its capacity for symbolically projecting more than the mere rudiments of dwelling. What is required is to ensure that people feel they can reside in a specific locale, a certain place, and, in short, can be at home.

In what follows, various dilemmas and paradoxes for the architecture of contemporary housing, brought about by conditions of modernity, will be examined in detail. In each section an attempt will be made to show how a particular paradox might be resolved, resulting in six underlying principles for the design of good modern housing.

Being and Becoming

One paradox of the modern era is that the closer in time circumstances are pulled together, the more distant becomes our experience of them (Ricoeur 1974). The undermining of indigenous building traditions by global practices, for instance, clearly places psychological distance between the built environment and local inhabitants (figure 231). Simply put, their environment is less familiar to them than it might otherwise have been. Flows of foreign capital on the world market tend to react internationally; as Frampton has clearly shown us, they are often used in ignorance of local building traditions and ways of making architecture inexpensively yet well (Frampton 1983, 1990). In Heidegger's terms, becoming, that dynamic and perennially future-oriented dimension of our lives, overcomes being, the place-specific, inherently situated aspect of our existence (Heidegger 1962).

Of equal concern is any contemporary tendency to slide into parochialism. Concerns for present custom and the local situation can be so strong that all sense of future opportunities from the outside is discouraged or disregarded. Building practices and architecture stagnate. Prospects for real reform wither and, worse, the desire to move forward expressively dies altogether. Being, in short, stifles becoming.

Architectural ways of resolving this dilemma should begin by symbolically referring away from the ever present, toward either a foothold in the future or an anchor in the past. Today, however, assertions regarding the timelessness of buildings seem difficult to substantiate, as we saw in chapter 3. Even within the most restricted conditions of a tectonic ontology—the stuff of buildings—one can still be unclear about the precise temporal niche of the technology concerned: does it make a backward reference toward craft or a forward one toward high technology? Fortunately, there are a number of plausible architectural strategies by which time's tendency to expressively impede the making of meaningful spatial and temporal distinctions can be symbolically arrested.

231
The contemporary dilemma of placelessness: an apartment complex on the outskirts of Frankfurt-am-Main.

The most straightforward way of dealing with the dilemma of the ever present is to securely anchor a work of architecture in its historical context—to find a way of establishing cultural continuity with the past. Fortunately there are several ways of designing that make good use of the past in order to temper modern time's tendency to symbolically homogenize space and nullify its familiar connections.

Among reasonably complete reuses of the past are various forms of revival, such as neoclassicism. For instance, Ricardo Bofill and the Taller de Arquitectura's contemporary housing projects of Le Viaduc and Les Arcades du Lac, built between 1974 and 1978 at Saint-Quentin-en-Yvelines on the outskirts of Paris, both monumentally deploy neoclassical themes and motifs. Indeed, the historicist form and sheer scale of the monumental archways and cornice lines (figure 232), among other elements of the buildings, distinctly convey the idea of palazzi for middle-class wage earners, as one observer put it (Dixon 1981). Behind this lavish formal surface detail, however, is a system of construction that is both highly sophisticated and efficient. Planning of the projects is straightforward and functionally rational. Apartments range in size but generally conform to French mass housing norms. In the end, the thoroughly revivalist interest in classicism is confined largely to the facades of the buildings and to the overall symmetrical composition of the housing blocks and their situation within the site surroundings. Unfortunately, here the extreme monumentality of the housing is least convincing, as it threatens to overwhelm intelligible integration of domestic architecture with other special functions for which a sense of monumentality might be more familiar. In these regards it fails to be as convincing as Pouillon's much earlier complex at Climat de France, with much the same monumental intentions.

Another way to reuse the past is by local emulation, either of the surrounding context or of historically significant buildings in the area. Many rehabilitation and housing infill projects, especially within traditional precincts of cities, closely emulate an existing neighboring context. Indeed, within specially designated historical districts emulation can be legally demanded, resulting in high degrees of exactitude. Affected buildings are usually either copies of what is around them or replicas of what was there before. The present residential circumstances are quite literally reconstructed from the past.

232
Neoclassicism and
monumentality: Le Viaduc at
Saint-Quentin-en-Yvelines by
the Taller de Arquitectura,
1974–1978.

Although revivalism and emulation clearly bring forward architectural norms and values of the past, at least superficially, they also do so selectively. Rarely, if ever, do the resulting projects present an enlarged historical survey of the architecture of an area. A specific period is chosen as somehow most appropriate for contemporary circumstances. Generally, it is a period of architectural distinction or a suitably heroic moment in a city's past. The sociocultural references are not casual and are usually selected precisely because they have the capacity to influence the symbolic direction of contemporary cultural enterprises.

The symbolic expression of American single-family homes, for instance, well illustrates such historical appropriations and the ideological purposes to which they can be put. Drawing upon two heroic moments in the American past—the colonial period of the eighteenth century and the time of the western frontier—the majority of American housing, although otherwise very modern, takes the outward form of either the colonial revival or the western bungalow and ranch house. Symbolically both command broad social understanding and respect, although with potentially different associations. The colonial revival, drawn largely from the history of the eastern United States, is perhaps most closely associated with solid respectability, social stability, and cultural continuity with earlier European beginnings. By contrast, houses drawn from the western frontier myth seem to emphasize informality, noble simplicity, and a progressive spirit (Rowe 1991).

233
American revivalist low-cost housing: Lewis Courts in Sierra Madre, California by Irving Gill, 1910.

In the arena of mass housing, a specific American revivalist example that effectively draws on both heroic themes is Irving Gill's Lewis Courts in Sierra Madre, California (Scully 1988). Constructed in 1910, slightly before the era of this book's central concern, Lewis Courts was a low-cost housing project strongly recalling the Spanish colonial architecture of the region— a legacy at once linked to the western frontier and to one branch of America's colonial European heritage. The square site was bounded by three streets, with the entire housing complex located toward the perimeter, surrounding a communal court (figure 233); the whole was extremely well planned. Housing units, although attached, are also separated by commonly held terraces, and each has a private outdoor garden. Without exception the intricate pattern of private and communal outdoor spaces forms a seemingly natural complement to the Spanish colonial architecture. Like that of the much later revivalist projects by Bofill, the construction of Lewis Courts was highly industrialized, emphasizing a prefabricated tilt-wall system. Unfortunately, strong market acceptance of the project pushed rents well above earlier affordable targets, much to Gill's chagrin (McCoy 1960).

Apart from offering their inhabitants a sense of familiarity and, indeed, pride, these historicist design strategies raise important issues of authenticity by the manner in which they connect the architectural and historical present to the past. For example, despite the ennobling polemics of the gesture, Bofill's and others' decisions to house middle-class wage earners in neoclassical palazzi may well be seen as a dubious papering over of the real contemporary structure of social power and continuing disparities among social classes. More generally, dwelling as if in another time brings with it symbolic responsibilities, and the meaning of the historicizing depends on its purpose. It may be one thing if it is a case of benign self-indulgence, or if it constitutes a logical part of a larger social enterprise, such as historic preservation, but quite another if it is a part of a broader apparatus for superimposing and maintaining social class distinctions.

Architectural traditions can also be deployed more selectively in dealing with the symbolic temporal dimension of contemporary housing. Probably the three most widespread strategies are eclecticism, quotation, and the use of type. In contrast to strict forms of historicism like revivalism, eclecticism draws from and combines various schools and design traditions. As in revivalist architecture, however, the selection of sources becomes important here. The very Greek root of the term means "to pick" or "choose out," conveying a sense of orchestrating from among a suite of alternatives, or of rearranging well-known architectural elements to convey a new sense of meaning and of place. Once again it is through the symbolic associations of historical and otherwise familiar references that architecture resists the complete hegemony of the modern present.

Quotation, a more limited application of borrowed architectural elements, has similar characteristics. However, rather than confecting an architecture from several known aesthetic orthodoxies, quotation is used more sparingly, like quotation in a written text. Like eclecticism, it often serves to confirm by appealing to another, presumably authoritative source, or to illustrate and connect by reference to some other example. Siza's Malagueira project quoted simultaneously in several directions. The street courtyard walls, with the variation of one- and two-story blocks behind, are clearly reminiscent of Oud's objective, aesthetic, and formal rhythms in the Ocean Boulevard Apartments proposal of 1917 (figure 234; Rowe 1988). As noted earlier, Siza also borrows elements from the nearby vernacular housing tradition of Portugal's Alentejo (Testa 1984). In fact it is precisely this bioptical vision, as it were, of the new by backward symbolic reference to the modern, and the present by parallel symbolic reference to the local, that makes the outward appearance of the Malagueira ultimately so appealing.

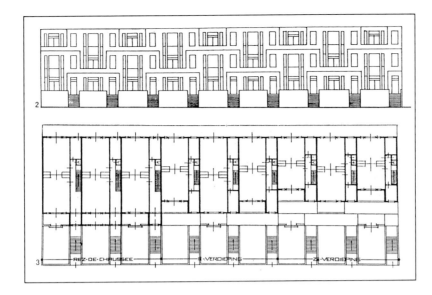

234
The Ocean Boulevard
Apartments proposal by
J. J. P. Oud, 1917.

In architecture as elsewhere, type is a venerable topic. The relationship of the one and the many, inherent in the idea of type, has been a subject of contemplation for centuries (Hirsch 1967). It is the capacity to maintain key features of an object in some essential and replicable way across numerous variations that makes the concept so useful in architectural design (Rowe 1987). To say that two buildings are of the same type means that, despite superficial dissimilarities, their spatial organization or formal composition is fundamentally the same. As a corollary, one can use an existing type as a model for a new design proposal without the risk of imposing irrelevant details. The row house, to use a common example, has many specific forms, both old and contemporary, but with very finite underlying organizational ideas.

Some authors differentiate between different typological procedures. Aymonino, for instance, distinguishes "stylistic and formal" types from those that are "organizational and structural." He, and others, also see types as existing in dialectical relationships with each other (Moneo 1978, Aymonino 1985). The relationship between housing types and urban form, for example, is not a constant. Housing types are clearly influenced by the prevailing and surrounding form of urban areas, and vice versa. As a strategy for dealing with the contemporaneity of modern housing circumstances, type can offer comfortable familiarity in the layout and surrounding of dwellings, at the same time insinuating changes in the urban form of an area. Ernst May's Römerstadt, for example, clearly did both, estab-

235
Modern housing for a
modern democracy:
El Silencio in Caracas,
Venezuela, by Carlos Raúl
Villanueva, 1942–1945.

lishing a new form of design for the urban periphery, within otherwise familiar surroundings for the inhabitants (Lauer 1988).

A large-scale project in which both quotation and typal arguments were used to splendid effect is El Silencio in Caracas, Venezuela, of 1942 to 1945, by Carlos Raúl Villanueva (figure 235). Built at the beginning of Venezuela's modern democratic period, during a moment of sociopolitical optimism not unlike that of Römerstadt and Frankfurt-am-Main under the Weimar Republic, El Silencio covers what became seven city blocks and contains some 780 large apartments and 200 commercial stores (De Sola Ricardo 1987). Although its architecture is unabashedly modern in most respects, the grand ground-floor portals and the surrounding arcade quote from earlier Spanish colonial examples (figure 236). In addition, moldings that project beyond the flat white surfaces of modern facades recall similar architectural devices, again in a Spanish colonial context at local coastal towns like Coro and Choroni. Well-composed, symmetrical facades, especially facing Plaza Urdaneta, and an axis with Torres del Centro Simón Bolívar also evoke a neoclassical grandeur entirely befitting the location

236
Quotation of the Spanish
colonial tradition at
El Silencio in Caracas,
Venezuela.

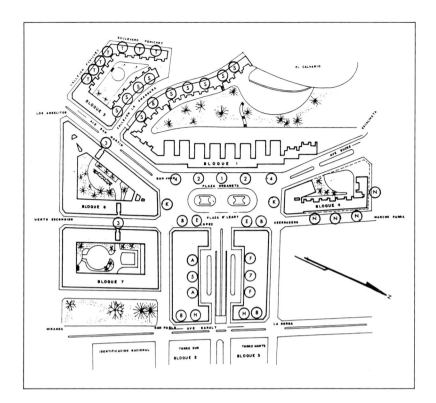

237
Overall plan of El Silencio in
Caracas, Venezuela.

(figure 237). Typologically, most buildings are modern slabs and several form perimeter blocks, reminiscent of earlier modern European and American examples. Individual dwelling units extend fully from back to front and are served, two to a floor, by internal stairways (figure 238). In an interesting juxtaposition of building types, the modern slab raised *sur pilotis* was merged with the traditional commercial arcade. The result is a vibrant residential and commercial environment that is architecturally well situated in both time and space.

Present-Future Ways of Making Architecture

An alternative way of spatially and symbolically dealing with the dilemma of the ever present is by extending a sense of the present toward the future. Instead of establishing familiarity through tradition and the past, architecture can seek to define the future, offering guidance about what's ahead and a certain sense of destiny. Both strategies situate dwellers, placing them conceptually in a certain time and place, if for no other reason than that they offer another temporal vantage point on contemporary conditions.

In principle there are two broad ways of extending the architectural present toward the future. One is by evolutionary extrapolation from present circumstances, whether actual or symbolic; the other is by making a radical break with both the past and present. The latter includes, by definition, strictly utopian proposals, whereas the former expresses varying assumptions about knowledge of the future (Mannheim 1936). Depending on how we choose to view the topic, a particular example may fit into either category. From the vantage point of looking forward in time, the *neue Sachlichkeit* architecture of the Weissenhofsiedlung, Kiefhoek, and Römerstadt may be interpreted both as a matter of timely necessity and as a form of extrapolation (figure 239). New but available materials and construction techniques were applied, essentially projecting present circumstances forward. Alternatively, from the vantage point of the past the *neue Sachlichkeit*, with all its new technology, can be seen as a radical symbolic shift away from earlier traditions and, therefore, a utopian experience. Indeed, as pointed out in the first chapter, this kind of distinction commonly divides discussions about avant-gardism in architecture. The stance being taken here, as earlier, is that architectural developments did not move in a manner that was drastically independent of broader sociotechnical and economic conditions. Consequently, a strict utopian position in Mannheim's terms was never really achieved and, while certainly imaginable and interesting in its own right, is largely irrelevant to this discussion.

As for extrapolation, it may have the past very much in mind, as in the continuation of vernacular traditions, or it may be based on present circumstances regardless of the past. We have already mentioned the architecture of the *neue Sachlichkeit* as a form of extrapolation deeply rooted in present technological and social developments. Römerstadt, for instance, was experimental, a way of palpably projecting the then-current thinking of Ernst May and his colleagues on how to solve a pressing housing shortage. It was a demonstration of what the future could be like, rationally harnessing new but reasonably well-developed planning and construction techniques. By being specific in both social and architectural terms, a claim was also being made that the near future could be known and determined.

238
Dwelling units and exterior play space at El Silencio.

239
An architectural look into the future: apartments by Mart Stam at the Weissenhofsiedlung in Stuttgart, 1925–1927.

240
Informal settlements with formal aspirations: the Granjeno Colonias in the Lower Rio Grande Valley, Texas, 1983.

Similar claims can be made for progressive forms of vernacular housing, although from a position that is usually much more deeply rooted in the past and also part of a mainstream. By and large, the vernacular is not experimental but rather more closely wedded to local building practice. In fact, it is the distinctly regional nature of most vernacular traditions that is advantageous in resisting the homogenizing influences of modernity, and hence a source of future possibilities. One rather extreme example can be found among the colonias of United States border communities with Mexico, although here the building style says less about resisting the temporal destruction of spatial distinctions than it does about aspirations to be in another place (figure 240). Briefly a colonia is a poor, inadequately serviced, neglected, and predominantly Mexican-American settlement of detached houses, which are often the first residence for immigrants coming across the border (Lyndon Baines Johnson School of Public Affairs 1977, Fernandez 1989). In appearance, these houses invariably imitate a perceived Anglo-American style of building, far removed from vernacular traditions on the other side of the border. In an already unstable world of labor-capital relations, from a colonista's point of view the symbolism of the dwelling provides an important and even crucial sense of social stability and arrival, albeit within a still-foreign land. Here the purpose of the imitation is much the same as in many other American single-family dwellings described earlier. It attempts to legitimize otherwise less than adequate conditions.

Many aspects of Sharratt's Villa Victoria complex in Boston's South End also constructively fall within a vernacular tradition, although the interest of the scheme lies in the forward projection of that tradition. First, the vernacular tradition drawn upon is not one to be found locally in the South End. Rather, the majority of the housing follows a distinctly suburban pattern of distinguishing individual housing units and of building at what appear to be spacious densities. The basic house type, however, is common to the South End, taking the form of a simple two- and three-story row house. Second, while the careful arrangement of units along streets is very much in a Boston housing tradition, the internal use of back spaces as communal garden and play areas is not common. This site strategy gives further spatial emphasis to the strong collective spirit of the place, at least during its early stages. Third, at a more detailed architectural level the reinterpretation of the row house front stoop, as we saw, was effectively to bring a stronger architectural character to rather modest dwellings.

Erskine's Byker Redevelopment, in spite of many of its peculiarities, also fits within a progressive vernacular tradition. The choice and detailing of the row houses on the hillside (figure 241), for example, takes on a suburban interpretation, as at Villa Victoria, but within a relatively high-density scheme. Furthermore, it is once again the details of doorways, external storage areas beside each unit, and the like that fashion connections at Byker to a vernacular tradition, but in new and often improved ways.

In addition to the architect's or planner's vision of the future, housing can be designed to accommodate (or at least seem to accommodate) actual modification on the part of the occupants. The modifications may be evolutionary, with the shape and appearance of housing changing incrementally over time, or they may occur more haphazardly and extemporaneously. In the first instance there is a sense that a guiding force, as it were, is at work, while in the second there is not. Both typically involve the actions of individual agents, namely homeowners or tenants, and both are largely reshaped by those actions. Neither, however, is simply a matter of a social building process waiting for completion.

241
Progressive vernacular in hillside housing: the Byker Redevelopment in Newcastle upon Tyne, England, by Ralph Erskine et al., 1969–1978.

The way in which sites-and-services projects become added to and change over time is a clear demonstration of an evolutionary practice at work in housing. Regular plots of land are laid out and provided with basic utilities and streets. From this basic framework dwellings are constructed in a rudimentary and sparse fashion at first, and then often with considerable sophistication and density (Caminos and Goethert 1976). The logic behind sites-and-services programs is that final outcomes are free to evolve, based on local circumstances. At the same time, a certain amount of control and predetermination of these final outcomes can also be exercised. Perhaps the closest analogy is to a biological process of growth and change, whereby an organism evolves but within a prescribed ecological niche.

Megastructural projects have often had a similar orientation. Moshe Safdie's extraordinary demonstration housing project in Montreal harbor of 1967, called Habitat, certainly neither allowed nor required the level of user autonomy embraced by sites-and-services projects. Nevertheless, at Habitat we were presented with an intricate system of interlocking dwelling units, garden terraces, and other housing components, which strongly insinuated a capacity and even an invitation for subsequent negotiation among inhabitants over shared turf and additions to the accommodations originally provided. Scully is correct when he likens Habitat to an Indian pueblo (Scully 1988). The comparison would seem to go further than merely one of image, however, and into an inherent idea about the social contract of building housing in an individual yet cooperative fashion.

In work that seems to combine evolutionary practices with strategies that make allowances for extemporaneous future changes, John Habraken sketched a broad proposal for individual dwellings within what he called "support structures." Simply put, "a support structure is a construction which allows the provision of dwellings which can be built, altered, taken down, independently of others" (Habraken 1972, p. 60). It is of roughly the same functional order as bridges, viaducts, and roads; conceptually, it forms the platform on which building plots are located and where dwellings are erected and inhabited. The proposal is evolutionary because certain broad stages of possible development are determined, and building outcomes, although likely to be highly varied, all flow from preestablished technical procedures, in this case from prefabricated elements. The proposal has an extemporaneous aspect in that specific dwellings can change and even disappear spontaneously, at the will of the inhabitants. No doubt the general appearance of such a system of dwellings and support structure could be ad hoc and unpremeditated.

242
The kit-of-parts aspect of the
Byker Redevelopment
Project.

Erskine's Byker Redevelopment also possesses an ad hoc visual aspect, especially in the kit-of-parts quality of many of the architectural details like stairs, balconies, porches, and even cladding materials. It looks as if parts can be changed and moved around at will (figure 242); there seems to be great potential for extemporaneous modification. Further, the project seems to invite expressive projection of all future changes onto its facades and into its community spaces. There is, nevertheless, a strong underlying rationale to the scheme and it is precisely the organic, architectural language of the project—with its hybrid forms of masonry and timber construction, simple building envelopes, distinctive balconies, and bold silhouettes—that blurs normal boundaries between original architectural deliberations and subsequent user transformations. The overall result is an unusual capacity for appearing simultaneously "populist" and yet architecturally predetermined. Detailed inspection, however, reveals that little seems to have changed from the original design. It just *appears* as if a process of user transformation might have taken place, thereby implying both a ready-made past for the project and a future direction for consideration by residents (Rowe 1988).

Tempering Being and Becoming

As many of the more complex examples presented thus far well illustrate, the potentially most appropriate strategies for designing modern housing are those that expressively accommodate both time and space. Although much of the discussion has revolved around the issue of symbolically and architecturally overcoming the ever present in modernity (i.e., of allowing being to temper becoming), the reciprocal expressive tendency must also be resisted. Revivalism and certain forms of slavish emulation, for instance, run a grave risk of symbolically fixing the present almost entirely within the past and of offering very little room for future cultural progression. Misuse of vernacular tradition only for its picturesque qualities, for example, can result in just such an outcome. More flexible and, indeed, practical design strategies, like the use of quotation and typological arguments, are inherently more permissive, establishing an expressive anchor in the past yet not encumbering efforts to design buildings oriented to the future. Becoming, in short, must also be allowed to temper being.

There still remains a question, however, as to whether a purchase on the future can create a heightened sense of being well situated in the world. Certainly like an anchor in the past it can create, conceptually speaking, a vantage point from which the present can be appreciated. But without the obvious advantages of tradition and familiarity, architecturally conveyed by vernacular expression and selective uses of the past, it is less clear that a sense of place, so vital for dwelling, can be created quite so readily. Indeed, most of the successful housing examples described thus far employ some form of past reference, even if only in a weak sense.

There are, nevertheless, several conditions through which concepts symbolizing the future can be used advantageously to create a strong sense of place. After all, if the site and surroundings of a place are embraced by inhabitants with confidence and enthusiasm, as at Römerstadt, it hardly matters if its symbolic references are more toward the future than to the past. In due course, acquaintance, knowledge, and appreciation will bring familiarity and a clear relationship with the present. This process is probably likely to be more didactic than visceral, but the outcome will be a viable dwelling place. Similarly the symbolic trace left by evolutionary and extemporaneous practices, which allow the future to be projected on the present, can also be didactic. If the architecture is not immediately familiar, as at the Byker Redevelopment, it can certainly intrigue and invite speculation. From that speculation may also come closer acquaintance and a corresponding sense of familiarity. Furthermore, the expressive trace of architectural production in evolutionary projects can almost instantaneously create a historical record and, therefore, a sense of a past.

In the final analysis it seems modern housing is less a matter of appropriate symbolic references to past or future or, for that matter, to some localized present condition. What is required is the expressive creation of a sufficient sense of place and of dwelling. Undoubtedly the past has been used with considerable vigor as an appropriate image and style for contemporary housing. Contextualism and historicism have gained a high degree of popular and professional appeal in recent years. Indeed, complete or selective uses of the past can be very effective in giving mass housing a familiar and human face. This, however, need not always be the case. At other times we have also turned to the future, fed up with the excesses of the past, in order to secure a better place to live. In short, to return to Heidegger's terms, good modern housing should always temper becoming with being, and vice versa.

Open-Endedness and Predetermination

Another contemporary dilemma in the design of housing is the balancing of individual expressive and programmatic freedoms with sufficient architectural standardization for projects to be practical. Essentially it is a matter of flexibility, although of two kinds. First, while a degree of programmatic and spatial open-endedness is undoubtedly a desirable feature of modern housing, there must also be sufficient architectural predetermination to achieve an immediate sense of permanence, and to provide architectural guidance for subsequent developments. Second, flexibility applies to the conception and early development of housing, where it suggests a balance between self-determination on the part of prospective inhabitants and technical decision making capable of exploring useful options. Flexibility, therefore, is an aspect both of the architecture itself and of an interactive process of design used to produce it.

Constituent Design Qualities and Strategies

A useful way of resolving the inherent tension between an open-ended and an entirely predetermined architecture is by analogy to the idea of constitutionality. As a form for organizing states, constitutions prescribe the necessary and sufficient principles for guiding citizens' freedom of action. In essence, they spell out the fundamental nature of the state and the principles for which it stands. When applied to housing, the concept suggests constituent qualities for dwelling, to which others may be subsequently added. Much as a political constitution sets out self-evident truths and universally held principles of social action, so the corresponding constituent properties of housing may represent bedrock principles for dwelling.

Attempts to explicitly articulate constituent properties of housing, however, usually result in vague and all-inclusive qualities. Enclosure, for example, is a property of all dwellings and, no doubt by definition, a constituent feature. Such a general characteristic, however, provides little further information. We can certainly speak of various degrees of enclosure (complete, incomplete, or partial) and forms of enclosure (heavy or light).

Any or all of these properties, however, can be rendered in numerous ways; overly abstract definitions provide little real architectural guidance. Fortunately, just as there are intermediary institutions and doctrines involved in the interpretation of state constitutions, analogous sources also exist for housing.

243
Habraken's "support structures": an SAR housing project at Lunetten in Utrecht, the Netherlands, 1971–1982.

As a first distinction, Habraken's "support structures," described earlier, clearly divide housing between "dwellings"—the domain of the individual household—and "supports"—the service and infrastructural responsibility of government. Habraken's formulation of the idea of supports was a reaction to the uniform, standardized, large-scale blocks of housing produced in the Netherlands after World War II. Development of this "mass housing," as he called it, misunderstood the real promise of advanced building technology and failed to establish a "natural relationship" between people and their environment (Habraken 1972). Within such a relationship, as dwelling needs change so can the housing (figure 243). As Habraken put it, "dwelling is building" (Habraken 1972, p. 18), a process and not simply a thing. Furthermore, by being mindful of the problem of averages, such a process must be individually directed. Consequently, it is the variety inherent in the assemblage of machine-produced building components that is of significance and not the standardization.

Here, as elsewhere, Habraken turns things around (Habraken 1972, 1985). Rather than seeing the constituent qualities of housing guiding and controlling the shape of dwellings, much as articles of a state constitution control lawmaking, he sees the day-to-day dwelling needs as controlling the essential environmental relationship. Indeed, Habraken appears to see no need for intermediaries between dweller and dwelling, reserving the functions of that role largely for the dwellers themselves. Moreover, it is a role that he regards them as performing instinctively.

In subsequent developments, the Dutch SAR (Foundation for Architectural Research) rigorously investigated basic questions of shelter provision, although rarely embracing the more symbolic and expressive aspects of housing. Consequently, there was always a need for upward translation, as it were, from these basic considerations into architectural form. Little guidance was offered beyond a still very conceptual framework. Only later did Habraken turn to a less first-principles stance toward architectural design, incorporating historical and traditional forms of knowledge (Habraken 1985).

A richer although not necessarily more fundamental source of guidance for the design of housing is the use of prevailing architectural conventions. Local building practices evolve over time and usually include common characteristics considered indispensable for good housing, whether aspects of plan and layout or the composition of facades or window detailing. A knowledgeable though cursory perusal of most places quickly reveals a pattern of such practices, although they are rarely, if ever, formally codified.

To return to first principles for a moment, the idea that dwelling is about shelter and maintaining one's body is intrinsically bound up with the idea of dwelling as a space to be occupied and, therefore, engaged by the body. From this it follows that design of dwellings translates bodily functions, together with the directness of experiencing an external environment, into a conceptual commentary or language about the body. Seen in this way, then, architectural conventions of the kind under discussion are widely held and habitual concepts about the body, rather than being about the body itself in a more direct sense. Furthermore, it is precisely this additional removal from direct bodily experience that sets conventions apart from the earlier first-principles formulation of dwelling. Here a reliance is placed on accumulated knowledge rather than upon empirical testing and theoretical speculation.

An inherent advantage of time-honored ways of dwelling and building housing is the lack of need for much translation. Reasonably complete guidance is offered and already in the language, so to speak, of architectural form. It is a matter of obeying easily understandable tacit rules of design and construction. The problem, however, is that such a conventional way of building may also be limiting, and not simply in an expressive sense. There may be a need, for instance, to build housing at a scale and density largely unknown to conventional means. As we saw earlier, there may be technological changes that require more than simple adoption of current housing practices, and here tacit rules are of little use.

More normally, however, like many other social practices, dwelling conforms to established patterns, where the potential conflict between architectural predetermination and open-endedness is relatively slight. More often than not, empowerment is more an issue of autonomy than of some other radical change. Except for the symbolism involved, it seems unlikely, therefore, that those who are newly empowered would immediately seek to invent entirely novel dwelling conditions. As we saw, even with the rise of socialism and the *neue Sachlichkeit* in Weimar Germany the program of accommodations for a house was not radically changed. On the contrary, emulation of some current or past practice, even if it is from some other sector of society, seems the more likely direction. Architecturally speaking, open-endedness, therefore, has reasonably narrow limits in a world of conventions, making a case for building explicitly and well.

Again the Malagueira Quarter serves as an interesting illustration (figure 244). First, the project has simultaneous senses of being complete and incomplete. The bold cubic volumes and ever-present visual datum of the infrastructural viaduct form the basis of well-made row houses situated on well-made streets. Nevertheless, the project also exhibits a clear understanding of likely subsequent architectural transformations. In comparison to nearby informal settlements, with a relative profusion of decorative detail around windows in the form of shutters and in pergolas, etc., the Malagueira seems like a broad white canvas, awaiting if not completion then some further broad brush strokes. It is at once determined and yet at the same time open to receive another round of local particularization.

The consideration of dwelling as social practice brings us to a further consideration of type and typology (figure 245). In fact, both the use of prevailing architectural conventions and the use of building types closely parallel one of Max Weber's general forms of social practice, namely "traditional action" (Weber 1947). According to Weber, traditional action is "carried out under the influence of custom and habit, [and] the meaning

244
The bold visual datum and cubic volumes of the Malagueira Quarter project in Evora, Portugal.

245
A clear example of house
type: row houses on Coleman
Street in the Dorchester area
of Boston.

of action is derived from ideals or symbols" (Giddens 1971, p. 153). The
parallel is particularly compelling when we also recall the eighteenth-
century architectural theorist Quatremère de Quincy's statement that "the
art of regular building is born of a preexisting source," that preexisting
source being the idea of type. Furthermore, "the word type presents less
the image of a thing to copy or imitate completely than the idea of an
element which ought itself to serve as a rule" (Quatremère de Quincy
1977, p. 148). Indeed, architectural types are less complete buildings
worthy of emulation than they are implicit rules of spatial organization
and architectural composition to be followed.

The advantages of type in this context of flexibility and architectural open-
endedness are reasonably obvious. First, a type can provide fundamental
guidance for housing design activity, but without predetermining the entire character of the final form. It is an essential yet only partial set of
rules. Consequently, typal arguments can be employed with an assurance
that final outcomes will remain open-ended. Certainly the degree of open-
endedness will depend on the typal arguments employed. The high-rise
slab building, for example, offers some degrees of design freedom with
respect to vertical access, double- rather than single-loaded corridors, and
building length. However, once certain choices are made, the remaining
organizing principles are usually well determined. The row house building
type also offers some degrees of design freedom (figure 246), although it
too carries constraints. Fortunately, if we return to the earlier argument
about just how much unencumbered design freedom is necessary or even
desirable, the usefulness of types can be more fully appreciated. Moreover,
the inherently higher degree of generality makes the use of type more

flexible than many other forms of architectural convention. The exception, once again, is clearly that new situation, like the railroad station in its day, for which no type had yet been invented (Frampton 1980).

User Sovereignty by Degrees

The tension between architecturally open-ended and predetermined forms of housing also dramatizes underlying differences and an ultimate complementarity between user sovereignty and technical expertise. Open-ended processes, incorporating high levels of user participation, usually allow for individually initiated modifications and accommodations to be made within an overall building process in a nondisruptive fashion. Predetermination of the architecture, on the other hand, represents the best judgment of technical experts about what is in the users' best interests. Naturally enough, various forms of architectural patronage exploit one or other or even both positions in this relationship. Under what might be called a normal model, clients generally define their needs to an architect,

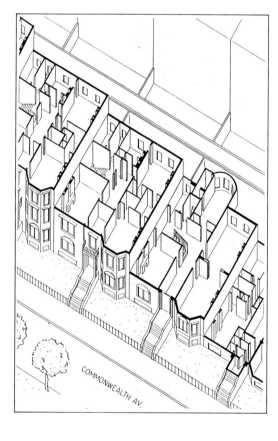

246
Spatial organization of the row house type: a nineteenth-century example from Boston's Back Bay district.

who then initiates a concrete proposal that becomes the basis for further discussion between the two parties, and so the process continues. Under ostensibly more politically liberating processes, users gain an increasing share of the conceptual design process until, under some versions of the process, technical experts become merely the facilitators of lay people's consensual processes (Goodman 1971, Kaplan 1973).

One obvious advantage of user sovereignty is that basic programmatic and design needs are likely to be met, at least for the user group directly concerned. The results for other, subsequent users may also be satisfactory, although such longer-term conditions cannot be guaranteed. Generally, the more specific and peculiar the requirements the less likely they are to meet with broad and lasting approval. The custom-made house, for instance, usually appeals to a fairly narrow clientele, especially when its design, layout, or program of accommodations breaks new ground or does not coincide with prevailing architectural norms and tastes. Nevertheless, across most housing requirements, consensus among otherwise diverse user groups is likely to be reasonably high.

Another advantage of design processes that confer high degrees of user sovereignty is avoidance of a cultural superimposition of values by well-meaning though misguided technical expertise. In the provision of low-cost housing, where decisions are made so often by one group of society for another, this can be an important issue. In Frankfurt's Praunheim housing estate, for instance, Ernst May and his colleagues deliberately installed the efficient though small Frankfurt kitchen described in chapter 2. This step was not immediately appreciated by the low-income tenants, many of whom were from rural backgrounds and vastly preferred the less efficient although far more convivial communal kitchen, where everyone congregated to cook and eat or simply to talk (Kauss and Reininger 1988). Similarly, in nearby Römerstadt and in several other modern housing estates in both Frankfurt and Berlin, residents accustomed to using large pieces of freestanding furniture found the relatively open layouts and built-in cabinets to be awkward (Lauer 1988). The first instance, at Praunheim, was clearly a case of members of one social group attempting to make another group conform to their way of living. The second instance was less a case of disparities among social groups, for they were all middle-class, as it was of traditional versus new ways of arranging a dwelling. In both instances, however, values were either assumed or superimposed by the designers concerned.

During the 1920s, designers consistently had trouble imposing collectivized open spaces and facilities outside of individual dwellings. At Spangen in Rotterdam (figure 247), for example, the allegedly "un-Dutch" character of Michiel Brinkman's complex and the communal aspect of almost all facilities met with opposition. There were also fears, apparently, that the gallery access to the upper maisonette units of the project (figure 248), as well as to the accessible flat roofs, would lead to loitering and dangers of a "moral character." These criticisms were then summarily dismissed by A. Plate, director of the Rotterdam Municipal Housing Agency, and by various socialist aldermen, both parties eager to forward the cause of collective housing (Groenendijk and Vollaard 1987). Similarly, most success was met in Ernst May's Frankfurt experience with the use of private outdoor spaces and allotment gardens. Today there is a noticeable difference, in places like Hellerhof, Heimat, and the Lindenbaum Siedlung, between communal outdoor areas and private gardens. The former are minimally maintained and sparse, whereas the latter are exuberant, varietal, and carefully nurtured. Subsequent developments at Sunnyside, New York, also resulted in a diminution of interest and support for community spaces as compared to private gardens (figure 249). Understandably, perhaps, this trend became more marked as the population of the complex became more heterogeneous (Kwartler and Havlicek 1984).

247
The Spangen project in Rotterdam by Michiel Brinkman, 1919–1922.

A third advantage of user sovereignty in the housing process is the provision, through direct involvement, of a sense of empowerment and self-determination. Rather than forcing them into a narrow acceptance of accommodations that were simply provided, user participation made the process of housing choice for less fortunate groups closer to that of people who commission their houses to be built, or who choose from among a range of marketplace alternatives. There was a sense of involvement, of personal investment, and most important, of autonomy. Within limits, there were genuine choices to be made.

Habraken's and the SAR's concept of "supports," to return to an earlier example, affords extensive user sovereignty over the housing process. In fact, it virtually requires potential households to make numerous decisions about their dwellings. With a basic structural framework and network of utilities, dwellings are assembled, conceptually anyway, as if from kits of parts. In one of the few large-scale applications, an estate of some 5,600 dwelling units was constructed, between 1971 and 1982, in the Lunetten sector of Utrecht in the Netherlands (figure 250). Nine separate housing associations and their membership participated as a joint venture, and extensive discussions were held with the users at all phases of the building

248
Gallery access and
maisonette units in
Brinkman's housing project
at Spangen.

process (Groenendijk and Vollaard 1987). Today the housing estate reflects this diversity of user impact, with a considerable number of different building types and an even greater degree of variation within each type.

On the other side of the relationship between user sovereignty and technical expertise, there is constantly a need for architectural knowledge and an ability to make housing convincingly. There are undeniably "expert" aspects of modern housing design, development, and provision. Most potential residents, for instance, are unlikely to be aware of the full range of housing choices available to them. While there is considerable comfort in housing that is familiar and well known, making a clean break with the past is difficult without considerable architectural knowledge. Residents of the Byker Redevelopment, for example, wanted precisely that— a discontinuation of past dwelling patterns. For them, their old and familiar houses were substandard and symbolically repugnant. They needed someone to help create an alternative dwelling environment with only certain existing community facilities remaining in place (Erskine 1981).

A lack of technical knowledge about building can also prove to be economically debilitating. Tried and true practices may indeed not be the most economical, especially during periods of rapid technological change within the building industry. In a strong critique of the self-help position on user autonomy, the geographer-economist Rod Burgess makes the point that low-technological building practices may well prove to be socially misplaced. Moreover, in a world where labor is already specialized, the aggregation of multiskilled individuals, required by many self-help and self-build programs, not only seems unlikely but also inappropriate (Burgess 1982). Even the construction of relatively straightforward American

249
Private gardens at Sunnyside,
New York, 1986.

tract houses was revolutionized during the early 1950s by the advent of vastly improved management procedures and a series of sweeping technical innovations (figure 251; Eichler 1982). Undoubtedly without these technical improvements, the housing circumstances of many Americans would have been far less satisfactory. Except in perhaps the most confined of material circumstances, perpetuation of the technical status quo is rarely, if ever, the most socially progressive policy for housing.

The ability to conceptualize the future architectural potential of housing is also particularly important when dealing with groups for whom there is a reasonable presumption of upward social mobility. Again the need to live in changed and better residential circumstances, as at the Byker Redevelopment, requires special design assistance of a kind that usually goes beyond technical experts serving merely as facilitators of lay people's consensual process. Even in the most politically liberating environments, architectural knowledge must keep pace with personal senses of empowerment.

A good example of this balance between self-determination and technical wherewithal to conceptualize the future took place under Oporto, Portugal's, now defunct SAAL declaration (Servico de Apoio Ambulatório Local) of 1974–1975. Under the provisions of this organization, local "technical assistance brigades," as they were called, worked with local inhabitants of poor urban areas to conceptualize, coordinate, and promote housing reconstruction projects. Operating essentially as a decentralized process, they initiated something like 174 projects in just a few years, involving as many as 41,758 families (Costa 1978). In the skillful hands of architects like Siza, Ferrera, Fernandez, and Ramalho, strong modern housing complexes began to emerge in various parts of the city. Siza's

250
An SAR housing project at Lunetten in Utrecht, the Netherlands, 1971–1982.

251
Improved management, technical innovation, and layout of American tract housing.

252
The Bouça housing project
built under the SAAL
declaration in Oporto,
Portugal, designed by Alvaro
Siza, 1975–1977.

128-unit Bouça project (figure 252), for example, built between 1975 and 1977, is a bold and sophisticated architectural work, well in advance and considerably different in design from the former, speculative *ilha* housing that it replaced. Unfortunately for many of Oporto's inhabitants, SAAL's operations were suspended in 1976, coinciding with a downturn in the popular urban movement that rose to the fore at the beginning of Portugal's recent revolution, and the resumption of housing provision by more traditional governmental institutions (Costa 1978).

Finally, in a related manner, the task of constantly offering a progressive cultural interpretation for housing would appear to remain largely in the hands of designers. It is not simply a matter of the accumulation of various building modifications proposed by a lay public, for that is usually only an expression of trends set firmly within a preexisting paradigm. To be sure there are often popular components involved. For example, the roofs, arcades, and plazas of Villa Victoria in Boston (figure 253) are clearly recognizable as local cultural motifs. Nevertheless, substantial and systematic shifts to new forms of housing, or to radical changes in the outward appearance of housing, tend to follow architectural disciplinary norms. The durable row house type, for instance, and the newer maisonette cross-sectional arrangement of apartments were both matters of architecture first and foremost, rather than the spatial resolution of external economic or technical forces. Moreover, the cultural authenticity of architecture essentially resides within the same autonomous realm. In the end, good modern housing always balances a programmatic and corresponding spatial open-endedness with an essential sense of architectural predetermination. The flexibility to respond to future conditions and local peculiarities is certainly required. However, there must also be sufficient architectural predetermination to achieve at least an initial sense of permanence and placedness.

253
Roofs, arcades, and plazas as
recognizable local motifs:
Villa Victoria in Boston by
John Sharratt, 1969–1982.

Redundancy and Precision

A common criticism of many modern housing projects, especially those thrown up during postwar booms on the outskirts of European cities or under the auspices of public agencies in the United States, is the desolate and nondescript character of available outdoor spaces. Too often the territory between dwellings lacks landscape quality and is unspecific in its subdivision and tenure, invariably becoming a behavioral no-man's land. The ambiguity in both ownership and supervision is usually acute, except when spaces are either clearly public or private and fenced off as such. Predictably, resulting levels of physical care and maintenance in the more ambiguous spaces are often extremely low. Furthermore, even when the issue of control becomes clearer, there can be a generic character to the appearance of the outdoor realm of housing projects that bears the imprimatur of budgetary constraints and bureaucratic provision. Often, little consideration, for instance, seems to be given to surrounding local circumstances. A modern dilemma in the design of mass housing, therefore, is how to avoid generic architectural qualities and a monotonous sameness, but still retain the necessary systematic characteristics required for economies of scale and egalitarian provision. Furthermore, in transcending those generic architectural qualities, conformance between the spaces that are created and the uses to which they are put must be both direct and manageable.

Creative Architectural Redundancy

By clearly going beyond the basic prescribed program of uses and accommodations, especially with respect to spaces lying within the communal and public domain, an effective level of creative architectural redundancy can be introduced into a housing project. Particularly when local themes and concerns are involved, this creative redundancy becomes a way of extending the design of housing beyond generic and nondescript origins. It is a way of enriching the communal and public spaces that are so often vital for a housing project's identity and for the practical amenity of its inhabitants. Even when the generic character of a project's origins is well founded, some form of creative design redundancy is a way of diminishing the universality of an architectural style, and of symbolically moving the project into specific local circumstances. Usually the result is to expressively connect the project to its surroundings and to give it distinction. Orthodox modernism, for instance, has many associated meanings, and modernity itself gave rise to strong metanarratives about our surroundings and our lives. Undercutting the starkness and generality of this presentation is a way of appropriately anchoring housing into the experience of its immediate cultural and physical environment. In short, it achieves the sense of placedness and permanence necessary for homes.

In all of the projects discussed in chapters 2 and 3, some measure of creative architectural redundancy was apparent. At Römerstadt, on the outskirts of Frankfurt-am-Main, for example, the very name of the estate ("Roman town") reflects the fact that the project site was occupied in antiquity by the Roman settlement of Nidda, which in turn gave its name to the adjacent river (Risse and Rödel 1987). Ernst May and his colleagues clearly took advantage of this circumstance and the need to deal with the topography of the river slope by creating an extensive flat plinth for the housing estate, with a large retaining wall (figure 254). In outline the plinth, retaining wall, and intermediate staircases allowing public access to lower levels closely resemble the battlements of a walled town. Other references to the original settlement of the site are also unmistakable in street names (e.g., Am Forum) and in the designation of specific housing blocks, such as at Hadrianstrasse. A similar local historical reference was made by Alvaro Siza in the viaduct-like structures of the Malagueira Quarter.

Kiefhoek and the Byker Redevelopment, by contrast, make no overt references to the historical circumstances of their sites, but achieve a certain level of creative architectural redundancy through the programmatic and urban-architectural deployment of nonresidential facilities. In the Netherlands, a nation that until recently was characterized by *verzuiling* or denominational segregation, Oud's inclusion of the Hersteld Apostolische church in the scheme for Kiefhoek was an effort to clearly establish an appropriate and unique sense of community (Barnouw 1940, Groenendijk and Vollaard 1987). At the Byker Redevelopment a similar emphasis was placed on existing local institutions. As we saw, many existing community facilities were either left in place or restored and expanded for a renewed role in the community. Both at Sunnyside and at Villa Victoria, in the United States, remnants of earlier developments were also preserved and restored, although in both instances creative redundancy in the open-space planning was perhaps better expressed through the invention of special places. At Sunnyside it was the well-marked rectangular common

254
Plinth and retaining wall
conforming to topography
and echoing an old Roman
town at Römerstadt,
Frankfurt-am-Main.

garden courts, and at Villa Victoria the plaza with its prominent surrounding loggia (figure 255).

As may be surmised, this idea of creative architectural redundancy does not entail the provision of incomplete spaces waiting for others, as it were, to fill in the blanks. It is not simply a matter of spatial oversupply, or a redundancy of accommodations in a general sense. The unfortunate experience with such incomplete places shows that they often remain unfinished, unused, uncared for, and vacant. On the contrary, the concept of creative redundancy requires a rationale, or, to use a literary analogy, a story line. It involves an architecture that can representationally signify a narrative that links the present conditions of a dwelling environment to some meaningful, broader, yet local cultural context. Aspects of such projects may well be multiuse, or may change function from time to time.

255

Prominent plaza and loggia
at Villa Victoria in Boston's
South End.

Nevertheless, they must be architecturally complete and specific. Otherwise their significance will be misunderstood and quickly lost.

Another advantage of such architectural specificity is the immediate direction offered for the use of community spaces by inhabitants. It can be
well argued that a certain amount of architectural predetermination, given
that it can be voted up or voted down by dwellers, is vastly preferable to
a blank slate to be filled in later. At the very least, attention is focused on
the outdoor public realm of a housing estate and people can become
actively and enjoyably engaged in the inevitably process of transformation.

A sense of completion, even if it is only momentary, is also crucial for
good housing projects, particularly in settings of relatively high social
mobility. The appearance of housing clearly in the process of completion
is now seldom convincing. During more socially cohesive times, the Lev-
ittowners of New York and the *Siedlungs-Bewohner* of Frankfurt may well
have been able to foresee verdant, well-paved avenues through their shared
optimism, amid minimally serviced lots. Today, without quite the same
bond of a pioneering spirit, the promise of a collective landscape is likely
to be far less palatable.

In the Malagueira Quarter, for instance, Siza was well aware of the combined needs of an instantaneous sense of the past and a monumental,
civic dimension to the project that transcended the aggregations of dwelling units (figure 256). He also clearly realized that such ideas must be
represented in architecturally specific forms—the viaducts and small plazas, for example—and that the general idea must be complete, but without
being finished in all its inevitable details (Siza 1988). In short, a civic

narrative was provided in sufficient architectural detail to both invite and guide further public installations as the project grew and matured.

Local Design Narratives

Within the representational realm of modern housing, appropriate local narratives for perceptually grounding projects in their environment would seem to derive from two primary sources: local history and tradition, and place-making aspects found at the site. In many cases there would seem to be an overlap between the two, but the latter category largely concerns geomorphological site conditions rather than cultural references. In either case, the process of local narrative begins with insights or particular understandings we might have about a place. It is precisely by noting how things are built in one place versus another that we gain some knowledge about them as locales. By reversing the process, logically speaking, we can also exploit what is known and peculiar about a place for practical building and dwelling, in order to further diminish the otherwise generic qualities of modern housing.

Probably the most widespread architectural use of historical references is concerned with the commemoration of events that took place in a locale, or with the recognition of nearby artifacts from other times (architecturally emulating in some way either their form or their functions). The monumental infrastructure at Malagueira (figure 257) is an obvious illustration in both respects. It resembles the arched form of the nearby eighteenth-century viaducts that provided water to the town of Evora and surrounding areas. It also has much the same function as the viaducts—the distribution of water and other utilities. The overall layout of Römerstadt, by contrast, clearly recognizes the ancient Roman encampment, but it is only recognition and not an explicit commemoration.

Three projects from the western hemisphere all make historical references, but in each case they remain strictly within the realm of architecture and the Spanish colonial tradition. Lewis Court in California and Villa Victoria in Boston were organized around a community place of Hispanic origin. At Lewis Court it was a patio, helping to render the entire housing complex as a singular entity, much like a *finca* or *hacienda*, with an organization of interdependent buildings around an internal courtyard. At Villa Victoria the reference is more civic, reminiscent of the town square, or *zócalo* of a Hispanic settlement. With El Silencio, the third example, architectural emulation is more limited in scope—the project owes little in spatial

256
Monument and public space at the Malagueira Quarter in Evora, Portugal, by Alvaro Siza.

organization to Hispanic towns—but it is more direct in its details. The main portals at the arcade level of the complex (figure 258) were literally copied from prominent Spanish colonial examples (De Sola Ricardo 1987). The remainder of the project, however, was unadorned. Quite naturally, the routines and rituals of daily life form one of the mainstays of tradition. Community functions and the activities people perform together make up the essential glue of a community. Normally, architecture accommodates these functions in a matter-of-fact manner. After all, one of its basic purposes is to house such activities in a direct and commodious fashion. Nevertheless, accentuation and symbolic enlargement of these commonplace architectural aspects can be a most effective method for emphasizing the circumstances of local daily life. The important question, usually, is how to make relevant distinctions.

In many of the Frankfurt housing estates from Ernst May and his colleagues, community spaces were prominent and symbolically exaggerated, presumably to emphasize shared activities. At the Hellerhof Housing Estate by Mart Stam, among the slab apartment blocks at Römerstadt, and at Lindenbaum by Walter Gropius, collective laundry and clothes-drying areas were used to articulate community open spaces, adjacent to dwellings, in a more than strictly functional manner. At both Lindenbaum and Hellerhof, for example, these areas are raised as berms, thus simultaneously enhancing exposure to sunlight and providing a much higher visual definition in cross section to the pathway running alongside the dwellings. In Römerstadt, these drying areas are paralleled by a beautiful vine arbor, a device that cleverly mediates between the sheer wall of a continuous five-story apartment complex and the semiprivate outdoor space beyond. Also at Römerstadt, the termination of the downhill pedestrian paths, which essentially divide the tiers of row houses into segments,

is celebrated in a relatively monumental manner by larger buildings and as a part of the earthworks and plinth mentioned earlier. At these junctions, the plinth and retaining wall bow outward to form public belvederes, with fine views across the Nidda River valley.

Spaces for less well determined community activities are also pronounced at Sunnyside Gardens in New York, and especially in the inner garden of the Phipps apartment complex. What might otherwise be regarded as circulation space in the Monte Amiata housing complex at the Gallaratese Quarter in Milan, by Carlo Aymonino and Aldo Rossi of 1969–1974, has also been amplified into arcades and public spaces with a theatrical quality (figure 259). In a project intended to house something like 2,400 people, these enlargements of commonplace corridors and galleries, according to the critic Pierluigi Nicolin, "were expected to promote some kind of communal life, half-way between the idea of 'palais social' and that of a civic center" (Nicolin 1977, p. 2). The ampitheather in the same complex was intended for use as a more collectivized rather than communal space, although it has now become simply a part of the outdoor space.

Of course, mythopoetic dimensions of dwelling and daily life also enter into the fabric of tradition. We have already seen, for instance, the role played by arcadian and pastoral themes in modern American life, whereby raw and stark realities of modernity have been tempered. It has been convincingly argued that the garden apartment housing type, America's major contribution to higher-density living, is a suburban and arcadian transformation of basic perimeter housing blocks of European origin (Plunz 1990). Indeed, much of the richness in exterior brickwork texture at the Phipps apartment complex near Sunnyside Gardens, New York, as well as the generous landscape in an English garden tradition, underlines this tempering of an otherwise pervasive modern technological atmosphere. The housing and transportation planning, for instance, are highly rational and technically advanced throughout Sunnyside. A similar tempering can also be found at Villa Victoria in Boston. Indeed, many modern housing projects in the garden city tradition reflect this merger between modern technology and an arcadian ideal. The neue Sachlichkeit architecture of the Frankfurt housing estates spread out along the Nidda River valley—Westhausen, Praunheim, Römerstadt, and Höhenblick—for instance, is boldly framed by garden plots and a bucolic landscape. The principal difference from American counterparts appears to be that the two parts of the merger have remained reasonably intact. The buildings reflect the promise of modern technology, whereas the garden landscape projects a romantic arcadian ideal. In America the romanticism usually extends further, as we saw at Sunnyside and elsewhere, into the buildings as well (Rowe 1991).

Place-making aspects found at the site can be organized largely according to the presence of significant resources and physical features, or according to a kind of practical reckoning with local circumstances required of dwelling. In areas with a harsh climate such as Saudi Arabia, for example, dwelling complexes, out of necessity, often assume a responsive and there-fore distinctive appearance (Talib 1984). Generally, a practical reckoning with local circumstances can have protective as well as conservationist dimensions, and sometimes both. In the Asir region of Saudi Arabia, the walls of rural houses are cloaked with tiles, jutting out at an angle and serving as rain deflectors in times of sudden storms (figure 260). This protection is necessary in order to preserve the relatively soft clay wall material underneath from damage. Nearby cisterns collect and conserve the otherwise precious water, as it is reticulated along and down the sides of the dwellings.

Other no less dramatic examples are also to be found in contemporary western contexts. The wall of apartments running along the northern boundary of the Byker Redevelopment in Newcastle, as we saw, was originally intended to shield the housing from the noise and disruption of an adjacent motorway. On the opposite southern exposure, apartments and balconies open up, for obvious climatic reasons and because of the fine view afforded out over the Tyne River valley. The important point here is that Erskine made the most of his practical reckoning, producing a memorable piece of architecture that is anything but generic.

260

Practical reckoning with local climatic circumstances: a rural house in the Asir region of Saudi Arabia.

As noted earlier, the local environmental features and local traditions are often intertwined. Traditional building practices, and particularly vernac-ular construction, almost always reflect the local availability of materials, the prevailing climate, and the need, if any, to conserve precious local resources (Upton and Vlach 1986). Corresponding architectural forms also tend to be recognizable place-specific and can even be used to exaggerate a particular local building condition for the purposes of appearing less generic. The Malagueira's viaduct structures are an obvious case in point; more subtle are the roofs of the predominant low-rise portions of the Byker Redevelopment. Here the patterns of light and shadow from a traditional tile roof, very common in northern England, are deliberately varied, pre-sumably in order to enrich the foreground view from those dwelling units on the hill immediately above. Similarly, local masonry patterns are ex-aggerated across the almost blank northern side of the Byker Wall, giving scale and diminishing the apparent size of the edifice.

261
Housing on the outskirts of
prewar Berlin: the Berlin
Britz development by Bruno
Taut et al., 1925–1933.

Significant natural features of a site can also be pressed into service to lend distinction to a settlement and tone down the generic quality of its layout. In fact, many memorable urban settlements, such as Italian hilltop towns, gain considerably as spectacles precisely because of the natural topography. Developments in many towns go further, using well-chosen architectural devices like the long stair at Caltagirone, for instance, to accentuate the public perception of a dominant natural feature. By providing a larger aspect to life, the terrain and the settlements within it provide a common sense of identity and of collective pride (Silvetti 1989).

Design emphasis on such features can be most important, especially during the modern era with such an instantaneous capacity for large-scale settlement. At the Berlin Britz development of 1925 through 1933, Bruno Taut and his colleagues appear to have well understood this importance. In general accord with Wagner's garden city principles, construction of this housing estate took full advantage of prevailing natural features on the site (figure 261). Three good-sized natural depressions and ponds were incorporated, enhancing the immediate sense of local focus for the relatively dense development (Huse 1987). One pond near the center of the development formed the centerpiece of the now famous "horseshoe" (*Hufeisen*) block (figure 262), from which the overall settlement derived its name (Hufeisensiedlung Britz). The added significance of this block is the essential monumental character of the space that was made, thus quickly converting a rural asset of the site into a palpable symbol of a new urban community. The other ponds were handled more informally and the swales running between them became part of the pedestrian network (figure 263). Today this open-space system terminates at the large Britzer Wiesen, or meadow, near the low-lying areas of the Tetlow canal.

With this aspect of the Britz estate, Taut and his team managed to achieve three objectives simultaneously. They provided a clear central axis and site-specific focus around which the highly rational layout of housing could be organized; they established an instantaneous, highly visible architectural symbol for the development, which was to have lasting effect; and they created a sense of urbanity and civic open space in an otherwise rural, small-town environment. All three objectives were probably crucial in enabling such a large project, of some 2,200 units, so immediately to assume the role of a viable community (Huse 1987).

Less dramatic architecturally, though no less effective in quickly helping to formulate a sense of community and of belonging to a place, was Alvaro Siza's way of dealing with the site terrain in the Malagueira Quarter. As site sections and local contact quickly reveal, the situation of streets running across shallow topographic depressions on a gentle hillside reinforces the sense of enclosure just enough to allow the residential street more easily to become a place and not a throughway. Similarly the location of dwelling units along the ridge line at Höhenblick, on the outskirts of Frankfurt-am-Main, one of Ernst May's first estates, takes full advantage of views and solar orientation. Moreover, the upper story of the three-floor row houses was set back with generous terraces (figure 264), allowing all the inhabitants to take full advantage of the project's extraordinary location.

Precision and Spatial Hierarchy

While a creative architectural redundancy over and above generic solutions and functional minima appears necessary to thoroughly situate the public aspect of housing into local environments, a complementary impulse is required in order to ensure lasting care and use. There must be a direct coincidence of the scale, type, and architectural conformation of community spaces with their use. Paramount, throughout, are questions about property tenure and a sense of turf; if not well handled, these can lead to dispute or to abandonment and neglect. Technically, the inherent hierarchy of public and private spaces within a community must match prevailing sociocultural norms and expectations with regard to desirable

262
Detail of the horseshoe block at the Berlin Britz development.

263
Natural swales and ponds incorporated into the Berlin Britz housing development as part of a pedestrian network.

territory, as well as a concomitant capacity for responsibility and maintenance. In affordable housing, for instance, it is quite conceivable that spaces may be desirable but responsibility for them may be beyond tenants' means or customs.

One general scale for describing space within housing environments graduates areas according to various degrees of public or private use (i.e., public space, semipublic space, semiprivate space, and finally private space, usually to be found in the immediate realm of a dwelling). Distinct cultural differences have been observed in the details of such a scale. In the United States, for example, a three-step hierarchy is often observed ranging for private to public through semiprivate spaces. The typical single-family dwelling usually follows that division (from house to yard to street). By contrast, in many areas of Europe a distinction is often much more sharply drawn between the private realm of the house and, say, the public realm of the street (Anderson 1972). Normally in this spatial formulation issues of the appropriateness of public-private distinctions revolve around conditions of ownership and control. The front lawn of an American suburban house, for instance, may be private because it belongs to the homeowner. Utility companies and municipal authorities, however, also usually have legal easements over part of it, and in the American tradition of unfenced front yards it is also visually a part of the public realm (figure 265). The playground in a public housing project, by contrast, theoretically belongs to a group of tenants and is, therefore, semipublic. Unfortunately, it often belongs to no one in particular, and a corresponding lack of responsibility is taken for it.

264
Terraces with a view: Höhenblick housing estate in Frankfurt-am-Main by Ernst May, 1926–1927.

The character of the public-private spatial hierarchy in a housing environment also closely relates to the principle of open-endedness concerning decision making and autonomy over projects. It immediately raises the question, for example, of how many people need to be persuaded before some aspect of the environment can be changed. A private backyard is clearly an individual homeowner's or tenant's concern. Common spaces between and among dwelling units require several or numerous parties to be persuaded, and so it goes on. Both de jure and de facto public spaces are somewhat different, because they are normally considered to be everyone's domain and, accordingly, are taken care of by some more remote authority. In practice it is usually those spaces requiring the approval of numerous parties for change, although not everybody's, that are most problematic, especially when the costs of making the change are reasonably high. This situation tends to make a strong argument for a two-step scale of privacy and autonomy on one side and public spaces on the other.

265
The public realm of the
American front yard: South
Boulevard in Houston, Texas,
1986.

As we saw earlier, semipublic spaces pose real problems in contemporary housing projects.

A clear spatial hierarchy of public and private spaces can strongly affect the basic choice of housing type. At median dwelling densities, the row house is well suited to this contemporary condition. With a capacity to form well-made public streets and allow relatively generous private back gardens, the row house has continued to evolve and perform serviceably from beginnings at least as far back as the eighteenth century (Frampton 1975). In fact, the walk-up, five-story apartment buildings in many of the modern housing estates were organized around the row house model, with a minimum number of units being served by a common entry and stairway. The common use of duplex, double-story units further helped to approximate the individuality of single-family, row house dwelling. Corresponding outdoor spaces in the form of upper-level terraces and balconies advanced the idea of a private house even further.

Of the projects already discussed in some detail, the immediate housing environment at Römerstadt and Praunheim among the Frankfurt estates, Kiefhoek in Rotterdam, Sunnyside Gardens in New York, and Villa Victoria in Boston more or less conforms to the standard pattern of public and private spaces associated with the row house. At both Praunheim and Römerstadt, residents added low walls and screens on the front of their

266
Mews entry to housing at the
Berlin Britz development.

houses to provide higher levels of privacy around the front entrances. As we have already seen, the elaborate front stoop arrangement at Villa Victoria accomplishes much the same purpose, but as an integral component of the original design. Variations on the standard arrangement of public streets and private backyards can be found among the majority of low-rise dwellings at the Britz estate in Berlin, at the Malagueira Quarter in Evora, and among sections of the Byker Redevelopment in Newcastle upon Tyne. In the last example, units have private front yards instead of back gardens, usually to improve solar orientation. At the Byker Redevelopment and the Britz estate individual dwellings are entered from the street via an alley or mews, and then through the front garden (figure 266). This arrangement simultaneously ensures both privacy and a sense of address. At the Malagueira Quarter, the double-level front courtyards, entered directly off the street, provide both an entry to the row houses and valuable outdoor garden space. Furthermore, because the units in a single row are placed back-to-back, there are no backyard spaces.

The serial arrangement of row house blocks in the standard model, such as at Praunhaim in Frankfurt, also ensures that private rear gardens, thus enlarging the overall, if vicarious, sense of communal outdoor space. In other arrangements, such as at the Heimats Siedlung in Frankfurt, the private realm of houses on one side of the street faces the front entrances of those on the other (figure 267). This awkward situation is architecturally resolved, however, with the introduction of a linear public park, including children's playing facilities, in between the street proper and the private garden fences of the adjacent row houses. Indeed, this device of private gardens facing onto community preserves is enlarged still further at Sunnyside Gardens, New York, but without the interruption of a street.

267
Asymmetrical street
condition at the Heimats
housing estate in Frankfurt-
am-Main, by Ernst May et al.

268
The productive strategy of communal spaces located adjacent to private outdoor spaces: the Heimats housing estate in Frankfurt-am-Main.

There are several notable exceptions to the largely dichotomous division between public and private space around dwellings. At the Weisse Stadt development in the north of Berlin, constructed between 1929 and 1930 by Ahrends under much the same auspices as the Britz estate, almost all the extensive garden around the dwelling units is communal or semi-private. In fact it is one of the few places where the desire for relatively high levels of a collective environment on the part of the modern pioneers seems to have been sustained. No doubt this orientation was also due to prevailing political ideology. Weisse Stadt is located in what was formerly East Berlin which allowed no private property ownership. Another project with a similar arrangement of outdoor space, discussed earlier, is El Silencio in Caracas, Venezuela. Unfortunately here, however, apart from several children's play areas, the semiprivate, community space has been woefully neglected.

Apart from institutional forms of development and maintenance at the scale of the larger community environments, proximity and the spatial relationships between various kinds of spaces would seem to strongly influence the subsequent quality of maintenance. The placement of communal spaces, like the linear park at the Heimats Siedlung (figure 268), directly adjacent to private outdoor spaces seems to be a fruitful strategy. By its very adjacency and similarity in vegetative character, the community space becomes coopted and, therefore, maintained. Simply put, it is in the adjacent dwellers' self-interest to care for it. Moreover, playground and other facilities, usually to be found in such community spaces, were intended for adjacent residents. By contrast, community spaces that are set apart from dwelling units, or are not directly accessible, even though they may be adjacent, seem to suffer most from abandonment and misuse. They are no one's property in particular, and the community pressures resulting in a kind of moral suasion are not present as they were in the case of the Heimats estate. Again these realities of jurisdiction and responsibility appear to argue for spatial hierarchies that are strongly-private and public, with community-held spaces verging closely onto the private realm.

Normalcy and Distinction

Today the populations of most industrialized and urbanized nations are becoming increasingly heterogeneous. A pronounced late modern attitude is recognition of this social pluralism, particularly in large urban centers. This, however, was not always the case. Indeed, we could well argue that an early social promise, if not effect, of modernity was quite the opposite: a widespread conformity in aspirations and a desire to reduce social differences. Furthermore, for many, this was a welcome change, offering equality of opportunity and other freedoms in the face of rigidly established and often discriminatory practices.

Against the background of the contemporary social flux, the balance between normalcy and distinction sometimes becomes precarious. On the one hand it is important to belong, but on the other there can be advantages to standing out. Housing is no exception, as the sometimes all too quick association of particular groups with particular houses so clearly demonstrates. In fact, a problem for many underenfranchised groups is how to distinguish themselves for the purposes of seeming special, but without fear of ridicule and cliché. Certainly, both distinction and normalcy are in the eye of the beholder. However, when confronted with the task of building modern mass housing, less idiosyncratic definitions are warranted.

To begin with, good modern housing is for a specific population, rather than for a specific type or category of population. It must also, however, avoid a superimposition of values and cultural stereotyping. Simultaneously, it must be housing as such, rather than housing for a particular socioeconomic class. Moreover, it must be housing of distinction: housing that can be referred to, proudly, as home.

Normalcy, Familiarity, and Standards

Normalcy in a housing environment is seldom conveyed or appreciated through any single characteristic but rather through a constellation of attributes, where the overall arrangement is also significant. It is important that these attributes and their relations conjure up an immediate sense of familiarity. They must not only be recognizable but must also not seem out of place and unusual. The overall shape and appearance of housing, for instance, should be of immediate familiarity, and not something that has to be struggled with interpretively. The typical American single-family house, for example, is certainly a vague or broad enough category, but we all usually know one immediately when we see it (figure 269), especially if we are American.

An immediate and broadly based sense of familiarity relies a good deal on the use of conventions. Conventionality can have two meanings. It can be based on a majority of similar cases, or it can refer to the incorporation of acceptable and widely held values. Either aspect is rarely independent of the other. We often promulgate values based upon an existing majority expression, and vice versa.

Housing standards such as those discussed in chapters 1 and 2 explicitly addressed, albeit abstractly, issues of acceptable values. Moreover, the legal intent was to make them hold for a majority of relevant cases. The more troublesome aspect of broad standard setting, as we saw, essentially concerned the kinds of values that should be incorporated and, in pluralistic societies, whose values should be reflected. Minimum standards avoid at least the latter issue by being absolute. They are claimed to hold as minima in all situations, no matter what the peculiarities. The problem in practice, however, is that they also seem to encourage building to a lowest common denominator, and offer no real guidance to building activities well above the standards.

269
The unmistakable attributes of a house type: the American single-family home.

270
A collective dimension to
residential life: a housing
estate in Hoek van Holland
by J. J. P. Oud, 1924.

In the application of minima, there is also an underlying conception of social mobility as an inevitable process leading to the assumption of normal mainstream values. Minimum standards only apply to the poorest of housing conditions, whose inhabitants will soon move on to better dwelling environments. Unfortunately, from the testament of thousands of homeless, downward mobility can also be a reality and, under these dreary circumstances, minimum standards can be an impediment, by institutionally cutting off a growing segment of the urban population from shelter relief. Effectively, the baseline becomes a line of demarcation between those who are within the system and those who are not.

The presence in an area of a majority of similar housing examples implies architectural conventions that cover a preponderance of familiar attributes. Fortunately, this can be achieved by a number of design strategies. The use of known and familiar housing types can quickly establish a normal residential environment. Duplexes and row houses, for example, are very common in most European and American residential environments. A significant issue then becomes how many aspects of a particular housing type constitute a sufficient preponderance to establish familiarity, short of complete correspondence with known examples. The row houses of architectural new realism, for instance, were undoubtedly row houses in spatial organization, distribution of public and private space, as well as overall size and density. They did not immediately look like more traditional examples of the same housing type, however, with, say, pitched roofs and individual facades. Under the doctrine of the *neue Sachlichkeit*, as we have seen, there was a strong commitment to a collective image for housing. J. J. P. Oud's Hoek van Holland project, for example, clearly emphasizes this dimension of residential life (figure 270). As several recent chroniclers predictably note, "in his design for housing Oud treats his facades not as an accumulation of individual dwellings but as an architectural whole in which the street wall functions as part of the urban fabric" (Groenendijk and Vollaard 1987, p. 180). The same case may also be made for Oud's Kiefhoek project of much the same time in Rotterdam. Certainly, the architecture of modern row house units was controversial. However, if Römerstadt is any guide, inhabitants rather quickly accepted the basic housing form or type. It was more the detailed finishing of the units that was contentious (Lauer 1988).

More directly in terms of superficial appearance, the use of quotations from familiar circumstances is another well-tried design tactic. Venturi and Scott Brown, for instance, exemplify this strategy in their embrace of popular culture (Venturi and Scott Brown 1971). Sharratt's Villa Victoria project places considerable emphasis on figuration of the individual row house units (figure 271), which are otherwise not dissimilar in layout and arrangement to those found at, say, Praunheim in Frankfurt in the late 1920s.

Building progressively in a vernacular tradition may well combine both approaches. Such dwellings are familiar in both their outward appearance and their spatial organization and layout. Problems can arise, however, when economic or other circumstances require significantly higher densities or kinds of housing that pose substantial breaks with traditional practices. As Colquhoun noted, vernacular architecture is essentially imitative of a "higher" architectural style or way of making buildings (Colquhoun 1989). Without that external impetus, following established vernacular approaches may prove to be too incremental to be effective when radical changes are necessary.

Meaningful Architectural Difference

An appropriate form of architectural distinction will fundamentally convey a sense of meaningful difference. It is simply not sufficient to make something look different, although that would clearly achieve a fair modicum of distinction. Meaningful architectural difference implies some notion of a baseline or datum from which difference can be appreciated in the first place, and against which its meaningfulness can be assessed. It is an active process of making judgments and not a sudden urge. The baseline also holds the keys to the expressive dimensions along which architectural

271
Bold figuration of individual row house units: Villa Victoria in Boston by John Sharratt, 1969–1982.

differences are accepted and found meaningful. Without this proviso we would be back to a concept of distinction according to any perceivable difference. Again the baseline is not a static concept but a set of spatial principles, quite probably tacitly held, that influence discriminating judgment.

In the example of the American single-family house, meaningful architectural differences among, say, colonial revival dwellings are those that fundamentally preserve basic attributes of this stylistic category, and not instances where the shape and appearance of the house change completely. In short, this datum or baseline is the generalized concept of normalcy discussed in the previous section. It may change over time, as accepted cultural concepts of normalcy expand or contract. Nevertheless, at any given moment the concept carries persuasive weight. It is what marks distinction.

Given this anatomy of architectural distinction, an important question in the architecture of housing concerns those aspects of a normal condition that can constitute fruitful points of departure for making works of distinction. If, for instance, a strong trait of a normal housing condition is the use of traditional building materials, like clapboard siding on wooden stud frames, then the sudden juxtaposition of galvanized iron would be, in all likelihood, a meaningfully different appearance. Many of Frank Gehry's California houses, for example, trade on this formulation of normalcy and meaningful architectural differences. In his own house in Santa Monica, built between 1977 and 1978, for instance, the use of metal siding and other commonplace materials, which are exotic in a suburban domestic context, draws attention to the house and cleverly relativizes accepted notions of American residential architectural norms (Cobb 1985, Arnell and Bickford 1986). In another example, the Norton House of 1983 to 1984, Gehry selectively exposes the timber stud wall beneath the siding, simultaneously revealing the membrane character of the outer stair and the relative flexibility of the American stud wall system, as well as strong connotations of impermanence and change, symbolically not usually associated with the American home (figure 272). For Gehry, manipulation of building materials and standard construction practices carries broad cultural as well as strictly architectural meanings.

Generally, there are several normal conditions in the architecture of housing that can form the basis of meaningful architectural difference and hence distinction in an honorific sense. In the work of Frank Gehry we have already seen examples of how the tectonic dimension of architecture

272
"Meaningful difference" and the material fabric of a house: the Norton House by Frank Gehry, 1977–1978.

273
Strong orderly articulation of
terraces and window
openings within a *neue
Sachlichkeit* aesthetic: Berlin
Britz housing development
by Bruno Taut et al.,
1925–1933.

can be exploited. Primarily this involves exaggeration and unusual juxtaposition within a palette of available materials and construction practices. Another example from the *neue Sachlichkeit* is the careful, orderly
composition and articulation of window and door openings within housing facades. In the case of, say, the Britz estate (figure 273), an overall
depiction of the wall as a single plane and surface is well established.
This, in turn, draws legitimate attention to fabrication through industrialized building systems and, by implication, to the economically productive
promise of new techniques. By remaining outside the framework of readily
available materials and construction techniques, the tectonic dimension
of housing can also be organized usefully to refer backward and forward
between traditional and modern methods of fabrication. Villanueva's project at El Silencio in Caracas clearly reflects, in material composition, the
perpetuation of culturally received ideas about the relative permanence
of the public and private domains. The base, with its arcade and grand
portals, for instance, is solid and made in the manner of a craft tradition
(figure 274). The housing above, by contrast, reflects the new (at the time),
forward-looking frame and reinforced-concrete slab construction. The resulting ensemble of materials and surface appearances thus exaggerates
tacitly accepted features of the urban realm in an architecturally distinctive fashion.

Another basic domain of architecture that can be exploited as the basis
for meaningful difference is the iconography of housing. During the Victorian era in the Anglo-American tradition, for example, a strong iconographic merger was made between romantic associations with the universe
at large and the role of family life. Under some aesthetic doctrines the
organic preponderance of decoration was seen to allow one to become
metaphysically lost in continuous detail and, therefore, to come closer in
feeling to nature's true complexity and grand design. Thus, elaborate
decorative programs were seen to be functional (Early 1965). The subsequent Progressive Era, by contrast, emphasized a modern functional sense
through honest, simple, and parsimonious uses of materials (Stickley
1909). Consequently the iconography of houses was less superficial and
more strongly tied to methods and materials of construction. The abstract
formalism of the International Style was to extend that functional concept
still further (Hitchcock and Johnson 1966). Clearly, the same terms and
organizing architectural principles carry different meanings from one era
to the next and are susceptible to manipulation. Amplification or diminution of the expressive program in housing thus allows current meanings
to be adjusted. With some oversimplification, a reduction in figuration, to
borrow a rhetorical term, usually conveys a more modern message. En-

richment of architectural surfaces, on the other hand, often conveys an orientation toward traditional values (Jencks 1987).

The underlying conditions of normalcy and architectural distinction can also operate in reverse. It is, after all, largely a self-referential and reciprocal set of cultural relations. Iconographically speaking, in many parts of the world there has been a trend to overlay a distinctive iconographic program onto otherwise conventional housing projects. Many public housing projects in the United States, like the large Columbia Point (now Harbor Point) complex in Boston, now have pitched roofs where they were once flat, and symmetrically composed facades where they were once organized informally (figure 275). The social impetus behind this renovation was the desire to somehow normalize the projects in the wake of the stigma associated with modernist public housing. Given the historical record, the affected public housing projects, paradoxically, are now more distinctive in order to achieve a broader sense of normalcy.

Finally, typological arguments can also be used to meaningfully differentiate aspects of housing projects, while still remaining within culturally

274
Relative permanence of public and private domains: the public arcade at El Silencio, Caracas, Venezuela.

275
Overlay of the cultural
iconography of pitched roofs
and symmetrical facades: the
Harbor Point redevelopment
project in Boston by Goody
and Clancy, 1985–1990.

recognizable architectural norms. They are "arguments" in so far as specific spatial layouts and forms allow certain social expectations to be
fulfilled, i.e., "this" does follow from "that." The row house type, for
example, brings with it specific, predictable spatial and architectural attributes. The same also applies to certain urban forms, such as various
types of plazas and gardens (Krier 1979).

The value of topological arguments for making distinctions in the architecture of housing is clearly demonstrated at an urban scale by the Villa
Victoria complex in the South End of Boston. Here, three basic urban
architectural types are deployed to meaningful effect: rectangular blocks
of row houses with fronts on residential streets; a well-defined urban plaza
with a central pedestrian area and a surrounding loggia; and high-rise
towers. The row houses, already typologically similar to dwellings in the
surrounding neighborhoods, create a sense of contextual harmony and
normalcy, whereas the urban plaza and arcade are more strongly in a
Hispanic tradition indigenous to the inhabitants' culture. Finally, the high-
rise towers create an appropriate sense of monumentality around the
commercial and residential core of the project surrounding the plaza.
Attached and semiattached courtyard housing, typical in much of Miami,
is another example of a cultural merger between building types. Here the
Latino courtyard configuration is incorporated into the earlier normal
Anglo condition of single-family dwellings (Stern 1981).

Throughout this discussion of architectural tectonics, iconography, and type, achievement of meaningful architectural difference has been approached largely as a matter of extending the existing frames of design reference. The question still remains, however, of how far afield such distinctions can go before they become clichéd, potentially subject to ridicule, and thus socially problematic. In strict cultural terms, boundary conditions for architectural distinction are already defined by the dimensions implied in the concept of meaningful difference. As we saw, matters of tectonics, iconography, and type were all culturally based constructs, subject to transformation by the creative imagination and ultimately by the ebb and flow of cultural politics. Therefore, given restless curiosity and a desire for change, it seems rather pointless to think of limits.

Socially, on the other hand, the matter of acceptable architectural distinction is likely to be more constrained. The way things look to a society, the socially structured figuration quickly becomes wrapped up in broad issues of identity, social status, and empowerment. Housing, as we have said, is no exception.

There do, however, appear to be two general conditions that must be met for architecturally distinctive aspects of housing environments to be regarded positively within a social milieu. First, the distinctions must celebrate redeeming and worthwhile aspects of the life and circumstances of the groups concerned. The architecture must allow a group to distinguish itself for what it is and what it wants to be. Furthermore, it must project a status actually aspired to by the group, rather than reflect architectural distinction by way of superimposed categories and stereotypical views. Second, residents and potential residents must be able to allow architectural distinctions to be made in their environments, against a sociopolitical background of being able to choose otherwise. This condition ensures both an autonomy and an authenticity of architectural expression, a condition so lacking in American public housing and in many peripheral developments around European cities.

Both the genesis and the results of the Byker Redevelopment and Villa Victoria conform well to these two conditions. For the Geordie of Newcastle, the light, gardens, open air, color, and imaginative architectural forms at the Byker were a welcome and premeditated release from dingy nineteenth-century bylaw flats. Moreover, although many existing facilities were maintained, it hardly can be argued that the Byker Redevelopment lacks distinction. Similarly at Villa Victoria, the Puerto Rican community retained part of their older tradition and were also able to purchase a piece of the American, suburban dream. A much earlier example, Eigen Haard by Michel de Klerk in Amsterdam, the Netherlands, built in two stages between 1913 and 1921, although totally dissimilar from Villa Victoria in appearance, had the same general distinctive characteristic (figures 276 and 277). According to one report, upon de Klerk's untimely death in 1923 a tenant wrote a letter to the daily newspaper mourning the departure of the builder of his house: "It is as if every brick calls out: Come all workers, and rest from your labors in the homes that await you. Is not the Spaarndammerplein [another name for the project] a fairy tale dreamt of as a child, as something we children never had?" (Groenendijk and Vollaard 1987, p. 148). Furthermore, Eigen Haard, meaning "our hearth," was the name of the housing association commissioning the project, some of whose members were the original occupants. Thus the second condition concerning empowerment was well satisfied, in spite of official governmental criticism that the housing project was too luxurious and exuberant (Groenendijk and Vollaard 1987).

276
A general view of the Eigen Haard housing project in Amsterdam by Michel de Klerk, 1913–1921.

277
Rich architectural detailing at the Eigen Haard housing project in Amsterdam.

Appreciable Abstraction

An inevitable aspect of the growing complexity of modern life, as we have seen, appears to be a need for abstraction. It is constantly manifested in day-to-day life and within our physical environments. More often than not the complexity of tasks in the workplace, for instance, is encompassed by special languages, the terms of which are intended to make those tasks more intelligible and tractable. Here computer applications are an obvious example. The practice also emerges of labeling broad aspects of contemporary life with simple words and phrases, again in order to reduce the apparent complexity. Unfortunately, this practice can sometimes result in a tragic oversimplification of social conditions. The term *homelessness,* for instance, may be a better label as labels go than *itinerant, hobo,* or *bum.* However, it also tends to sanitize a much more complex, deep-seated, and desperate set of personal circumstances.

Opportunities within modern cities brought people together, often from very different social and cultural backgrounds. Consequently, as Raymond Williams so vividly noted, the only aspects of life these people could find in common, and from which they derived a singular sense of identity, were necessarily abstract (Williams 1973). Again conversation regarding the city, even among neighbors, make rather constant casual references to generic systems and events like traffic, crime, pollution, and schools. Thus a move toward abstraction, now in social terms, results not so much from complexity per se as from sociocultural heterogeneity. Even our neighbors tend to come from different places, thus reducing the effectiveness of local colloquial terminology.

The need to reduce the complexity of building in order to build quickly and at a large scale has also been an imperative of modern life, especially for the social promise that such a process seems to hold for ill-housed populations. The resulting simplification, repetition, and standardization of housing is often represented by an expressive abstraction of the task of building that has met, as we have seen, with mixed popular success. A challenge, then, for modern mass housing is to seem familiar and homelike and yet enable efficiencies of production, as well as economies of scope and scale, to be realized. Unfortunately, abstraction, unless it can be appreciated adequately, quickly leads through a lack of understanding to a sociocultural distancing and possible alienation. Appreciable architectural abstraction, therefore, is a necessary quality of good modern housing.

Architectural Abstraction and Reduction

The difference between architectural abstraction and reduction can sometimes be slippery. Essentially, abstraction involves the process of reduction, as in reduction to salient properties, although usually not in the pejorative sense of a phrase like "the program of accommodations for the housing was severely reduced." Abstraction, therefore, is an expression of essentials rather than the diminution to essentials implied by reduction. Moreover, the simplification involved in abstraction invariably has an expressive purpose and is not simply the by-product of cost cutting. Abstraction, in short, is simultaneously a simplification and a more intense focus on one or more specific characteristics.

Once a focus has been established and extraneous elements have been either reduced or eliminated, the process of architectural abstraction usually operates in reverse, by amplification. Eisenman's numbered houses from the early 1970s, for instance, are all explorations of formal geometric properties of solid figures and planar shapes. Eisenman has even spoken of them as attempting to locate and express the "syntactic structure" of platonic solids and other forms (Gutman 1977, Eisenman 1979). They were an attempt to deliberately evolve the expressive language of architecture and resulted in buildings that, although highly abstract, were also very complex and intricate in appearance. Abstraction, then, does not mean "to make plain," even though many examples of abstraction from, say, *neue Sachlichkeit* architecture appear to be plainer than other presumably less abstract structures.

At issue here, however, is not so much a process of architectural abstraction as the conceptual dimensions or physical features along which abstraction has taken place. If, for example, the feature is the wall planes of a house then the result may well appear to be plainer than a neighboring house without the same abstract expressive interests in its design. On the other hand, architectural abstraction may involve an intricate decorative program that attempts to essentially describe people's relationship to the cosmos. The result, such as might be found in a Gothic church, may be no less an effort at abstraction, even though its appearance is far more intricate and varied (Panofsky 1967).

In order not to become merely reduction, architectural abstraction must be intelligible throughout. It is, after all, first and foremost a process of making sense of things and, ultimately, of enhancing understanding. The results can be apprehended and "read," as it were. Abstraction in scientific fields of endeavor, for example, clearly have this orientation. The detail of the natural world is abstracted in order for us to understand its underlying functions more clearly. Appreciable architectural abstraction, however, goes beyond this aspect of sense making to incorporate feelings of satisfaction and even liking. It is appreciable in two senses: it can be simultaneously understood and enjoyed. In this regard, one of the problems with much American public housing was a sense of enforced simplification within the residential environment. Certainly by comparison to other forms of housing, the apparent terms of design reference for dwelling were reduced and clearly seen as simply cost cutting, rather than as an attempt to provide low-cost housing of quality with an abstract architectural form.

Finally, architectural abstraction can also be used and appreciated for a capacity to blur distinctions and blunt the directness or completeness of the formal design references that are adopted. In cases where historical circumstances should be incorporated into the architecture of a housing project, while also allowing for a contemporary feel, abstraction of both sets of references may prove useful.

278
Contemporary housing creating well-defined urban streets: Back of the Hill project in Mission Hill, Boston, by William Rawn, 1989.

William Rawn's Back of the Hill row houses of 1989, built for the Bricklayers' and Laborers' Non-Profit Housing Company in the Mission Hill area of Boston, take such an approach. To begin with, 165 row house units are arranged in four blocks so as to create a sequence of well-defined urban streets (figure 278) linking two areas of Mission Hill, a streetscape that harks back to much earlier examples in Boston's well-known Back Bay and Beacon Hill (Campbell 1990). The architecture is certainly not a copy of these earlier districts, for that would have been unaffordable, and yet abstractly speaking the same basic relationships of building to sidewalk and street are incorporated. The individual townhouse units are then aggregated to form something like a nineteenth-century terrace, within which different kinds of projecting bays and porches provide localized variety among the streets of the project, again very much in keeping with historical examples (figure 279). The overall appearance of the project, however, is modern, with simple building silhouettes and a continuity in the exterior wall surfaces clearly only allowed by contemporary construction techniques. The span and opening dimensions of generous windows within the front facade are also clearly from modern times and not the nineteenth century. Essentially, historical references have been well placed and abstracted within an otherwise modern framework of architectural forms, materials, and building practices. The result is most pleasing because it allows a twofold reading, establishing continuity with tradition and yet simultaneously advancing a vision of the future.

279
Nineteenth-century terrace housing in a modern manner at Mission Hill, Boston.

Forms and Purposes of Appreciable Abstraction

As might be expected among housing projects, architectural abstraction may be understood and appreciated very differently in different places. Nevertheless, there are at least four general architectural strategies of abstraction that have experienced relatively widespread use during the modern era.

The first involves what might be termed tectonic essentialism and closely corresponds, for example, to the architecture of the new realism. According to Frampton, "the tectonic" is the poetic or expressive aspect of statics and methods of construction. He also sees it as being at the same categorical level as "type" and "context" among major dimensions in an autonomous discussion of architecture (Frampton 1990). While contingent upon structure, material appropriateness, and a direct reckoning with techniques of construction, the tectonic nevertheless transcends mere functional necessity. In the *neue Sachlichkeit*, as we saw earlier, the resulting architectural objectivity is more than one of form following function. Both the formal and functional relationships involved are expressively accentuated and not a mechanical by-product of putting pieces of building together. As may be obvious, the second term, "essentialism," refers to a focus, in the process of abstraction, upon fundamental characteristics of building, in this case statics and methods of construction.

Like so many other estates in Frankfurt-am-Main constructed during the 1920s, Römerstadt closely reflected Ernst May's highly organized system of production and fabrication. The continuous walls, punctuated by doors and windows, along with the boxlike appearance of individual units, directly corresponds to the relative plasticity and structural integrity of reinforced concrete, as well as to the simplicity required of low-cost, repetitive assembly. This example of tectonic essentialism was made even more dramatic by the composition and detailing of fenestration which accentuates the appearance of having been cut from a single wall slab, rather than having been made from an aggregation of other materials such as masonry. Also consistent is the insistence upon flat roofs and decks, lyrically culminating in the Hadrianstrasse block by Schuster, with its strong iconographic references to the enclosed, rounded decks and other contoured elements of modern ships (figure 280). Overall, the abstract qualities of the buildings were accentuated still further by the bucolic surrounding landscape, suggesting veritable machines in the garden (after Marx 1964).

A similar kind of tectonic essentialism can also be found at Oud's Kiefhoek estate in Rotterdam, although here the expressive aspect concerns the frame and outer skin of the row house buildings. The front facade of each row house block is composed into three bands: a base, a middle, and a top (figure 281). The base is a repetitive array of windows and doorways set within the structural frame of the building and expressive of the frame's regularity and inherent thinness. The top consists of a full clerestory of rectangular windows, which together with the vertical dimensions and glazing of the base clearly convey the idea of a light frame running the entire length of the building along the facade. The blank, horizontal middle band further reinforces that essential idea, by giving the appearance of a thin skin or membrane laid across the frame of the facade. Other aspects of the row houses, like the flat roof and blank side walls, also help simplify and form the architectural expression of frame and skin. In addition, the serial arrangement of columns, windows, and doors within the front facade further suggest an idea of continuous extension, in itself an inherent property of a simple rectangular structural frame.

280
Iconographical references to
modern transportation
technology: the
Hadrianstrasse Block by
Schuster at Römerstadt in
Frankfurt-am-Main, 1927.

A second strategy for projecting appreciable abstraction within a housing
environment is with the use of a kind of architectural essentialism that
gives rise to a sense of civic monumentality. Usually, the purpose behind
such a strategy is to establish a clear architectural relationship between
individual households and the community at large, with an obvious emphasis on the latter. As we have seen, the spine and vertebrae of the
Malagueira project, formed by the service viaduct and the large walls
separating each unit, create a monumental and civic presence. Inhabitants
seem to be dwelling within a common structure as much as within individual units. A similar result was achieved at the Niederrad estate of 1926
to 1927, on Bruchfeldstrasse in southern Frankfurt-am-Main, another of
Ernst May's extraordinary social housing projects, although by quite different means. Here May and Rudloff, the architect in charge, symmetrically
arranged most of the 654 five-story apartment units around a central open
space of considerable civic proportions. The space itself had a strong axis,
reinforced by an orderly arrangement of gardens within and terminated
by a monumental gateway and ornamental pool (Risse 1984). A repetitive,
oblique arrangement of the primary blocks of the apartment complex along
the flanks of the large central space parallel to Bruchfeldstrasse accentuated still further the line of the monumental axis, and its preferred
viewing point in front of the pool. The architectural result symbolically
reinforced the intended idea of community living, although in subsequent
years the central garden space has been subdivided for more private use.

Both a defined outdoor place and a heightened sense of common structure
can be found in Jean Nouvel's contemporary Némausus complex in Nîmes
of 1989 (figure 282). Taking cues from the surrounding suburban context,

281
Tectonic essentialism within
a row house block: the
Kiefhoek estate in Rotterdam
by J. J. P. Oud, 1925–1930.

282
A common sense of structure
in housing: the Némausus
complex in Nîmes by Jean
Nouvel, 1989.

283
Apartment slabs festooned by
metal balconies and screens
at the Némausus complex in
Nîmes.

the two large apartment slabs, festooned with metal balconies and screens,
turn housing into a monument (figure 283; Anderton 1990). Rising five
stories above grade on stilts, with parking underneath, the complex includes in its cross section extraordinary units with double- and triple-
height living areas. The latter are even sufficiently spacious to enclose
full-grown trees. Between the two buildings is a paved area, through which
there is a line of plane trees. In spite of an obvious economy of means,
this urban space truly marks the center of the complex, blurring the usual
distinction between street and concourse into a fine public place.

Finally, in Rossi's residential block at the Gallaratese Quarter in Milan,
reliance is placed less on the aggregation of elements into a monumental
civic presence, as at Malagueira and Niederrad, than the transformation
of an existing building type in a monumental direction. Here a relatively
conventional horizontal slab block arrangement of apartment units, not
dissimilar from many in the surrounding area, is elongated still further
and raised up upon regularly spaced nib walls and several large drumlike
columns (Futagawa 1977). The resulting loggia both created a community
space, symbolically underpinning the remaining private portions of the
buildings, and lent undeniable monumental and civic presence to the
overall complex (figure 284). Abstraction of the wall surface, with deep
window reveals and the strip cut-out appearance around column walls,
intensifies the play of light and shadow, increasing the grandeur and visual
drama of the facade. Furthermore, the closely spaced, thin column walls,

running several stories up into the building, seem too slender and insubstantial to provide adequate structural support, adding a surreal dimension to the architecture. Effectively, the transformation of the original residential slab block type was so complete that its domestic status was undermined in favor of the appearance of a public building with a characteristic overall unity and presence (Tafuri 1989).

A third strategy of appreciable architectural abstraction involves the simultaneous simplification and amplification of architectural elements within an otherwise conventional framework. Here the purpose often seems to be to sharpen the rhetorical focus of the architecture on themes of social symbolic significance. Thus the front stoops and pitched roofs of the row houses at Villa Victoria were simplified into basic yet quintessential forms, and then increased in scale. The result had the effect of taking what is conventional about local townhouse living and underlining its merger, so to speak, with the image of suburban dwelling. The symbolic social aspiration appears to encompass normalization on both fronts: the surrounding context of Boston row houses, and the more general American suburban dream.

Those elements that contribute to the kit-of-parts character of the Byker Redevelopment, such as the stairs, decks, and balconies, have all been simplified into very basic forms and arranged in a manner that draws attention to their essential qualities. Protruding balconies, for example, make few if any concessions to adjoining wall surfaces, preserving the architectural integrity of the illusion of clip-on pieces. Rather than becoming resolved, specific discrepancies between the various architectural ele-

284
Monumental and civic
presence: Monte Amiata
complex at the Gallaratese
Quarter in Milan.

285
Simplification and
rearticulation of building
forms: garden facade at
Weisse Stadt in Berlin by
Ahrends, 1930–1932.

ments are usually exposed and even exaggerated. The horizontal alignment of balconies and decks, for instance, occurs without any particular regard for consistency within the overall form of a facade. Instead, they are placed where they need to be, with regard to internal functional arrangements, and the inconsistencies are taken up directly by short fights of stairs and short bridges. The resulting symbolism is unmistakable, underlining the social and architectural potential for continuous growth and change (Rowe 1988).

A fourth and final strategy for achieving appreciable architectural abstraction involves both simplification and rearticulation of primary architectural forms, usually as an alternative means of place making within a housing project. Unlike the earlier thrust toward civic monumentality, this strategy usually concerns the creation of private and semiprivate spaces. In general concept, the early American garden apartments of the late teens and twenties are excellent examples. The greater generosity of private outdoor space, including apartment units set back from the street, more closely matched prevailing suburban circumstances than courtyard and perimeter blocks within adjacent urban areas (Plunz 1990). Nevertheless, relatively high residential densities could still be retained, especially with the aggregation of tracts of land into superblocks (Wright 1933).

Among the housing projects already examined in some detail, the various building complexes at Sunnyside Gardens clearly illustrate this approach. The rational yet varied arrangement of straightforward apartment buildings, each more or less in the form of a basic rectilinear block within the heart of Sunnyside, sets up a framework of exterior outdoor and garden space with a corresponding variety and functional integrity. The sense of definition and enclosure that is provided within the private outdoor space of each unit, for instance, is enhanced by breaking an otherwise continuous line of regular apartment buildings. Distinctions between back and front are also maintained while preserving an overall suburban garden setting. In addition, coincidence between pedestrian thoroughfares and more public community areas within the project helps to further preserve the integrity of private outdoor spaces. At the neighboring complex of the Phipps Garden Apartments, the potential of the garden apartment is even more fully realized. A regular T-shaped arrangement of dwellings in plan emerged from the consolidation of vertical circulation, efficient arrangement of units, and a need for varied outdoor space around the inner perimeter zone of the project. Repetition of this T-shaped arrangement across the site, with some simple variations, results in a community garden space of pleasing variety and picturesque complexity. Each unit, in turn, also incorporates a private outdoor balcony or garden space, the seclusion of which is enhanced by the larger community garden area.

At a smaller scale of consideration, the garden facades of apartment buildings within Ahrends's Weisse Stadt in Berlin use the same strategy of simplification and rearticulation of basic building forms to create private balconies and semienclosed exterior spaces (Huse 1987). Here the facade of a basic slab block, with entry stairs at regular intervals, is strongly articulated parallel to the original plane of the exterior wall, pulling out, as it were, generous roomlike enclosures as simple cubic forms (figure 285). Appreciation of this process of transformation on the sunny side of each block is further aided by the presentaiton of a similar unarticulated condition on the opposite facade (figure 286). Here vertical strips of windows running the length of each stairwell, and both the horizontal and vertical composition of windows to individual apartments, cleverly establish a virtual gridwork within the facade's flat plane that then forms the basis of the articulated balconies on the other side of the building. A similar formal strategy was performed along the back of Bruno Taut's Rote Front complex of 1926 to 1927 within the Berlin Britz estate, and also in the remarkable apartment blocks at Siemenstadt in the same city of 1930, by Hans Scharoun. Indeed, at various scales, the abstraction of building volumes into concise simple geometric forms, which can then be rearticulated in combination with each other, constitutes a very basic modern architectural strategy, and one, as we have seen, that can produce considerable visual variety and practical outdoor amenity.

286
Apartment block facade as a
virtual gridwork at Weisse
Stadt in Berlin.

Projects in the City

One of the advantages of urban life is undoubtedly the general efficiency associated with high levels of production and consumption. The relatively large numbers of people required by a work force can live in reasonable proximity to their places of employment. The flows of goods, services, and information among firms can be handled in an expeditious manner, and the scale of support necessary for a variety of leisure time activities can be that much larger.

There are also other more social and personal advantages to be gained from urban life. For instance, bringing people together from different ethnic origins, occupations, and religious persuasions can produce a broad understanding of general social conditions and, consequently, heighten prevailing senses of tolerance and personal awareness. As Sennett cogently argues, it is only through personal contact and even confrontation with people different from oneself that a fuller sense of self-realization can be achieved (Sennett 1977). The modern dilemma, however, what might be called the philosophical problem of the public, is how to prevent the same differences and social heterogeneity from disabling a broader social discourse and passage of self-discovery, through the isolation of different factions living separate and very different existences (Sennett 1977).

Projects and Pieces of the City

Distinctions can be made between "projects" and "pieces of the city" in terms of functional homogeneity or heterogeneity, physical separation or connection, and a relative singularity of appearance (figure 287). Projects are usually clearly identifiable and often suggest a degree of architectural autonomy from surrounding circumstances. Pieces of the city, on the other hand, are just that, continuations with some modification of what is already in place.

There is nothing inherently deficient in the concept of projects. After all, from a developmental point of view, most cities are composed, almost by definition, of numerous projects. Problems arise, however, when unnecessary or exaggerated conditions of self-containment and architectural

287
Conspicuous appearance yet heterogeneity of use at Weisse Stadt, Berlin.

autonomy begin to emerge. This usually occurs when projects deliberately form distinct social enclaves, and when an interest in creating a highly specific image becomes idiosyncratic, without broad, socially redeeming features. Many of the inwardly oriented apartment complexes that dot the American suburban landscape, built around supposedly marketable popular themes, are clear illustrations of these phenomena. Unfortunately, the impact goes well beyond visual kitsch by establishing a residential environment clearly at odds with broader social purposes.

Modern planning doctrines of functional separation among uses, broadly enshrined by "as of right" forms of zoning, often contribute indirectly to a distinct project orientation in the physical conformation of a city. Housing is certainly encouraged to extend without the necessity of considering boundaries and edges with other nonconforming uses that may pose a threat of blight and nuisance. Rarely, however, do such well-zoned developments allow for mixtures of uses and especially the processes whereby singular uses, such as residential, become despecialized over time, as a neighborhood assumes a well-rounded functional character. Furthermore, the inevitable boundaries between one section of a residential zone and another are likely to persist, without the ameliorative effects of other spontaneous supportive uses and interstitial developments. Superficial architectural distinctions among projects within the same functional zone can also be encouraged by an insistence upon a singularity of uses, for the purposes of better differentiating housing as products in a marketplace. The results are artificial discontinuities in both the formal organization and visual appearance of an urban area.

Early successes within the modern city of eradicating squalor and blight, as well as rationalizing processes of production and consumption, lent considerable credence to an orderly separation and dispersal of uses. A confidence also emerged in the capacity for centralized, large-scale planning (Boyer 1983). As a result it was easy to conceive of the city-building process from a vantage point of separate well-made projects, all carefully connected through a well-planned modern infrastructure. Indeed for much of the twentieth century that is how many cities proceeded, until this confidence in large-scale, holistic plan making was shaken by mounting urban system dysfunctions (Goodman 1971). Against this earlier background, then, it was understandable how the common practice of creating totally planned, separate projects became ingrained. Unfortunately, this practice also often exaggerated socioeconomic segregation within urban areas (Wingo 1963).

Paradoxically, perhaps, precisely the reverse modern impetus toward functional integration resulted in much the same outcome. The search for the appropriate submultiple of integrated functions to accompany housing, a hallmark of post–World War II community design, often resulted in functional contrivance and a condensation of community activities to a scale that could be architecturally realized. Le Corbusier's *unité*, for example, was certainly notable in both regards. Unfortunately, this pursuit of the submultiple often also resulted in both an unwelcome singularity of appearance and a real isolation within a city (figure 288).

Prevailing conditions within real estate markets of many contemporary cities also favor distinctive, enclavelike forms of development for at least three reasons. First, inward-oriented building complexes allow market uncertainties associated with surrounding properties to be minimized. A clear focus inside a project, for instance, allows the orientation of the remainder to turn away from surrounding developments. Second, in a related manner, enclaves can be secured readily from unwanted outside intrusions. Third, as described above, real estate competition encourages quickly establishing a singular marketable image for a project that is markedly different from those around it.

All three conditions also contribute to a privatization of residential environments whereby they become set apart from the rest of the city. While there is nothing wrong with a close sense of community, it is essentially a social phenomenon that may come and go, depending upon the dispositions and fortunes of those in the community. It cannot be physically prescribed for all time, and in both principle and practice it can be severely

288
Singularity of appearance
and relative isolation of
housing blocks at Brasília.

limited by physical overdetermination. Instead, a rough continuity in the scale of development and architectural character would seem to offer the most socially balanced approach to urban development. Indeed, the criticism that can be leveled at a project like Ernst May's Niederrad complex on Bruchfeldstrasse in Frankfurt concerns the overwhelming idiosyncrasies of its form. The scale is roughly commensurate with surrounding areas. However, the closed overall form and the zigzag plan configuration of apartment complexes clearly set it apart from the remainder of the city, running the risk of unnecessary social distinctions. De Klerk's Eigen Haard project is also distinctive in appearance from its neighbors. It is not, however, significantly different in overall form, building type, or construction materials. Here the distinctions are made tolerable by concentrating architectural expression in a way that does not interfere with social processes of community formation. Indeed, judging from the tenant responses cited earlier, the effusive architectural expression has made Eigen Haard a desirable place to live.

Critical Contextualism

Continuity and architectural similarity can run the risk, however, of becoming a slavish form of contextualism, which merely perpetuates the predominant surrounding forms of development in an unpremeditated manner. Unfortunately, throughout many cities, large tracts of development can be found that are monotonous in their relentless repetition. Moreover, they are usually housing estates of one kind or another. Sometimes this slavish conformity to the surrounding context reflects uncertainty about marketplace tolerance for difference, while on other occasions it seems to be less premeditated and more a matter of simple convenience. Rarely does there appear to be a compelling economic rationale based upon, say, economies of scale. Few of these large homogeneous tracts are built at once, or by the same entity.

As an architectural ideology rather than simply an exigency of building practice, strict forms of contextualism largely relate back to the past. The past is repeated in the belief that tried and true building practices should prevail and that the overall character and appearance of an area is worth maintaining and perpetuating. Technological circumstances may change, as they certainly have in the past 50 years. However, it is important to retain the look and feel of what was there before. Social circumstances and the character of family life may also change, but the basic style of residential accommodations should persist. Usually this is not an unknowing or uncritical response. On the contrary, it often reflects deeply held beliefs in maintaining not only the status quo but traditional patterns of living. There is a firm commitment to the past as somehow offering appropriate guidance for the future, as well as a certain confidence in the persistence of particular universally applicable arrangements of housing. On this latter point there are grounds for this confidence. As we have seen on a number of occasions, the persistence and evolution of the row house building type supports a claim of general applicability. In addition, easy internal conversion of existing row house units from one spatial arrangement to another allows new social circumstances to be met and another benchmark to be established for subsequent development. The magnificent dwellings of the Back Bay in Boston, for instance, were once large and commodious single residences. Today many are subdivided into several apartments, although the overall external appearance of the housing stock is little changed. New residential infill developments, in turn, reflect the economy and social appropriateness of these changed circumstances, while also preserving the established external architectural forms.

At another extreme we have a housing complex like the Monte Amiata section of the Gallaratese Quarter in Milan. Here the desolate surrounding context of postwar apartment blocks is directly challenged, and in its place we find a strong, dynamic arrangement of building structures and public spaces (figure 289). The usual isolation and repetitive arrangement of apartment towers and multistory slab blocks, each with separate car parking areas and other ancillary facilities, were eschewed in favor of a far more consolidated attempt to create public space. The typical separation of functions was deliberately blurred and avoided where possible, in

289
A dynamic arrangement of building structures and public spaces at the Gallaratese Quarter in Milan.

order to firmly establish a more complete precinct in the city. Although very different from its surroundings, the housing complex is clearly contextual because of the emphasis placed upon a critical assessment of these surroundings as a point of departure. Physical difference with surrounding developments, then, is not necessarily merely a dismissal of contextual responsibility. It may result from disagreement over how a context should be established most appropriately.

There appear, then, to be at least any one of three characteristics required of critical contextualism. First, there must be an openness to the city-building process and not simply acquiescence to surrounding circumstances and urban architectural norms. The need for change at an urban as well as at the local scale of building should be recognized and incorporated into new projects. Perceived economic advantages to be gained from industrialized mass production remained a strong part of Ernst May's housing program in Frankfurt-am-Main, for instance, even though the predominant form was the row house, not uncommon in many parts of Germany at the time. A similar observation could also be made about Martin Wagner's contemporaneous city-building process in Berlin. Adoption of garden city principles in both cases, for reasons of decentralization and of natural amenity, were clearly prompted by concerns about a residential context. There was, nevertheless, an undeniable openness to new or other ideas. In neither case was there the kind of wholesale destruction of existing residential contexts that we associate with various forms of postwar urban renewal and urban expansion.

A second characteristic of critical contextualism is not only a sense of continuity with the past but also an openness toward the future. Indeed, new housing projects as pieces of a city should attempt to chart a specific direction for future housing, not by novelty for its own sake but by deliberately attempting to improve upon existing living conditions. Villanueva's El Silencio complex did this admirably. It was at once a substantial new district in the city of Caracas. It clearly offered improvements in comfort and amenity to many prevailing residential circumstances, and yet it offered connections to the past through traditional forms of spatial organization and iconography.

Finally, almost by definition, critical contextualism must also allow for useful self-reflection: an ability to diagnose current problems and to cast them constructively into relief. Critically contextual projects must present palpable alternatives to existing situations and in a manner that makes an unambiguous link between both the existing problems and the new opportunities. Aymonino and Rossi's Gallaratese project clearly established such a link and thus remains a serious proposition about living in the city (Nicolin 1977).

Openness to the City-Building Process

Beyond the generalities and attitudinal orientation of a critical form of contextualism, a question still remains regarding how to continue to be architecturally open to the city-building process. It is clear that once urban complexes are constructed they usually remain for some time to come. There is inevitably both a longevity and a finitude to most urban buildings, especially those of any significance or, like housing, of habitual occupation. How then can such fixed and permanent structures somehow remain open to the processes or urban change that seem to occur with some frequency?

First, in spite of some real estate conditions to the contrary, housing environments should not be developed in an insular or enclavelike fashion. They should remain a part of a city and at least not give the appearance of being exclusive or aloof from the day-to-day ebb and flow of urban life. Forms of spatial organization that extrapolate and actively extend the public presence of a city should be favored. Open street grids, for example, and buildings with fronts onto such streets clearly establish a normal division between public and private space, without the other levels of discrimination of most residential enclaves. The public realm is public, and not subject to further physical subdivision into public at large versus the public of the community living inside the enclave.

290
A sufficiency of structure and yet an openness to future development at the Malagueira Quarter in Evora, Portugal.

Second, projects as pieces of the city should be finished but not necessarily complete. They should appear to be resolved architecturally and fit for occupation but not so definitive as to discourage any subsequent additions and modifications. As we saw at the Malagueira Quarter there must be a sufficiency in the architecture to clearly establish a sense of place and a direction for future developments (figure 290). The architecture should not, however, foreclose any possible further elaboration, as it does in the strongly wrought edifices at Le Viaduc and Les Arcades outside of Paris. Here it is not the neoclassical aspect of these complexes that appears to prevent further change but rather the completeness and pristine idiosyncrasy of their form. The projects seem to be both finished and complete, once and for all. Kiefhoek suffers from the same potential drawback, although to nowhere near the same degree. The elegant, taut front facades

291
Incorporation of institutional facilities: the community center complex at the Byker Redevelopment project in Newcastle upon Tyne.

and simple rectangular forms of the row houses seem to defy any tampering. In fact their appearance today is much as it was over 60 years ago. The rear of the houses have changed and become more elaborate, however, as needs have surfaced and resources have become available.

A third way of remaining open to city-building processes is to promote and preserve a heterogeneity of use at a grain commensurate with other areas of the city. Providing for a heterogeneity of use makes easier the functional change and diversification that will inevitably become necessary with changes of living patterns. Furthermore, by allowing substitutions of urban activities to occur relatively easily, a functional variety can be maintained that is supportive of urban street life. Accommodation of mixed uses is not always successful, however. In several modern housing estates from the 1920s, such as Westhausen in Frankfurt and Kiefhoek in Rotterdam, well-designed space was provided for nonresidential activities. But with changes in the size and distribution of retail services over the intervening years, these facilities proved to be inadequate and are now no longer used. More centrally located and functionally commercial projects like El Silencio in Caracas, the Hadrianstrasse block at Römerstadt, or the shopping plaza at Villa Victoria have fared much better. Provision of residential support facilities like kindergartens, schools, recreation facilities, and community centers also contribute to the functional diversity of a viable residential environment. Nowhere among the projects discussed is this better illustrated than at the Byker Redevelopment (figure 291). Here there are something on the order of 20 institutional facilities incorporated within the project, including the Shipley Street Baths, four churches, a YWCA, four schools, day nurseries, two geriatric units, a library, a community center, and a number of social clubs.

A fourth way of remaining open to city-building processes is through the provision of redundant, architecturally engaging and yet non–functionally designated spaces. The monumental loggia and several of the exterior public spaces at the Gallaratese complex have these qualities. They are forms that emerge from the architecture directly, more than from a strictly functional program of accommodations. They add a civic dimension to the project, but one that is not in any way finite or predetermined. The architecture produces an aura that can be taken advantage of in a number of ways, for different functions at different times, but by no one function on a permanent basis. Thus the public face of the complex remains open to be perpetually engaged—written on and erased, so to speak—by inhabitants as they see fit. Many of the more informal, recreationally oriented open spaces at the Byker Redevelopment have similar qualities. It is space that has its own landscape architectural integrity and spatial feeling, like the large meadows up toward the northeast corner of the development, but that invites various extemporaneous uses. Again the space appears not to have been designed for any function in particular but as a general urban architectural proposition about a place.

Finally, topological clarity, especially if it is already familiar within an area, is a fifth approach for maintaining a degree of openness to the rest of the city. When a project provides architectural continuity with surrounding developments, the urban landscape of a city is enlarged and distinctions between new and old developments are made less obvious. Familiarity also brings with it the almost certain knowledge that architectural transformation over time can and will be accommodated, thus allowing the rawness of newness to be more easily accepted than it might be with idiosyncratic and peculiar forms of architecture. Peculiarity is not so much a matter of style as it is of housing type. Again Eigen Haard in Rotterdam is instructive. Its exterior expression is certainly exotic, but the layout of dwelling units and their spatial organization around a city block is quite conventional (figure 292). In fact, de Klerk's project was roundly criticized by younger architects of Oud's generation as being too conventional and meager in its accommodations (Groenendijk and Vollard 1987). Furthermore, emphasis on the clarity of a building type as the constituent quality of housing can liberate the remaining architecture to take on and reflect not only surrounding local circumstances but changes that occur through time. Housing at Römerstadt and even more in the Malagueira Quarter clearly exemplify this open-ended urban characteristic.

292
Unusual exterior expression with a straightforward layout of dwelling units: Eigen Haard in Amsterdam.

Modern Housing In Situ

The design of good modern housing always tempers becoming, the tendency for time to eliminate spatial distinctions, with being, a strong sense of place, and vice versa. Furthermore, it always balances a programmatic open-endedness with a strong sense of architectural predetermination. It is not a matter of either the user or the designer knowing best. Paradoxically, perhaps, good modern housing must also exhibit sufficient redundancy in its design to allow the architecture to reach beyond the immediate program and yet maintain a functional precision in the spatial arrangements that are made. In addition, it is built for a specific population rather than for a specific kind of population and must avoid a misplaced superimposition of sociocultural values and stereotyping. Architectural distinction is also important, but so is normalcy, and, expressively, a balance must be struck between architectural abstraction and empathy that avoids the nostalgia of other times and other places. On the one hand, there must be a surrender to the inevitable urge toward abstraction occasioned by modern conditions, and yet on the other there must be an architectural clarity and appropriateness about what is being abstracted. It is not a question of architectural language per se, but rather of the mode of representation. Finally, good modern housing suggests a way of continuing the project of the city as an integral and yet not slavishly contextual piece of urbanism.

Underlying these principles are two broad relationships that seem to lie near the heart of the modern condition, particularly as it effects the way we dwell. One governs the locus of our actions, orchestrating between individualism and the need for collective expressions of behavior. The other concerns a balance between rational and sensible ways of knowing the world and is closely linked with the two sides of modernism discussed earlier. On the rational side of this balance are tendencies toward generality in scope, universality in sense of place, and abstraction by way of expression. On the sensible side, by contrast, are to be found more specific, local, and empathetic proclivities.

As in other cultural fields, the modern crisis of meaning in architecture seems to have come about because of a chronic imbalance in the rational-sensible equation demanded of architectural modernism, and an exhaustion of directions leading toward general solutions, a universality of applications, and formal abstraction (Klotz 1989). In a word, the rational-sensible equation was grossly weighted toward the rational side at the exclusion of sensible adjustments of a more local and traditional kind. At the outset this orientation was not a problem, as the stridency of modernism seemed entirely necessary to unseat moribund traditional forms of architecture. Later, and certainly by the late 1960s and early 1970s, the imbalance became a problem, as the conditions and results of a by now well-established modernism spiraled out of local control and ran their course. If not accurate, it was probably fitting that Charles Jencks declared an end to architectural modernism with the blowing-up of Pruett Igo in St. Louis—one of America's rational brave new worlds of modern public housing (Jencks 1984).

This impasse need not be endemic, however, for the rational-sensible relationship possesses a capacity both for self-regulation and for providing critical insight. By turning our attention to the future, the rational side can prevent contemporary complacency and backward slides into nostalgia for the past. The sensible side for its part tempers excessive abstraction with empathy and seeks ways of grounding the universality of modernism in local circumstances. In principle anyway, each side of the philosophical arrangement can work on the other. Indeed, in most of the cases of modern housing we have discussed, rational and sensible characteristics commingle. At Römerstadt, for example, we have already seen how the overall landscape and site work made strong yet lyrical local historical references to prior settlements, as well as sensibly tempering the relatively uncompromisingly objective aspects of the building architecture. The industrially produced, abstract rational character of the architecture, on the other hand, clearly befitted the contemporary era, both practically and symbolically offering the promise of social progress and expanded levels of well-being.

Critical insight is also a by-product of a self-regulatory process. As one side of the relationship exerts pressure on the other, the underlying character of both sides usually becomes more distinct. With that clarity can come deeper insight into broader cultural as well as sociopolitical underpinnings of a project. Returning for a moment to Römerstadt, the juxtaposition between the landscape and the buildings (figure 293) draws

293
Juxtaposition of landscape
and buildings at Römerstadt
in Frankfurt-am-Main.

294
Modern arcadianism at work
in the Union Carbide office
complex in Danbury,
Connecticut, by Kevin Roche,
John Dinkeloo and
Associates, 1976–1982.

immediate attention to the limits of each and simultaneously makes us aware of the scope and responsibilities involved in the social undertaking. A rational, repetitive assembly of mass-produced dwellings, especially on the scale of Römerstadt, required other ingredients to fit the project into its surroundings and to convey a sense of place and of belonging. Those other ingredients, in turn, could not stand on their own and needed the discipline of the building blocks and the sheer sameness of appearance in order to clearly project the egalitarian, individual, and collective social motives of the housing, not to mention clearly defining the divisions of private and public responsibility for the open space.

Less generally, there are at least two versions of the rational-sensible relationship, each more or less corresponding to unique conditions on either side of the Atlantic. In the United States and much of North America, the relationship expresses itself as a form of modern pastoralism or modern naturalism (Rowe 1991). The modern technological orientation is tempered by pastoral and arcadian ideals of living in the countryside (figure 294). The merger is abundantly clear in most forms of suburban-metropolitan development, by far the most expansive cultural environment in America today. Both technology and its applications, as well as pastoral idealism, tend to be ubiquitous and not associated with any place in particular. There is inevitably variety among different local and particularly regional renditions of modern pastoralism. Nevertheless, it is a relatively fixed concept and one most closely associated with activities rather than places. Moreover, this seems to be well suited to a culture that refers to itself more by activities than by locales and history. There is also a process orientation to both sides of the modern pastoral equation that has to do more with the general functions of dwelling in the world than with specific differences among locales.

Although no less modern in technological orientation, Continental Europe, by contrast, would seem to have stronger associations with *genius loci*. Here the rational-sensible relationship expresses itself as a form of modern localism. Even housing projects like many of the estates in Germany and the Netherlands from the 1920s that owed a considerable debt to the garden city movement—clearly a form of modern pastoralism—invariably made strong references to a particular locale and its history. Römerstadt is already an obvious example, but so is the Britz estate and its topography, not to mention the Malagueira and its particular references, as well as the Byker Redevelopment (figure 295). Localism is about place but not in any generalized sense. It is far less abstract and culturally matches a long European sense of history, and of the historical layers that lend a palpable directness to the idea of "this" place versus "that" place. It is not enough, for instance, to dwell in an arcadian landscape. It must be a particular location within that landscape category. This is, of course, not surprising in a continent that has maintained considerable cultural differences and a real prominence to local circumstances, rather than searching for the homogenizing forces of the American melting pot.

All six of the above principles for the design of good modern housing flow from the rational-sensible relationship and, within the scope of this philosophical construct, serve to adjust and address the balance between the two sides of the equation. It is not a precise mapping, however, as these are design principles and not simply abstract concepts. Universality and abstraction of expression for instance, together with generality and precision in programmatic scope, tend to be rational traits, as are architectural predetermination, autonomy, coherence to norms, and the idea of planned self-contained projects in a city. Concerns for local circumstances, distinction, and a potential open-endedness and idiosyncrasy in expression, by contrast, err in the sensible direction, helping to particularize modern housing and lend empathy to its interpretation and appreciation.

Collective-Individual Action and Expression

The other broad dimension underlying the design of modern housing is the essential tension created between individual and collective forms of action and expression. Particularly during the modern period, the question regarding for whom housing is being built has become both important and universal. It is constantly confronted by government officials in their housing policies, by speculative real estate entrepreneurs competing in the residential marketplace, and by architects and builders charged with the responsibility for giving housing form. As many prior examples have shown, architecture, especially in mass housing, can lend an appearance and reality to individual living or, alternatively, it can provide a strong sense of community expression, where individual tastes and requirements are subordinated to a larger, collective order.

There are at least four distinct levels at which the relationship between collective and individual action can be expressed in the design of modern housing. First, the architecture of specific housing blocks, or aggregations of dwellings, can be inflected to emphasize either individual units or the collection of units as a whole. Row houses, for example, through architectural devices like porches, bay fronts, the composition of windows on the facade, and so on, usually express the idea of individual units joined together to form a row of individual houses; hence the name. Often there are subtle and not so subtle differences between specific arrangements of these architectural elements that sharpen still further the individual identity of each unit. In the style of the typical Boston row house, for example, the appearance of a chamfered bowfront facade would be quite striking next to, say, a relatively flat, unrelieved Italianate facade. By contrast, the individual row houses may be organized to express a larger identity. The tying together of individual dwellings under a single huge pediment, as at Regency Terrace in London, is a clear illustration of such an identity. The architecture of Hoek van Holland by J. J. P. Oud also falls within this category, the rounded ends and prominent commercial space at the middle of this housing row establishing clear limits and a strong center to a coherent collective architectural identity.

A second expression of the relationship between collective and individual action comes during the process of housing design, as well as during phases of subsequent occupation. Here the issue basically concerns who decides and how much is built in a predetermined form. Here the role of the collective is usually filled by a government agency and bureaucracy, whereas individual users usually represent themselves. Some confusion can arise under collective kinds of user participation. Nevertheless, the collective-individual relationship still persists in relative terms. A metropolitan jurisdiction served by a single agency, for instance, invariably consists of numerous collections of users. Usually at issue, architecturally, is the adequate provision of allowance for design variations and subsequent transformations of the basic housing units.

A third expression of the relationship between collective and individual action is more general and concerns architectural perpetuation of inherent

295
Reference to an earlier
history of place at the Byker
Redevelopment project in
Newcastle upon Tyne.

cultural differences within a multicultural society. Here the boundaries of the collection of users almost always extend well beyond a specific group and the issues correspond more closely with standard political practices like majoritarian self-rule and pluralistic protection of minority interests (Nelson 1982). Moreover, there is a contingent quality to the collective-individual relationship, as the potential for cultural difference may or may not be pressed into action. At Villa Victoria in Boston, as we saw, there was a constructive symbolic ambiguity on this score (figure 296). The spatial organization and much of the architectural iconography of the commercial plaza make clear references to Hispanic culture, whereas the adjacent quasi-suburban row houses blur such a distinction, by clearly referring to a much broader American mainstream.

Fourthly, the collective-individual dimension also crops up around the most general issues of public and private responsibility for the various spatial domains encompassed by housing. Choices of housing type each bring generic layouts of public and private space. In fact, this book has favored the predominant use of row houses precisely because their emphasis on private indoor and outdoor space was so well suited to the prevailing social milieu in Europe and the United States. Moreover, the architecture of housing is not completely malleable, nor can precedents be easily ignored. For the day-to-day ritual of simple occupation, each house type brings with it a particular and inherent responsibility for collective and individual action.

The design principles espoused here for good modern housing also reflect the collective-individual dimension, and in a manner that can bring an appropriate sense of balance to the relationship. The tension, during the process of designing, between open-endedness and predetermination of housing architecture is a rather clear example, as are architectural tradeoffs between normalcy and distinction. Housing as a piece of the city, rather than as a semiautonomous project, clearly points in favor of a broader collective view, while the lines along which architectural abstraction can be widely appreciated are similarly inclined in a collective direction. Furthermore, time-space distinctions between local and universal can also take on obvious social identities, local corresponding to individualism and universal to a collective. In short, the six design principles can be cast to represent and orchestrate the potential for various architectural construals of collective and individual action in housing.

Moving into the broader realm of policy planning, strong parallels can be seen between the architectural principles of good modern housing and contemporary attitudes toward housing policy. As observed throughout this book, such a parallelism is not surprising, given the pervasive qualities of modernity as a basic condition of life, not the least of which were the tendencies toward universalism, standardization, and functional control that have more recently given way to localism, diversity, and flexible management. Furthermore, although emphases on the spatial and aspatial dimensions of housing have rarely been congruent in the highly specialized modern world, when policy does coincide with the physical realm a commonality of interests logically emerges.

One of the important lessons learned from this modern period concerns the need to separate housing production and housing assistance, even though subsidies may go, and, indeed, probably should go to both sectors of a housing program. In certain ways this distinction parallels the differ-

296
The collective-individual
relationship at Villa Victoria
in Boston's South End.

ence between architectural open-endedness and predetermination. To build "low-income housing," for instance, is to link social distinctions of income with production cost. The outcome, as we saw in the United States and parts of Europe, has been disastrous. Public housing was soon referred to as "the projects" or some similar term, and became stigmatized and set apart from other forms of housing. This is not to say, however, that housing production should not be subsidized. Indeed, the idea of most government-sponsored programs is to produce housing units that could not be produced otherwise. Another potential result is that this generally increased level of production will substantially benefit economically marginal buyers and renters of housing. The point, however, is not to so merge the two aims that one must necessarily coincide spatially with the other.

A second and related aspect of many contemporary housing policies is the need to maintain a diversity of housing stock within as local a geographic area as possible. In addition to the spatial hierarchy commonly associated with the public and private realms of a dwelling, a similar kind of hierarchy also exists among various housing types. Standards of accommodation, for instance, among dwellings within residential hotels, apartment blocks, row houses, and single-family houses are often different and represent different housing opportunities. Theoretically, there is a wide palette of potential units and housing types available to a community. Furthermore, the ideas of redundancy and diversity of available types go hand in hand. The concept of housing diversity, although it might appear to be a market-driven term aimed at realizing a higher degree of precision between household needs and available products, can also productively operate, in broader social terms, precisely where markets are marginal. Simply put, housing diversity, at any given moment, usually brings with it redundancy. Moreover, with redundancy can come satisfactory provision on the economic margins. Residential hotels, for example, have come and gone as a center of marketplace attention. Nevertheless, they have continued to provide housing for a broad range of tenants, both with and without adequate means (Cromley 1990).

The integration of housing within a city, and the integration of housing as a policy dimension among others, can be traced in many nations' stances toward urban planning and administration. As we clearly saw during the post–World War II era, concerns for housing gradually became integrated with concerns for other functions. From a planning perspective the treatment of integrated urban systems became more emphatic as it became more complex. The architectural parallels with mixed-use development have already been mentioned, as have the failures of both views.

Today the necessity of adequately relating housing and community services, as well as places of work and places of residence, is well known. To make pieces of a city in a holistic and even ad hoc sense seems to be far more relevant than the rationalizations of planning for separate uses.

Finally, large master plans have generally been eschewed for planning at a local level, closer to the political interests of constituencies. Just as the universalizing influences of modern architecture created the need to make local distinctions, so too in planning the need for local distinctions and accommodations rose to the fore (Castells 1983). The closer the sovereignty of public decision making reached down to a local level the better off many citizens felt. Heterogeneous populations with multicultural backgrounds, especially in a nation like the United States, understandably place different claims on the common weal, necessitating local rather than universal plans. In addition, the style of public decision making and planning has often changed away from the abstractions and generalities of former comprehensive plans. In their place are to be found an emphasis on project-by-project negotiation, and a far greater flexibility in the prior designation of allowable practices within various districts of a city. Here the stances of the Boston Redevelopment Authority and the city of Barcelona are two good cases in point. Both jurisdictions have plans in a broad and general sense, and yet both ultimately rely on direct negotiations and project-by-project involvements. What is more, there is a growing awareness of the limitations to both collective and individualistic forms of housing provision.

Returning for a final brief moment to the three parallel themes that began this book, we can now see that modernity and the architecture of housing need not be out of harmony. The rise of technocracy and conditions of space-time compression do raise problems for the design of appropriate housing. Distinctions between one locale and another, and between one form of architecture and another, are difficult to maintain. Nevertheless, there are consistent ways of finding our place in the world and of creating a palpable physical sense of belonging. Furthermore, the rise of subject-centered reason away from metaphysical foundations, and an almost inexorable modern impulse toward abstraction, have certainly posed problems for finding an adequate expressive architecture. For modern housing, however, the issue of language and meaning is probably secondary. Both in principle and in practice, there are numerous ways of striking a balance among the expressive urges and attitudes already inherent in modernism itself. It is not the monolith of much received wisdom. Moreover, its quite distinct historical phases must be recognized. Modernism of the 1920s was a joyous, liberating, and universalizing reaction to Victorian morality, the *Gründerzeit*, and traditional values from the past. Later modernism of the 1970s, by contrast, was a flat-out reaction to the totalizing, impoverishing, and alienating excesses of what had become of early modernism. Both, however, were moments of extensive work on the architecture and the scope of what could be accomplished in modern housing: an architecture and sense of provision that continues to evolve. The principal remaining issue, however, lies elsewhere and concerns the adequate support of housing in these contemporary times. After fine starts during the predepression years of the twenties, followed by virtual surpluses in the seventies, both the United States and many European countries find themselves delinquent on their social promises of adequate housing for all. As we have clearly seen, the design and, indeed, the planning of good modern housing can no longer be cast as a question of architectural and developmental shortcomings. It is now a matter of political will—but that is another story.

Appendix A

Profiles of Selected
Housing Projects

The following are short summaries of each of the significant housing projects described or referred to in the text. The purpose of each summary is to provide a readily accessible statistical and factual profile of each project, more or less in a consistent format. Important sources of further information are also noted. Citations about each project are also contained in the preceding text. For convenience of reference, the housing projects are described in alphabetical order. Abbreviations used in the descriptions are as follows: E=entrance, K=kitchen, T=toilet, B=bath, LR=living room; BR=bedroom, DR=dining room, R=room.

Les Arcades du Lac

Place	La Sourderie, Montigny-le-Bretonneux, St. Quentin-en-Yvelines, France.
Date	1974–1978.
Architect	Taller de Arquitectura.
Client	Le Foyer du Fonctionnaire et de la Famille; financing provides subsidized condominium units to eligible families.

Project Description

General	Perimeter block housing with the addition of an "aqueduct" housing block extending into an artificial lake adjacent to the site.
Project	Floor area: 50,000 m^2 (538,000 sq. ft.); 4 stories; 700 units in the perimeter blocks, 60 units in the "aqueduct"; studio to 5-room units (predominance of 3- and 4-room units); "aqueduct" units are two- and three-level units.
Units	Double exposure, through-block apartments.
Materials/construction	Concrete bearing wall structure with brick and precast concrete panel facade treatment.

Sources: *Architecture d'Aujourd'hui* no. 187, October-November 1976; Dixon 1981.

Bergpolderflat

Place	Abraham Kuyperlaan/Borgesiusstraat, Rotterdam, the Netherlands.
Date	1932–1934.
Architect	J. A. Brinkman, Cornelis van der Vlugt, and W. van Tijen.
Client	Rotterdam contractor.

Project Description

General	Slab-shaped high-rise housing block; planning of urban and dwelling spaces developed with user participation.
Project	9 stories; 72 units; single-loaded access gallery; skip-stop elevator; includes storage spaces, washing and drying facilities, children's nursery, communal gardens.
Units	48 m^2 (516 sq. ft.); plan 6 × 8 m; typical unit: E, K, T, B, LR, 2 BR, balcony.
Materials/construction	Steel frame, lightweight sandstone partition walls; alternating wood and concrete floors; prefabricated concrete stairs, access galleries and balcony floors; prefabricated steel and wood facade.

Sources: *Bouwkundig Weekblad*, 1934, p. 361; *De 8 en Opbouw*, 1934, p. 45; *Het Bouwberijf*, 1934, p. 173; 1935, p. 243; Geurst 1983; Groenendijk and Vollaard 1987.

Britz Hufeisensiedlung

Place	Berlin-Neuköln (Britz), Germany.
Date	1925–1927 (phase 1: 1925–26, phase 2: 1926–27).
Architect	Architect: Bruno Taut, Martin Wagner; landscape architect: Vageler.
Client	GEHAG (Gemeinnützige Spar und Bau AG).

Project Description

General	Housing estate.
Project	2 and 3 stories; 1,027 units; 46% single family, 54% multifamily (95% of the multifamily units have 1 or 2 rooms, and 5% have 3 and 4 rooms in addition to the kitchen and bath); includes stores and garages.
Units	Area of single-family units: 51% at 79 m^2 (850 sq. ft.), 49% at 89 m^2 (957 sq. ft.); area of multifamily units: 95% at 49–65 m^2 (527–700 sq. ft.), 5% at 80–96 m^2 (861–1,033 sq. ft.); typical unit: E, K, B, 1–2 BR, LR; central heating.

Sources: Berning, Braum, and Lütke-Daldrup 1990; Huse 1987.

Bruchfeldstrasse (Niederrad)

Place	Niederrad/Bruchfeldstrasse, Frankfurt-am-Main, Germany.
Date	1926–1927.
Architect	Master plan: Ernst May, Herbert Boehm; architects: Ernst May, C. H. Rudloff; interior design: Ferdinand Kramer; landscape architect: Max Bromme.
Client	Aktienbaugesellschaft für Kleine Wohnungen.

Project Description

General	Perimeter block housing around interior communal, multifunctional open space.
Project	3 stories; 654 units: 7% single-family houses, 1% studios, 28% 2-room units, 62% 3-room units, 2% 4-room units; includes shops, library, nursery and kindergarden, reading rooms, central radio installation, washhouse, and central heating station.
Units	Area of single-family houses: 107 m^2 (1,152 sq. ft.); 2-room unit: 56 m^2 (603 sq. ft.); 3-room unit: 65 and 90 m^2 (700–970 sq. ft.); 4-room units: 105–115 m^2 (1,130–1,240 sq. ft.); typical unit: E, K, B, LR, 1–4 BR; central heating, central radio, attic rooms; most units have gardens or roof gardens.
Materials/construction	Brick construction, timber or concrete slab roof.

Sources: Dreysse 1988, Risse 1984.

Place	Newcastle upon Tyne, United Kingdom.
Date	1969–1982 (phase 1–4: 1970–75; final phase and some landscaping: 1975 and 1982).
Architect	Planner and architect: Ralph Erskine, in association with Vernon Gracie and Roger Tillotson; landscape architects: Par Gustavson, Gery Kemp, Arne Nilsson, and Derek Smith.
Client	Newcastle upon Tyne Metropolitan District Housing Committee.

Project Description

General	Redevelopment of existing worker housing community. New housing typologies: 8-story "inhabitable wall" (perimeter block), low-rise "link" housing, low-rise terrace housing. Planning objectives: rental units, a complete and integrated environment at the lowest possible cost to the community and with their collaboration, maintenance of traditions and characteristics of the existing neighborhood, rehousing of former residents.
Project	81 hectares (200 acres) of which 19% consists of housing: population: 6,300; 237 p per hectare (100 p per acre); 2,000 units; 75 units per hectare in areas of built-up development (30 units per acre); includes parking, recreational open space, baths, churches, a YWCA, schools, 2 geriatric units, a library, a community center, clubs and social facilities.
Units	Perimeter block: 3-room units on two levels accessed by outer galleries; "link": 5-room units on two levels with 2-room units above; terrace: 5-room row housing units with garden at ground level both sides.
Materials/construction	Perimeter: brick and plywood facing; terrace: wood frame with brick and plywood facing, and steel roof decking.

Sources: *Architecture d'Aujourd'hui* no. 187, October-November 1976; Dunster 1979; Rowe 1988.

Climat de France

Place	Algiers, Algeria.
Date	1953–1957.
Architect	Fernand Pouillon.
Client	The city of Algiers.

Project Description

General	Low-income housing district; freestanding bar and tower buildings composed around squares and streets surrounding a monumentally scaled residential courtyard building.

Project   30 hectares (74.1 acres); 3,500 units; 3 to 6 stories; includes ground-floor shops in the courtyard building and in others throughout the site.

Materials/construction   Reinforced concrete and hollow brick bearing wall with stone and brick facing; stone; load-bearing brick partitions.

Source: Dubor 1986.

Corviale

Place   Via Portuense, Rome, Italy.

Date   1974 onward.

Architect   Group coordinated by Mario Fiorentino.

Client   GESCAL IACP.

Project Description

General   Linear housing blocks.

Project   Population: 6,000 inhabitants. Project included commercial facilities in addition to a range of residential apartments.

Materials/construction   Mixed construction of frame and in situ concrete.

Source: de Guttry 1978.

Eigen Haard

Place   Spaarndammerplantsoen, Amsterdam, the Netherlands.

Date   1913–1920 (phase 1, Spaarndammerplantsoen 1913–15; phase 2, Zaan-straat 1915–16; phase 3, Oostzaanstraat 1917–20).

Architect   Michel de Klerk.

Client   Phase 1: contractor K. Hille; phase 2 and 3: Eigen Haard Housing Association.

Project Description

General   Three housing blocks situated in a northwest section of Amsterdam.

Project   3 to 5 stories; includes school, post office, meeting hall. Housing is organized around communal courtyards and contains apartments of various sizes. Phase 2 consisted of 102 units with 18 different apartment types.

Materials/construction   Brick load-bearing construction.

Sources: *Wendingen,* 1919, no. 2; 1924, no. 9/10; *Domus,* September 1984; *Architecture Vivante,* 1926, no. 11; *Global Architecture* no. 56, 1984; Groenendijk and Vollaard 1987.

Place	Gallaratese Quarter, Milan, Italy.
Date	Designed 1967–1969; built 1969–1974.
Architect	Carlo Aymonino and Aldo Rossi.
Client	Private development showcase construction based on a program drawn up with the local town council. Purchased by the Milan Town Council for city employee housing shortly after completion.

Project Description

General	4-block rental housing complex.
Project	Population: 2,400; Aymonino: 7- to 9-story buildings; Rossi: 4-story bar building.
Units	Three blocks by Aymonino in the Amiata complex: double-loaded floors with maisonettes on the bottom floors, gallery units on the middle floors, and courtyard and duplex units on the top floors, with E, K, B, laundry/ storage room, pantry, LR/DR, 2–4 BR, balcony or courtyard; block by Rossi: single-loaded floor with gallery access, 2–4-room units on one level with E, K, B, LR, 1 or 3 BR, balcony.
Materials/construction	Reinforced concrete bearing wall with plaster stucco finish.

Source: *Global Architecture* no. 45, 1977.

Les Gratte-Ciel de Villeurbanne

Place	Lyon-Villeurbanne, France.
Date	Designed 1930–1931; built 1931–1934.
Architect	Môrice Leroux.
Client	Société Villeurbannaise d'Urbanisme (mixed public and private corporation authorized by national law for the purpose of improving sanitary and hygienic conditions in cities).

Project Description

General	Low- and moderate-income housing district defining a new town center; high-rise stepped-back linear blocks and 2 towers; residential blocks aligned along central avenue.
Project	Floor area: 45,000 m^2 (484,380 sq. ft.); 8.8 hectares (21.7 acres); typical block: 10 to 12 stories; towers: 20 stories; 1,500 units; includes city hall, completion of the Worker's Palace, ground-floor shops, municipal heating.

Units	2 to 7 rooms; 85% of units have 3 rooms or less; elevators, disposal, lifts, hot water, electric kitchens, central heating.
Materials/construction	Steel frame with hollow brick infill; cement stucco finish.

Sources: Delfante, Meuret, and Lagier 1984; *Urbanisme* no. 16, 1933.

Hansaviertel District

Place	Hansaviertel, Berlin, Germany.
Date	1953–1957 (master plan competition 1953; buildings designed 1954; completed 1957).
Architect	Master plan: G. Jobst, W. Kreuer; architects: international roster of architects (47); landscape architects: Hermann Mattern, Otto Valentien, Hertha Hammerbacher, Gustav Lüttge, Wilhelm Hübotter.

Project Description

General	International housing exhibit by the city of Berlin in a redevelopment area; freestanding linear apartment blocks and apartment towers, and detached or row house single-family units in park.
Project	23 apartment blocks or towers of 2, 3, 4, 8, 9, 16, and 17 stories; 18 units of single-family, 2-story row houses; 33 single-family 1- and 2-story detached houses; includes day care center, cinema, shops, restaurant, 2 churches, a library, a 20-room school, and a congress hall.
Units	Typical units: E, K, B, LR/DR, 1–3 BR, balcony; a significant number of studio units were also built.
Materials/construction	Typically poured-in-place reinforced concrete structure with different facade treatment, including enameled steel and glass curtain walls.

Source: Benevolo 1985, p. 738.

Harbor Point/Columbia Point

Place	Columbia Point, Boston, Massachusetts, USA.
Date	Designed 1950; built 1951–1954; redeveloped 1983–present.
Architect	Original project: M. A. Dyer Company; redevelopment plan: Goody, Clancy and Associates, and Mintz Associates.
Client	Original owner: Boston Housing Authority; redevelopment: Peninsula Partners (private development team benefiting from public financing).

Project Description

General Original project: low- and moderate-income housing estate of detached high-rise and walk-up buildings. Redevelopment project: town houses and apartments in new construction and rehabilitated original buildings.

Project Original project: 37.5 acres (15.2 hectares); population: 6,500; 27 buildings: 1,120 units in 15 7-story elevator-accessible buildings (3½ to 5½ rooms); 384 units in 12 3-story walk-up buildings (4½ to 7½ rooms); 13% 2-room units, 40% 3-room units, 32% 4-room units, 12% 5-room units, 3% 6-room units; includes central heating facility, 4.5-acre (1.8-hectare) outdoor recreational area. Redevelopment project: selective demolition of 15 buildings; 1,283 units; 62% market rate units; 1- to 7-room apartments (78% 1- and 3-room units).

Units Original project: typical floor layout: double split-wing cross plan; typical unit: E, K, BR, LR, 1–5 BR, equipped kitchen, central heating.

Materials/construction Original project: Reinforced concrete structure with brick and cinder block perimeter walls; brick facing.

Source: Lari 1989.

Hillside Homes

Place Bronx, New York, USA.

Date Designed 1932; built 1933–1935.

Architect Architect: Clarence Stein; landscape architect: Marjorie S. Cautley.

Client Hillside Housing Corporation (builders: Starrett Brothers and Eken).

Project Description

General Low/moderate-income housing estate; perimeter block.

Project Area: 14.18 acres (6 hectares); population: 5,250; 303 p per acre (757 p per hectare); floor area: 1,247,815 sq. ft. (115,900 m^2); 5-floor walk-up; 1,416 units, 12% 2-room units, 35% 3-room units, 46% 4-room units, 7% 5-room units; includes storage, laundries, incinerator and boiler rooms, workshops, offices, 2.5-acre (1-hectare) playground, wading pools, nursery school, community rooms.

Units Garden apartment on basement floor with storage and utilities; 3 units per floor per stair above; units have double exposure; typical unit: E, K, B, LR, 1–4 BR; 2-room units: 443 sq. ft. (41 m^2), 3-room: 665 sq. ft. (61.7 m^2), 4-room: 886 sq. ft. (82.3 m^2), 5-room: 1,108 sq. ft. (103 m^2).

Materials/construction Brick walls on concrete foundation; reinforced cinder block concrete floors; built-up roofing.

Sources: *American Architect,* February 1936; Stein 1957.

Höhenblick

Place	Niddatal, Frankfurt-am-Main, Germany.
Date	1926–1927.
Architect	Ernst May, et al.
Client	Aktienbaugesellschaft für Kleine Wohnungen.

Project Description

General	Housing estate.
Project	176 units (43% single-family units, 57% apartments).
Units	Single-family units include garden. Organized in row houses along neighborhood streets.
Materials/construction	Light frame, cinder block with stucco finish.

Source: Dreysse 1988.

Internationalen Bauausstellung Berlin (Neubau-IBA)

Place	South Tiergarten and south Friedrichstadt districts, Berlin, Germany.
Date	1979–present.
Architect	Master plan: Joseph P. Kleiheus; architects: international roster as well as local architects.
Client	Internationalen Bauaustellung Berlin.

Project Description

General	Redevelopment and reconstruction of urban districts; 21 open and invited competitions for predominantly residential projects.
Project	Dominance of perimeter block and infill proposals.

Source: Kleiheus and Klotz 1986.

Karl Marxhof

Place	Vienna, Austria.
Date	1926–1933 (phase 1 and 2: 1926–30; phase 3: 1933).
Architect	Karl Ehn.
Client	Vienna City Council.

Project Description

General	Superblock housing estate; perimeter buildings enclose garden courtyard.
Project	Floor area: 156,000 m^2 (1,679,000 sq. ft.); 23% site coverage; population:

5,000–6,000; 1,382 units; includes public baths, youth hostel, dental clinic, pharmacy, library, post office, guest quarters, 25 work spaces, gardens, laundry, hospital, consultation rooms, mother counseling center.

Source: *Lotus* 10, 1975.

Kiefhoek Housing

Place	Kiefhoekstraat/Lindstraat, Eemstein 23, Rotterdam, the Netherlands.
Date	Designed 1925; built 1928–1930.
Architect	J. J. P. Oud.
Client	Rotterdam Municipal Housing Authority.

Project Description

General	Low-income housing estate; elongated rows of standardized 2-story dwelling units.
Project	300 units; includes 2 shops, central water heating installation, two raised playgrounds, church.
Units	Area: 61.5 m² (662 sq. ft.); floor plan: 7.5 × 4.1 m (25 × 13.5 ft.); typical unit: E, K, T, and LR on ground level, 3 BR on upper level.
Materials/construction	Painted plaster finish, brick and frame construction.

Sources: *Bouwkundig Weekblad,* 1930, p. 369; *Architecture Vivante,* 1933, no. 1; Oud 1984; Groenendijk and Vollaard 1987.

Levittown, New York

Place	Levittown, Hempstead, New York, USA.
Date	1947–1950.
Client and Architect	Levitt and Sons (developer, builder).

Project Description

General	Suburban single-family tract development.
Project	1,400 acres (566 hectares); 6,000 units; single-family housing on curvilinear street pattern.
Units	60 × 40 ft. (18 × 12 m) lots with 12% coverage; typical dwelling area: 750 sq. ft. (70 m²); 4½ rooms; typical unit: K, B, LR, 2 BR, central heating.
Materials/construction	Wood frame on concrete floor slab at grade; asbestos siding and asphalt shingle roofing.

Sources: Plunz 1990; Rowe 1991.

Lewis Courts

Place	Sierra Madre, California, USA.
Date	1910.
Architect	Irving Gill.
Client	F. B. Lewis.

Project Description

General	Low-cost garden court housing estate; single-family rental cottages set around central garden court.
Project	Contiguous cottages at perimeter of north and west sides of the property; contiguous cottages set back from block perimeter at east and south sides; less than 30% lot coverage; includes community pavilion.
Units	Only one unit type: E, K, B, LR, BR, loggia, private garden.
Materials/construction	Stucco finish over wood frame.

Source: McCoy 1960, Scully 1988.

The Malagueira Quarter Housing Project

Place	Evora, Portugal.
Date	Designed 1977; built 1977–present.
Architect	Architect and planner: Alvaro Siza Vieira.
Client	Municipal Government of Evora.

Project Description

General	Low-cost, single-family row house housing in linear block configuration; housing available for rent or purchase through a housing cooperative.
Project	27 hectares (67 acres); 75 units per hectare of built-up development (30 per acre); 1,200 units; one- or two-story units on 96 m^2 (1,033 sq. ft.) plot of land; 100 units per block or fragment (neighborhood); includes community facilities, commercial spaces, public parks.
Units	Unit typology: two courtyard configurations; type 1: courtyard adjacent to street; type 2: courtyard at rear of plot; both types have a second-story patio; street parking.
Materials/construction	Concrete block on poured concrete slab, stucco finish.

Sources: Rowe 1988, Testa 1984.

Place	Boston, Massachusetts, USA.
Date	1989.
Architect	William Rawn.
Client	Bricklayers and Laborers Non-Profit Housing Co.

Project Description

General	Row house estate.
Project	165 row house units arranged on a steep hilly site, in 4 blocks creating a sequence of well-defined urban streets. All units are served by an inner service court, with limited car parking, laundry facilities, etc.
Materials/construction	Frame construction, masonry front facades, clapboard cladding at rear.

Source: Campbell 1990.

Némausus Quarter

Place	Nîmes, France.
Date	1989.
Architect	Jean Nouvel, Jean-Marc Ibos.
Client	Nemosem (experimental project of the Ministry of Infrastructure, Housing, and Planning, in coordination with the city of Nîmes).

Project Description

General	Experimental low-rise subsidized rental housing project.
Project	Site: 10,000 m^2 (107,640 sq. ft.); floor area: 10,300 m^2 (110,830 sq. ft.); 5 stories; 114 units; 2 linear block buildings on pilotis over parking with gallery access.
Units	17 unit types of 1, 2, and 3 levels; typical 2-room unit, 52 m^2 (560 sq. ft.), K, T, ½ B, LR/DR/BR; typical 3-room 2-level unit, 94 m^2 (1,012 sq. ft.), K, T, B, LR/DR, 2BR, terrace; typical 4-room 3-level unit, 116 m^2 (1,246 sq. ft.), K, T, B, ½ B, LR/DR, 3 BR, terrace; typical 5-room 2-level unit, 170 m^2 (1,823 sq. ft.), K, T, 1½ B, LR/DR, 4BR; double orientation.
Materials/construction	Poured in place concrete sheer walls on concrete pilotis; exterior curtain wall of corrugated aluminum, insulation and plywood on gallery side; wall of folding garage doors on terrace side; built-up roofing with aluminum sunscreens.

Source: *Architecture d'Aujourd'hui* no. 252, September 1987.

Oud-Mathenesse

Place	Aakstraat/Baardsestraat/Barkasstraat, Rotterdam, the Netherlands.
Date	1922–1923 (demolished ca. 1987).
Architect	J. J. P. Oud.
Client	Rotterdam Municipal Building Authority.

Project Description

General	Temporary housing; variations of a freestanding duplex unit.
Project	2-story units in a triangular site arrangement; steep pitched roofs. Community facilities and play areas included in site plan. Housing units arranged as row housing with private gardens at rear.
Materials/construction	White stucco, red tile roofs.

Sources: *Bouwkundig Weekblad*, 1924, p. 418; *Plan*, 1927, no. 9; *Architecture Vivante*, 1925, no. 1; Oud 1984; Groenendijk and Vollaard 1987.

Het Pentagon

Place	Sint Antoniesbreestraat/Zandstraat, Amsterdam, the Netherlands.
Date	1975–1983.
Architect	Theo J. J. Bosch.

Project Description

General	Perimeter block in the form of a pentagon around a semipublic internal court.
Project	88 units in 6 stories; includes 5 shops around the base of the project. Site located on prominent canal within Amsterdam forming part of a recent neighborhood redevelopment.

Sources: *Bouw*, 1985, no. 24; *Architectural Review*, 1985, no. 1; *Architectural Record*, 1985, no. 1; Groenendijk and Vollaard 1987.

Phipps Garden Apartments

Place	Sunnyside, Queens, New York, USA.
Date	1931.
Architect	Architect: Clarence Stein; landscape architect: Marjorie S. Cautley.

| Client | The Society of Phipps Houses, developer of "housing accommodations for the working classes." |

Project Description

General	Perimeter block around central garden court.
Project	Floor area: 184,000 sq. ft. (17,094 m²); 43% site coverage; 6 6-story elevator buildings and 16 4-story walk-up wings; includes social hall, nursery, and community room; incinerators in each stairwell.
Units	Elevator building: single-orientation units; walk-ups: double-orientation I-shaped units; typical unit: K, B, LR, 1–2 BR.
Materials/construction	Solid brick exterior walls and fire walls; slate roofing.

Source: Stein 1957.

Praunheim

Place	Praunheim, Frankfurt-am-Main, Germany.
Date	1926–1929 (phase 1: 1926; phase 2: 1927–28; phase 3: 1928–29).
Architect	Planners: Karl May, Herbert Boehm, Wolfgang Bangert; architects: K. May, Eugen Kaufmann, Adolf Meyer, Anton Brenner, C. H. Rudloff, Martin Weber; landscape architects: Leberecht Migge, Max Bromme.
Client	City of Frankfurt-am-Main; Hochbauamt (Municipal Building Department) and Aktienbaugesellschaft für Kleine Wohnungen.

Project Description

General	Predominantly single-family, experimental housing estate of row houses in linear blocks alternating with private gardens.
Project	1,441 units; phase 1: 154 3-story single-family houses (59% 3-room units, 39% 4-room units, 2% 5-room units), 10 2-story 3-room houses, and 9 upper-story apartments over 3 shops and a restaurant, church; phase 2: 253 2-story single-family 4-room houses, 189 3-story single-family houses (25% 4-room units, 65% 4-room units with internal studio units, 10% 5-room units), 123 apartments, 4 upper-story apartments over 2 shops, washhouse; phase 3: 464 2-story single-family houses (77% 3-room units, 10% 4-room units, 13% 5-room units), 235 apartments with gallery access, 8 shops, heating station, washhouse, playground.
Units	Typical units: single-family house with internal studio, 103 m² (1,106 sq. ft.), E, K, 2T, B, LR, 2 BR, storage room, studio (29 m²), terrace; single-family house, 76 m² (816 sq. ft.), E/DR, K, B, LR, 2 BR; single-family house, 54.5 m² (580 sq. ft.), basement, E, K, B, LR, 2BR.
Materials/construction	Phase 1: prefabricated concrete slab construction; phase 2: 42% brick

construction, 58% prefabricated concrete slab construction; phase 3: 35% brick construction, 65% prefabricated concrete slab construction.

Sources: Dreysse 1988; Risse 1984; Risse and Rödel 1987.

Radburn

Place	Fairlawn, New Jersey, USA.
Date	1928.
Architect	Master plan: Clarence Stein, Henry Wright; architects: Clarence Stein (head) with Frederick L. Ackerman, Andrew J. Thomas, James Tenwick Thomson.
Client	City Housing Corporation.

Project Description

General	Planned, medium-income, residential subdivision of detached two-family houses and row houses.
Project	2 square miles (5.2 km^2); superblock area: 20–30 acres (8.1–12.1 hectares); projected population: 25,000; two-family houses or row houses clustered around a cul-de-sac; houses open onto cul-de-sac on one side and communal central "green" on the other.
Units	Typical unit: E, K, B, LR, 1–3 BR, garage, cellar storage, porch.
Materials/construction	Wood frame over cellar; wood siding, brick veneer, and asphalt shingle roof.

Source: Stein 1957.

Ritterstrasse North/South

Place	Berlin-Kreuzberg, Germany.
Date	North: 1982–1989; South: 1978–1980.
Architect	Master plan: Rob Krier; landscape planning: North, Halfmann-Zillich; South, Halfmann-Zillich, Müller-Heinze and Partner; architects: various architects.
Client	North: Klingbeil-Gruppe; South: H. Buschmann, contractor.

Project Description

General	Project built for Internationalen Bauausstellung Berlin, 1987; perimeter blocks.
Project	Population 1987 (phase 1): 539; density: 115 p per hectare (46 p per acre);

North: 315 units (2% 1 and 1.5 rooms, 20% 3 rooms, 40% 4 and 4.5 rooms, 14% 5 rooms, 1% 6 rooms); South: 125 units (30% 2 rooms, 36% 3 rooms, 23% 4 rooms, 7% 5 rooms, 4% 6 rooms); 4 to 6 stories.

Units
Units vary from 49 to 123 m^2 (520–1,324 sq. ft.); varied plans generally have double orientation.

Source: Berning, Braum, and Lütke-Daldrup 1990.

Roehampton

Place
London, United Kingdom.

Date
1951–1959 (built in phases).

Architect
J. L. Martin and Hugh Bennett.

Client
London County Council.

Project Description

General
Large-scale housing estate with mixed development.

Project
Clarence Avenue development: 100-acre (40.5-hectare) site; 1,875 dwelling units at an overall density of 28 units per acre (70 units per hectare), 100 p per acre (250 p per hectare); 55% high-rise apartments; 33% 4-story maisonnettes; 12% single-family dwellings. Portsmouth Road development: 25-acre (10.1-hectare) site; 737 dwelling units; 60% high-rise; 30% 4-story maisonettes, 10% terrace houses.

Sources: Barr 1958, Benevolo 1985.

Römerstadt

Place
Römerstadt, Frankfurt-am-Main, Germany.

Date
1927–1928 (preservation order 1972).

Architect
Master plan: Ernst May, Herbert Boehm, Wolfgang Bangert; architects: Ernst May, C. H. Rudloff, Albert Winter, Karl Blattner, Gustav Schaupp, Franz Schuster, Martin Elsaesser, Walter Schütte; landscape architect: Leberecht Migge.

Client
Aktienbaugesellschaft für Kleine Wohnungen.

Project Description

General
Housing estate in satellite town of Niddatal; rental units; linear terraced row houses and apartment blocks frame streets and interior private gardens.

Project	1,182 units in 2–4 stories (50% in 4-room single-family houses, 4% in 2-family houses with 3 and 4 rooms, 46% in 2- and 3-room apartments); includes 10 shops and an elementary school.
Units	Units have central heating, radio connection, and electrical supply (lighting, hot water, stove); typical units: E, K, B, LR, 1–4 BR; generally double orientation.
Materials/construction	Plaster stucco over solid brick construction with flat timber roofs.

Sources: Dreysse 1988; Lauer 1988; Risse 1984; Risse and Rödel 1987.

Sar Methodieken

Place	Brennerbaan, Hondsrug e.o., Utrecht-Lunetten, the Netherlands.
Date	1971–1982.
Architect	Project architect: F. van der Werf; concept initiated and developed along principles established by the Foundation for Architectural Research (Dutch initials SAR) of theoreticians Habraken and Carp.
Client	Joint venture of nine housing associations.

Project Description

General	Housing estate; urban design and dwelling units developed through discussions with the users.
Project	5,600 units of housing at mixed densities, and in mixed housing types, ranging from apartment slabs to single-family row houses.

Sources: *de Architect*, 1979, no. 11; 1982, no. 9; Groenendijk and Vollaard 1987.

Scheepvaartstraat Housing

Place	2e Scheepvaartstraat, Hoek van Holland, the Netherlands.
Date	Designed 1924; built 1926–1927.
Architect	Architect: J. J. P. Oud.
Client	Rotterdam Public Works.

Project Description

General	2-story residential block, one unit deep.
Project	Row housing estate, includes shops and library.

Units	3-room units with garden on ground floor at the rear; 2- and 4-room units with balcony on the upper level.
Materials/construction	Brick and concrete, with stucco finish.

Sources: *Bouwkundig Weekblad,* 1926, p. 386; 1927, pp. 45, 281, 284; *De Stijl,* 1927, nos. 79/84; *Architecture Vivante,* 1928, no. 11; Oud 1984; Groenendijk and Vollaard 1987.

Sharpstown

Place	Sharpstown, Texas, USA.
Date	1954–present.
Client and Architect	Frank W. Sharp, developer.

Project Description

General	Moderately priced planned residential subdivision of detached single-family houses for private ownership.
Project	6,500 acres (2,630 hectares); 25,000 units; includes shopping complex, office space, recreational space and facilities, schools.
Materials/construction	Wood frame and concrete floor slab at grade; brick veneer and asphalt shingle roofing.

Sources: Papademetriou 1972; Rowe 1991.

El Silencio

Place	Caracas, Venezuela.
Date	1942–1945.
Architect	Planner and architect: Carlos Raúl Villanueva.
Client	Banco Obrero.

Project Description

General	Slum redevelopment project to house low-income residents; typically mixed-use perimeter block buildings partially or fully enclosing central garden court.
Project	Area: 9.5 hectares (23.5 acres); building: 32%, streets: 25%, open space: 43%, 4 perimeter blocks and 3 linear blocks; typically 4-story flat-roof buildings, with 2 6- and 7-story buildings; 845 units (30% 4 BR, 51% 3 BR, 19% 2 BR); includes 400 spaces for shops or small industry.

Units	Typical units: E, K, B, LR/DR, 2–4 BR, loggias and balconies; double orientation.
Materials/construction	Reinforced concrete structure with hollow brick infill.

Source: De Sola Ricardo 1987.

Spangen Housing

Place	Justus van Effenstraat, Rotterdam, the Netherlands.
Date	1919–1922 (renovation 1982–1983).
Architect	Michiel Brinkman, L. de Jonge.
Client	Rotterdam Municipal Housing Agency; renovation: State Service for the Care of Monuments.

Project Description

General	Closed housing block.
Project	Block area: 12,500 m² (134,500 sq. ft.); 273 units; 2-story unit at ground level with 2-story maisonette above, reached by third-floor open-access gallery; 4 floors total; includes central heating plant, baths, bicycle sheds, 2 lifts, cloth-drying balconies. Renovation: baths transformed into a creche and clubhouse.
Units	Typical unit: K, T, LR, 3 BR, rubbish chute, outdoor space (garden or balcony). Renovation: Two maisonettes combined into one large unit for families.

Sources: Groenendijk and Vollaard 1987; *Bouwkundig Weekblad*, 1920, p. 45; *Tijdschrift voor Volkshuisvesting*, 1924, p. 197; *Forum*, 1960/61, p. 159; *Casabella*, July-August 1985.

Stuyvesant Town

Place	Lower East Side, Manhattan, New York, USA.
Date	1943–1949.
Architect	Project team: Gilmore D. Clark (team head), Irwin Clavin, H. F. Richardson, George Gore, Andrew J. Eken.
Client	Metropolitan Life Insurance Company.

Project Description

General	Middle-income, freestanding high-rise housing estate: "towers in the park."

Project   Population: 24,000; site coverage: 23%; 35 13-story buildings; 8,755 units; 945 1–2-bedroom units; 6% units 3 or more bedrooms; varied core types combined into single large blocks.

Units   Typical unit: E, K, B, LR, 2 BR; single orientation.

Materials/construction   Brick veneer facade over frame construction.

Source: Plunz 1990.

Sunnyside Gardens

Place   Queens, New York, USA.

Date   1924–1928.

Architect   Planners: Clarence Stein and Henry Wright; architects: Clarence Stein (chief architect), Frederick Ackerman.

Client   City Housing Corporation (limited-dividend company organized to build an American garden city and which later administered mortgage and rental payments).

Project Description

General   Housing estate consisting of single or multifamily houses for private ownership and rental apartments; linear rows of single-family row houses and apartment blocks were laid out on the perimeter of the existing standard city block, creating inner courts open for gardens and leisure activities.

Project   55.82 acres (22.6 hectares); 1,202 units; 2-story 1-, 2-, and 3-family houses, and 3- and 4-story apartment blocks; includes park and community building.

Units   Limited and standardized unit types; 1-, 2-, and 3-family houses: 2-story over basement with double orientation and garden (E, K, B, LR, 1–3 BR); apartments: 4 rooms (E, K, B, LR, 2 BR) with double orientation; standard dwelling width: 25 ft. (7.6 m), length: 28 ft. 4 in. (8.5 m).

Materials/construction   1924: brick bearing walls; 1925–1928: wood frame with brick facing.

Source: Stein 1957.

Toulouse Le Mirail

Place   Toulouse Le Mirail, France.

Date   Planning 1960–1966; development corporation created and land purchases began 1966; construction 1966–present.

Architect   Master plan: Georges Candilis, Alexis Josic, Shadrach Woods; architects: Bellefontaine quarter: Georges Candilis, Association Paritaire d'Architectes Urbanistes, R. Fort, Atelier 4; Reynerie quarter: Association Paritaire d'Architectes Urbanistes.

Client
La Société d'Equipement Toulouse-Midi-Pyrénées (planning, development, construction, and administration semipublic nonprofit corporation for the city of Toulouse); final stages increasingly privatized.

Project Description

General
Satellite community of Toulouse; commercial, residential, and retail "linear center" surrounded by low-density residential construction (single-family and low-rise apartment buildings); separation of pedestrian and vehicular circulation by the creation of a raised pedestrian slab above grade.

Project
Program: population: 100,000; 800 hectares (1,977 acres); 23,000 units; 75% collective units in linear center (5-, 9-, and 15-story buildings); 12% collective units (2-, 3-, and 5-story buildings) and 13% row houses and individual houses (1- and 2-story buildings) in the peripheral zones; includes shopping centers, 16 schools, cultural center, recreation and sports facilities, community centers and exhibit space, administrative center, and several peripheral industrial and commercial activity areas.

Units
Double orientation for most collective units; internal patios for most row houses and individual houses.

Sources: Candilis, Josic, and Woods 1975; *Entreprise* no. 744, 13 December 1969.

Town Center Housing, Runcorn New Town

Place
Runcorn New Town, United Kingdom.

Date
1969–1976.

Architect
James Stirling and Partners, Michael Wilford, Peter Ray.

Client
Financing: Ministry of Housing; planning: Runcorn New Town Corporation.

Project Description

General
New town housing development; linear blocks (housing "terraces") are set at 90 and 135 degrees to create residential garden "squares"; third-level pedestrian access gallery links all the blocks to one another and to the commercial and retail town center.

Project
30 hectares (74 acres); population: 6,000; 1,500 units; 117 p per acre (292 p per hectare); 5 stories; each block groups different size units at each stair well; 33% 2- and 3-person apartments, 33% 4-person "maisonettes,"

33% 5–6-person "houses"; district heating; includes 2 shops and 2 public houses.

Units — All main living spaces face south or west; double orientation; garages and automobile circulation at ground level; "houses" for 5 or 6 persons on first and second levels with private garden (E, K, T, B, LR, 4 BR); maisonettes for 4 persons on the third and fourth levels with private terrace (E, K, B, LR/DR, 3BR); studios or apartments for 1 to 3 persons on the fifth level with private terrace (E, K, B, LR, BR).

Materials/construction — Precast concrete facade panels; heavy precast concrete structural walls; wood floors inside two-story units; glass-reinforced polyester panels in pedestrian galleries.

Sources: *Architecture d'Aujourd'hui* no. 187, October-November 1976; *Lotus 10*, 1975.

Unité d'Habitation Marseilles

Place — Marseilles, France.

Date — Designed 1945; built 1947–1952.

Architect — Le Corbusier.

Client — Ministry of Reconstruction, as part of a national, state-sponsored program for the construction of prototypical housing projects.

Project Description

General — Experimental freestanding high-rise middle-income housing block for private ownership.

Project — Population: 1,600; 337 units; 17 stories over pilotis; includes professional offices, shops, nursery, gymnasium, outdoor theater, running track.

Units — 23 unit types; all units on two levels; typical 4-room unit: E, K, T, 1½ B, LR/DR, 3 BR, terrace.

Materials/construction — Poured-in-place reinforced concrete structural framework with prefabricated concrete facade elements; individual units are assembled within the structural framework from prefabricated wood and sheet rock panels.

Source: Benevolo 1984 and 1985.

Villa Victoria

Place — Boston, Massachusetts, USA.

Date — 1969–1982 (built in six phases).

Architect	John Sharratt.
Client	Emergency Tenants Association.

Project Description

General	Urban redevelopment and renewal neighborhood-sponsored housing project; perimeter block housing with semipublic common gardens in center.
Project	19 acres (7.7 hectares); 736 units; 40 units per acre (180 units per hectare); 19% studios, 62% 1–2 bedroom units, 19% 3–5 bedroom units; phase 1: 17 low-income units and 54 moderate-income units; phase 2: 18-story elderly housing apartment building (ground floor includes shop and recreational facilities); phase 3: mid-rise residential block and 181 townhouse units; phase 4: 9 townhouses converted to 36 apartments; phase 5–6: balance of units; includes common gardens, play areas, central plaza.
Units	Row house unit: 3-, 4-, or 6-bedroom duplex over 1–2-bedroom apartments at ground level, front yards belong to ground-floor unit, rear yards to upper-level units, central wet core of kitchen and bath with living rooms at front and bedrooms at back.
Materials/construction	Row houses: lightweight steel framing with load-bearing masonry walls, painted stucco upper-level exteriors.

Source: Sharratt 1980.

Weissenhofsiedlung

Place	Stuttgart, Germany.
Date	Planning 1925–1926; designed and built 1926–1927.
Architect	Peter Behrens, Victor Bourgeois, Richard Döcker, Josef Frank, Walter Gropius, Ludwig Hilberseimer, Le Corbusier and Pierre Jeanneret, Ludwig Mies van der Rohe, J. J. P. Oud, Hans Poelzig, Adolf Rading, Hans Scharoun, Adolf G. Schneck, Mart Stam, Bruno Taut, Max Taut.
Client	Berlin Werkbund.

Project Description

General	Prototypical housing exhibit.
Project	6 housing types (A–F) with 61 units in 27 blocks; 5 3-story duplexes of 6 dwellings each, 3 2-story duplexes of 4 dwellings each, 19 1- and 2-story houses.
Units	8 type "A" apartment units: K, B, 4 R, servant's room; 34 type "B" apartments: K, B, 3 R, servant's room (on roof level); 13 type "C" single-family houses: K, B, 4 R, servant's room (on roof level); 3 type "D" 2-story houses: K, B, 6 R, servant's room; 2 type "E" 2-story houses: K, B, 5 R, servant's room; 1 type "F" 1-story single-family house: K, B, 3 R, servant's room.

Source: Joedicke 1989.

Weisse Stadt

Place | Reinickendorf district, Berlin, Germany.

Date | 1929–1931 (phase 1: 1929–30; phase 2: 1930–31).

Architect | Architects: phase 1: Otto Rudolf Slavisberg, Wilhelm Büning, Bruno Ahrends; phase 2: Wilhelm Büning, Bruno Ahrends; landscape architect: Ludwig Lesser.

Client | Gemeinnützige Heimstättengesellschaft Primus mbH.

Project Description

General | Rental, multifamily housing district; L-shaped and perimeter linear blocks.

Project | Site area: 115,532 m² (1,243,590 sq. ft.); floor area: 75,922 m² (817,224 sq. ft.); 3 and 4 stories; phase 1: 6% 1–1½ rooms; 77% 2–2½ rooms; 15% 2½–3 rooms; 2% 3½–5½ rooms; phase 2: 76% 1 room; 11% 1½ rooms; 13% 2½ rooms; includes 24 stores, central heating plant, laundry, health clinic, day care.

Source: Huse 1987.

W e s t h a u s e n

Place | Westhausen, Frankfurt-am-Main, Germany.

Date | 1929–1931 (phase 1: 1929–30 (by ABG); phase 2: 1930–31).

Architect | Master plan: Ernst May, Herbert Boehm, Wolfgang Bangert; terrace houses: Eugen Kaufmann, L. Becker; apartment blocks with access galleries, wash-house: Ferdinand Kramer, Eugen Blanck; landscape architect: Leberecht Migge.

Client | Phase 1: Aktienbaugesellschaft für Kleine Wohnungen. Phase 2: Nassauische Heimstätte.

Project Description

General | Housing estate; 2-family row houses and apartments in freestanding linear blocks.

Project | 1,116 rental apartments in row houses (2-story over basement) and apartment blocks (4-story); 19% 3-room units; 77% 2½-room units; 4% 3½-room units; includes central laundry and heating plant.

Units | 3-room units in apartment blocks with access gallery, 47 m² (505 sq. ft.): E, B, K (Frankfurt), LR, 2 BR, balcony, central heating, hot water; 2½-room units in 2-family terrace houses, 40–42 m² (430–450 sq. ft.): E, B, K (reduced Frankfurt), LR, 1½ BR, stove heating, balcony; 3½-room units in

2-family terrace houses, 54 m^2 (580 sq. ft.): E, B, K (Frankfurt), LR, 2½ BR, stove heating, balcony.

Materials/construction 34% prefabricated concrete slab construction; 66% brick construction.

Sources: Dreysse 1988; Risse 1984.

Williamsburg Homes

Place   Brooklyn, New York, USA.

Date   1937–1938.

Architect   Design team: Richard H. Shreve, William Lescaze, Matthew Del Gaudio, Arthur Holden, James Bly.

Client   Public Works Administration.

Project Description

General   Limited-income rental housing estate; 20 freestanding H- and T-shaped blocks set in 3 superblocks.

Project   25-acre (10.1-hectare) site with lot coverage of 32.1%; 1,622 units of housing; 4-story walk-up apartments. School and other community facilities included within the development.

Materials/construction Masonry walls, poured-in-place concrete floors.

Sources: Architectural Forum 1938; Plunz 1990.

Profiles of Housing Production

The following tables present a statistical summary of housing production in countries relevant to the preceding narrative. Specifically the profiles include: United States (1920–1975), Germany (1920–1938), the Netherlands (1921–1963), Great Britain (1930–1973), Italy (1951–1972), and Spain (1960–1971). In each case, data is presented in a form consistent with earlier discussion in the text.

United States

Year	Housing Starts (dus)	Annual Change (%)	Normalized (du/1,000 population)	Public (%)	Single-Family Dwellings (%)
1920	247,000				82
1921	449,000				71
1922	716,000				61
1923	871,000				59
1924	893,000				60
1925	937,000				61
1926	849,000				58
1927	810,000				56
1928	735,000				58
1929	509,000				62
1930	330,000				69
1931	254,000				74
1932	134,000				88
1933	93,000				82
1934	126,000				87
1935	221,000				83
1945	209,000		1.5	0.6	88
1949	1,025,000	10.1	6.8	3.5	77
1950	1,396,000	7.2	9.2	3.1	83
1955	1,328,000	neg.	8.0	1.5	89.9
1960	1,296,000	neg.	7.2	3.4	78
1961	1,365,000	5.3		3.8	72
1962	1,492,000	9.3		2.0	67
1963	1,614,000	8.2		2.1	62
1964	1,535,000	−4.9		2.1	62
1965	1,509,000	−1.7	7.9		63
1966	1,195,000	−20.8			65
1967	1,322,000	10.5			64
1968	1,545,000	16.9			58
1969	1,499,000	−3.0	7.4	2.0	54
1970	1,469,000	−2.0		0	56
1971	2,084,000	41.9			55
1972	2,379,000	14.2	±11.4		55
1973	2,058,000	−13.5			55
1974	1,353,000	−34.3			66
1975	1,172,000	−13.4	5.5	0.8	76
1989	1,374,000		5.5		73

Source: U.S. Department of Commerce 1955; annual figures from U.S. Department of Labor, Bureau of Labor Statistics (1945–).

Germany

Year	Housing Starts (dus)
1920	neg.
1921	neg.
1922	20,000
1923	95,000
1924	130,000
1925	173,000
1926	200,000
1927	287,000
1928	310,000
1929	320,000
1930	309,000
1931	288,000
1932	150,000
1933	136,000
1934	192,000
1935	210,000
1936	274,000
1937	307,000
1938	389,000

Source: Benevolo 1984; Bauer 1934.

The Netherlands

Year	Housing Starts (dus)	Annual Change (%)	Normalized (du/1,000 population)	Public (%)	Municipal (%)
1921	40,364				
1922	45,500				
1923	43,132				
1924	46,712				
1925	47,190				
1926	49,593				
1927	51,099				
1928	48,165				
1929	48,068				
1930	52,238				
1931	51,543				
1932	42,317				
1933	45,610				
1934	53,814				
1935	46,459				
1936	31,071				
1945	566			17.2	26
1950	47,300		5.9	65	37
1951	58,666	24	4.1	70	41
1952	69,372	64			26
1953	77,160	12	7.0±		26
1954	61,254	−21			34
1955	76,430	25			22
1956	86,437	13	7.1±		17
1957	84,783	−2			27
1958	83,396	−2			33
1959	87,085	5			29
1960	86,025	−1			22
1961	101,768	17	7.2±		17
1962	91,880	−10			14
1963	93,766	2	6.5		16

Source: Ministry of Housing and Building 1964; Ministry of Reconstruction and Housing 1953.

Great Britain

Year	Housing Completions (dus)	Annual Change (%)	Normalized (du/1,000 population)	Public (%)
1930	190,000			
1931	210,000			
1932	220,000	5		
1933	362,000	65	9 to 10	
1934	350,000			
1935	375,000			
1936	365,000			
1946	60,000			50
1947	135,000	125		70
1948	225,000	67		84
1949	200,000	−11		85
1950	200,000	0		85
1951	195,000	−3	4.5±	87
1952	240,000	23		87
1953	320,000	33	7.0±	82
1954	350,000	9	7.9±	73
1955	315,000	−10	7.7±	63
1956	300,000	−5	6.8±	58
1957	300,000	0	6.8±	57
1958	241,525	−20		55
1961	268,832		6.8	
1963	298,872		6.3±	42
1964	373,676	25	8.0±	42
1965	382,297	2.4		44
1966	385,509	0.8		47
1967	404,356	5		50
1968	413,715	2	7.8±	46
1969	366,793	−13	7.1	51
1970	350,433	−4		51
1971	350,520		6.6	45
1972	319,097	−9		38
1973	293,571	−8		37

Source: 1930–1935: Benevolo 1984, p. 508; 1946–1957: Barr 1958, p. 23; 1958, 1961; Alderson 1962; 1963–1973: Pepper 1975, p. 95.

Italy

Year	Investment (trillion lire, 1963 values)	Annual Change (%)	Public (%)
1951	0.51		25
1952	0.63	24	26
1953	0.75	19	21
1954	0.9	20	16
1955	1.09	21	12
1956	1.21	11	10
1957	1.36	12	10
1958	1.41	4	14
1959	1.51	7	21
1960	1.53	1.3	17
1961	1.67	9	11
1962	1.93	16	7
1963	2.16	12	4
1964	2.29	6	4
1965	2.15	−6	6
1966	2.12	−1.4	7
1967	2.21	4	7
1968	2.47	12	7
1969	2.85	15	5
1970	2.67	−6	3.6
1971	2.35	−12	3.5
1972	2.39	1.7	3.3

Source: Garavini 1975.

Spain

Year	Housing Completions (dus)	Annual Change (%)	Normalized (du/1000 population)	Public (%)
1960	144,000		4.8	
1961	148,000	3	4.8	
1962	162,000	9	5.3	8.9
1963	206,000	27	6.6	14.2
1964	257,000	25	8.1	5.4
1965	283,000	10	8.9	6.8
1966	268,000	−5	8.9	7.7
1967	204,000	−24	6.3	8.8
1968	248,000	22	7.5	8.8
1969	270,000	9	8.1	8
1970	308,000	14	9.1	6.8
1971	319,000	4	9.4	

Source: Bohigas 1975, p. 152.

References

Abercrombie, Sir Patrick.
1959.

Town and Country Planning. 3d ed. London: Oxford University Press.

Adorno, Theodor W.
1967.

"Looking Back on Surrealism." In Irving Howe (ed.), *The Idea of the Modern in Literature and the Arts.* New York: Horizon Press.

Aiken, Henry D.
1956.

The Age of Ideology: The Nineteenth Century Philosophies. New York: Mentor Books.

Alderson, Stanley.
1962.

Britain in the Sixties: Housing. London: Penguin.

Alexander, Christopher.
1964.

Notes on the Synthesis of Form. Cambridge, Massachusetts: Harvard University Press.

Alexander, Christopher.
1979.

The Timeless Way of Building. New York: Oxford University Press.

Alexander, Christopher, et al.
1977.

A Pattern Language. New York: Oxford University Press.

Alexander, C., S. Ishikawa, and M. Silverstein.
1968.

A Pattern Language Which Generates Multi-Service Centers. Berkeley, California: Center for Environmental Structure.

Allen, Frederick Lewis.
1959 (1931).

Only Yesterday: An Informal History of the 1920's. New York: Harper and Row.

American Public Health Association.
1939.

"Basic Principles of Healthful Housing Officials." In National Association of Housing Officials, *Practical Standards for Modern Housing.* Chicago: National Association of Housing Officials.

Amery, Colin.
1974.

"Housing, Byker, Newcastle upon Tyne." *Architectural Review,* December, pp. 346–362.

Anderson, Stanford Owen.
1968.

"Peter Behrens and the New Architecture of Germany, 1900–1917." Ph.D. dissertation, Columbia University. Copyright 1970.

Anderson, Stanford (ed.).
1972.

On Streets. Cambridge, Massachusetts: MIT Press.

Anderton, Frances.
1990.

"A Tailoring of Two Cultures." *Architectural Review,* May, pp. 70–73.

Archer, John.
1987.

Building a Nation: A History of the Australian House. Sydney: Collins.

Architectural Forum.
1938.

"Public Housing." *Architectural Forum,* vol. 68, no. 5, May, pp. 345–424.

Architectural Record.
1932.

"Portfolio of Apartment Houses." *Architectural Record,* vol. 71, no. 3, March, pp. 167–208.

Architectural Review.
1974.

"Byker by Erskine." *Architectural Review,* December, pp. 346–353.

Architecture d'Aujourd'hui.
1956.

"Unité d'Habitation at Nantes-Reze and Bron Parilly." *Architecture d'Aujourd'hui,* July, pp. 2–13.

Architecture d'Aujourd'hui.
1957.

"LCC Projects." *Architecture d'Aujourd'hui,* November, pp. 46–60.

384

Arnell, Peter, and Ted Bickford (eds.).
1986.

Frank Gehry, Buildings and Projects. New York: Rizzoli.

Aronovici, Carol.
1914.

"German Housing Reform." *Journal of the American Institute of Architects* (reprint), pp. 3–8.

Atterbury, Grosvenor.
1936.

"Bricks without Brains: A Challenge to Science, and the Factory-Made House." *Architecture,* vol. 78, no. 4, April, pp. 193–196.

Auerbach, Erich.
1953.

Mimesis: The Representation of Reality in Western Literature. Princeton, New Jersey: Princeton University Press.

Aymonino, Carlo.
1985.

"Type and Typology." *Architectural Design,* 55, May–June, pp. 49–51.

Babcock, Richard F.
1966.

The Zoning Game. Madison, Wisconsin: University of Wisconsin Press.

Bahrdt, Hans.
1968.

Humaner Stadtbau. Hamburg: Wegner Verlag.

Banham, Reyner.
1960.

Theory and Design in the First Machine Age. London: Penguin.

Barazzetta, Giulio.
1991.

"Le Duecento Colonne Climat de France, 1955–57." *Phalaris,* no. 16, pp. 26–29.

Barbieri, Umberto.
1986.

J. J. P. Oud. Bologna: Zanichelli Editore.

Barnett, Jonathan.
1986.

The Elusive City: Five Centuries of Design, Ambition and Miscalculation. New York: Harper and Row.

Barnouw, Adriaan J.
1940.

The Dutch: A Portrait Study of the People of Holland. New York: Columbia University Press.

Barr, A. W. Cleeve.
1958.

Public Authority Housing. London: B. T. Batsford, Ltd.

Barzun, Jacques.
1961 (1943).

Classic, Romantic and Modern. Chicago: University of Chicago Press.

Baudelaire, C.
1964 (1863).

The Painter of Modern Life and Other Essays. Translated and edited by J. Mayne. London: Penguin.

Baudrillard, Jean.
1983.

Simulations. Translated by Paul Foss and Paul Patton. New York: Semiotext.

Bauer, Catherine.
1934.

Modern Housing. New York: Houghton Mifflin Company.

Beddington, Nadine.
1981.

Design for Shopping Centers. London: Butterworth Scientific.

Behar, Richard.
1990.

"Who Invented Microprocessors?" *Time,* 10 September, p. 62.

Bemis, Albert Farewell.
1934.

The Evolving House. Cambridge, Massachusetts: The Technology Press.

Benevolo, Leonardo.
1984.

History of Modern Architecture. Vol. 2 (*The Modern Movement*). Cambridge, Massachusetts: MIT Press.

Benevolo, Leonardo.
1985.

The History of the City. Cambridge, Massachusetts: MIT Press.

Beniger, James R.
1986.

The Control Revolution: Technological and Economic Origins of the Information Society. Cambridge, Massachusetts: Harvard University Press.

Benjamin, Walter.
1969 (1955).

Illuminations. Translated by H. Zohn. New York: Harcourt, Brace and World.

385

Benjamin, Walter.
1978.

One-Way Street. Translated by E. Jephcott and K. Shorter. New York: Harcourt Brace Jovanovich.

Berning, Maria, Michael Braum, and Engelbert Lütke-Daldrup.
1990.

Berliner Wohnquartier: Ein Führer durch 40 Siedlungen. Berlin: Dietrich Reimer Verlag.

Bernstein, Richard J.
1976.

The Restructuring of Social and Political Theory. New York: Harcourt Brace Jovanovich.

Bernstein, Richard J.
1983.

Beyond Objectivism and Relativism: Science, Hermeneutics and Praxis. Philadelphia: University of Pennsylvania Press.

Bernstein, Richard J.
1986.

Philosophical Profiles: Essays in a Pragmatic Mode. Philadelphia: University of Pennsylvania Press.

Black, C. E.
1966.

The Dynamics of Modernization: A Study in Comparative History. New York: Harper and Row.

Blackshaw, Maurice B.
1951.

A Comparative Study of the Utilization of Space in Current Types of Dwellings in 14 European Countries (1948–1949). Geneva: United Nations Housing Sub-committee.

Blatt, Sidney J.
1984.

Continuity and Change in Art: The Development of Modes of Representation. Hillsdale, New Jersey: Lawrence Erlbaum Associates.

Blum, John M., et al.
1963.

The National Experience. New York: Harcourt, Brace and World.

Bohigas, Oriol.
1975.

"Barcelona, Residential Area. *Lotus International*, no. 10, pp. 146–155.

Borgmann, Albert.
1984.

Technology and the Character of Contemporary Life: A Philosophical Inquiry. Chicago: University of Chicago Press.

Boston Redevelopment Authority.
1967.

Housing in Boston. Boston: Planning Department, Boston Redevelopment Authority, July.

Bowly, Devereux, Jr.
1978.

The Poorhouse: Subsidized Housing in Chicago, 1895–1976. London: Feffer and Simons, Inc.

Boyer, Christine.
1983.

Dreaming of the Rational City. Cambridge, Massachusetts: MIT Press.

Braghieri, Gianni.
1982.

Aldo Rossi. Barcelona: Editorial Gustavo Gili, S.A.

Braun, Helmut, and Hans-Georg Heimel (et al.).
1977.

Bauen in Frankfurt-am-Main. Frankfurt-am-Main: Verlag von Waldemer Kramer.

Bromberg, Paul.
1942.

Architecture in the Netherlands. New York: Whitney.

Brownell, Baker, and Frank Lloyd Wright.
1937.

Architecture and Modern Life. New York: Harper and Brothers Publishers.

Bruner, James E., Jr.
1972.

Industrialism: The American Experience. New York: Benzinger.

Buchanan, Peter.
1981.

"Byker: The Spaces Between." *Architectural Review*, vol. 170, no. 1018, December, pp. 334–343.

Buekschmitt, Justus.
1963.

Bauten und Planungen—Band 1—Ernst May. Stuttgart: Verlagsanstalt Alexander Koch, GmbH.

Burgess, Rod.
1982.

"Self-Help Housing Advocacy: A Curious Form of Radicalism. A Critique of the Work of John F. C. Turner." In Peter M. Ward (ed.), *Self-Help Housing: A Critique*. London: Mansell Publishing Limited, pp. 55–97.

Burns, Wilfred (ed.).
1964.

Housing: A Review of Current Problems and Policies. 4 vols. Newcastle upon Tyne: City and Council of Newcastle upon Tyne.

References

386

Burstein, Daniel.
1988.

Yen! Japan's New Financial Empire and Its Threat to America. New York: Simon and Schuster.

Caminos, Horacio, and Reinhard Goethert.
1976.

Urbanization Primer for the Design of Sites and Services Projects. Washington, D.C.: World Bank Urban Projects Department.

Campbell, Robert.
1990.

"Thoughtful Designs for City and Suburb." *Boston Globe,* 12 March, pp. 60–61.

Candilis, Georges.
1977.

Baton la vie: Un architect temoin de son temps. Paris: Stock.

Candilis, Georges, Alexis Josic, and Shadrach Woods.
1975.

Toulouse Le Mirail: La naissance d'une ville nouvelle. Stuttgart: Karl Krämer.

Casabella.
1938a.

"Two Buildings in Rotterdam." *Casabella,* November, pp. 18–25.

Casabella.
1938b.

"La sistemazione di una piazza nuova a Genoa." *Casabella,* November, pp. 12–15.

Casabella.
1938c.

"Proposta di piano regolatore per la zona Sempione-Fiera, a Milano." *Casabella,* December, pp. 2–7.

Casciato, Maristella.
1987.

La scuola di Amsterdam. Bologna: Zanichelli Editore.

Cassirer, Ernst.
1951.

The Philosophy of the Enlightenment. Princeton, New Jersey: Princeton University Press.

Castells, Manuel.
1983.

The City and the Grassroots: A Cross-Cultural Theory of Urban Social Movements. Berkeley: University of California Press.

Chandler, Alfred D.
1977.

The Visible Hand: Revolution in American Business. Cambridge, Massachusetts: Harvard University Press.

Chandler, Alfred D., Jr.
1987.

"Technology and the Transformation of Industrial Organization." In Joel Colton and Stuart Bruchey (eds.), *Technology, the Economy and Society: The American Experience.* New York: Columbia University Press.

Chandler, Alfred D., Jr.
1990.

Scale and Scope: The Dynamics of Industrial Capitalism. Cambridge, Massachusetts: The Belknap Press.

Cherry, Gordon E.
1988.

Cities and Plans: The Shaping of Urban Britain in the Nineteenth and Twentieth Centuries. London: Edward Arnold.

City Housing Corporation.
1924a.

Good Homes and Good Citizenship. New York: City Housing Corporation, November 14.

City Housing Corporation.
1924b.

Sunnyside: The New Garden Homes of Queens. New York: City Housing Corporation, October 17.

City Housing Corporation.
1925.

Sunnyside: A Step Towards Better Housing. New York: City Housing Corporation.

City Housing Corporation.
1926.

Housing Notes. New York: City Housing Corporation, October 1.

City Housing Corporation.
1927a.

Sunnyside: A Step Towards Better Housing. New York: City Housing Corporation, March 15.

City Housing Corporation.
1927b.

Expert Opinion. New York: City Housing Corporation, December 15.

City Housing Corporation.
1927c.

Block Plan of Third Unit of Sunnyside Gardens. New York: City Housing Corporation.

City Housing Corporation.
1927d.

Third Annual Report. New York: City Housing Corporation.

City Housing Corporation.
1928.

Sunnyside Gardens. New York: City Housing Corporation.

City of Newcastle upon Tyne.
1981.

The Byker Redevelopment. Newcastle upon Tyne: City of Newcastle upon Tyne.

City Planning Commission of Los Angeles.
1947.

Year Book. Los Angeles: City of Los Angeles.

Clark, Clifford Edward, Jr.
1986.

The American Family Home: 1800–1960. Chapel Hill: University of North Carolina Press.

Clark, T. J.
1982.

"Clement Greenberg's Theory of Art." *Critical Inquiry,* vol. 1, no. 9, September, pp. 139–156.

Clawson, Marion, and Peter Hall.
1973.

Planning and Urban Growth: An Anglo-American Comparison. Baltimore: Johns Hopkins University Press.

Clémençon, Anne-Sophie, Florence Curt-Patat, and Alain Lagier (et al.).
1988.

Villeurbanne Gratte-Ciel. Lyons: Conseil Régional Rhône-Alpes.

Cobb, Henry N.
1985.

The Architecture of Frank Gehry. New York: Rizzoli.

Cohn, Sidney.
1968.

Practice of Architectural Control in Northern Europe. Chapel Hill: University of North Carolina Press.

Collingwood, R. G.
1946.

The Idea of History. New York: Oxford University Press.

Collymore, Peter.
1983.

Ralph Erskine. Barcelona: Editorial Gustavo Gili.

Colquhoun, Alan.
1989.

Modernity and the Classical Tradition: Architectural Essays 1980–1987. Cambridge, Massachusetts: MIT Press.

Colton, Joel, and Stuart Bruchey (eds.).
1987.

Technology, the Economy and Society: The American Experience. New York: Columbia University Press.

Connor, Steven.
1989.

Postmodernist Culture: An Introduction to Theories of the Contemporary. Oxford: Basil Blackwell.

Conrads, Ulrich.
1964.

Programs and Manifestos on 20th Century Architecture. Cambridge, Massachusetts: MIT Press.

Cooke, Catherine.
1983.

Chernikhov: Fantasy and Construction. London: AD Profile.

Copleston, Frederick.
1963.

A History of Philosophy. Vol. 7 (*Modern Philosophy, Part I, Fichte to Hegel*). New York: Doubleday and Company.

Corn, Joseph J. (ed.).
1986.

Imagining Tomorrow: History, Technology, and the American Future. Cambridge, Massachusetts: MIT Press.

Costa, Alves.
1978.

"The Oporto Experience." *Lotus International,* no. 18, pp. 66–70.

Cowan, Ruth Schwartz.
1982.

"The Industrial Revolution in the Home: Household Technology and Social Change in the Twentieth Century." In Thomas J. Schlereth (ed.), *Material Cultural Studies in America.* Nashville, Tennessee: American Association for State and Local History, pp. 222–397.

Cromley, Elizabeth Collins.
1990.

Alone Together: A History of New York's Early Apartments. Ithaca: Cornell University Press.

Day, Michael G.
1981.

"The Contribution of Sir Raymond Unwin and R. Barry Parker to the Development of Site Planning Theory and Practice c. 1890–1918." In Anthony Sutcliffe (ed.), *British Town Planning: The Formative Years.* Leicester: Leicester University Press, pp. 156–199.

388

de Guttry, Irene.
1978.

Guida di Roma moderna: Architettura dal 1870 a oggi. Rome: De Luca Editore.

Delfante, Charles, Bernard Meuret, and Alain Lagier (et al.).
1984.

"Les Gratte-Ciel de Villeurbanne." *Urba*, vol. 204, November, pp. 49–64.

Department of Housing.
1950.

Historical Sketch of Housing in Rotterdam from the Middle Ages to the Present Day. Rotterdam: Municipality of Rotterdam.

Department of Housing of the Municipality of Rotterdam.
1950.

Rotterdam: Its Dwellings during the Last Ninety Years. Rotterdam: Department of Housing.

De Sola Ricardo, Ricardo.
1987.

La Urbanizacion "El Silencio": Cronica, 1942–1945. Caracas: Ernesto Armitano.

DiBacco, Thomas V.
1987.

Made in the U.S.A. New York: Harper and Row.

Dilthey, Wilhelm.
1959.

Schiller. Göttingen: B. G. Teubner.

Dixon, John Morris.
1981.

"Wage-Earner's Versailles." *Progressive Architecture*, October, pp. 94–97.

Döblin, Alfred.
1931 (1929).

Alexanderplatz, Berlin. Translated by Eugene Jolas. New York: Frederick Unger Publishing.

Drabble, Margaret (ed.).
1985.

The Oxford Companion to English Literature. 5th ed. New York: Oxford University Press.

Dreysse, D. W.
1988.

Ernst May Housing Estates: Architectural Guide to Eight New Frankfurt Estates (1926–1930). Frankfurt-am-Main: Fricke Verlag.

Dubor, Bernard Félix.
1986.

Fernand Pouillon. Milan: Electa Moniteur.

Dudley, Earl of.
1944.

Design of Dwellings. London: H. M. Stationery Office.

Dunster, David.
1979.

"Walled Town." *Progressive Architecture*, vol. 8, pp. 66–73.

Early, James.
1965.

Romanticism and American Architecture. New York: A. S. Barnes and Co.

Egelius, Mats.
1977.

"Ralph Erskine: The Humane Architect." *Architectural Design*, vol. 47, nos. 11 and 12.

Eichler, Ned.
1982.

The Merchant Builders. Cambridge, Massachusetts: MIT Press.

Eisenman, Peter.
1978.

"Postscript: Graves of Modernism." *Oppositions*, no. 12, Spring, pp. 22ff.

Eisenman, Peter.
1979.

"Aspects of Modernism: Maison Domino and the Self-Referential Sign." *Oppositions*, nos. 15/16, pp. 118–129.

Eisenman, Peter.
1985.

Romeo and Juliet Project. Venice Biennale.

Ernst and Sohn, Wilhelm.
1986.

Ernst May und das neue Frankfurt 1925–1930. Berlin: Helm.

Erskine, Ralph.
1968.

Memorandum on the Byker Redevelopment Project. Housing Committee, City of Newcastle upon Tyne, November.

Erskine, Ralph.
1981.

The Byker Redevelopment. Newcastle: City of Newcastle upon Tyne.

389

Fernandez, Raul A.
1989.

The Mexican-American Border Region. Notre Dame, Indiana: University of Notre Dame Press.

Fischer, W.
1965.

"Das Werk von J. J. P. Oud." *Bauen + Wohnen* 2, vol. 1, no. 4, pp. 10ff.

Fish, Gertrude S. (ed.).
1979.

The Story of Housing. New York: Macmillan.

Fisher, Leonard Everett.
1985.

Masterpieces of American Painting. New York: Exeter Books.

Five Architects.
1972.

Five Architects: Eisenmann, Graves, Gwathmey, Hejduk and Meier. New York: Wittenborn Art Books, Inc.

Foard, Ashley A., and Hilbert Fefferman.
1966.

"Federal Urban Renewal Legislation." In James Q. Wilson (ed.), *Urban Renewal: The Record and the Controversy.* Cambridge, Massachusetts: MIT Press.

Forty, Adrian.
1986.

Objects of Desire: Design and Society from Wedgewood to IBM. New York: Pantheon Books.

Foster, Hal.
1985.

Recodings: Art, Spectacle, Cultural Politics. Seattle, Washington: Bay Press.

Foulke, William Dudley.
1911.

"A German City Worthy of Emulation: A Study of Frankfurt-on-the-Main as an Example in Municipal Administration." *Seventh Annual Convention of the American Civic Association,* Washington, D.C., December 13.

Foulke, William D.
1912.

"A German City Worthy of Emulation." *American City,* vol. 6, no. 1, January, pp. 412–419.

Frampton, Kenneth.
1975.

"The Evolution of Housing Concepts, 1870–1970." *Lotus International,* no. 10, pp. 24–33.

Frampton, Kenneth.
1980.

Modern Architecture: A Critical History. New York: Oxford University Press.

Frampton, Kenneth (ed.).
1982.

Modern Architecture and the Critical Present. New York: St. Martin's Press.

Frampton, Kenneth.
1983.

"Towards a Critical Regionalism: Six Points for an Architecture of Resistance." In Hal Foster (ed.), *The Anti-Aesthetic: Essays on Postmodern Culture.* Port Townsend, Washington: Bay Press, pp. 16–30.

Frampton, Kenneth.
1986.

"Poesis and Transformation: The Architecture of Alvaro Siza." In Pierluigi Nicolin, *Alvaro Siza: Poetic Profession.* New York: Rizzoli, pp. 10–23.

Frampton, Kenneth.
1990.

"On the Architectural Tectonic." Public lecture, Graduate School of Design, Harvard University.

Franck, Karen A., and Sherry Ahrentzen (eds.).
1991.

New Households New Housing. New York: Van Nostrand Reinhold.

Frederick, Christine.
1920.

Scientific Management in the Home: Household Engineering. London: Dummet.

Friedrich, Otto.
1972.

Before the Deluge: A Portrait of Berlin in the 1920's. New York: Harper and Row.

Frisby, David.
1986.

Fragments of Modernity: Theories of Modernity in the Work of Simmel, Kracauer and Benjamin. Cambridge, Massachusetts: MIT Press.

Futagawa, Yukio.
1977.

Carlo Aymonino/Aldo Rossi: Housing Complex at the Gallaratese Quarter, Milan, Italy. 1969–1974. Tokyo: Global Architecture, ADA Edita.

Futagawa, Yukio (ed.).
1984.

Byker Redevelopment, Byker Area of Newcastle upon Tyne, England, 1969–82. Tokyo: Global Architecture.

Gadamer, Hans-Georg.
1982.

Reason in the Age of Science. Translated by Frederick G. Lawrence. Cambridge, Massachusetts: MIT Press.

390

Galbraith, John Kenneth.
1972.

The New Industrial State. 2d ed. Boston: Little, Brown.

Gans, Herbert J.
1962.

The Urban Villagers: Group and Class in the Life of Italian-Americans. New York: The Free Press.

Garavini, Roberto.
1975.

"Mass Low-Cost Housing and Urban Land Rent in Post-War Italy." *Lotus International*, no. 10, pp. 42–55.

Gartenstadt, AG.
1935.

25 Jahre Gartenstadt-Gesellschaft, Frankfurt am Main A-G (1910–1935). Frankfurt-am-Main: Gartenstadt Gesellschaft.

Gay, Peter.
1968.

Weimar Culture: The Outsider as Insider. New York: Harper and Row.

Geist, Johann Friedrich, and Klaus Kürvers.
1984.

Das Berliner Mietshaus, 1862–1945. Munich: Prestel-Verlag.

Geurst, J.
1983.

Van der Vlugt, Architect, 1894–1936. Delft: Molenaar.

Giddens, A.
1971.

Capitalism and Modern Social Theory. New York: Cambridge University Press.

Giedion, Sigfried.
1931.

Walter Gropius. Paris: Editions G. Crès et Cie.

Giedion, Sigfried.
1948.

Mechanization Takes Command. New York: Oxford University Press.

Giedion, Sigfried.
1970 (1941).

Space, Time and Architecture: The Growth of a New Tradition. Cambridge, Massachusetts: Harvard University Press.

Gilles, Mary Davis (ed.).
1946.

Let's Plan a Home. Toledo, Ohio: Surface Combustion Corporation.

Glaab, L. N., and A. T. Brown.
1967.

A History of Urban America. New York: Macmillan.

Goldberg, Michael, and Peter Horwood.
1980.

Zoning: Its Cost and Relevance for the 1980s. Ottawa, Canada: The Fraser Institute.

Goodman, Robert.
1971.

After the Planners. New York: Simon and Schuster.

Gowans, Alan.
1986.

The Comfortable House: North American Suburban Architecture, 1890–1930. Cambridge, Massachusetts: MIT Press.

Green, Gil.
1976.

Portugal's Revolution. New York: International Publishers.

Gregotti, Vittorio.
1979.

Alvaro Siza: Architetto 1954–1979. Milan: Idea Editions.

Grinberg, Donald I.
1980.

"Modernist Housing and Its Critics: The Dutch Contributions." *Harvard Architecture Review*, 1, Spring.

Grinberg, Donald I.
1982.

Housing in the Netherlands, 1900–1940. Delft: Delft University Press.

Groenendijk, Paul, and Piet Vollaard.
1987.

Gids voor Moderne Architectuur in Nederland. Rotterdam: Uitgeverij 010 Publishers.

Gropius, Walter.
1955.

Scope of Total Architecture. New York: Harper and Row.

Gutman, Robert.
1977.

"House VI." *Progressive Architecture*, June, pp. 57–68.

Habakkuk, H. J.
1962.

American and British Technology in the Nineteenth Century. Cambridge, Massachusetts: MIT Press.

391

Habermas, Jürgen.
1981.

"Modernity versus Postmodernity." *New German Critique*, no. 22, Winter, pp. 3–14.

Habermas, Jürgen.
1987.

The Philosophical Discourse of Modernity: Twelve Lectures. Translated by Frederick Lawrence. Cambridge, Massachusetts: MIT Press.

Habraken, N. J.
1972.

Supports: An Alternative to Mass Housing. New York: Praeger Publishers.

Habraken, N. John.
1985.

The Appearance of the Form. Cambridge, Massachusetts: Attwater Press.

Hall, Edward T.
1969.

The Hidden Dimension. Garden City, New York: Anchor Books.

Hall, Peter, and Ann Markusen (eds.).
1985.

Silicon Landscapes. Boston: Allen & Unwin.

Hartlaub, Gustav F.
1925.

Introduction to *Neue Sachlichkeit.* Chemnitz: Chemnitz Kunsthütte.

Harvey, David.
1989.

The Condition of Postmodernity. London: Basil Blackwell.

Hawkes, Nigel.
1971.

The Computer Revolution. New York: Dutton.

Hawking, Stephen W.
1988.

A Brief History of Time: From the Big Bang to the Black Holes. New York: Bantam Books.

Hayden, Dolores.
1982.

The Grand Domestic Revolution: A History of Feminist Designs for American Homes, Neighborhoods and Cities. Cambridge, Massachusetts: MIT Press.

Heidegger, Martin.
1959.

An Introduction to Metaphysics. New Haven: Yale University Press.

Heidegger, Martin.
1962.

Being and Time. Translated by John Macquarie and Edward Robinson. London: SCM Press.

Heidegger, Martin.
1971.

Poetry, Language, Thought. Translated by Albert Hofstadter. New York: Harper and Row.

Herbert, Gilbert.
1984.

The Dream of the Factory-Made House: Walter Gropius and Konrad Wachsmann. Cambridge, Massachusetts: MIT Press.

Heskett, John.
1980.

Industrial Design. New York: Oxford University Press.

Hess, Hans.
1974.

George Grosz. New York: Macmillan.

Hirsch, E. D., Jr.
1967.

Validity in Interpretation. New Haven: Yale University Press.

Hiss, Anthony.
1990.

The Experience of Place. New York: Vintage.

Hitchcock, Henry-Russell, and Philip Johnson.
1966 (1932).

The International Style. New York: W. W. Norton.

Höpfner, Rosemarie, and Volker Fischer (eds.).
1986.

Ernst May und das Neue Frankfurt 1925–1930. Berlin: Wilhelm Ernst and Sohn Verlag.

Höpfner, Rosemarie, and Gerd Kuhn.
1988.

"Vergangene Gegenwart: Sequenzen städtischer Geschichten—1928 bis 1958." In Walter Prigge and Hans-Peter Schwartz (eds.), *Das Neue Frankfurt.* Frankfurt-am-Main: Vervuert Verlag, pp. 16–89.

Hounshell, David.
1985.

From the American System to Mass Production. Baltimore, Maryland: Johns Hopkins University Press.

Howard, Ebenezer.
1902 (1898).

Garden Cities of Tomorrow. Paternoster Square, England: Sonnen Schien & Company.

392

Howard, Ebenezer.
1945 (1914).

Garden Cities of Tomorrow. London: Faber and Faber.

Huntoon, Maxwell C., Jr.
1971.

PUDs: A Better Way for the Suburbs. Washington, D.C.: The Urban Land Institute.

Huse, Norbert (et al.).
1987.

Vier Berliner Siedlungen der Weimarer Republik. Berlin: Argon Verlag.

Huyssen, Andreas.
1986.

After the Great Divide: Modernism, Mass Culture, Postmodernism. Bloomington, Indiana: Indiana University Press.

International Garden Cities and Town Planning Association.
1915.

First Annual Report. London: International Garden Cities and Town Planning Association.

Jackson, Kenneth T.
1985.

Crabgrass Frontier: The Suburbanization of the United States. New York: Oxford University Press.

Jansen, Wolfgang.
1987.

Glanzrevuen der Zwanziger Jahre. Berlin: Kapele Verlag.

Jencks, Charles (ed.).
1980.

Post-Modern Classicism. London: Garden House Press.

Jencks, Charles (ed.).
1984.

The Language of Post-Modern Architecture. London: Academy Editions.

Jencks, Charles.
1987.

Post-Modernism: The New Classicism in Art and Architecture. New York: Rizzoli.

Joedicke, Jürgen.
1989.

Weissenhof Siedlung Stuttgart. Stuttgart: Karl Krämer Verlag.

John Sharratt Associates.
1991.

Villa Victoria: Statistical Profile. Boston: John Sharratt Associates.

Joint Center for Housing Studies of Harvard University.
1985–1991.

The State of the Nation's Housing. Cambridge, Massachusetts: Joint Center for Housing Studies of Harvard University.

Kaplan, Justin D. (ed.).
1958.

Aristotle. New York: Washington Square Press.

Kaplan, Marshall.
1973.

Urban Planning in the 1960s: A Design for Irrelevancy. Cambridge, Massachusetts: MIT Press.

Kauss, Uwe, and Susanne Reininger.
1988.

"Vom fortschrittlichen Bauen zur einheitlichen Vielfalt. Zur Sozialgeschichte der Siedlung Praunheim." In Walter Prigge and Hans-Peter Schwartz (eds.), *Das Neue Frankfurt.* Frankfurt-am-Main: Vervuert Verlag, pp. 41–59.

Kennedy, G. Donald.
1944.

Here's How You Can Help Redevelop Your City with Modern Highways. Washington, D.C.: Chamber of Commerce of the United States.

Kilham, Walter Harrington, and James Hopkins.
1913.

"Two Groups of Houses Built for the Boston House Company." *Bricklayer*, vol. 22, no. 4, pp. 93–96.

Kleiheus, Josef Paul, and Heinrich Klotz.
1986.

International Building Exhibition Berlin 1987: Examples of a New Architecture. New York: Rizzoli.

Klotz, Heinrich.
1989.

"New German Painting." In Andreas Papadakis (ed.), *German Art Now.* London: Academy Editions, pp. 6–13.

Kostof, Spiro (ed.).
1977.

The Architect: Chapters in the History of the Profession. New York: Oxford University Press.

Kracauer, Siegfried.
1930.

"Schreie auf der Strasse." *Frankfurter Zeitung*, 19 July.

Kracauer, Siegfried.
1964.

Strassen in Berlin und anderswo. Frankfurt: Suhrkamp.

393

Kracauer, Siegfried.
1977 (1927).

Das Ornament der Masse. Essays. Frankfurt-am-Main: Suhrkamp.

Kramer, Lore.
1986.

"Rationalisierung des Haushaltes und Frauenfrage—Die Frankfürter Küche und zeitgenössische Kritik." In Rosemarie Höpfner and Volker Fischer (eds.), *Ernst May und das Neue Frankfurt 1925–1930.* Berlin: Wilhelm Ernst and Sohn Verlag, pp. 77–84.

Krasnowiecki, Jan Z., and Richard F. Babcock.
1965.

"Legal Aspects of Planned Unit Development: With Suggested Legislation." *Urban Land Institute, Technical Bulletin,* 52, May.

Krier, Rob.
1979.

Urban Space (Stadtraum). New York: Rizzoli.

Krimerman, Leonard I.
1969.

The Nature and Scope of Social Science: A Critical Anthology. New York: Appleton-Century-Crofts.

Krueckeberg, Donald A. (ed.).
1983.

Introduction to Planning History in the United States. New Brunswick: Center for Urban Policy Research.

Kwartler, Michael, and Franklin Havlicek.
1984.

"Sunnyside Gardens: The Politics of Common Open Space." *Space and Society,* June, pp. 108–119.

Lane, Barbara Miller.
1968.

Architecture and Politics in Germany 1918–1945. Cambridge, Massachusetts: Harvard University Press.

Lane, Barbara Miller.
1986.

"Architects in Power: Politics and Ideology in the Work of Ernst May and Albert Speer." In Robert I. Rotberg and Theodore K. Rabb (eds.), *Art and History: Images and Their Meaning.* New York: Cambridge University Press.

Lari, Mihail S.
1989.

"Public Housing in the United States—The Columbia Point Housing Project, Dorchester." Undergraduate thesis, Harvard University.

Lasdun, Denys.
1984.

Architecture: In an Age of Scepticism. New York: Oxford University Press.

Lauer, Heike.
1988.

"Neu-Marokko zur Vorseige—Siedlung par excellence. Zur Sozialgeschichte der Siedlung Römerstadt." In Walter Prigge and Hans-Peter Schwarz (eds.), *Das Neue Frankfurt.* Frankfurt-am-Main: Vervuert Verlag, pp. 19–27.

Le Corbusier.
1959 (1923).

Towards a New Architecture. London: Architectural Press.

Le Corbusier.
1964 (1933).

The Radiant City. New York: The Orion Press.

Le Corbusier.
1975 (1924).

"The New Spirit in Architecture." In Timothy Benton and Charlotte Benton (eds.), *Architecture and Design, 1890–1939.* New York: Wittenborn, pp. 135ff.

Le Goff, Jacques.
1980.

Time, Work and Culture in the Middle Ages. Translated by Arthur Goldhammer. Chicago: University of Chicago Press.

Levitt and Sons, Inc.
1951.

"Background Memorandum on Levittown, Pennsylvania." Mimeographed. Frances Loeb Library, Harvard University.

Liebs, Chester H.
1985.

Main Street to Miracle Mile. Boston: Little Brown.

Löwith, Karl.
1964 (1941).

From Hegel to Nietzsche: The Revolution in Nineteenth-Century Thought. Translated by David E. Green. New York: Holt, Rinehart and Winston.

Lunn, Eugene.
1982.

Marxism and Modernism. Berkeley: University of California Press.

Lynch, Kevin.
1972.

What Time Is This Place?. Cambridge, Massachusetts: MIT Press.

Lyndon, Donlyn.
1982.

The City Observed: Boston. New York: Vintage Books.

Lyndon Baines Johnson School of Public Affairs.
1977.

Colonias in the Lower Rio Grande Valley of South Texas: A Summary Report. Austin: University of Texas at Austin.

394

Lyotard, Jean-François.
1984.

The Postmodern Condition. Minneapolis: University of Minnesota Press.

McComb, David G.
1981.

Houston: A History. Austin: University of Texas Press.

McCoy, Esther.
1960.

Five Californian Architects. New York: Reinhold.

McQuade, Walter.
1966.

"Urban Renewal in Boston." In James Q. Wilson (ed.), *Urban Renewal: The Record and the Controversy.* Cambridge, Massachusetts: MIT Press.

Mandelker, Daniel R.
1962.

Green Belts and Urban Growth. Madison, Wisconsin: University of Wisconsin Press.

Manguin, William (ed.).
1970.

Peasants in Cities. Boston: Houghton Mifflin.

Manguin, William, and J. F. C. Turner.
1968.

"Barriada Movement." *Progressive Architecture*, vol. 5, May, pp. 154–162.

Mannheim, Karl.
1936.

Ideology and Utopia. New York: Harcourt, Brace and World.

Mariani, Riccardo.
1982.

"Life in Architecture: People's Housing in Naples." *Abitare*, November, pp. 76–81, 94.

Marx, Leo.
1964.

The Machine in the Garden: Technology and the Pastoral Ideal in America. New York: Oxford University Press.

Masnick, George, and Mary Jo Bane.
1980.

The Nation's Families: 1960–1990. Cambridge, Massachusetts: Joint Center for Urban Studies.

Mason, Joseph B.
1982.

History of Housing in the U.S., 1930–1981. Houston, Texas: Gulf Publishing Company.

Masotti, Louis H., and Jeffrey K. Hadden (eds.).
1974.

Suburbia in Transition. New York: New Viewpoints.

May, Ernst.
1926.

"Das Neue Frankfurt." *Das Neue Frankfurt*, 1, pp. 2–11.

Meyrowitz, Joshua.
1985.

No Sense of Place: The Impact of Electronic Media on Social Behavior. New York: Oxford University Press.

Miller, Mervyn.
1981.

"Raymond Unwin 1863–1940." In Gorden E. Cherry (ed.), *Pioneers in British Planning.* London: The Architectural Press, pp. 72–102.

Ministry of Housing and Building.
1964.

Housing in the Netherlands. The Hague: Ministry of Housing and Building.

Ministry of Reconstruction and Housing.
1948.

Housing in the Netherlands and Relevant Acts and Regulations from 1900 Onwards. The Hague: Information Department of the Ministry of Reconstruction and Housing.

Ministry of Reconstruction and Housing.
1950.

The Netherlands Dwelling. New York: Netherlands Information Bureau.

Ministry of Reconstruction and Housing.
1953.

Introduction to the Housing Problem in the Netherlands. The Hague: The Netherlands Government Information Service.

Moneo, Rafael.
1978.

"On Typology." *Oppositions*, no. 13, Summer, pp. 22–45.

Morris, Kelly, and Amanda Woods.
1989.

Art in Berlin 1815–1989. Seattle: High Museum of Art.

Moynihan, Daniel P.
1969.

Maximum Feasible Misunderstanding: Community Action in the War on Poverty. New York: Free Press.

Mott, Seward.
1941.

"Neighborhood Planning." *American Society of Planning Officials National Conference on Planning*, pp. 156–162.

References

Muller, Peter O.
1981.

Contemporary Suburban America. Englewood Cliffs, New Jersey: Prentice-Hall.

Mullin, John R.
1975.

"German City Planning in the 1920s: A North American Perspective of the Frankfurt Experience." Occasional Paper No. 16, Faculty of Environmental Studies, University of Waterloo, Canada.

Mumford, Lewis.
1970.

The Culture of Cities. New York: Harcourt, Brace and Jovanovich.

Muthesius, Hermann.
1979 (1904).

The English House. New York: Rizzoli.

National Association of Housing Officials.
1939.

Practical Standards for Modern Housing. Chicago: National Association of Housing Officials.

National Housing Authority.
1945.

Minimum Physical Standards and Criteria for the Planning and Design of FPHA-Aided Urban Low-Rent Housing. Washington, D.C.: Federal Public Housing Authority.

Nelson, William E.
1982.

The Roots of American Bureaucracy 1830–1900. Cambridge, Massachusetts: Harvard University Press.

Nevins, A., and E. F. Hill.
1957.

Ford. 2 vols. New York: Scribners.

Nicolin, Pierluigi (ed.).
1975.

"The House." *Lotus International,* nos. 8–10.

Nicolin, Pierluigi.
1977.

"Housing Complex at the Gallaratese Quarter." In Yukio Futagawa (ed.), *Carlo Aymonino/Also Rossi: Housing Complex at the Gallaratese Quarter, Milan, Italy. 1969–1974.* Tokyo: Global Architecture, ADA Edita.

Nicolin, Pierluigi.
1986.

Alvaro Siza: Poetic Profession. New York: Rizzoli.

Norberg-Schulz, Christian.
1988 (1986).

Architecture: Meaning and Place, Selected Essays. New York: Rizzoli.

Novak, Barbara.
1976.

"The Double-Edged Ax." *Art in America,* January-February, pp. 44–50.

OECD.
1987.

Statistical Bulletin. Paris: Organization for Economic Cooperation and Development.

OMB.
1980.

Economic Report to the President, Washington, D.C.: Office of Management and the Budget.

O'Neill, William L.
1971.

Coming Apart: An Informal History of America in the 1960's. Chicago: Quadrangle Books.

Oud, Hans.
1984.

J. J. P. Oud: Architekt 1890–1963 Feiten en herinneringen gerangschikt. The Hague: Nijgh & Van Ditmar.

Oud, J. J. P.
1917.

"Art and Machine." *De Stijl.*

Panofsky, Erwin.
1967 (1951).

Gothic Architecture and Scholasticism. Cleveland: Meridian Books.

Papademetriou, Peter C. (ed.).
1972.

Houston: An Architectural Guide. Houston: Houston Chapter of the American Institute of Architects.

Pepper, Simon.
1975.

"British Housing Trends, 1964–1974." *Lotus International,* no. 10, pp. 94–103.

Perry, Clarence Arthur.
1939.

Housing for the Machine Age. New York: Russell Sage Foundation.

Pevsner, Sir Nikolaus.
1963.

Pioneers of the Modern Management. London: Pelican Books.

Plunz, Richard.
1990.
A History of Housing in New York City: Dwelling Type and Social Change in the American Metropolis. New York: Columbia University Press.

Podro, Michael.
1982.
The Critical Historians of Art. New Haven: Yale University Press.

Poggioli, Renato.
1968.
The Theory of the Avant-Garde. Cambridge, Massachusetts: The Belknap Press.

Polano, Sergio.
1977.
"Notes on Oud, Re-reading the Documents." *Lotus International,* no. 16, September, pp. 16ff.

Preiser, Wolfgang (ed.).
1978.
Facility Programming. Stroudsburg, Pennsylvania: Dowden, Hutchinson and Ross.

Preminger, Alex (ed.).
1965.
Princeton Encyclopedia of Poetry and Poetics. Princeton, New Jersey: Princeton University Books.

Prigge, Walter, and Hans-Peter Schwarz (eds.).
1988.
Das Neue Frankfurt: Städtebau und Architektur im Modernisierungs-prozess 1925–1988. Frankfurt-am-Main: Vervuert Verlag.

Progressive Architecture.
1980.
"Gallaratese Housing, Milan." *Progressive Architecture,* no. 10, pp. 10–18.

Quatremère de Quincy.
1977 (1825).
"Type." Translated from an essay in the *Encyclopédie Méthodique. Oppositions,* no. 9, pp. 148ff.

Querrien, Gwenaël.
184.
"Climat de France." *Bulletin d'Informations Architecturales de l'IFA,* no. 15, pp. 18–21.

Quilici, Vieri.
1975.
"Regional Character and National Role of Housing Co-operatives." *Lotus International,* no. 10, pp. 74–75.

Rae, John B.
1965.
The American Automobile: A Brief History. Chicago: University of Chicago Press.

Rae, John B.
1971.
The Road and the Car in American Life. Cambridge, Massachusetts: MIT Press.

Rapaport, Amos.
1969.
House, Form and Culture. Englewood Cliffs, New Jersey: Prentice-Hall.

Rayon, Jean-Paul.
1982.
"Il Quartiere Malagueira a Evora." *Casabella,* vol. 46, March, pp. 3–15.

Relph, Edward.
1987.
The Modern Urban Landscape. Baltimore: Johns Hopkins University Press.

Ricoeur, Paul.
1974.
The Conflict of Interpretations: Essays in Hermeneutics. Evanston, Illinois: Northwestern University Press.

Riis, Jacob A.
1957 (1890).
How the Other Half Lives. New York: Hill and Wang.

Risse, Heike.
1984.
Frühe Moderne in Frankfurt am Main 1920–1933. Frankfurt: Frankfurter Societäts-Druckerei GmbH.

Risse, Heike, and Ingrid Rödel.
1987.
Frankfurt. Stuttgart: Baedeker.

Roche, Camille.
1934.
"Le centre urbain de Villeurbanne." *Sciences et Monde,* vol. 161, June, pp. 379–381.

Ross, W. D.
1942.
The Works of Aristotle. 12 vols. London: Oxford University Press.

Rossi, Aldo.
1982.
The Architecture of the City. Translated by Diane Ghirardo and Joan Ockman. Cambridge, Massachusetts: MIT Press.

Rowe, Colin, and Fred Koetter.
1978.
Collage City. Cambridge, Massachusetts: MIT Press.

Rowe, Peter G.
1972.

"A Question of Architecture, a Matter of Style." *Architectural Design*, August, pp. 466ff.

Rowe, Peter G. (et al.).
1978.

Principles for Local Environmental Management. Cambridge, Massachusetts: Ballinger Publishing Company.

Rowe, Peter G.
1987.

Design Thinking. Cambridge, Massachusetts: MIT Press.

Rowe, Peter G.
1988.

The Byker Redevelopment Project and the Malagueira Quarter Housing Project. Cambridge, Massachusetts: Harvard Graduate School of Design.

Rowe, Peter G.
1991.

Making a Middle Landscape. Cambridge, Massachusetts: MIT Press.

Ruttenbaum, Steven R.
1986.

Mansions in the Clouds: The Skyscraper Palazzi of Emery Roth. New York: Balsam Press.

Schaal, Rolf, Stephen Pfister, and Giovanni Scheibler.
1990.

Siedlungen. Basel: Birkhäuser.

Schiller, Friedrich von.
1961.

Ästhetische Schriften. Paderborn: Schöningh.

Schlandt, Joachim.
1975.

"Economic and Social Aspects of Council Housing in Vienna Between 1922 and 1934." *Lotus International*, no. 10, pp. 161–175.

Schlesinger, Arthur M.
1933.

The Rise of the City 1878–1898. New York: Macmillan.

Schmertz, Mildred F.
1978.

"Housing." *Architectural Record*, February, pp. 78–94.

Schulze, Franz.
1985.

Mies van der Rohe: A Critical Biography. Chicago: University of Chicago Press.

Scott, Mel.
1969.

American City Planning since 1890. Berkeley: University of California Press.

Scully, Vincent.
1988.

American Architecture and Urbanism. Rev. ed. New York: Henry Holt.

Sennett, Richard.
1977.

The Fall of Public Man. New York: Knopf.

Sennett, Richard.
1990.

Conscience of the Eye. New York: Knopf.

Sharratt, John.
1980.

"Urban Neighborhood Preservation and Development." *Process Architecture*, no. 14, pp. 28–32.

Sharratt, John.
1991.

Personal interview with author. July.

Short, John R.
1982.

Housing in Britain: The Post-War Experience. London: Methuen.

Silvetti, Jorge (ed.).
1989.

Architectural and Urban Environments of Sicily. Cambridge, Massachusetts: Harvard Graduate School of Design.

Simmel, Georg.
1902.

"Tendencies in German Life and Thought since 1870." *International Monthly*, vol. 5, pp. 93–111, 116–184.

Simmel, Georg.
1968.

The Conflict in Modern Culture and Other Essays. Translated and edited by P. K. Etzkorn. New York: Scribners.

Siza, Alvaro.
1987.

"Built on the Site." *Lotus International*, no. 37.

Siza, Alvaro.
1988.

Public Presentation of the Malagueira Quarter Project during the Awarding of the Prince of Wales Prize in Urban Design. Cambridge, Massachusetts: Graduate School of Design, Harvard University, October.

398

Soltan, Jerzy.
1988.

"Modernism and the Past—Were They Really Enemies" (lecture). New York: AIA New York Chapter.

Sparke, Penny.
1987.

Design in Context. Secaucus, New Jersey: Quatro Publishing.

Sparke, Penny.
1988.

Italian Design: 1870 to the Present. London: Thames and Hudson.

Spears, Monroe K.
1970.

Dionysus and the City: Modernism in Twentieth-Century Poetry. New York: Oxford University Press.

Stamm, Gunther.
1978a.

J. J. P. Oud Bauten und Projekte 1906 bis 1963. Berlin: Bei Florian Kupferberg.

Stamm, Gunther.
1978b.

The Architecture of J. J. P. Oud, 1906–1963. Tallahassee: University Presses of Florida.

Stangos, Nikos (ed.).
1974.

Concepts of Modern Art. 2d ed. New York: Harper and Row.

Stein, Clarence S.
1966 (1957).

Towards New Towns for America. Cambridge, Massachusetts: MIT Press.

Stern, Robert A. M. (ed.).
1981.

The Anglo-American Suburb. London: Architectural Design Profile.

Stickley, Gustav.
1909.

Craftman Homes. New York: Craftman Publishing Co.

Strong, Ann Louise.
1971.

Planned Urban Environments: Sweden, Finland, Israel, the Netherlands and France. Baltimore: Johns Hopkins University Press.

Tafuri, Manfredo.
1980.

Vienna Rossa. Milano: Electa.

Tafuri, Manfredo.
1989.

History of Italian Architecture, 1944–1985. Cambridge, Massachusetts: MIT Press.

Tafuri, Manfredo, and Francesco Dal Co.
1976.

Modern Architecture. New York: Electa/Rizzoli.

Talib, Kaiser.
1984.

Shelter in Saudia Arabia. London: St. Martin's Press.

Taut, Bruno.
1979.

Die neue Baukunst in Europa und Amerika. Stuttgart: Julius Hoffman Verlag.

Taylor, Frederick W.
1911.

Principles of Scientific Management. New York: John Wiley.

Testa, Peter.
1984.

"The Architecture of Alvaro Siza." *Thresholds.* Working Paper no. 4, Department of Architecture, Massachusetts Institute of Technology.

Thrall, William Flint, Addison Hubbard, and C. Hugh Holman.
1960 (1936).

A Handbook to Literature. Rev. ed. New York: The Odyssey Press.

Toffler, Alvin.
1970.

Future Shock. New York: Bantam Books.

Toulmin, Stephen.
1961.

Foresight and Understanding. Bloomington, Indiana: Indiana University Press.

Trilling, Lionel.
1961.

Beyond Culture. New York: Viking.

Tunnard, Christopher, and Boris Pushkarev.
1963.

Man-Made America: Chaos or Control. An Inquiry into Selected Problems of Design in the Urbanized Landscape. New Haven: Yale University Press.

Turner, John F. C.
1972.

Freedom to Build: Dweller Control of the Housing Process. New York: Macmillan.

Turner, John F. C.
1976.

Housing by People: Towards Autonomy in Building Environments. New York: Pantheon Books.

U.S. Bureau of the Census.
1940–1990.

Census of Population: Summaries. Washington, D.C.: U.S. Bureau of the Census.

U.S. Bureau of the Census.
1975.

Historical Statistics. Washington, D.C.: U.S. Bureau of the Census.

U.S. Department of Commerce.
1955.

Construction Review Statistical Supplement: Construction Volume and Costs 1915–54. Washington, D.C.: U.S. Department of Commerce.

U.S. Department of Commerce.
1976.

Construction Review Statistical Supplement. Washington, D.C.: U.S. Department of Commerce (annual publication).

U.S. Department of Labor.
1959.

How American Buying Habits Change. Washington, D.C.: U.S. Department of Labor.

Unwin, Raymond.
1911.

Town Planning in Practice: An Introduction to the Art of Designing Cities and Suburbs. London: T. F. Unwin.

Upton, Dell, and John Michael Vlach (eds.).
1986.

Common Places: Readings in American Vernacular Architecture. Athens, Georgia: University of Georgia Press.

Urbanisme.
1933.

"Le Nouveau Centre de Villeurbanne." *Urbanisme*, no. 16, pp. 211–215.

Vaile, Roland S., and Helen G. Canoyer.
1938.

Income and Consumption. New York: Henry Holt.

Vance, James E., Jr.
1977.

This Scene of Man: The Role and Structure of the City in the Geography of Western Civilization. New York: Harpers College Press.

Vatter, Harold G.
1987.

"Technological Innovation and Social Change in the United States, 1870–1980." In Joel Colton and Stuart Bruchey (eds.), *Technology, the Economy and Society: The American Experience.* New York: Columbia University Press.

Vattimo, Gianni.
1988 (1985).

The End of Modernity: Nihilism and Hermeneutics in Postmodern Culture. Translated by Jon R. Snyder. Baltimore: Johns Hopkins University Press.

Veiller, L.
1910.

Housing Reform: A Handbook for Practical Use. New York: Scribners.

Venturi, Robert.
1966.

Complexity and Contradiction in Architecture. New York: Museum of Modern Art.

Venturi, Robert, and Denise Scott Brown.
1971.

"Ugly and Ordinary Architecture, or the Decorated Shed (Parts 1 and 2)." *Architectural Forum*, November, pp. 64–67, and December, pp. 48–53.

Venturi, Robert, Denise Scott Brown, and Steven Izenour.
1972.

Learning from Las Vegas. Cambridge, Massachusetts: MIT Press.

von Moos, Stanislaus.
1979.

Le Corbusier: Elements of a Synthesis. Cambridge, Massachusetts: MIT Press.

Ward, Colin.
1974.

Tenants Take Over. London: Architectural Press.

Ward, Colin.
1976.

Housing: An Anarchist Approach. London: Freedom Press.

Ward, Colin.
1990.

Talking Houses: Ten Lectures. London Freedom Press.

Ward, Peter M. (ed.).
1982.

Self-Help Housing: A Critique. London: Mansell Publishing Limited.

Warner, Sam Bass, Jr.
1962.

Street-Car Suburbs: The Process of Growth in Boston (1870–1900). Cambridge, Massachusetts: Harvard University Press.

400

Watterson, Thomas.
1990.

"Don't Feed the Bear Your Lunch in a Down Market." *Boston Globe,* 30 August, pp. 61, 67.

Webber, Melvin M.
1964.

"Order in Diversity: Community without Propinquity." In Lowdon Wingo (ed.), *Cities and Space.* Baltimore: Johns Hopkins University Press.

Webber, Melvin M., John W. Dyckman, and Donald L. Foley (et al.).
1964.

Explorations into Urban Structure. Philadelphia, Pennsylvania: University of Pennsylvania Press.

Weber, Adna Ferris.
1967 (1899).

The Growth of Cities in the Nineteenth Century: A Study in Statistics. Ithaca, New York: Cornell University Press.

Weber, Max.
1947.

The Theory of Social and Economic Organization. New York: Free Press.

Welfeld, Irving H.
1972.

European Housing Subsidy Systems: An American Perspective. Washington, D.C.: Office of International Affairs, U.S. Department of Housing and Urban Development.

Wellmer, Albrecht.
1991.

The Persistence of Modernity. Cambridge, Massachusetts: MIT Press.

Whitehill, Walter Muir.
1959.

Boston: A Topographical History. Cambridge, Massachusetts: Harvard University Press.

Wilbur Smith and Associates.
1961.

Future Highways and Urban Growth. New Haven: Wilbur Smith and Associates.

Willett, John.
1978.

Art and Politics in the Weimar Period: The New Sobriety, 1917–1933. New York: Pantheon Books.

Williams, Raymond.
1973.

The Country and the City. London: Oxford University Press.

Wilson, James Q. (ed.).
1966.

Urban Renewal: The Record and the Controversy. Cambridge, Massachusetts: MIT Press.

Wingler, Hans M.
1969.

The Bauhaus. Cambridge, Massachusetts: MIT Press.

Wingo, Lowdon, Jr. (ed.).
1963.

Cities and Space: The Future Use of Urban Land. Baltimore: Johns Hopkins University Press.

Woods, Shadrach.
1965.

"Free University Berlin." In *World Architecture,* vol. 2. New York: Viking Press.

Woods, Shadrach.
1975.

The Man in the Street: A Polemic on Urbanism. New York: Penguin.

Worringer, Wilhelm.
1967 (1908).

Abstraction and Empathy: A Contribution to the Psychology of Style. Cleveland: Meridian Books.

Wright, Frank Lloyd.
1945.

When Democracy Builds. Chicago: University of Chicago Press.

Wright, Gwendolyn.
1981.

Building the Dream: A Social History of Housing in America. Cambridge, Massachusetts: MIT Press.

Wright, Henry.
1933.

"Housing—Where, When and How?" *Architecture,* vol. 68, no. 1, July, pp. 1–32, and August, pp. 79–110.

Yeomans, Alfred B.
1916.

City Residential Land Development: Studies in Planning. Chicago: University of Chicago Press.

Zweig, Ferdynand.
1961.

The Worker in an Affluent Society. London: Heineman.

Illustration Credits

Figure 1: Bohigas 1975, p. 149.

Figures 2 and 174: Bowly 1978, pp. 29 and 125 respectively.

Figure 3: Risse 1984, p. 272.

Figures 4 and 5: Rae 1965, pp. 53 and 49 respectively.

Figure 7: Kennedy 1944, p. 2.

Figure 10: Photography by Nina Leen, LIFE Magazine, copyright 1947 Time, Inc.

Figure 11: Corn 1986, p. 55.

Figure 12: Gilles 1946, p. 64.

Figures 13 and 34: Hassner 1970, pp. 35 and 21 respectively. Courtesy of the Museum of the City of New York.

Figure 15: Liebs 1985, p. 11. Courtesy of Huntington Library, San Marino, California.

Figure 15: Courtesy of the Astrocard Company, Inc., Houston, Texas.

Figure 16: With permission of the Philadelphia Museum of Art.

Figure 17: Jansen 1987, p. 70.

Figures 18, 74, 91, 94, 106, 108, and 122; Buekschmitt 1963, pp. 50, 43, 37, 52, 49, 47, and 52 respectively.

Figure 19: Photograph by J. R. Eyerman, copyright 1953 Time, Inc.

Figures 22, 31, 51, 116, 135, 144, 161, and 167: Benevolo 1985, p. 857, 443, 929, 877 (and photography by KLM), 931, 878, 883, and 956 respectively.

Figure 23: Braghieri 1982, pp. 120–121.

Figure 24: Unknown.

Figure 27: With permission of the Museum of Modern Art.

Figure 28: Cooke 1983, pp. 69 and 80.

Figure 30: Five Architects 1972, p. 37.

Figures 32 amd 37: Bauer 1934, pp. 44 and 25 respectively.

Figure 35: Illustration from original Scribner edition of Jacob Riis, *How the Other Half Lives* (1890).

Figures 36, 125, and 133: Plunz 1990, pp. 49, 217, and 255 respectively.

Figure 38: Geist and Kürvers 1984, p. 65. Photograph by Willy Römer, 1910.

Figure 39: Ministry of Reconstruction and Housing 1953, p. 4.

Figures 41, 60, 93, 101, 103, 104, and 105: Gartenstadt AG 1935, pp. 33, 4, 50, 24, 22, 29, and 24 respectively.

Figure 42: Le Corbusier 1964, p. 145.

Figures 43, 44, and 134: Courtesy of the Frances Loeb Library, Harvard University.

Figures 49 and 58: Ministry of Reconstruction and Housing 1950, pp. 12 and 6 respectively.

Figure 50: Courtesy of the Planning Department, Township of Framingham, Massachusetts.

Figure 53: Gowans, 1986, p. 47.

Figure 55: Herbert 1984, p. 46.

Figure 56: Christine Frederick, *Scientific Management in the Home: Household Engineering* (1870), and Forty 1986, p. 217.

Figure 57: After Bauer 1934, p. 37, and Benevolo 1984, p. 519.

Figure 59: Foulke 1911, p. ix.

Figure 61: After Howard 1902 and Cherry 1988.

Figures 65, 143, 160, 166, 171, and 289: Tafuri and Dal

Co 1976, pp. 170, 208, 351, 345, 377, and 380 respectively.

Figure 71: U.S. Department of Labor 1959, p. 17.

Figures 75, 77, and 85: City Housing Corporation 1924a, pp. 2, 3, and 17 respectively.

Figure 76: City Housing Corporation 1927a, frontispiece.

Figures 78, 80, 82, and 84: City Housing Corporation 1928, pp. 2, 7, 5, and 8 respectively.

Figures 79, 88, 89, 90, 149, 150, and 158: Stein 1966, pp. 29, 90, 86, 70, 58, 42, and 97 respectively. Photographs by Gretchen von Tassel of Washington, D.C.

Figure 81: City Housing Corporation 1927c.

Figure 98: Braun and Heimel 1977, p. 31.

Figures 99, 117, 119, 201, 205, and 234: Drawn by Christopher Procter. Figures 99 and 234 based on illustrations in Dreysse 1988 and Oud 1984, respectively.

Figure 112: After Department of Housing 1950. Redrawn by Jacqueline Tatom.

Figure 114: Oud 1984, p. 75. Copyright J. J. P. Oud/VAGA, New York, 1993.

Figures 126, 156, and 157: Architectural Forum 1938, pp. 351, 411, and 352, respectively.

Figure 132: Photograph by William Fried. Dover Publications, 1980.

Figure 138: Gropius 1955, figure 40.

Figure 139: Giedion 1931, plate 14.

Figures 141, 142, and 163: Courtesy of Joan Busquets.

Figure 147: Kilham and Hopkins, 1913, p. 94.

Figure 148: Scott 1969, p. 351.

Figure 151: Regional Planning Commission of the County of Los Angeles, *Landscape Design* (1929), p. 29.

Figure 152: Clark 1986, p. 223. Photograph by Ben Martin, Time Magazine.

Figure 153: Unknown.

Figure 154: Courtesy of the Fondren Library, Rice University.

Figure 159: Casabella 1938c, p. 2.

Figure 162: Dubor 1986, p. 77.

Figure 164: Photograph by Lauretta Vinciarelli.

Figure 165: Courtesy of Landslides of Boston.

Figure 169: Candilis, Josic, and Woods 1975, p. 53.

Figures 172 and 173: Nicolin 1975, pp. 118, 121, and 110, respectively.

Figure 175: Courtesy of the Boston Housing Authority.

Figure 177: Alexander, Ishikawa, and Silverstein 1968, p. 18.

Figures 183 and 217: Drawn by Vasilios Tsakalos.

Figures 185, 188, 189, and 190: Courtesy of Ralph Erskine.

Figures 186, 192, and 194: Erskine 1981, pp. 4, 6, and 8 respectively.

Figure 187: Architectural Review 1974, p. 346.

Figures 204 and 209: Courtesy of John Sharratt and *Architectural Record*, February 1978, pp. 88 and 93 respectively.

Figures 213, 215, 219, 227, 256, and 290: Photographs by Roberto Collovi of Palermo, Italy, 1988.

Figure 223: Nicolin 1986, p. 6.

Figure 225: Courtesy of Alvaro Siza.

Figure 232: Detail from *Progressive Architecture*, October 1981, p. 95. Photograph by Deidi von Schaewen.

Figure 233: Photograph by Dennis Pieprz.

Figure 237: De Sola Ricardo 1987, p. 242.

Figure 246: Drawn by Masami Kobayashi.

Figure 247: Groenendijk and Vollaard 1987, p. 233.

Figures 261 and 263: Huse 1987, pp. 34 and 133 respectively.

Figures 282 and 283: Photographs by Paul Naecker.

Figure 288: Photograph by L. G. Rowe.

Figure 294: Courtesy of Kevin Roche, John Dinkeloo and Associates.

Index